The Politics of Public Health in the United States

The Politics of Public Health in the United States

Kant Patel and Mark E. Rushefsky

With a Foreword by Deborah R. McFarlane

M.E.Sharpe
Armonk, New York
London, England

Library of Congress Cataloging-in-Publication Data

Patel, Kant, 1946–
    The politics of public health in the United States / Kant Patel and Mark E. Rushefsky.
        p. cm.
    Includes bibliographical references and index.
    ISBN 0-7656-1135-X (hardcover : alk. paper) — ISBN 0-7656-1136-8 (pbk. : alk. paper)
        1. Public health—United States. 2. Public health—Political aspects—United States.
    3. Medical policy—United States. [DNLM: 1. Politics—United States. 2. Public
    Health—trends—United States. 3. Public Health Administration—trends—United
    States. 4. Health Policy—trends—United States. WA 100 P295p 2004]
    I. Rushefsky, Mark E., 1945– II. Title.

    RA445.P37 2004
    362.1′0973—dc22   2004009724

Printed in the United States of America

The paper used in this publication meets the minimum requirements of
American National Standard for Information Sciences
Permanence of Paper for Printed Library Materials,
ANSI Z 39.48-1984.

                                    ∞

        BM (c)   10   9   8   7   6   5   4   3   2   1
        BM (p)   10   9   8   7   6   5   4   3   2   1

Contents

Figures and Tables

Figures

Tables

Foreword

The Politics of Public Health in the United States addresses both an under-valued policy area and an understudied political arena. Public health mea-sures have had an enormous impact on American lives. In the past century, life expectancy in the United States has risen from forty-seven to seventy-seven years (CDC 2004). Of those thirty years added to the average American's life, twenty-four years can be attributed to public health measures. Medical care on the other hand has been estimated to have increased life expectancy by about six years (Bunker et al. 1994; Bunker 1995).

In spite of the tremendous contributions of public health, which are well documented by Patel and Rushefsky, only a small fraction of Ameri-can health expenditures is directed toward public health.[1] To date, this phenomenon has not been well explained. While a voluminous literature addresses the tools and techniques of public health, very little work has focused on the politics that surrounds the field. For the most part, scholars of health policy and politics have ignored the field of public health and chosen instead "to follow the money"[2] by studying medical care policies. Given the fact that medical expenditures have increased dramatically over the past few decades and funding for public health has stagnated, this situ-ation is unfortunate but understandable.

Although it receives less support, public health offers solutions that medi-cal care alone cannot provide. If we as a nation wish to improve our health status and increase our life expectancy, we must face our misplaced priorities in health spending. American health expenditures per capita are the highest in the world, yet the United States ranks twenty-fifth among other nations in infant mortality and twenty-fourth in life expectancy.

This is a situation that will not be substantially improved by new technol-ogy. Indeed, faith in advanced technology has contributed to high levels of health expenditures while other important factors have been neglected. In order to make substantial gains in health status, we would need to turn to public health functions and principles as well as address lifestyle issues and disparities in population health.

What is public health? Patel and Rushefsky (2004, 7) report that less than

1 percent of Americans can specify the mission of public health. Even among public health professionals there is no universal definition. This lack of consensus can complicate the political message, particularly when public health agencies request public resources. Because policymakers do not understand the relative efficacy of public health and medical care, they are more likely to fund the latter, which they view as having a greater urgency (Gordon 1993, 262). In a sense, public health has fallen victim to its own silent successes, and current public health advocates have not convincingly made the case for obtaining adequate resources.

Making the case for adequately supporting public health requires a coherent message. Noted public health scholar and practitioner Larry Gordon offers clear demarcations when it comes to public health, environmental health and protection, and health care services. These distinctions are necessary if coherent messages are to be conveyed to policymakers. *Public health* is the art and science of preventing disease and injury, and promoting health and efficiency through organized community effort. *Environmental health and protection* is the art and science of protecting against environmental factors that may adversely impact human health or the ecological balances essential to long-term human health and environmental quality. *Health care services* involve the diagnosis, treatment, or rehabilitation of a patient under care, accomplished on a one-to-one basis (Gordon 1993, 261–62). Gordon has even developed a health services continuum that is useful for explaining both the differences among and the relationships between environmental health and protection, health promotion, disease prevention, and health care (Gordon 1997, 301).

More emphasis on public health in the policy arena would represent a real departure from the status quo. Although estimates vary, only about 2–3 percent of all health expenditures in the United States is directed toward public health functions; the rest is devoted to curative care. If this ratio is to change, it will require not just clear definitions and documented results, but also public health professionals who are adept at working within the political system. The fact remains that public health involves collective action and often produces nondivisible goods, so government is an important source of revenue for most public health programs (McFarlane and Gordon 1992).

More involvement by public health professionals in politics would also mean a significant change from the status quo. In fact, many public health professionals do not even participate in activities that they perceive as political because they are ignorant or disdainful of politics. This lack of involvement has had very serious consequences. One result is that many policymakers do not consider appropriate technical advice when they develop health policies (Institute of Medicine 1988; McFarlane and Gordon 1992). Patel and

Rushefsky rightly point out that sound public health policies require reliance on solid technical and scientific data, evidence that is best presented by public health professionals themselves (2004, 51).

In this book, Patel and Rushefsky explain the political realities associated with changing the capacity of public health and they skillfully present the substantive challenges. Among the most important realities is that American political institutions are designed more for checks and balances than for collective action. This institutional fact complicates the development and implementation of public health programs, which require collective action to improve community health. The federal structure of American government itself presents serious constraints and some opportunities for public health policies (McFarlane and Meier 1993). Successfully building capacity in this American public health also requires addressing the power of private interests in a liberal state.

While Patel and Rushefsky well understand and thoroughly explain the political constraints, they are not naysayers. They describe the current status of public health programs as well as what needs to happen for public health policies to improve. They note the irony in the fact that the 9/11 tragedy and the subsequent anthrax mailings have provided a political opportunity for strengthening the neglected and inadequate public health system.

In short, Patel and Rushefsky have given us a study that is firmly rooted in existing political institutions and norms, yet it is also focused on the possible and the imaginable. The book is completely up-to-date in terms of the technical challenges of the Human Genome Project and bioterrorism, but it also explains how public health developed scientifically and organizationally in the unique American political culture. Patel and Rushefsky explain many of the controversies in the field such as whether public health departments should assume the role of safety net medical provider and how the tension between individual liberties and community health plays out in real-life settings.

In terms of existing literature, this book offers a unique contribution. The politics of public health have been sorely neglected by scholars and policy analysts. While there has been ample funding for the study of policies related to health care services and medical expenditures, the American politics of public health have been largely ignored. As in their previous work in the politics of health care services, Patel and Rushefsky have assembled and integrated a vast amount of literature while offering their own valuable insights. Although the book is focused on American public health politics and policies, Patel and Rushefsky certainly recognize that pathogens and disease have never recognized political borders. In the face of new challenges such as globalism and bioterrorism as well as old threats such as unsafe food and water, public health remains a vitally important policy area. Understanding the context and dynamics of public health politics will be necessary if significant improvements are to be made in American health status.

Deborah R. McFarlane
University of New Mexico

Notes

1. Estimates vary widely here, and that fact alone indicates how marginalized public health has become. Larry Gordon (1993) estimates that approximately 3 percent of all health dollars go to public health, while Patel and Rushefsky rely on Levitt et al. who estimate this figure to be around 7 percent.

2. Following the money trail is a term used by Larry Gordon to critique American schools of public health as they have deviated from their collective mission of training practitioners of public health (Gordon and McFarlane 1996).

Preface

When we finished writing our previous book, *Health Care Policy in an Age of New Technologies* (2002), we ended the preface with a brief reference to the September 11, 2001, terrorist attacks. We mentioned the anthrax incidents that occurred shortly thereafter, the threat of bioterrorism, and the newly placed emphasis on public health. To quote ourselves (Patel and Rushefsky 2002, xix): "Public health in the twenty-first century will be a major player in ways that it has never been before."

The present book is our examination of the politics of public health in the United States. That had not been a focus of our previous works, and this plugs a hole in our efforts at understanding health care in the United States. As we worked on this project, we made two important findings—at least for us. First, public health is an integral part of health care with many important achievements. The infrastructure of public health is elaborate and exists at all levels of government. Our second finding is that public health in the United States has many problems. Perhaps the most important of all is that it is underappreciated. Much of the enhanced health that Americans enjoy is due to public health efforts, as much as or perhaps even more so than to more traditional medical care. But we take public health for granted. Related to that is the enormous fragmentation of public health. As with many areas of public policy in the United States, it developed piecemeal; it can hardly be called a system.

Most important of all, we have neglected public health. In 1988 the Institute of Medicine (IOM) issued a report on public health. It made observations and a series of recommendations. Fifteen years later, it issued a follow-up report and noted that not much had changed in the interim. Only in the aftermath of the 9/11 terrorist attacks has critical attention once more turned to public health. Our book examines many of these problems and offers a series of recommendations.

This book is also the continuation of a successful working relationship and friendship, something that does not always occur together. One thing that has cemented our friendship has been, as we have explained before, sports. Patel is from Houston, Rushefsky is from New York. Both are basketball fanatics, but also like baseball and other sports. This has made for lively, friendly competition. That has become more interesting in what can only be called a merger of franchises. Three former New York Knicks currently play for the Houston Rockets. The head coach of the Rockets is the former head coach of the Knicks. An assistant coach is one of the all-time great Knick players. Two observations: though most of those ex-Knicks have been to the finals of the NBA playoffs, they have not won. Second, only one ex-Rocket plays for the Knicks. Further, half of the starting pitching rotation for the Houston Astros were half of the starting rotation for the New York Yankees. Here there are more grounds for optimism for the Astros. All of this makes for interesting conversation.

We do need to update our readers on one story. In our first book, *Health Care Politics and Policy in America* (Patel and Rushefsky 1999), we told the story of the birth of Rushefsky's younger daughter. During the course of writing this preface, that daughter, Leah, now married, presented Rushefsky with his first grandchild. Echo Nichol Vaughn was born five weeks prematurely and thus spent the first weeks of her life in the neonatal intensive care unit of one of the local hospitals. Among other things, Rushefsky received an intimate lesson in the miracles of modern medicine as well as in the high costs of that care. Rushefsky and his wife are experiencing the joys of grandparenthood.

We should note, finally, that there are still health care issues that remain to be resolved or even addressed. Recent reports have pointed out inequities that exist in the American health care system. At some point, hopefully, those will be placed on the policy agenda.

Acknowledgments

As is typical of any book, this one is not the product of its authors only. We would like to thank Debbie Underwood for her editorial work on several of the chapters, and Michael Sahmel, our graduate assistant, for his work on the chronology of public health events and laws along with the list of abbreviations. Our thanks also to Deborah McFarlane for her graciousness and willingness to write the foreword. We would also like to express our great appreciation to Patricia Kolb, editorial director at M.E. Sharpe. She and Sharpe have continued to support our work. Thanks also to her editorial assistant, Amy Albert, and to Henrietta Toth, production editor, and Dean Curtis, copyeditor. Of course, any remaining errors are ours.

Acronyms

AAHP	American Association of Health Plans
AAPHD	American Association of Public Health Dentistry
AAPHP	American Association of Public Health Physicians
ACLU	American Civil Liberties Union
ACPM	American College of Preventive Medicine
ACSH	American Council on Science and Health
ADA	Americans with Disabilities Act
AHCPR	Agency for Health Care Policy and Research
AID	Agency for International Development
AIDS	Acquired Immunodeficiency Syndrome
AMA	American Medical Association
APAA	Armor Piercing Ammunition Act
APHA	American Public Health Association
ASPH	Association of Schools of Public Health
ASTHO	Association of State and Territorial Health Officials
ATPM	Association of Teachers of Preventive Medicine
ATSDR	Agency for Toxic Substances and Disease Registry
BATF	Bureau of Alcohol, Tobacco, and Firearms
BHVPA	Brady Handgun Violence Prevention Act
CAHP	Cooperative Action for Health Program
CAL/EPA	California's Environmental Protection Agency
CBER	Center for Biologics Evaluation and Research
CDC	Centers for Disease Control and Prevention
CDC	Communicable Disease Center
CDER	Center for Drug Evaluation and Research
CDRH	Center for Devices and Radiological Health
CEHN	Children's Environmental Health Network
CFSAN	Center for Food Safety and Applied Nutrition
CHA	Children's Health Act
CIA	Central Intelligence Agency
CLAA	Cigarette Labeling and Advertising Act
CPTED	Crime Prevention Through Environmental Design
CRG	Council for Responsible Genetics

CUP	Conditional Use Permits
DES	Diethylstilbestrol
DHEW	Department of Health, Education, and Welfare
DHHS	Department of Health and Human Services
DHS	Department of Homeland Security
DHSS	Missouri Department of Health and Senior Services
DNR	Department of Natural Resources
DPA	Drug Policy Alliance
DRGs	Diagnostic Related Groupings
EAF	Environmentally Attributable Fraction
EIS	Epidemic Intelligence Service
ELSI	Ethical, Legal, and Social Issues
EPA	Environmental Protection Agency
EPO	Epidemiology Program Office
ETS	Environmental Tobacco Smoke
FBI	Federal Bureau of Investigation
FDA	Food and Drug Administration
FDVGA	Federal Domestic Violence Gun Act
FEMA	Federal Emergency Management Agency
FERA	Federal Emergency Relief Administration
FRC	Family Research Council
GAO	General Accounting Office
GCA	Gun Control Act
GFSZA	Gun-Free School Zone Act
HAA	Hormonally Active Agent
HGP	Human Genome Project
HIV	Human Immunodeficiency Virus
HMO	Health Maintenance Organization
HSA	Health Systems Agencies
HSA	Highway Safety Act
IOM	Institute of Medicine
IPCC	Intergovernmental Panel on Climate Change
IRB	Institutional Review Board
JAMA	Journal of American Medical Association
MCOs	Medical Care Organizations
MCWA	Malaria Control in War Areas
MHHDREA	Minority Health and Health Disparities Research and Education Act
MHS	Marine Hospital Service
MSEHPA	Model State Emergency Health Powers Act
MSPHPA	Model State Public Health Privacy Act
NAAG	National Association of Attorneys General

NACCHO	National Association of County and City Health Officials
NASA	National Aeronautics and Space Administration
NBI	National Biological Institute
NCBDDD	National Center for Birth Defects and Developmental Disabilities
NCCDPHP	National Center for Chronic Disease Prevention and Health Promotion
NCEH	National Center for Environmental Health
NCHS	National Center for Health Statistics
NCI	National Cancer Institute
NCID	National Center for Infectious Diseases
NCIPC	National Center for Injury Prevention and Control
NCSL	National Conference of State Legislatures
NEI	National Eye Institute
NEPA	National Environmental Protection Act
NFA	National Firearms Act
NGA	National Governors' Association
NHANES	National Health and Nutrition Examination Survey
NHGRI	National Human Genome Research Institute
NHI	National Heart Institute
NHLBI	National Heart, Lung, and Blood Institute
NIA	National Institute on Aging
NIAAA	National Institute on Alcohol Abuse and Alcoholism
NIAID	National Institute on Allergy and Infectious Diseases
NIBR	National Institute of Biological Research
NIDA	National Institute on Drug Abuse
NIDR	National Institute of Dental Research
NIH	National Institutes of Health
NIMH	National Institute of Mental Health
NIOSH	National Institute for Occupational Safety and Health
NIPO	National Immunization Program Office
NOW	National Organization of Women
NSF	National Science Foundation
NVPO	National Vaccine Program Office
OEP	Office of Emergency Preparedness
OGHA	Office of Global Health Affairs
OHAP	Office of HIV/AIDS Policy
OHRP	Office for Human Research Protection
OHS	Office of Homeland Security
OIRA	Office of Information and Regulatory Affairs
OMH	Office of Minority Health
OMHRC	Office of Minority Health Resource Center

OPA	Office of Population Affairs
OPHP	Office of Public Health Preparedness
OPHS	Office of Public Health and Science
ORI	Office of Research Integrity
OSG	Office of the Surgeon General
OSHA	Occupational Safety and Health Administration
OWH	Office on Women's Health
PCPFS	President's Council on Physical Fitness and Sports
PFSA	Pure Food and Safety Act
PHIA	Public Health Improvement Act
PHLA	Public Health Law Association
PHLI	Public Health Leadership Institute
PHPPO	Public Health Practice Program Office
PHS	Public Health Service
PHTERA	Public Health Threats and Emergencies Relief Act
PKU	Phenylketonouria
PPS	Prospective Payment System
PRO	Peer Review Organization
PSRO	Professional Standards Review Organization
RCT	Randomized Clinical Trial
SCHIP	State Children's Health Insurance Program
SDA	Safe Drinking Act
SHHS	Secretary of Health and Human Services
SIECUS	Sexuality Information and Education Council of the United States
SOPHE	Society for Public Health Education
STDs	Sexually Transmitted Diseases
TB	Tuberculosis
TPMSPHA	Turning Point Model State Public Health Act
UN	United Nations
USAID	U.S. Agency for International Development
USDHEW	U.S. Department of Health, Education, and Welfare
USDHHS	U.S. Department of Health and Human Services
USDHUD	U.S. Department of Housing and Urban Development
USDOE	U.S. Department of Education
USPHS	U.S. Public Health Service
USPHSCC	U.S. Public Health Service Commissioned Corps
VCCEA	Violent Crime Control and Enforcement Act
WHO	World Health Organization
WMD	Weapons of Mass Destruction
WPA	Works Progress Administration

The Politics of
Public Health
in the
United States

CHAPTER 1

The Politics of Public Health in the United States

> Laws and regulations in a democracy are only as good as public support for them. Where the public is informed, educated, and socially aware, the level of personal and community health is generally high. Unless the majority of citizens is convinced of the value of a particular law or regulation, it becomes meaningless. (Duffy 1990, 313)

The American health care system is built around two complementary yet, unfortunately, often competitive models of health care. The first model—the curative model—emphasizes treatment and cure of illness and diseases. It is built around efforts designed to improve diagnostic and treatment/cure capabilities through the discovery of better drugs, surgical techniques, and life-sustaining and prolonging technologies. The second model—the preventive model—emphasizes prevention of illness, diseases, and promotion of health. It is built around efforts designed to prevent illness and diseases through promotion of a healthy lifestyle at the individual level and to discover and address environmental factors that contribute to ill health at the community level. The activities and services associated with prevention of illness, diseases, and promotion of health are what is generally referred to as public health. Public health has often been defined to include all knowledge and measures designed to foster health or prevent disease. This includes the recognition that "health" means much more than just the absence of disease (Winslow 1977).

These two models have competed for preeminence in the American health care system. Despite the accomplishments and successes of public health services in the United States, the curative model has dominated the American health care system since the second half of the twentieth century. In contrast, the public health system in the United States has suffered significant damage due to the politics of benign neglect.

Accomplishments of the Public Health System

Public health in the United States has had many successes and accomplishments to its credit. During the twentieth century, public health activities helped significantly improve the quality of life in America. According to an annual report released by the Centers for Disease Control and Prevention (CDC), Americans are healthier today than they were twenty-five years ago because of fewer smokers, less hypertension, lower cholesterol levels, better infant survival, and longer life expectancy ("CDC report finds Americans . . ." 2001). During the twentieth century, life expectancy increased by almost thirty years. In fact, life expectancy for persons in every age group also increased (U.S. Department of Health and Human Services 2000). Of the thirty-year gain in life expectancy, twenty-five years of the gain is attributable to advances in public health ("Public health achievements" 1999). Smallpox has been eradicated and polio has not been seen in the United States since 1979. Cardiovascular deaths have also declined significantly (Lee 1994).

According to the CDC, the top ten accomplishments of public health in the United States during the twentieth century include elimination of several infectious diseases due to the widespread use of vaccines, decreases in deaths related to motor vehicle accidents, declines in rate of fatal occupational injuries due to safer workplaces, better control of infectious diseases due to better sanitation, fewer coronary and stroke deaths, safer and more healthful foods, dramatic decreases in maternal and infant mortality, better family planning, significant decline in tooth decay and tooth loss with the addition of fluoridation to drinking water, and prevention of millions of smoking-related deaths due to increased recognition of the hazards of smoking ("Medical triumphs" 1999; "Ten great public health achievements" 1999). The 1980s alone saw a major decline in death rates for three of the leading causes of death among Americans—heart disease, stroke, and unintentional injuries. Some childhood diseases were nearly eliminated, and infant mortality also declined (U.S. Department of Health and Human Services 1990).

Shortcomings of the Public Health System

Despite these accomplishments, many problems remain. According to the World Health Organization (WHO), the overall life expectancy for babies born in 1999 in the United States is seventy years. The United States ranks only twenty-fourth in healthy life expectancy ranking[1] among all member states (WHO Press Release 2000). Despite the fact that the United States ranks first among all WHO member states in health expenditures per capita in international dollars, it ranks fifteenth on the index of overall health-system attainment,[2] seventy-second on the index of performance on the level of health,[3] and thirty-seventh on the index of overall health system performance[4] (World Health Organization 2000).

Almost half of the deaths in America have been attributed to an unhealthy lifestyle. Of the total number of deaths from all causes in America in 1988, almost half were attributed to deaths from cancer, heart disease, pulmonary disease, and motor vehicle accidents. Smoking alone accounts for one out of every five deaths in America (Houston 1991).

During the 1990s, many criticisms were voiced of the U.S. public health system. Many of these criticisms attributed the decline of the public health system in the United States during the last half of the twentieth century to the politics of neglect. According to some critics, the U.S. public health system is inadequately prepared to deal with many of the health problems of today or of the future due to a decline in the very foundation of the public health system (Cahill 1991). They charge that the present public health system has taken on the role of a safety-net medical provider to the disenfranchised, the elderly, the uninsured, the poor, the homeless, and people addicted to drugs (Cahill 1991).

According to a report of the Institute of Medicine (1988), the role and mission of the public health system is not clearly defined nor fully supported. Many health departments suffer problems of health care delivery, financing, and quality of personal health services. Public health services have fallen into disarray and the ability of the public health system to take effective actions to deal with continuing and emerging public health threats is questionable. According to the report, public health as a vital function is in trouble and many public health issues have become inappropriately politicized. In addition, public health responsibilities have become highly fragmented, and the public health system suffers from a hodgepodge of fractionalized interests, organizational turmoil, and unbalanced appropriations. A recent report by the Institute of Medicine (2002) concludes that not a great deal has changed since its 1988 report. The report argues that public health law at all levels of government is outdated and internally inconsistent creating inefficiency and lack of coordination. It further argues that the public health workforce is not receiving appropriate education and training to perform its current role. The current infrastructure burdens the work of the state and local public health agencies with too many administrative requirements. Furthermore, the report concludes that the Department of Health and Human Services (DHHS) currently lacks the capacity for conducting regular evaluation of the adequacy and ability of the governmental public health infrastructure.

Critics also argue that the American public health system, once the envy of the world, has fallen into despair with government laboratories running short on funds and equipment, and emergency preparedness plans that are antiquated (Kluger, Bjerklie, Dorfman, and Goldstein 2002). According to a recent report issued by the Institute for the Future (2000), public health is likely to continue to be underfunded and marginalized; efforts designed to address some of the underlying problems will continue to be incremental rather than dramatic.

The CDC has listed ten public health goals for the twenty-first century. They include eliminating health disparities, establishing a rational system of health care, focusing on children's physical and emotional development, achieving a longer "healthspan," integrating physical activity and promoting a healthy lifestyle, cleaning up and protecting the environment, preparing to respond to emerging infectious diseases, reducing the toll of violence in society, recognizing the contribution of mental health to overall health, and making wise use of scientific knowledge and technology (Koplan and Fleming 2000).

A report by the Institute of Medicine (2002) calls for action and change in six areas to address the present and future challenges faced by the American public health system. The six areas for action include adopting a population-based approach that considers multiple determinants of health, strengthening the government's public health infrastructure, building new intersectional partnerships, developing a system of accountability, decision-making based on evidence, and enhancing and facilitating communication between health professionals and community members.

The goals and challenges facing the U.S. public health system outlined by the CDC and the Institute of Medicine are daunting challenges, and meeting these challenges will require a strong political will, a significant commitment of monetary resources, and public health leadership.

The United States spends more money on health care than any other country in the world. National health care expenditures for the year 2000 were $1,299.5 billion. Private and public sector spending accounted for $712.3 million and $587.2 million, respectively, of the total amount. Of the $587.2 million spent by the federal government on health care, spending for public health activities accounted for only $42.2 million, a mere 7 percent of total national expenditures (Levit et al. 2002).

Of course, most public health activities in the United States are carried out at the state and local government levels. Historically, it has been very difficult to obtain uniform information about public health spending, especially state and local government spending on public health activities. Previous attempts to characterize public health expenditures failed to differentiate between expenditures for personal health care and population-based health services. Currently, efforts are under way to develop and test a new methodology to collect consistent and complete expenditure data on state and local health agency expenditures for personal health care services (Public Health Foundation 2000, 1998, 1997).

Public opinion polls suggest that Americans favor a health care system that spends more money on prevention and health promotion and less on treatment. According to a Harris poll, 91 percent of respondents considered prevention of infectious diseases very important, and 88 percent of respondents considered conducting research into the causes and prevention of diseases very important. Similarly, 87 percent of respondents considered immunization to be a key issue ("Americans support . . ." 2000). Unfortunately, despite the public's support for public health activities, public opinion polls also show that barely 1 percent of the public can specify the mission of public health (Young 1998).

It is clear that the public health system in the United States has suffered from political neglect in the last fifty years or so, and the revitalization of the U.S. public health system will necessitate confronting many of the challenges facing it in the twenty-first century. To understand these challenges, it is first necessary to examine the evolution of public health services and public health policies in the United States.

History of Public Health Policy in the United States

"The history of public health in America has not been one of constant and steady upward progress. One has only to glance at present public health statistics to realize how much still remains to be done. Yet public health, like politics, is the art of the possible" (Duffy 1990, 315). One of the best and most comprehensive accounts of the history of American public health is provided by John Duffy in *The Sanitarians* (1990). Duffy identifies three themes that run through the history of American public health. The first theme centers around the fact that public and community reactions to periodic public health crises have alternated between apathy and strong collective responses. For example, during the colonial period the public reacted strongly to yellow fever and smallpox by taking collective preventive actions. Yet, the diseases responsible for most of the sickness and death, such as malaria and respiratory infections, did not generate much public and community reaction. Since America is a land of immigrants of different cultures, the second important theme in the history of American public health is the impact of acculturation upon public health, that is, how various groups of immigrants have been integrated into American society with re-

spect to how to live and interact with their environment. The third theme is
the constant friction between individual and civil liberties on the one hand
and public welfare on the other as the government tries to regulate individual behavior in order to protect community health. This issue is certainly
at the heart of a democratic society. The task of public health officials in the
United States is made more difficult by the general American distrust of
government laws and regulations (Cantril and Cantril 1999; Wills 1999).

Duffy (1990) also argues that American public health policy has been
influenced by three key factors. First, at any given point in time, public
health measures and policies to be used are always influenced by the medical concepts predominant at that point in time. For example, if a sickness or
disease is attributed to the gods, then prayers and sacrifices may be considered the most appropriate responses for treatment. A second factor that
shapes public health policies is the prevailing social attitude. If the public
equates certain sicknesses or diseases with individual failings and sins, as
was the case with venereal disease in the past, society may show no inclination to try to cure or prevent it. The slow response to the AIDS crisis in the
United States to some extent reflected such societal attitudes (Shilts 1987).

The third factor that shapes public health policies is role of government
in a country's economy. Government regulatory policies are influenced by
what the dominant political ideology views to be the proper relationship
between government and business or industry. For example, in American
society, mistrust and suspicion by the citizens of government in general and
national government in particular do not allow the national government to
play a major role in the national economy except during a period of crisis.
The mistrust of government is a reflection of the constant tension between
the philosophy of Lockean liberalism, in which government is supposed to
play a neutral role to allow individual self-interest to prevail in the marketplace, and the philosophy of republicanism, which advocates a more positive role for the government in order to ensure the primacy of the
commonwealth. The result is that businesses in the United States are sub-
jected to piecemeal regulations for specific purposes without a clear overall
purpose (Ballam 1994).

We add a fourth factor—prevailing politics—as another important factor
that shapes the formulation of public health policies. Which party is in
power and which political ideology is dominant at any given point in time
determines how confidently government wields its authority and deploys its
regulatory power to protect public health (Scheiber 1997). The formulation, adoption, and implementation of public health policies are influenced
by social and political processes (Nathanson 1996). The political culture of
a country is important to the conception of policy solutions because policy

innovation is guided by what is culturally imaginable, and policy implementation is guided by structural constraints and opportunities (Dobbin 1994).

The Colonial Period: Seventeenth and Eighteenth Centuries

The first two hundred years of American history were a period of rapid population growth marked by the dramatic appearances of diseases such as diphtheria, measles, smallpox, and yellow fever. They often had devastating effects and wiped out as much as 10 percent of a community's population in a few months. Smallpox and yellow fever were two of the most feared diseases. However, the diseases that were the main killers on a regular basis included malaria, dysentery, typhoid, and smallpox. Death rates were horrendous during the early colonial period. Data complied from 1778 to 1795 in Rhode Island indicated that 20 percent of deaths were in persons younger than one year while about 15 percent of deaths occurred in people older than sixty years (Mermann 2000). The first colonists reported unprecedented epidemics among the native people.

During this period, colonists believed that all diseases were an expression of Divine Providence (Jimenez 1997). For example, in 1633 a New England colonist reported that "it pleased God to visit these Indians with great sickness" (Taylor 2001, 41). Health, sickness, recovery, and death, even in children, were considered acts of God that served a divine purpose. For example, a smallpox epidemic in 1689 was considered the work of God. Similarly, following the yellow fever epidemic in 1798, the Common Council of the City of New York declared February 5, 1799, a day of thanksgiving, humiliation, and prayer (Bloch 1974).

Thus, it is not surprising that health guides and medical advice tracts of the time urged their readers to avoid behaviors and emotions that could lead to disease. Strong emotions such as anger, fear, grief, and envy were often linked to ill health (Jimenez 1997). The desire to ensure that the welfare of the colony, that is, community, prevailed over that of the individual led colonial governments not only to direct business activities but also to engage in extensive supervision of personal conduct and behavior (Ballam 1994).

One of the first public health laws in Massachusetts limited the number of passengers on a ship according to the size of the vessel, recognizing that overcrowded conditions posed serious health problems on long ocean voyages. Concern over aesthetics and a vague sense of connection between sickness and purification also led the town of Boston in 1634 to prohibit residents from depositing fish or garbage near common landings (Duffy 1990).

This was the beginning of many colonies passing a variety of sanitation laws. Butchers and slaughterhouses were ordered to keep their premises clean. Scavengers were appointed by local authorities to impound stray cows and horses and remove dead animals from the street. Similarly, as the export of food increased, inspectors were appointed to supervise the packing of barrels of flour and meat (Duffy 1990).

Another strategy used by the colonists to deal with epidemics was the use of quarantine. Colonial quarantine regulations were adopted around the same time as other sanitary measures. The quarantine function during colonial times was left entirely in the hands of state and local authorities. This continued until the nineteenth century (Cumming 1921). Thus, by the end of the seventeenth century, several colonial towns had passed rudimentary but basic sanitation laws, and quarantine regulations were enforced during a health crisis.

During the eighteenth century there was an immense growth in the colonial population. This led to the creation of a more complex society as communities grew into towns and towns grew into small cities. Local authorities passed more specific ordinances and regulations governing sanitation, food, and water supplies. The need to take care of the poor and sick also led to the development of almshouses. The 1700s also witnessed the establishment of several hospitals. However, they mainly became places where the sick went to die. An expanding population and crowded conditions provided a potent ground for the spread of diseases.

The development of business in colonial America was shaped by a philosophy of mercantilism in which trade was the driving force (Ballam 1994). The growing trade with Europe, Africa, and the West Indies also led to importation of many diseases to the colonies. Two of the diseases that aroused the most attention were smallpox and yellow fever. Diphtheria was another major concern. However, the most important threat to health and life during the colonial period was from malaria. Ironically, the lack of roads or a modern transportation system also made it possible to confine the spread of disease by an effective quarantine at port cities. In many local communities, quarantine laws were strengthened. For example, cities such as Philadelphia and New York adopted strict quarantine regulations. Under such regulations, ships arriving from an infected port or with sickness aboard were required to get permission from local authorities before they were allowed to land passengers or goods at port.

Sanitation and lack of adequate drainage in communities also became major concerns. Drains and open sewers had become fertile grounds for the spread of diseases. The growth of the population combined with the waste produced by the emergence of slaughterhouses, fishmongering, and butchering added to the problems. Water supply was also an area of major concern. However, the majority of local authorities were reluctant to impose regulations and fines against businesses. Water supply remained primarily a citizen responsibility, although some local authorities had begun to take on responsibilities for public wells and adopt some regulations about water supply.

Even though the effectiveness of inoculation in limiting the devastation caused by smallpox was demonstrated as early as the 1721 epidemic, it remained a very controversial procedure. In fact, the careless use of inoculation often helped spread the disease and thus many communities opposed such measures. Nonetheless, the practice of inoculation slowly spread throughout the colonies and had become widely accepted by the time of the revolution for independence.

The disruption of civic life caused by the Revolutionary War led to widespread epidemics. Crowded army camps were ideal grounds for the spread of disease. As the fighting moved into the Southern colonies, troops from the North suffered a great deal from malaria (Duffy 1990). The smallpox epidemic also accompanied the American Revolution between 1775 and 1782. George Washington had to decide between variolation or quarantine as the best method to protect American troops. Variolation of the troops could increase the exposure to the rest while inoculation would have made American troops defenseless for weeks against British attacks. Britain had opted for variolation for their troops. In the beginning, George Washington opted for quarantine over variolation, which proved to be ineffective. Given the fact that American troops were more vulnerable to smallpox, Americans suspected that the British practiced a crude form of biological warfare by sending infected civilians and clothing within American lines (Fenn 2001). Ultimately, the general use of inoculation brought smallpox under control.

For a few years after the Revolutionary War, the basic pattern of sanitary regulations that was established during colonial times continued to be enforced with few modifications because the new nation was occupied with establishing a national government and state constitutions. However, the situation changed with the emergence of a potentially catastrophic yellow fever epidemic that afflicted Philadelphia in 1793 (Scutchfield and Keck 1997). Yellow fever attacked several other port cities such as Baltimore, New Haven, and New York in 1794 and 1795, but the one in Philadelphia was the most serious since the city was the capital and cultural center of the newly independent nation, and virtually the entire government was forced to desert the city. More than one-tenth of the city's population died despite sanitation and quarantine measures used by the city (Shonick 1993). The city of Baltimore, in response to yellow fever in 1794, built its first quarantine station under a legislative mandate (Markel 1995). Local health committees established to deal with the crisis in other cities, such as New York, also used quarantine measures to prevent the spread of diseases. The dramatic situation created by the yellow fever epidemic during the 1790s forced local and state governments to assume greater responsibilities in the area of public health activities. It also provided a major impetus to the sanitary reform movement.

The origins of the federal government's involvement in public health can be traced to the provision of medical and hospital care of merchant seamen and sailors. In 1798, Congress passed the Act for the Relief of Sick and Disabled Seamen to finance the construction and operation of public hospitals in port cities. The act created a tax on the salaries of sailors, and the revenue generated through the tax was to be used for the construction of public hospitals and medical care of merchant seamen. This was the first time that the federal, state, or local government had established a program for a specific group of people rather than a general health program (Anderson 1990). This established the Marine Hospital Service. Initially the service was a loosely knit group of hospitals for merchant seamen. In 1870 it was reorganized, and the administration of the hospitals was centralized in Washington, DC. A supervising surgeon was appointed head of the service in 1871, and in 1912 the Marine Hospital Service was renamed the Public Health Service (PHS) (Gist 1998; Parascandola 1995; Lee 1994).

The Nineteenth Century

Sanitation reformers stressed the need for clean water and air, and pure food. Cleanliness came to be viewed as necessary for the preservation of life and health. A connection was beginning to be seen between the quality of water, air, food, and illnesses. This led to increased support for the strengthening local government structures to prevent or palliate the epidemics. However, this is not to suggest that a sanitary revolution was well under way. The major emphasis to prevent epidemics remained on quarantine measures and isolating disease victims in pest houses. The high cost of sanitary measures also worked against sanitary reforms (Duffy 1990).

In addition, unlike their predecessors, antebellum writers stressed health promotion and disease prevention. Health reformers were especially concerned with growing urbanization, commercialization, full-scale manufacturing, and increased immigration. Interest in public health grew out of health problems connected with urban growth in the early nineteenth century (Rosen 1958). The surge of epidemics led locally appointed health boards to look for causes of diseases. Antebellum urban sanitary reform was the first stage of the public health movement (Jimenez 1997). Early sanitary engineers sought to provide pure water—the urban sanitary infrastructure's triad—water supply, water treatment, and solid waste disposal—as a public good (Melosi 1999). Prior to 1850, local public health activities were largely a reaction to the onset of epidemics, and local authorities were content with passing quarantine and sanitary measures (Shonick 1993).

Smallpox was brought under control with inoculation, and the introduction of a vaccine in 1798 opened the path for prevention. In fact, in 1813 the federal government passed a law to encourage the use of vaccination to prevent smallpox. By 1830, vaccination had become a generally accepted practice.

The first third of the nineteenth century witnessed only limited advances in the functions and responsibilities of municipal government, such as the emergence of garbage collection and street-cleaning, temporary health boards, quarantine systems, public or private water systems, and nuisance inspections. The period from about 1830 to the start of the Civil War witnessed the emergence of vital statistics as an important public health tool and the increasing role of medical societies. Improvement in the collection of vital statistics was aided by the American Medical Association (AMA), established in 1847, and the rapid growth of insurance companies around the middle of the nineteenth century (Duffy 1990). Between 1857 and 1860, several national sanitary conventions were held that called for sanitary and hygiene reforms.

However, the outbreak of Civil War in the spring of 1861 delayed the establishment of any national health organization. In the bloody Civil War, about six hundred thousand men lost their lives. Sickness killed twice as many people as did battle wounds. Crowded army camps produced widespread outbreaks of mumps, measles, scarlet fever, smallpox, and other disorders. Soldiers also suffered from diarrhea, dysentery, typhoid, and other illnesses due to poor food and unsanitary conditions. President Lincoln in June 1861 gave his approval for the creation of the United States Sanitary Commission, which provided direct assistance to soldiers. The commission also helped reform the Army Medical Corps.

The end of the Civil War helped usher in the sanitary revolution in the United States. By the end of the 1860s, several cities had established effective health boards, and the sanitary movement was well under way. The next thirty years witnessed the emergence of state health boards and the rapid expansion of urban local health departments.

The American Public Health Association (APHA) was established in 1872, which ultimately led to the professionalization of public health. By the 1870s, public health reformers were pushing for the formation of a national system of quarantine and a national health board. In 1879 the United States Congress created the National Health Board, and it was given the power to enforce interstate quarantine laws that previously were the responsibility of the Marine Hospital Service (Anderson 1990). The board was responsible for formulating quarantine regulations but it soon became embroiled in a political battle over the issue of states' rights because local governments were unwilling to give up their powers to the national government. Finally, in 1883, the National Health Board was abolished and its quarantine powers were returned to the Marine Hospital Service (Fee 1997).

In 1876 the discovery of the germ theory of disease by Louis Pasteur established the empirical causal link between germs and diseases (Gorham 1921). In his 1878 celebrated lecture to surgeons on the germ theory, Louis Pasteur warned of the dangers caused by the germs of microbes on the surface of every object (Walker 1930). In 1880 he published his germ theory of disease, in which he argued that all contagious diseases were caused by microscopic organisms (Garrett 2000). This provided public health with an empirical foundation.

In 1887 the first research facility, the Hygiene Laboratory, was established at the Staten Island Marine Hospital. In 1891 it was moved to Washington, DC. In 1889 the United States Public Health was commissioned with a regular corps of physicians (Hinman 1990). The sanitary revolution was fully under way during the last twenty years or so of the nineteenth century. City health departments were establishing vaccination programs and testing water, and the sanitation movement was beginning to improve the quality of life in America. Morbidity and mortality rates in large cities were declining.

However, it should be stressed that during the 1880s and 1890s the successful implementation of vaccination programs was often delayed by the antivaccination movement led largely by irregular physicians and laypersons (Garrett 2000; see also Allen 2002). The movement was successful in opposing compulsory vaccination in schools. The antivaccination movement was also successful in using courts and legislatures to delay action on vaccination programs. Nonetheless, public health was becoming both institutionalized and professionalized, and public health departments were increasingly involved in educating the public about public health hazards (Duffy 1990).

The Twentieth Century

The rise of bacteriology combined with advances in pathology, physiology, chemistry, and other fields was beginning to enhance the understanding of the causes of various diseases as many pathogenic organisms were identified. Laboratory testing of water, milk, and other foods had become an important function of local health departments. The rise of bacteriology and other scientific advances also contributed to the professionalization of public health (Fee 1997). Advances in bacteriology and pathologic science also created an appreciation of the importance of laboratory facilities to identify agents of communicable diseases. Local public health departments became responsible for maintaining public health laboratories. In fact, by the first quarter of the twentieth century, most of the causes and methods of transmission of leading communicable diseases had been identified, and preventive measures had been developed. In the early 1900s the new public health movement expanded its role from environmental sanitation and concern with infectious disease to control of communicable diseases (Cassedy 1962).

State health boards, which were weak and ineffective agencies staffed by volunteers, were transformed into strong state departments led by public health professionals between 1900 and the 1940s. Several factors contributed to this transformation, including the Progressive movement, which demanded better government and a better quality of life; urbanization, requiring more attention to be focused on sanitation and health; the influence of strong local health leaders who had moved into state governments; and the efforts of private foundations and the federal government (Duffy 1990).

The bacteriological revolution combined with other developments in medicine also strengthened the position of the medical profession, and physicians came to dominate public health. For example, during the early years of the APHA, a large majority of its membership was made up of physicians. The new method of identifying disease through microscopes and the demonstrated diagnostic power of public health laboratories moved the focus away from environmental reform and narrowed the distance between medicine and public health, creating conflict and tension between the two as physicians increasingly became resentful of public health officials' claims to diagnose and treat infectious diseases (Fee 1997). For example, physicians strongly opposed and tried to defeat passage of the Sheppard-Towner Act of 1921, which authorized federal grants to state health departments for maternal and infant hygiene, because they saw this as a threat to their profession and income.

As the demand for public health professionals increased, separate schools of public health were established through financial support from private donations. For example, the Harvard School of Public Health was funded by philanthropists (Garrett 2000). The Johns Hopkins School of Hygiene and Public Health was established in 1916 by a Rockefeller Foundation grant. Soon, several other schools of public health were established following the Johns Hopkins model. This combined with other developments ultimately helped public health establish an identity separate from that of private medicine (Duffy 1990).

By the beginning of the twentieth century the federal government was also becoming more active. In 1902 a permanent Census Bureau was established by the federal government to collect vital statistics. The Federal Food and Drug Act was passed in 1906 to supplement state control and regulation of food and to encourage cooperative efforts between the federal and state governments. The Hygiene Laboratory established in 1887 became the National Institute of Health (NIH) in 1909. In 1912 the name of the United States Marine Hospital Service was changed by Congress to the United States Public Health Service (USPHS) and it was authorized to study and investigate causes of diseases and provide information for the public. During the same year the Children's Bureau was established in the Department of Commerce and Labor to address concerns raised about child labor laws. The bureau was soon involved in health-related activities such as maternal and child welfare and infant mortality. In 1921, Congress passed the Sheppard-Towner Act to provide federal grants-in-aid to states for maternal and child health programs to reduce maternal and infant mortality.

By 1935, not only had public health become professionalized, it had also become an important government function performed by agencies at the local, state, and to some extent, national levels. All major cities had public health departments and laboratories. Most states had established state health boards and were supervising and monitoring local public health activities. The federal government was working closely with state governments in performing quarantine services and providing some federal financial aid to improve sanitary services. The federal government also provided funds to states for public health training, which helped develop programs for controlling specific diseases, expand local health departments, and increase training of personnel, among other improvements (Fee 1997).

The Social Security Act of 1935 was the first broad-based social welfare legislation passed in the United States. It provided old-age benefits, unemployment insurance, and public health services. Under the law, federal funds were made available to states for maternal and child health services and expansion of other public health services. In 1937 the establishment of the National Cancer Institute (NCI) expanded public health services' involvement in laboratory and field research, but more important, it provided grants-in-aid to nongovernmental institutions for research to improve the general public health (Snyder 1994a).

World War II also provided public health services with an opportunity to play a major role in American health affairs. During the war years the PHS was responsible for medical and sanitary support for the different branches of the armed forces. The PHS also instituted a training program for nurses. In fact, in 1943, Congress created the Cadet Nurses Corps within the PHS, and between 1943 and 1948, 124,065 nurses graduated from the Cadet Nurses Corps (Willever 1994).

Post–World War II, medical research and science had become the hallmark of health care and medicine in the United States as large sums of grants were awarded by the federal government for basic research and medical technology. Public health professionals were confronted with new community health problems such as alcoholism, drug addiction, smoking, exposure to radiation, heart disease, cancer, mental illness, and environmental hazards, among others.

Changed societal conditions following World War II necessitated a new definition for the role of public health professionals. This came in the form of two laws passed by Congress. The first law—Public Law 78-184 signed in November 1943—reorganized the Commissioned Corps along military lines and integrated PHS functions into four subdivisions: Office of the Surgeon General, the NIH, the Bureau of Medical Services, and the Bureau of State Services (Snyder 1994a). Under this law, the PHS turned into a tightly knit bureaucracy managed by public health professionals. The second law—Public Law 78-410, the Public Health Service Act, passed in 1944—codified all of PHS's responsibilities and strengthened the hand of the surgeon general (Snyder 1994a, 1994b).

The 1944 law gave public health its mission and was a significant innovation in national policy. It helped make scientific research a major area of priority by providing funding for biomedical research at private institutions, the training of public health professionals, and the building of new health care facilities. The USPHS became the leader in implementing national policy based on the new consensus that medical science was the main cause of progress in the fight against disease. In 1946, Congress passed the Hill-Burton Act, which led to the expansion of hospital capacity. The same year the Communicable Disease Center (CDC) was established (Fox 1994). In 1948, Congress established the National Heart Institute (NHI), the National Biological Institute (NBI), and the National Institute of Dental Research (NIDR) as part of the National Institute of Health. The National Institute of Health itself was renamed National Institutes of Health (NIH). The National Institute of Mental Health (NIMH) was added to the NIH in 1949. The budget of the NIH grew from $46.3 million in 1950 to $400 million during the next decade. Americans placed their hope in the belief that the magic of science and money in terms of biomedical research would lead to finding cures for leading killers such as cancer and heart disease. The curative model of health care began to replace the preventive model.

One issue that did gain prominence in the field of public health was that of community or social medicine (Henig 1997). Epidemiology came to be viewed as an essential discipline for dealing with both chronic and infectious diseases. The idea that community health can be quantitatively measured helped broaden the scope of epidemiology to place more emphasis on the social environment, giving rise to medical ecology. However, under the onslaught of biomedical research, the theoretical innovations of social medicine—the idea that advances in diet, housing, and public health nursing were more important than building hospitals—were not translated into effective public health programs, and public health services suffered from neglect (Fee 1997).

During the 1950s, public health professionals showed political naivete by not taking credit for controlling infectious diseases and other scientific achievements during World War II. In the public's mind, many of these successes came to be attributed to scientific medicine and not to public health. Public health expenditures also failed to keep pace with the increase in population because public health professionals failed to assert a strong political presence or even recognize the importance of politics to public health. In recognition of this fact, the annual meeting of the APHA in 1958 was devoted to the discussion of the politics of public health (Fee 1997).

Similarly, many of the new health and social programs created in the 1960s, such as the War on Poverty programs along with Medicaid and Medicare, bypassed the structure of public health agencies and created new agencies to deal with federal–local government relations. The same was the case with environmental issues in the 1970s. For example, a separate Environmental Protection Agency (EPA) was created to deal with environmental problems. Mental health agencies were often separate from public health agencies (Fee 1997). In fact, by the 1960s those medical areas most immediately connected to public health, such as family practice, infectious disease, pediatrics, and medical social work, had lost prestige and status while medical specialties connected with hospitals such as oncology, surgery, cardiology, and the like had risen to the top in terms of money, prestige, and status (Garrett 2000).

While during the 1960s and 1970s the focus was on expanding the capacity to deliver health services, during the 1970s and 1980s the focus turned to cost containment, quality control, practice guidelines, and peer review (Henig 1997). This was reflected in various government policies such as the establishment of health maintenance organizations (HMOs), health system agencies (HSAs) for the planning of health care facilities, peer review organizations

(PROs), and the prospective payment system (PPS), also known as diagnostic related groupings (DRGs) for Medicare reimbursement to hospitals. During the Reagan administration, funding for public health programs was cut, and state health departments were left with the task of managing the Medicaid program that delivered health care services to the uninsured and indigent populations, severely straining state budgets. The Medicare program shifted American health expenditures toward end-of-life care and away from public health's most important activity, that is, prevention. The AIDS epidemic in the 1980s and the failure of the public health system to respond quickly to the crisis revealed significant weaknesses in the public health system. The Institute of Medicine's report *The Future of Public Health* (1988) highlighted many of the major shortcomings of the U.S. public health system.

The euphoria for the overhaul of the American health system and health care reform that gained momentum during the presidential campaign of 1992 and the election of Bill Clinton to the presidency faded when Congress failed to pass any of the competing health care reform proposals during the summer of 1994. During the 1990s, managed care and managed competition became the new buzzwords for health care cost containment, with marketplace medicine taking center stage. What role public health will play in such a marketplace is still evolving.

As we discussed earlier in the chapter, by the late 1980s and 1990s, significant criticisms of the public health system had emerged, pointing to many shortcomings. At the beginning of the twenty-first century, the American public health system resembled a hodgepodge of programs and agencies rather than a coherent system. The emphasis on individualism and individual rights had led to the neglect of the crucial role played by public health activities in maintaining and promoting community health. Most of the legal authorities of the public health system had been stripped by the 1950s. The America that had been the role model for designing and implementing the public health program in the 1890s had become a nation that had neglected its public health system by the 1990s. The American public health system, once an envy of the world, was in shambles by the end of the twentieth century (Garrett 2000).

In 2000 the APHA became more active in promoting laws designed to improve public health ("APHA promotes public health legislation" 2001). Congress passed several key laws to benefit public health activities. The Minority Health and Health Disparities Research and Education Act of 2000, also known as the Health Care Fairness Act, established a new center for research on minority health and health disparities. The Children's Health Act of 2000 was designed to expand research and treatment on childhood issues such as diabetes, asthma, and autism, among others.

The Public Health Improvement Act of 2000 passed by Congress contains a comprehensive package of public health laws. One is the Public Health Threats and Emergencies Relief Act. It is designed to strengthen the country's capacity to detect and respond to serious public health threats such as bioterrorist attacks and bacterial resistance to antimicrobials. Under the Twenty-First Century Research Laboratories Act, the NIH will provide grants to improve the infrastructure of United States' research institutions by renovating biomedical and behavioral research facilities throughout the country. Other laws are designed to expand and intensify research and other activities with respect to lupus, prostate cancer, Alzheimer's disease, and to develop treatments for sexually transmitted diseases through NIH research ("Public Health Improvement Act of 2000" 2001; "Legislation to Benefit Key Public Health Issues" 2001; Benjamin 2001).

The terrorist attacks of September 11, 2001, on the Twin Towers of the World Trade Center in New York and on the Pentagon in Washington, DC, followed by the anthrax-laced letter mailed to Sen. Tom Daschle (D-South Dakota) and the death of five citizens exposed to anthrax, raised the specter of a bioterrorist attack in the United States and questioned the preparedness of United States' public health agencies to deal with such an attack. The significant amount of media coverage dealing with the anthrax exposure cases and the public health agencies' handling of these cases put the spotlight on the American public health system and helped raised public awareness about the role of public health. This was reflected in an interactive poll conducted by the Harris Poll in which 77 percent of the respondents indicated that it was very or extremely important to strengthen the United States' public health system to detect, diagnose, treat, and prevent infectious and other diseases ("Health Care Priorities" 2002).

The Bush administration's budget request for the fiscal year (FY) 2003 proposed $5.9 billion to improve the nation's public health system to defend against the deliberate use of disease as a weapon. The bioterrorism budget request included $1.8 billion for federal agencies and $1.6 billion for state and local public health agencies involved in bioterrorism defense. It also proposed to spend $650 million to expand the nation's stockpile of vaccines and antibiotics, to construct containment laboratories, and to conduct basic and applied research in new drugs (Miller 2002). President Bush also requested an increase of $3.7 billion, or 15.7 percent, for the NIH, with a significant amount of that money going to the National Institute on Allergy and Infectious Diseases (NIAID) for basic and applied research (Stolberg 2002). In May 2002 the House and the Senate reached a compromise on a bioterrorism bill that included funding to expand the government's stockpile of antibiotics and vaccines and to tighten regulations of laboratories that handle deadly microbes. The bill also includes measures to improve food safety and protect water systems. Under the bill, states would get $1.5 billion in federal grants to prepare for a biological attack. Money is also provided to buy hospital equipment and to train medical workers to deal with a bioterrorist attack and to prepare for medical emergencies. Finally, the bill also provided $300 million to CDC to upgrade its laboratories and scientific equipment (Pear 2002).

Federal funding to state and local governments for bioterrorism-related programs and activities has increased significantly. In fact, the largest share of federal funding is dedicated to this cause. On the negative side, this has led to neglect of other needs. According to Georges Benjamin, executive director of the American Public Health Association (APHA), "We are funding preparedness and cutting everything else" ("Public Health: Costs of Complacency" 2004, 26). Public health budgets derived from state general funds have been reduced in states like Oklahoma, Indiana, and Massachusetts (ibid).

Thus it appears that at the dawn of the twenty-first century, the U.S. public health system is again in the spotlight as it attempts to address many of the shortcomings created by years of neglect. How successful it will be in confronting these challenges remains to be seen. The success or failure of the American public health system will depend on how the politics of public health shapes future public health policies. The ability, capacity, and willingness of public health professionals to enter the political arena to influence and shape public health policies will be a determining factor in their success or failure. Before examining the politics of public health and the challenges confronting public health in the twenty-first century, it is useful to first understand the organization of the U.S. public health system.

The Organization of the U.S. Public Health Service

The tradition of the Public Health Service (PHS) started in 1798 with the establishment of the Marine Hospital Service (MHS) to provide medical care for sick and disabled seamen. The original mission of the MHS was to create, staff, and manage a series of hospitals to treat the illnesses of merchant seamen. However, from early on, providing medical care became linked with research and disease prevention. The Marine Hospital Service helped fight yellow fever, cholera, and smallpox epidemics (Koop and Ginzberg 1989). In 1889, Congress established the United States Public Health Service Commissioned Corps (USPHSCC). Originally the corps was created as a uniformed nonmilitary service. In 1912 the Marine Hospital Service was renamed the Public Health Service (PHS). President Roosevelt in 1939 placed the PHS in the Federal Security Agency (FSA).

Public Law 78-184 passed by Congress in 1943 encouraged the organization of the Commissioned Corps along military lines and helped centralize various functions of the PHS. Public Law 78-410 passed by Congress in 1944 provided a legal framework for all of the PHS's responsibilities and authorities (Snyder 1994a). Under the law, the PHS assumed primary responsibility for advancing the nation's public health through subsidizing biomedical research at private institutions, training health professionals, and building health care facilities. It authorized the surgeon general to conduct clinical research and establish new institutes (Snyder 1994b). The 1944 law gave PHS its mission and made it a leading agency in advancing medical science as the primary cause of progress in the struggle against disease. It helped transform scientific research from an accidental or emergency function into a permanent function and major priority (Fox 1994).

In 1953 the FSA was renamed the Department of Health, Education, and Welfare (DHEW). In 1979, during the Carter administration, the DHEW was split into two departments—the Department of Education and the Department of Health and Human Services (DHHS). Today the PHS is located within the DHHS.

The functions and missions of the USPHS have evolved over time. Originally it was mainly concerned with infectious diseases. Today its focus has shifted to cardiovascular diseases, cancer, and AIDS, among others. The broad mission of the USPHS is to protect and advance the health of the American people. The USPHS tries to achieve its mission through biomedical research, promoting a healthy lifestyle, prevention of disease, care and treatment of patients, and performing other traditional public health activities such as vaccination. The USPHS works with state and local authorities to solve various health problems (Koop and Ginzberg 1989).

The National Government

In theory, the United States Constitution established a national government that had limited powers. In reality, however, the expansion of the national government's powers over the last two hundred years has given the national government significant authority to act in the interest of citizens' public health and safety, that is, to prevent injury and disease and promote the nation's health. Over the years the national government has played a major role in the identification, control, and elimination of public health threats in the United States (Foreman 1994).

Most of the national government's constitutional powers in the area of public health are indirect and derived from its power to tax, spend, and regulate commerce (Gostin 2000a). The power to tax and spend allows the national government to raise and allocate resources for its various public health activities. The power to tax also gives the national government the means to penalize, either directly or indirectly, private activities that endanger public health by levying higher taxes (for example, federal taxes on cigarettes, alcohol, and air pollution), thus discouraging citizens and industries from engaging in such activities. Similarly, tax incentives can be used to encourage health-promoting activities (for example, employer-sponsored health insurance, preventive care, etc.). The national government can also use federal grants as a tool to induce state governments to meet federal performance standards (for example, highway and occupational safety, Medicaid). Congress's power to regulate commerce allows the national government to exercise its authority in areas such as environmental protection, occupational health, and safety of food and drug products, among other priorities, in the name of protecting public health and safety. The limitations on the national government's power and authority derive from the Constitution's guarantees of privacy, liberty, and property (Gostin 2000a).

Today almost all public health activities of the national government are carried out by five agencies within the DHHS—Office of Public Health and Science (OPHS), Centers for Disease Control and Prevention (CDC), National Institutes of Health (NIH), Office of Public Health Preparedness (OPHP), and the Food and Drug Administration (FDA). Each of the agencies contains many divisions/centers/institutes and performs a variety of functions. Outside of the DHHS, another agency involved in public health issues is the Occupational Safety and Health Administration (OSHA).

The Office of Public Health and Science

The OPHS is headed by the assistant secretary for health, who serves as the senior adviser on public health and science issues to the secretary of DHHS. The office provides leadership, gives directions, and coordinates many of the program activities carried out by many of its different divisions. The OPHS includes many offices that perform a variety of functions related to public health (U.S. Department of Health and Human Services 2002) (Table 1.1).

Today the most visible office is that of the Office of the Surgeon General (OSG) of the United States. The surgeon general is the national spokesperson on public health issues. The original MHS was a loose collection of many hospitals. It was reorganized in 1870, and the administration of all the hospitals under the MHS was centralized in Washington, DC. In 1871 the title of the head of MHS was changed to supervising surgeon general. In 1875 the title was changed to surgeon general (Parascandola 1995). How-

Table 1.1

Offices Located Within the Office of Public Health and Science

Office of Disease Prevention and Health Promotion
Office of Emergency Preparedness
Office of Global Health Affairs
Office of HIV/AIDS Policy
Office for Human Research Protection
Office of Minority Health
Office of Population Affairs
Office of Research Integrity
Office of the Surgeon General
Office on Women's Health
Office of Military Liaison and Veterans Affairs
National Vaccine Program Office
President's Council on Physical Fitness and Sports
Regional Health Administrators

Related Programs
    Advisory Committee on Blood Safety and Availability
    Pharmacy Professional Advisory Committee
    Secretary's Advisory Committee on Genetic Testing
    U.S. Public Health Service Nursing

Source: Department of Health and Human Services, www.hhs.gov/agencies/ophs.html.

ever, it was not until the public health service reforms of the 1940s that the surgeon general's role in public health policymaking was enhanced.

The surgeon general is appointed by the president of the United States with the advice and consent of the Senate. He serves a four-year term and reports to the assistant secretary for health. He also holds the rank of vice admiral in the United States Public Health Service Commissioned Corps (USPHSCC). Qualifications include a medical degree from an accredited medical school, at least one year of postgraduate medical training, and license to practice medicine in one of the fifty states. The surgeon general is responsible for administering the USPHSCC. He is also expected to provide leadership and management oversight of the Commissioned Corps' involvement in emergency preparedness and response activities. In addition, his duties also include protecting and advancing the nation's health through education of the public, disease prevention and health promotion, advising the secretary of HHS and the president on public health issues, and improving public health practices through advancement of professional standards and establishment of research priorities (U.S. Department of Health and Human Services 2002).

The Office of Disease Prevention and Health Promotion is responsible for strengthening disease prevention and health promotion priorities of the DHHS through collaborative efforts with other agencies. The Office of Emergency Preparedness (OEP) is responsible for managing and coordinating federal medical and health-related social services during major emergencies and federally declared disasters such as natural and technological disasters, major transportation accidents, and terrorism. The Office of Global Health Affairs (OGHA) is responsible for working with governments of other countries and the private sector on refugee health issues, providing leadership and coordination for bilateral programs with other countries, and working with the U.S. Agency for International Development (USAID).

The Office of HIV/AIDS Policy (OHAP) acts as a principal adviser to the assistant secretary for health and the surgeon general on HIV/AIDS issues such as budget, research, care and treatment services, and training. It is also responsible for implementing HIV/AIDS programs across all agencies within the DHHS. The Office for Human Research Protection (OHRP) is responsible for developing, monitoring, and exercising compliance oversight with DHHS's regulations for the protection of human subjects in research conducted or supported by any agencies of the DHHS. It is also responsible for coordinating DHHS regulations, establishing criteria for assurance of compliance, and evaluating the effectiveness of DHHS programs and policies for the protection of human subjects in research ("Office of Public Health and Science, and National Institutes of Health, Office of the Director; Statement of Organization, Functions, and Delegation of Authority" 2000).

The mission of the Office of Minority Health (OMH) is to improve the health of racial and ethnic minorities through the development of health policies and programs designed to eliminate disparities in health care. The Office of Minority Health Resource Center (OMHRC) within the OMH has become the largest source of minority health information. The Office on Women's Health (OWH) is the focal point for women's health issues and works to reduce inequalities in research and health care services and to promote education on women's health issues.

The Office of Population Affairs (OPA) is responsible for advising the secretary and the assistant secretary on reproductive health issues including adolescent pregnancy family planning and sterilization. The Office of Research Integrity (ORI) promotes the integrity of biomedical and behavioral research by the USPHS at four thousand institutions worldwide. It monitors investigation of institutional research misconduct and helps promote responsible conduct of research through educational and regulatory activities.

The President's Council on Physical Fitness and Sports (PCPFS) is responsible for promoting, encouraging, and motivating Americans to become physically active by participating in sports through education and development of community recreational, physical fitness, and sports programs. It also works with businesses and government agencies to establish innovative programs to reduce the financial and health care costs associated with physical activities.

The National Vaccine Program Office (NVPO) is responsible for carrying out the national goals of the national vaccine plan in order to prevent outbreaks of infectious diseases through immunizations.

Centers for Disease Control and Prevention

The Communicable Disease Center (CDC) was created in 1946. Its name was changed to the Centers for Disease Control (CDC) in 1970. It was an outgrowth of an agency called Malaria Control in War Areas (MCWA). During its first year, CDC was preoccupied with malaria control. It soon focused on other tropical diseases and ultimately assumed responsibility for a wide range of contagious disorders. From the beginning, one of the major functions of the CDC included training state and local health care workers in disease control through the application of the science of epidemiology (Etheridge 1992). The fear of biological warfare during World War II necessitated adding an Epidemic Intelligence Service (EIS) to the Division of Epidemiology. The Vietnam War moved the CDC onto the international scene due to the threat of different forms of malaria to American soldiers in Southeast Asia and to Peace Corps workers in Africa. One of the great successes of the CDC is the role it played in the worldwide eradication of smallpox (Etheridge 1992).

The mission of the CDC is to promote health and quality of life by preventing and controlling disease, injury, and disability. The CDC includes eleven centers, institutes, and offices, and is headed by a director who also serves as administrator for the Agency for Toxic Substances and Disease Registry (ATSDR), a sister agency of the CDC. The CDC performs many of the administrative functions of the ATSDR.

The Office of the Director includes various offices such as Associate Director for Minority Health, Associate Director for Science, Freedom of Information Act Office, Information Resource Management Office, Management Analysis and Services Office, National Vaccine Program Office, Office of Women's Health, Office of Communication, Technology Transfer Office, Office of Health and Safety, and Washington, DC Office (Centers for Disease Control and Prevention 2002).

The CDC is a complex agency with many major centers, institutes, and/

Table 1.2

Offices/Centers Located Within the Centers for Disease Control and Prevention

Office of the Director
  Office of Global Health
  CDC Washington Office
  Office of Program Planning and Evaluation
  Office of Communication
  National Vaccine Program Office
  Office of Women's Health
  Office of Health and Safety
  Office of Equal Employment Opportunity
  Office of Program Services
  Office of Management and Operations
  Financial Management Office

Epidemiology Program Office
National Immunization Program Office
Public Health Practice Program Office

National Center for Birth Defects and Developmental Disabilities
National Center for Chronic Disease Prevention and Health Promotion
National Center for Environmental Health
National Center for Health Statistics
National Center for Infectious Diseases
National Center for Injury Prevention and Control
National Center for HIV, STDs, and TB Prevention
National Institute for Occupational Safety and Health

Source: Centers for Disease Control, www.cdc.gov/od/cdcchart.htm.

or offices (Table 1.2). The primary responsibility of the Epidemiology Program Office (EPO) is to strengthen the public health system by coordinating public health surveillance at the CDC and training experts in surveillance, epidemiology, applied public health, and prevention effectiveness. The mission of the National Center for Chronic Disease Prevention and Health Promotion (NCCDPHP) is to prevent and control chronic diseases. The center conducts scientific studies to understand the causes of various diseases and monitors the health of the nation through surveys. It also supports programs to promote healthy behavior. The National Center for Environmental Health (NCEH) is responsible for promoting health and quality of life by preventing or controlling diseases, birth defects, disabilities, or deaths that result from interactions between people and their environment. The National Center for Health Statistics (NCHS) compiles statistical information to guide actions and policies to improve the health of our people (Centers for Disease Control and Prevention 2002).

The National Immunization Program Office (NIPO) is responsible for the planning, coordination, and conducting of immunization activities nationwide. The focus of the Public Health Practice Program Office (PHPPO) is on creating an effective organizational structure, public health workforce, public health laboratories, and management of public health information and knowledge. The National Center for Birth Defects and Developmental Disabilities (NCBDDD) promotes the health of babies, children, and adults. This center is responsible for identifying the causes of birth defects and developmental disabilities, and promoting health and well-being among people of all ages who have disabilities. The mission of the National Center for Infectious Diseases (NCID) is to prevent illness, disability, and death caused by infectious diseases in the United States and around the world. The National Center for Injury Prevention and Control (NCIPC) works to reduce morbidity, disability, mortality, and costs associated with injuries. The National Center for HIV, STDs, and TB Prevention is responsible for public health surveillance, prevention research, and programs to prevent and control human immunodeficiency virus (HIV) infection and acquired immunodeficiency syndrome (AIDS), other sexually transmitted diseases (STDs), and tuberculosis (TB). The National Institute for Occupational Safety and Health (NIOSH) is responsible for conducting research and making recommendations for the prevention of work-related disease and injury (Centers for Disease Control and Prevention 2002).

National Institutes of Health

The forerunner to the National Institutes of Health (NIH) was the Hygiene Laboratory established in 1887 at Staten Island Marine Hospital. The laboratory was moved to Washington, DC, in 1891. The NIH was created in 1909. The National Cancer Institute was established in 1937. The National Heart Institute, the National Institute of Dental Research, and the National Institute of Biological Research (NIBR) were created by Congress as part of the National Institute of Health in 1948, and the name of the National Institute of Health was changed to the National Institutes of Health.

The NIH is headed by a director who is responsible for setting policy for NIH and for, planning, organizing, managing, and coordinating the programs and activities of its various institutes and centers. The NIH is the world's leading medical research center and the focal point for medical and behavioral research in the United States. The primary mission of the NIH is to discover new knowledge by conducting research in its laboratories, supporting research of scientists in universities, hospitals, and research institutions throughout the United States and the world, training research investigators, and encouraging communication of medical information. The goal of NIH research is to discover new scientific knowledge that can help prevent, detect, diagnose, and treat various forms of diseases and disabilities. To this end the NIH provides federal grants and contracts for biomedical research. Most of the NIH budget supports individual research projects conceived of and conducted either by government scientists working on the NIH campus or by scientists working in other settings such as universities; medical, dental, nursing, and pharmacy schools; schools of public health; and nonprofit research institutions or private research laboratories. In 2001 the NIH spent about $21 billion in support of research. The NIH has been credited for significant reductions in heart disease and deaths caused by strokes, and for improved treatment and detection methods for cancer, among other diseases, in the United States (National Institutes of Health 2002).

The NIH has twenty-seven institutes and/or centers specializing in specific fields of research (Table 1.3). Some of the major institutes/centers are the National Cancer Institute (NCI), the National Eye Institute (NEI), the National Heart, Lung, and Blood Institute (NHLBI), the National Institute on Aging (NIA), the National Institute on Drug Abuse (NIDA), the National Institute on Alcohol Abuse and Alcoholism (NIAAA), the National Human Genome Research Institute (NHGRI), and the National Institute of Mental Health (NIMH).

The Office of Public Health Preparedness

The Office of Public Health Preparedness (OPHP) is headed by a director and its mission is to prepare for, protect against, respond to, and recover from all acts of bioterrorism and other public health emergencies that affect the American civilian population. The functions and responsibilities of the OPHP include advising the secretary of DHHS on matters relating to bioterrorism and public health emergencies. The OPHP also acts as a liaison with the Office of Homeland Security (OHS) and directs implementation of a strategy designed to protect the civilian population from acts of bioterrorism and other public health emergencies ("Office of Public Health Preparedness: Organization, Functions, and Delegation of Authority" 2002).

The Food and Drug Administration

The Food and Drug Administration's (FDA) mission is to promote and protect public health by making sure that only safe and effective products

Table 1.3

Offices/Centers/Institutes Located Within the National Institutes of Health

Office of the Director of NIH
  Program Office
    Office of Research on Women's Health; Office of AIDS Research; Office of Behavioral and Social Science Research; Office of Disease Prevention; Staff Offices; Office of Extramural Research; Office of Intramural Research; Office of Management; Office of Science Policy; Office of Budget; Office of Communication and Public Liaison; Office of Equal Opportunity and Diversity Management; Office of Program Coordinator; Office of Legislative Policy and Analysis; Office of Community Liaison; Executive Office; Office of the Ombudsman

Institutes/Centers
  National Cancer Institute
  National Eye Institute
  National Heart, Lung, and Blood Institute
  National Human Genome Research Institute
  National Institute on Aging
  National Institute on Alcohol Abuse and Alcoholism
  National Institute of Allergy and Infectious Diseases
  National Institute of Arthritis and Musculoskeletal and Skin Diseases
  National Institute of Biomedical Imaging and Bioengineering
  National Institute of Child Health and Human Development
  National Institute on Deafness and Other Communication Disorders
  National Institute of Dental and Craniofacial Research
  National Institute of Diabetes and Digestive and Kidney Diseases
  National Institute on Drug Abuse
  National Institute of Environmental Health Sciences
  National Institute of General Medical Services
  National Institute of Mental Health
  National Institute of Neurological Disorders and Strokes
  National Institute of Nursing Research
  National Library of Medicine
  Center for Information Technology
  Center for Scientific Review
  John E. Fogarty International Center
  National Center for Complementary and Alternative Medicine
  National Center on Minority Health and Health Disparities
  National Center for Research Resources
  Warren Grant Magnuson Clinical Center

Source: National Institutes of Health, www.nih.gov/about/NIHoverview.html.

Table 1.4

Centers Located Within the Food and Drug Administration

Center for Food Safety and Applied Nutrition
Center for Drug Evaluation and Research
Center for Biologics Evaluation and Research
Center for Devices and Radiological Health
Center for Veterinarian Medicine

Source: Food and Drug Administration, www.FDA.gov.

reach the market and by monitoring products for continued safety after they are in use. The FDA is one of the oldest consumer protection agencies. The FDA regulates everything from the most common food ingredients to complex medical and surgical devices, lifesaving drugs, and radiation-emitting consumer and medical products. Its regulatory approach takes a variety of forms. The FDA also regulates cosmetics products after they are marketed. The FDA regulates certain products such as drugs and medical devices to make sure that they are safe before they are allowed to enter the marketplace. Some regulations are designed to make sure that products such as x-ray machines and microwave ovens are safe and measure up to performance standards. The FDA performs its regulatory and other functions through its different centers (U.S. Food and Drug Administration 2002) (Table 1.4).

The Center for Food Safety and Applied Nutrition (CFSAN) promotes safe food-handling practices by producers and consumers and detection practices that are effective in tracking and preventing food-borne illness. The FDA safeguards the nation's food supply by making sure that all ingredients used in foods are safe and that food is free of contaminants like disease-causing organisms, chemicals, or other harmful substances. The agency must approve new food additives before they can be used in foods. The FDA also monitors the safety of dietary supplements and the content of infant formulas and medical foods.

The Center for Drug Evaluation and Research (CDER) is responsible for ensuring that prescription and over-the-counter drugs are safe and effective. This center serves as a watchdog by evaluating and approving all new drugs before they are sold in the marketplace. The center also monitors drug advertisements on TV and radio and in print to ensure that they are truthful and balanced. It provides information to health professionals and consumers for the appropriate and safe use of the drugs.

The Center for Biologics Evaluation and Research (CBER) regulates biological and related products such as blood, vaccine, tissue, allergenic, and biological therapeutics. It is responsible for ensuring that the nation's blood supply and any products derived from it are safe. In addition, the CBER is also responsible for production and approval of safe childhood vaccines, proper oversight of human tissue for transplants, for ensuring the safe supply of allergenic materials and antitoxins, and for biological therapeutics including biotechnology-derived products. In contrast to drugs that are chemically synthesized, biologics are derived from living sources such as humans, animals, and microorganisms.

The Center for Devices and Radiological Health (CDRH) is responsible for the development, safety, effectiveness, and regulation of medical devices and electronic products that produce radiation. Its main activities involve the review, monitoring, evaluation, surveillance, and regulation of the medical device industry.

The Occupational Safety and Health Administration

OSHA was created in 1971 to ensure safe and healthy workplaces in America through the Occupational Safety and Health Act of 1970. OSHA is located within the United States Department of Labor (USDL), and its mission is to save lives, prevent injuries, and protect the health of American workers. OSHA works with state governments in partnership to accomplish its mission. OSHA and its state partners employ about two thousand inspectors and many complaint discrimination investigators, engineers, physicians, educators, and others who work in over two hundred offices nationwide. The staff of OSHA writes regulatory policies and establishes protective standards designed to ensure worker safety and health. OSHA also enforces these standards and provides education and consultation services to employers and employees throughout the country. The agency had a budget of $443 million in fiscal year 2002 and had a staff of 2,316, of which 1,123 were inspectors. In addition, twenty-six states also run their own OSHA programs, employing 3,105 employees, including 1,378 inspectors (OSHA facts 2002).

State Governments

The Tenth Amendment to the U.S. Constitution reserves for the states all powers that are not given to the national government nor denied to the states. One of the most important powers that states enjoy is the police power to promote the general welfare of society. This police power gives states and localities an important role providing public health services because it includes all laws and regulations intended to lessen morbidity and mortality in the population. Thus, states and localities have the authority to promote public health in wide-ranging areas including injury and disease prevention, enforcement of inspection laws, sanitation, prevention of water and air pollution, and proper waste disposal (Gostin 2000a). State governments have significant power to protect public safety and health in order to promote the public good. Their powers are limited only by judicial rulings that require that states must not act arbitrarily, discriminate against a class of people such as a racial minority, or infringe on fundamental individual rights. The electronic accumulation and exchange of personal health data can also lead to discrimination in employment, insurance, and government programs. Federal privacy protections do not adequately protect public health data, and existing state privacy laws are very fragmented and often inconsistent (Gostin, Hodge, and Valdiserri 2001).

Today all states have health agencies, generally called state health departments. However, it is important to note that state health agencies are often called by different names in different states. They may be titled department of health, department of public health, department of health services, department of human services, and so forth depending upon the specific organizational structure within a state. For our purposes, we will refer to them as departments of health. Similarly, the title of the chief executive officer of the state health agency also varies from state to state. In most states they are called director or commissioner. In some states the chief executive officer is referred to as state health officer or secretary. In most states the chief executive officer is appointed by the governor.

Originally the functions of state health departments were limited and focused primarily on the collection of vital health statistics, control of communicable diseases, environmental sanitation, maternal and child health care, public health education, and laboratory services. During the 1950s the functions of state health departments expanded as the federal government started to provide categorical grants to support specific groups of people suffering from specific diseases such as heart disease, mental illness, and diabetes (Dandoy 1997).

Typical responsibilities of state health departments can be classified under five basic categories. One category is health information, which includes recording and issuing certificates for births and deaths, collecting and publishing health statistics, and keeping birth defect and cancer registries. The second category of responsibilities has to do with prevention of disease and disabilities. Here state health departments perform functions such as immunization programs, AIDS screening, counseling and partner notification, tuberculosis control, investigation of disease outbreak, laboratory testing for infectious diseases, and the like. Third, state health departments engage in activities such as issuing permits for sewage disposal systems, monitoring drinking water supplies, inspecting dairies, licensing hospitals, nursing homes, and home health care agencies, inspecting clinical laboratories, and examining and certifying emergency medical personnel. Under the category of health promotion, state health departments provide family planning services, prenatal care for low-income families, and promote a variety of health educational programs. Finally, state health departments also work to improve health care delivery systems through issuing certificates of need for construction of health care facilities and the development of rural health care services (Dandoy 1997).

In addition to state health departments, several states also have state boards of health. State boards of health are typically responsible for making and enforcing rules and regulations pursuant to state health codes. During the 1970s and 1980s, reorganization of health departments in many states led either to consolidation of state boards of health with other departments or their elimination. Today, among states that do have a health board, some still make policies while others have been confined to advisory roles. Thus state health boards today do not play as strong a role as they once did (Dandoy 1997).

The 1988 report by the Institute of Medicine titled *The Future of Public Health* argued that the role and mission of the public health system was not clearly defined and many of the health departments suffered problems of health care delivery, financing, and quality of personal health services. The report also charged that the public health profession had failed to provide leadership in policy development. A 1994 study of forty two state health departments' mission statements concluded that state health departments generally do a good job of identifying their customers, markets, and major products and services. However, they fail to present their organization's philosophy and mission clearly to the public and they do a poor job of communicating the departments' self-image or desired public image to the larger community (Duncan, Ginter, and Kriedel 1994). Another study of the role of state health departments in formulating policy concluded that, contrary to the Institute of Medicine's 1988 report, state departments appear to play an effective role in areas where they have primary legal responsibilities and when given adequate resources (Robins and Backstrom 1994).

Today, state public health departments are facing many changes due to the emergence of managed care for publicly insured populations under Medicaid and Medicare, and welfare reforms. As state legislatures have adopted managed care in response to state budget crunches, the role of state health departments is changing from providing direct health care services to providing fiscal and programmatic oversight for the managed care organizations (MCOs).

State governments are increasingly leaning toward privatization as an answer to the public's desire for reducing the growth of government (Kotkin-Jaszi 2001). For example, today, many states already privatize mental health services (Bachman 1996). Four strategies of privatization include load shedding, developing alternative delivery systems, imposing user charges for goods and services, and restoring competition by minimizing government monopolies (Savas 1982). Under the load-shedding strategy, health departments may simply withdraw from providing certain goods and services and make patients rely on the private market or not-for-profit organizations to fill the void.

Under the second strategy, public health departments can encourage development of alternative delivery systems through provider grants, vouchers, and contracts and thus limit government's role as a direct service. Under the third strategy, public health departments can encourage the creation of alternative delivery systems by imposing user fees in the form of copayments for health services. The fourth strategy of minimizing government monopoly in order to encourage true alternatives is not a likely possibility in public health since traditionally public health departments have operated as providers of last resort, and they provide services to populations that otherwise would not be served (Kotkin-Jaszi 2001). How state health departments respond to challenges posed by managed care remains to be seen.

Local Governments

Local health departments are governmental entities of towns, cities, counties, and/or districts and their general mission is to protect, promote, and maintain the health of the population under their jurisdiction. An overwhelming majority of local health departments are entities of county governments or county-related jurisdictions. Local health departments enforce public health laws and regulations of federal, state, and local governments. Local health departments derive their authority from their state health departments and from the city or county government of which they are a part. The nature of the relationship between state and local health departments varies considerably from state to state. In some states, local health departments enjoy a considerable amount of autonomy and act independently of state health departments. In other states, local health departments are treated as entities of the state, and they work in an interdependent fashion. It should be noted that many charter cities have city health departments whose authority differs from county health departments (Rawding and Wasserman 1997).

The National Association of County and City Health Officials (NACCHO) has outlined that local health departments themselves should provide certain services or ensure that these services are provided by others. These services include conducting community diagnoses, preventing and controlling epidemics, promoting a safe and healthy environment, measuring the performance, effectiveness, and outcome of health services, promoting healthy lifestyles, providing health education, laboratory testing, and personal health services, and mobilizing the community for action when necessary (*Blueprint for a Healthy Community* 1994). Thus, local health departments provide a wide range of services including assuring the safety of food and milk products, inspecting restaurants, assuring the safety of public and private water supplies, and providing solid waste management, animal control, and management of the sewage disposal system as well as pollution prevention, family planning, dental and prenatal care, and HIV counseling and treatment.

Depending upon the locality, local boards of health can be policymaking or advisory bodies. They act as a link between local public health agencies and the community and help develop local health department services. In most jurisdictions, local health boards have authority to establish local health policies, fees, and regulations.

Just like state health departments, local health departments are confronting new challenges posed by managed care. Many local health departments are losing a portion of their clientele because managed care systems are providing many of the services traditionally provided by local public health departments, such as immunization, maternal and child health care, and tuberculosis treatment. How can a population-based system of health care be achieved in light of managed care since managed care organizations are responsible only for their enrolled population while the public health care system is responsible for the entire population (Goldberg 1998)? One strategy is for local health departments to work collaboratively with managed care organizations, citizen groups, physicians, health and human service providers, and other community organizations to share responsibility for the community's health because such collaboration with certain types of partners promotes better public health performance (Lovelace 2000). It has been suggested that an adversarial relationship often exists between local hospitals and local health departments, and low priority is assigned to developing a better working relationship between the two. What is needed is a better collaborative relationship between local public health departments and local hospitals because local public health leaders and hospital administrators play a major role as community opinion leaders in health policy development and health politics (Crum and Somani 1992).

Politics and Public Health

The primary mission of public health is to prevent and control disease and promote the health of the community as a whole. Success in fulfilling this mission depends largely on the establishment of sound and effective public health policies. Public health policies play a vital role in meeting the objectives of promoting community health through disease prevention and control. The political and social environment of a society significantly influences the formulation, adoption, and implementation of public health policies. What types of policy alternatives are considered and adopted as potential solutions to public health problems and how they are implemented takes place in a political arena in the midst of competing political ideologies, cultural and moral values, and private economic interests (Nathanson 1996). Public health needs to recognize that the political culture of a society plays a major role not only in defining the meaning of disease but also in setting limits on what the government can do in the name of promoting the public's health (Burris 1997). Promoting and protecting the community's health requires that public health professionals venture beyond their scientific training and enter into the forest of democratic politics. For public health officials and other public health professionals, there are often many dangers lurking in this forest.

One of the dangers includes the possibility of powerful private markets overrunning community welfare. For example, as we have discussed in the last section, the rise of managed care that caters only to its clientele conflicts with public health's focus on the welfare of the community as a whole. Nancy Milo uses an interest group model of politics to assess the performance of public health and argues that there needs to be a reformed public health system to meet the challenges of marketplace health care and fiscal retrenchment (2000). The famous report by the Institute of Medicine (1988) on *The Future of Health Care* also argued that public health's success in creating conditions in which people can live a healthy life depends on how interest group actions and conflicts shape the politics of public health policy. The environment of fiscal retrenchment and the public's desire for shrinking the size of the government make it difficult for public health officials at state and local levels to oppose market intrusion and also make it tempting to accept privatizing of public health policies that provide public or social goods.

Lawrence Weiss (1997) blames the problems of the American health care system on a capitalist system in which for-profit corporations and well-financed business interests control not only the financing and delivery of health care but also the political power structure for their own personal end, that is, profit. The failure of the Clinton health care reform effort was largely a demonstration of how powerful private interests can triumph over the public interest by manipulating public opinion to defeat reform desired by a majority of the people (Johnson and Broder 1996). Similarly, Patricia Thomas (2001) has argued that bureaucratic fears, political timidity, petty rivalries between the theorists of academic science and the empiricists of applied research, and concerns about corporate profits and liabilities are responsible for the slow development of an AIDS vaccine.

A second possible danger is the prospect of electoral politics giving rise to political power centered around cultural politics based on religious moralism that can threaten the realm of privacy or put limits on free democratic discussion. This is reflected in the politics surrounding abortion and contraceptive policies and what can be said and discussed in public health education programs about HIV, birth control, and so on (Beauchamp 2002). The controversy surrounding abortion policy often reflects a combination of interest group politics and a clash of conflicting moral values (O'Connor 1996). Deborah McFarlane and Kenneth Meier (2001) have provided an excellent analysis of the politics of morality surrounding family planning and abortion policies. The initial slow response of the public health service to the spread of AIDS also reflected the politics of morality and phobia (Costanza 1992).

The third possible danger lurking in the forest of democratic politics is whether the public health system can protect and promote community health without endangering basic civil liberties (Callahan 2000). Public health policies must constantly struggle to balance the interests of the community as a whole, that is, the community or public good, and individual autonomy (Gostin 2000b). A significant portion of diseases and early deaths in many societies stems from risk-taking behavior by individual citizens. Attempts by the public health system to deal with such lifestyle risks create significant political controversies in democratic political systems. Compulsory vaccination laws, fluoridation of the water supply, seat belt requirements, requiring motorcycle riders to wear helmets, and antismoking laws are just a few examples where such controversies arise. In Western democracies, paternalistic public health policies designed to restrict such lifestyle choices have always generated a considerable amount of opposition because political individualism operates on the assumption that the political community is an association of self-determining individuals (Beauchamp 1997).

At what point can public health policy limit individual liberty in order to promote the collective or community good? Do individual citizens have a duty and obligation toward one another and society as a whole to conduct themselves in ways that are not harmful to themselves, to others, and the community at large as argued by communitarians? Communitarians such as Amitai Etzioni (1993) have argued that the right to be free of government intervention does not mean that individual citizens are free from the moral claims of the community. In fact, civil society requires that we be each other's keepers. Can coercive government measures such as mandatory testing, isolation, or quarantine of individuals infected with HIV virus, and antisodomy laws be justified in order to prevent the spread AIDS? (Bayer 1991) What, if anything, can the government do to address the public health problem of smoking during pregnancy? (Oaks 2001)

During the 1950s and 1960s the Warren Supreme Court tended to lean in favor of protecting individual rights and civil liberties against too much government encroachment. Today courts engage in the strict scrutiny of government policy if a public health policy invades the fundamental rights of a citizen or discriminates against a suspect class such as a minority group. The state in its exercise of police power must demonstrate that it has a compelling interest in limiting individual liberty or autonomy and that the intervention is the least restrictive alternative (Gostin 2000a).

The politics surrounding public health is reflected in other areas as well. For example, in recent years some have charged that lack of research funding for breast cancer, because it is overwhelmingly a women's disease, has led to inadequate diagnosis and treatment. There is more research funding support for men's diseases compared to women's diseases like breast cancer (Stabiner 1997; Altman 1996). How and why did the issue of increased funding for breast cancer research emerge on the national policy agenda only in the late 1980s? It is because the advocates of increased funding for breast cancer research were able to improve the political climate for their cause by arguing that women's issues were being neglected by the male-dominated political establishment. Thus, often it is the politics rather than the merit that determines the course of public health policy (Casamayou 2001).

The making of sound public health policies requires reliance on solid technical and scientific data. However, as the above discussion shows, politics pervades almost every aspect of the U.S. public health system. Public health policies are ultimately set by the elected representatives of the people, that is, politicians who have political goals in mind. The dynamics of American politics make it difficult to make sound public health policies based solely on hard technical and scientific evidence. Public health policymaking is often driven by crisis and hot issues; interest group politics and policy decisions are made largely based on bargaining and compromises rather than comprehensive analysis (Garrett 2000).

As we embark upon the twenty-first century, the American public health system faces many challenges. The CDC has outlined specific public health goals for the twenty-first century such as eliminating health disparities, focusing on children's physical and emotional development, achieving a longer healthspan, promoting physical activity and a healthy lifestyle, environmental protection and cleanup, and reducing violence (Koplan and Fleming 2000). The purpose of our book is much broader. In this book we discuss the major political challenges confronting the U.S. public health system in general and public health professionals in particular. The success of the American public health system in meeting the public health goals for the twenty-first century outlined by the CDC will require that public health professionals confront these political challenges in ways that will allow them to become important players in public health policymaking.

Organization of the Book

In the following chapters we examine and discuss the political challenges confronting the American public health system in the twenty-first century. In chapter 2, we examine the role of leadership in influencing public health policymaking. Historically, public health professionals have not played a significant role in the development of public health policies. The chapter discusses factors that explain this lack of leadership role by the public health professionals. It also examines the existing tension between professional expertise and politics prevalent in the current U.S. public health system. We argue that public health officials and professionals must become effective policy advocates by becoming more engaged in the thicket of democratic politics.

The history of the relationship between private medicine and public health in the United States can best be characterized as history of cooperation, apprehension, tension, conflict, and at times open hostility. Chapter 3 examines this relationship and discusses the factors that have led to competition rather than cooperation between the two fields. We argue that the curative model of health care pursued by private medicine and the preventive model followed by public health must become complementary instead of operating in competition. Private medicine and public health must find ways to work in a more cooperative sprit to address public health problems.

Chapter 4 analyzes the relationship between law and public health. Discussed are the weaknesses of current public health laws and the need for public health law reform in the United States. This chapter also examines how law can be used as a tool in the political arena to promote public health in areas such as drug and alcohol abuse, gun violence, and smoking and tobacco use. The use of litigation as a public health strategy is also discussed. We argue that public health professionals must learn to make creative use of the law to promote public health.

Development of sound public health policies requires comprehensive analysis based on solid technical and scientific data. Chapter 5 analyzes the role of science and public health policymaking. It examines the evolution of public health research and the role science can play in the development as well as evaluation of public health policies. The chapter discusses some of the difficulties in the use of technical and scientific data for public health policymaking in the rough-and-tumble of politics. We argue that public health professionals must learn to use their scientific expertise to become effective advocates for the development of sound public health policies.

Chapter 6 provides an analysis of the role of genetics in public health. It discusses the Human Genome Project, developments in genetic science, the value of genetic testing in public health, the cost-effectiveness of genetic testing, the use of genetic technologies for tracking emerging infectious diseases, and improving diagnosis, treatment, and prevention. The chapter analyzes legal, ethical, and political issues involved in epidemiological studies such as privacy and confidentiality of genetic information, informed consent, and individual autonomy. Also discussed are issues such as the potential for discrimination based on genetic information and inequality that may result from unequal access to genetic technologies. We argue that public health professionals must be sensitive to these concerns.

Chapter 7 examines environmental politics and public health. It discusses environmental degradation and its impact on public health and the politics of environmental regulation. The chapter discusses the role of lifestyle choices versus the environmental factors in public health. Also examined are the social ecology, that is, the relationship between people and their environment, and the construction of social capital and building community capacity for improving public health. We argue that public health must focus on addressing public health problems created by environmental degradation by working to improve the quality of the environment in which people live.

Chapter 8 discusses one of the most important challenges confronting public health, that of dealing with potential as well as actual acts of bioterrorism. The chapter discusses the history of bioterrorism, types of biological weapons, and analyzes the current preparedness of the American public health system to deal with a bioterrorist attack. The role of national, state, and local governments in dealing with bioterrorism is examined. Developments in the public health field since the September 11 terrorist attack are discussed. We argue that American public health has suffered considerably from the politics of neglect and that the public health system must do much more to deal with future bioterrorism threats.

Chapter 9 provides a summary of our major arguments and discusses how the American public health system can be reinvigorated within the context of American politics. One of our main conclusions is that the preventive model of public health must be elevated and accorded the same, if not higher status, as the curative model of health care that has dominated the American health care system in the last half century.

Notes

1. Health life expectancy ranking is based on the World Health Organization's Disability Adjusted Life Expectancy (DALE). DALE summarizes the expected number of years to be lived in what might be termed the equivalent of "full health." To calculate DALE, the years of ill health are weighted according to severity and subtracted from the expected overall life expectancy to give the equivalent years of a healthy life.

2. Overall health system attainment is a composite measurement of achievement in the level of health (25 percent weight), the distribution of health (25 percent weight), the level of responsiveness (12.5 percent weight), distribution of responsiveness (12.5 percent weight), and fairness of financial distribution (25 percent weight) constructed from the survey of over one thousand public health practitioners from over one hundred countries.

3. The index on the performance of the level of health reports how efficiently health systems transfer expenditures into health as measured by DALE. Performance on the level of health is defined as the ratio between achieved levels of health and the levels of health that could be achieved by the most efficient health system.

4. Overall performance of the health system is measured using a similar process, relating overall health system achievement to health system expenditures.

Study Questions

1. What is the mission of public health? What are the major accomplishments and failures/shortcoming of public health in the United States?
2. Write an essay in which you trace the evolutionary history of public health in the United States. What have been some of the major milestones?
3. How have the goals and strategies of public health changed over the years?
4. Write an essay in which you explain the organization of the U.S. public health system at the federal, state, and local levels. In your discussion, be sure to include the roles and functions of some of the major agencies and organizations.
5. How do politics shape public health policies in the United States? What are some of the political challenges confronting public health in the United States as it tries to meet the goals outlined by the Centers for Disease Control and Prevention for the twenty-first century?

CHAPTER 2

Leadership, Politics, and Public Health

Public health with its related disciplines of prevention, epidemiology, and biostatistics was shunted to the world of policy and politics, where it has languished because of limited leadership, poor funding, and inadequate advocacy. In short, public health was formally relegated to the porch. Too often, it was the back porch. (Smith 1994, 726)

Historically, public health professionals have not played a significant leadership role in the development of health policies. This lack of leadership role has been attributed to several factors. First, it has been suggested that health care providers have monopolized the development of health policy. Medical and hospital associations along with many private health-related interest groups are the most visible and dominant groups at legislative forums. They have often used seasoned legislative liaisons and lobbyists to influence health policymaking. In contrast, public health professionals have been less visible. In addition, they often lack sophistication and skills in lobbying strategies and as a consequence are less influential in shaping health policy development (Williams-Crowe and Aultman 1994).

The second factor is that many public health officials have a short tenure in office, making it difficult for them to sustain leadership (Williams-Crowe and Aultman 1994). For example, almost half of all local health officials have a tenure of less than five years with a particular agency (National Association of County Health Officials and Centers for Disease Control 1990), and state health officials have an even shorter tenure in office (Public Health Foundation and Centers for Disease Control 1990).

The third factor often cited is the conflict faced by public health professionals between sound professional judgment and the bargaining style of political decisionmaking, that is, policymaking. According to this argument, public officials have often failed to or declined to participate at all in policymaking because of their belief or conviction that their neutral scientific knowledge should not be undermined through negotiations and compromises that are inevitable in the political arena (Stivers 1991).

A tension exists between professional expertise and politics throughout the public health system in the United States. A central tenet of professional ethics of the public health profession is to use expert knowledge derived from epidemiology and biostatistics to identify and deal with the health needs of the population and to help improve the quality of life in a community. The political arena in which policymaking takes place operates by a different set of rules and in a very different environment. Policymaking in the public health area, like many other areas, is often driven by crisis, hot issues, and organized interest groups. Decisionmaking in such an environment is often based on competition, bargaining, and compromises rather than a dispassionate, objective, comprehensive systematic analysis. Public health professionals often feel uncomfortable operating in an environment where decisions are based on prevailing political dynamics and not strictly on expert analysis based on scientific knowledge alone (Institute of Medicine 1988).

However, the inclination of public health professionals to distance themselves from the ordinary processes and elected leaders of government was not always the norm. Prior to the bacteriological revolution of the nineteenth century, making and implementing health policy was a collaborative activity between physicians in private and public health practice, lawmakers, lawyers, urban planners, civil engineers, and business leaders (Fox 2002). As the steady progress of science came to be viewed as the primary cause of improvements in preventing, detecting, and treating most diseases, public health professionals as well as the public came to accord medicine and other health occupations a higher stature than the occupations of law and politics. Unfortunately, the public's faith in science and technology to improve personal health services did not translate into increasing the capacity of public health. Public health came to be accorded lower priority by government with respect to funding (Fox 2002).

Cutbacks in federal, state, and local funding not only endangered the health safety net protecting the poor and disadvantaged but also significantly eroded the very fabric of the public health system in the United States. The failed attempt at reforming the nation's health care system by the Clinton administration and the arrival and growth of managed care on the scene, combined with a potential bioterrorism threat, have created new challenges for public health. While the terrorist attacks of September 11, 2001, in New York and Washington, DC, and the anthrax scare have led to an increase in public health funding, especially for activities designed to prevent and deal with potential bioterrorist attacks, it is clear that future public health funding will not be guided solely by technical assessment and community views; politics will play an important role in deciding winners and losers. Programs that have a strong constituency may survive while those with weak constituencies may suffer (Brown 1997). To protect against the further erosion of public health and successfully face new challenges will require strong leadership on the part of public health professionals.

In this chapter we discuss the politics of leadership in public health. First, we examine the role of leadership as it relates to public health. Second, we examine the leadership role of public health officials in federal, state, and local governments, and the politics surrounding their roles. Third, we analyze the leadership role played by professional associations in the field of public health. The chapter concludes with a discussion of the interrelationships between leadership, politics, and public health.

Leadership and Public Health

As public health professionals, we must reassert our leadership over public policies that affect the public's health. Whether we are practitioners or scientists, whether we work in the university or service organizations, whether we are in public or private-sector agencies or community-based organizations, we have a responsibility to be public health leaders.

Leadership is required to invigorate public health agencies with a commitment of effectiveness and innovation. Leadership is required to build collaboration with other sectors of the community. And leadership is essential to advocate effectively for policies that meet public health needs to build coalitions, make the media our allies, and persuade policymakers to support health promoting public policies. This leadership agenda is both urgent and feasible. (Brown 1997, 555)

Leadership has been defined in a variety of ways. One view of leadership describes it as a process through which a leader intentionally attempts to influence other individuals/groups to accomplish some goals. Thus, according to this view, leadership is a process; it entails influencing others, it is intentional, and the objective of leadership is goal accomplishment. Leadership is not the same as management. Leadership is one of many roles a manager performs. In addition, leadership is multidimensional and downward focused (Pointer and Sanchez 1997).

Another approach to leadership is to associate it with certain traits and skills. Many of the studies on leadership in the first half of the twentieth century focused on certain traits of physical characteristics, personality, and the ability to distinguish leaders from followers. Studies of leadership focused on traits such as height, weight, and appearance along with personality traits such as alertness, originality, intelligence, and self-confidence. This led to an unsuccessful search for universal leadership traits. By the beginning of the second half of the twentieth century the trait approach was discredited (Longest Jr. 1996).

Others have argued that leadership is more than the attributes or personal characteristics of an individual. This approach has tended to focus on the behavior of leaders and whether they tend to be autocratic, benevolent, consultative, and participative, or democratic (Likert 1977). Likert also identified two styles of leadership behavior as either "job centered" or "employee centered" (1961). Others have argued that leadership is behavior that goes beyond required performance. Leadership is more than a mechanical compliance with the directives of the organization. It involves going beyond the requirements. In public health, this translates to going beyond mandated services and traditional organizational boundaries to improve the health of the community. Leadership can occur at individual as well as at organizational levels (Upshaw, Sollecito, and Kaluzny 2001).

Another approach to leadership has focused on situational influences or contingencies that affect leadership effectiveness. One of the most well known of such theories is Fiedler's leadership model, which argues that effective leadership is contingent upon a proper match or fit between a particular situation and particular traits of the leader. In other words, certain leadership traits fit particular situations to produce an effective leader while the same traits under a different situation may not produce effective leadership (Fiedler 1967; Fiedler and Chemers 1964).

Some have equated leadership with developing executive strategies for managing responsible change. This view tends to equate effective leadership with effective management (Simendinger 1997). However, others have argued that difficult times require leaders, not simply managers, suggesting that effective leadership involves more than effective management. According to this view, leaders differ from managers because leaders emphasize intangibles such as values, vision, and motivations. This is particularly true of public health. In medicine, those at the highest administrative levels tend to be from narrow fields of specialization, while in public health, the higher the level, the greater the need for leaders who have a broader knowledge of the entire field (Legnini 1994). One of the hallmarks of effective leadership is not just an ability to articulate a vision from the top but to help an organization build a sense of shared destiny (Kerfoot 2000). An essential element of effective leadership is the ability of a leader to create a shared sense of purpose requiring creative collaboration (Bennis 1996). Effective leadership also involves building successful partnerships with other groups and organizations by creating a consensus around shared values and a common agenda (Lashof 1992; Gardner 1990).

Most studies of leadership, while admitting that the leadership process may sometimes be political in nature, tend to imply that the best leadership is above politics. Few studies of leadership have tried to understand the political nature of leadership. For example, James McGregor Burns (1978) argues that leadership is a sociopolitical process in which transactional leaders tend to emphasize maintenance of the status quo while transformational leaders transform the existing values into higher, moral forms that help produce better individuals and communities. Similarly, Robert Tucker (1995) has suggested that we need to view leadership as a political phenomenon. Robertson and Tang have also argued that leadership is a highly political process that requires organizational leaders to use political skills to be effective or successful (1995). However, David Weaver (2000) goes further than all other scholars in arguing that we need to view leadership as inherently political in nature and recognize that politics is the central, common element in all leadership. Indeed, he argues that politics is the essence of leadership.

As we discussed earlier, public health professionals have not played a leadership role in the development of public health policies. Reinvigorating public health will require strong political and professional leadership. Public health professionals and policymakers both face many challenges in addressing broad public health issues. Some of the trends that present public health with dangers as well as opportunities include the financing and organization of health care and human services; revolutionary changes in biotechnology, genetics, and information and communication technologies; the rise of alternative and complementary health care; an increasingly diverse and aging population; globalization of the economy; the decline of civic and other nongovernmental organizations; deterioration of the sociocultural environment; a crisis of values; and the changing role of government. Responses to these challenges will require public health professionals to be good listeners, to educate and inform, to advocate for strong public health policies, and to develop partnerships with like-minded public health groups and organizations. This in turn will require promoting values of social justice and community responsibility, a clear vision of safe and healthy communities, and leadership that translates these values and visions into actual public health policies (Levy 1998).

Public health professionals will need to play an important leadership role in identifying, quantifying, and reducing the risks to health resulting from social, behavioral, and environmental factors, and working with policymakers to make sure that the public health perspective is integrated into policy formulation (Beaglehole and Bonita 2000). According to the Institute of Medicine's report (1988), public health agencies must perform three important roles—evaluate data to help establish specific public and environmental health problems in a community; promote the use of scientific knowledge in health policymaking; and make sure that goals set out under policy are achieved through the provision of services, regulation, and working with others. Fulfilling the three roles will require a strong leadership role by public health professionals. Public health leaders will need to educate the public and the policymakers about the need to incorporate the scientific knowledge base in the development of public health policies (Kotchian 1993).

However, public health policymaking will not be guided simply by technical assessments and a scientific knowledge base. Politics will play a major role in determining winners and losers. For example, politically powerful religious and conservative ideological groups have tried to substitute their own social norms for sound and effective public health policies. Such groups have strongly opposed explicit sex education programs even though such programs may prevent sexually transmitted diseases among young adults (Brown 1997). Similarly, issues such as abortion, drug addiction, needle exchange programs, and HIV/AIDS touch public nerves and involve large, organized interests in society.

Inevitably, public health policy formulation and practice become involved in the politics of the time and public health professionals, whether they like it or not, must become political players (Mullan 2000). The task of public health professionals is to use scientific knowledge and discoveries to protect and promote public health. They cannot do this in a laboratory; they must do this in a public arena, that is, in a political arena. The political arena is governed not by calm, objective analysis and neutrality, but by many political forces and by policymakers who have political agendas that are often larger and more varied than that of public health professionals. Public health professionals, especially public health officials, must play three different roles as one—a determined idealist locked into his mission like Don Quixote, a cunning political strategist with the pragmatic cynicism of Machiavelli to promote the public good, and a Robin Hood-like agent who reallocates resources from the wealthier sectors of the society to the poor sectors (Mullan 2000).

Public Health Leadership at the National Level

The last twenty years have witnessed an increased politicization of some of the most important public health positions in the federal government. This is reflected in the fact that after almost ten months in office, the Bush administration had failed to fill some of the most important vacant public health positions in the federal government. This was all the more glaring in light of the terrorist attack of September 11, 2001, and the anthrax scare that had gripped the nation. The Food and Drug Administration

(FDA) had no commissioner. The National Institutes of Health (NIH) had been without a director for two years. The position of surgeon general was also vacant. No replacement had been named to replace Jeffrey P. Koplan, director of the Centers for Disease Control and Prevention (CDC), who had resigned his position due to criticisms of his handling of the anthrax attack and that the CDC's response to the bioterrorism threat was inadequate (Asch-Goodkin 2002).

The absence of leadership in such key positions had raised concerns that key decisions on vaccine development, cloning, prescription drugs, stem-cell research, and the abortion pill Mifepristone, among other issues, were being postponed or lacked input from some of the best scientific minds in the country (Connolly 2002). For example, when Tommy Thompson, secretary of the Department of Health and Human Services (DHHS), met with drug companies to discuss the development of important drugs and vaccines, FDA officials were not present at the meeting (Schultz 2001). The delay in filling these vacancies illustrates how many aspects of science and medicine have become increasingly politicized, making it all the more difficult to find outstanding scientists willing to navigate the political forest that comes with the top public health jobs in the federal government (Connolly 2002). For example, candidates for the FDA job were asked their views on RU-486, the controversial abortion drug, and stem-cell research (Schultz 2001). According to Paul Berg, a Nobel laureate in chemistry and a researcher at Stanford University, most people were suspicious that in order to get the job with the Bush administration, one had to pass a litmus test, and anyone who was pro-choice, pro–stem-cell research, or pro-cloning was not welcomed (Connolly 2002). It was only after many months of delays that Julie Geberding was appointed as director of the CDC and Elias Zerhouni was appointed as director of NIH. It was not until July 2002 that Richard Carmona was confirmed by the Senate as surgeon general of the United States (Piotrowski, 2002a; Nerf 2002).

Such criticisms and suspicions were reaffirmed recently on February 18, 2004, when more than sixty influential scientists, including twenty Nobel laureates, issued a statement in which they charged that the Bush administration had systematically distorted scientific facts to serve the administration's policy goals. They accused the Bush administration of censoring and suppressing reports by its own scientists and stacking advisory panels with unqualified political appointees (Glanz 2004). This bipartisan group of scientists accused the administration of politicizing science and called for an independent congressional investigation of federal science-advisory policies (Vergano 2004). On February 21, 2004, the Bush administration admitted that it had improperly altered a report documenting large racial and ethnic disparities in health care and indicated that it will publish the full, unexpurgated document (Pear 2004). When President Bush on February 27, 2004, replaced two members of the president's Council on Bioethics that advises him on issues such as cloning and stem-cell research, critics charged that the President was stacking the bioethics group with ideologically friendly members (Loven 2004).

In this section we examine the leadership role played by some of the important public health officials at the national level in shaping public health policies, how politics has affected their leadership role, and how they have attempted to navigate the tricky and often murky political waters. Our examination focuses on the roles of the surgeon general, the commissioner of FDA, and the directors of NIH and CDC.

The Surgeon General

The Act for the Relief of Sick and Disabled Seaman of 1798 laid the foundation for the establishment of the U.S. Public Health Service. In 1870, Congress established a tightly organized Marine Hospital Service (Jensen 1997). In 1871, John Woodworth was appointed as the first surgeon general (at that time the position was called supervising surgeon) by the treasury secretary. The process of appointing the surgeon general was changed in 1875, requiring presidential appointment and Senate confirmation. Today the surgeon general is the administrator of the Public Health Service, located within the Department of Health and Human Services (DHHS), and is directly accountable to the assistant secretary for health (Sofalvi 1997). Prior to the 1930s the position of surgeon general did not attract much controversy. Some controversy had begun to emerge with respect to the surgeon general's position during the 1930s. The position of surgeon general has become one of the most controversial and most politicized in the nation since the 1980s (Sofalvi 1997). The surgeon general is the most visible public health official at the national level. Attempts by surgeon generals to promote public health education, a healthy lifestyle, and specific public health policies based on scientific data have generated a significant amount of political controversies. This in turn has highly politicized the position of the surgeon general with respect to Senate confirmation and tenure in office. Such politicization threatens the very independence of the surgeon general's position that is necessary for a sound public health practice ("Independence of the U.S. Surgeon General" 1997). Since the 1980s the office of the surgeon general has become such a political hot potato and litmus test for social values that attempts have been made to eliminate the position altogether. For example, in June 1995, Sen. Conrad Burns

(R-Montana) introduced a bill designed to eliminate the position by arguing that the office had been used by both political parties as a political football (MacPherson 1995).

The first controversial surgeon general of the United States was Dr. Thomas Parran, who was nominated for the position by President Roosevelt and confirmed by the Senate in March 1936. However, his nomination was opposed by some physicians because of his support for socialized medicine ("New Surgeon General" 1938). Prior to his appointment as the surgeon general, he was embroiled in a controversy when the Columbia Broadcasting System prohibited him from discussing syphilis on the radio. Ultimately his statements about syphilis were published in newspapers around the country (Sofalvi 1997).

His tenure as surgeon general was controversial because of his efforts to consolidate and professionalize the Public Health Service when it became tied into a debate about national health insurance. The Wagner-Murray-Dingell Bill introduced in 1943 proposed a totally federal system of social insurance with the surgeon general playing the role of gatekeeper for the provision of medical services. The bill was strongly opposed by the American Medical Association (AMA), and its chief editorialist compared the proposed role of surgeon general under this bill to that of a "virtual gauleiter" of American medicine (Snyder 1994).

To distance the PHS from the controversy surrounding national health insurance, it was proposed that the PHS's authorities and duties be codified under a new Public Health Service Act. Such a bill ultimately passed both houses of Congress and was signed into law by President Roosevelt in 1944. Skillful political maneuvering by Dr. Thomas Parran and his allies in Congress made it possible to expand the role of the federal government in public health and put the PHS into the business of advancing public health through subsidizing biomedical research at private institutions, building health care facilities, improving the training of health professionals, and expanding coordination with state and local health departments. Under the act, the National Health Institute was elevated from a division to a bureau, and the surgeon general was authorized to conduct clinical research and create new institutes (Snyder 1994).

The release of the report of the Surgeon General's Committee on Smoking and Health in January 1964 by Surgeon General Luther Perry became very politically controversial because the report concluded that smoking was causally related to lung cancer in men and probably in women as well, and it implicated smoking in a number of disease conditions. This was the first time that the name of the surgeon general of the PHS was associated with a formal statement about the health hazards of tobacco, and the report became a signpost in the campaign against tobacco because the report hit the country like a bombshell (Parascandola 1997). The report ultimately led Congress to require warning labels on cigarette packs about the potential harmful effects of smoking.

As can be seen from the above discussion, controversy surrounding the Office of the Surgeon General is not new. However, since the 1980s the position has become a political lightning rod. It began with President Reagan's nomination of Dr. C. Everett Koop as surgeon general. Koop had come to Washington with a reputation of being an antiabortion crusader, and in books and articles he had written during the 1970s he had argued that society's tolerance of abortion leads to euthanasia (Glastris 1987). He had also denounced women's liberation and gay pride for encouraging "antifamily" trends in the country. The New Right and the right-to-life movement had hailed him as a bearded Ahab who would slay the white whale of liberalism (Judis 1989). Political conservatives were thrilled by his nomination. Liberals were equally appalled by Koop's appointment.

Koop's nomination was opposed by major newspapers such as the *New York Times* and the *Los Angeles Times*, liberal interest groups including the AFL-CIO, the National Organization of Women (NOW), and the American Public Health Association (APHA). This was the first time the APHA opposed a nominee for the position of surgeon general. In fact, the director of APHA said that he would rather see the position abolished than see Koop confirmed (Judis 1989). Koop's confirmation process, which was expected to last a few days, lasted nine months as liberals engaged in stalling tactics. He was called a right-wing crank, a pro-life nut, a religious zealot, scary, Dr. Unqualified, and inexperienced. Such name-calling and personal attacks were fueled by pro-choice advocates who feared his opposition to abortion (Carlson 1989). Despite this fierce opposition, Dr. Koop was confirmed by the Senate by a vote of 68 to 24 ("Senate Confirms Koop" 1981). Koop characterized his confirmation as a form of political and personal harassment the likes of which he had never experienced in his whole life (Koop 1991).

When Koop was confirmed as surgeon general, he was expected to be a figurehead like most surgeon generals before him, since the position carries very little statutory authority. However, the surgeon general's office does carry the weight of medical authority, and Dr. Koop used his visibility and medical authority to shake things up in a number of areas.

After only a few months following his confirmation, Koop issued his first report on smoking, which was the strongest indictment of cigarettes since the 1964 report. In May 1984 he issued a scorching condemnation of smoking, the tobacco industry, and the negative effects of passive smoking (secondhand smoke), and launched a crusade for a smokeless society by the year 2000. He endorsed smoking prohibition in the workplace and other public places (Judis 1989). His crusade against smoking was a headache for the Reagan administration because in a 1980 campaign appearance Ronald Reagan had promised to end the antagonistic relationship between the federal government and the tobacco industry (Glastris 1987). It also irritated free market conservatives.

In October 1986, Koop released his now-famous report on AIDS. Instead of moralizing about the disease's wicked causes, as many had expected him to do given his personal views, his report was not only frank but also compassionate, arguing that it was important to remember that we were fighting a disease and not people. He denounced the idea of quarantining AIDS victims, which many conservatives had advocated. Instead, he advocated the use of condoms and called for a serious program of sex education starting at the lowest grade level possible (Glastris 1987). This was a health report based on science and not a political report. Gary MacDonald, executive director of the AIDS Action Council, said that he had not previously seen such moral leadership by the PHS (Glastris 1987). Conservatives were stunned by the candor of the report and furious that Koop did not preach abstinence alone and with the report's conclusion that there was no evidence to suggest that the practice of homosexuality was psychologically harmful (Carlson 1989). The *National Review* accused Koop of criminal negligence for recommending the use of condoms. Dr. Koop in turn accused the *National Review* of letting politics and ideology supersede science (Judis 1989).

On the issue of abortion, the antiabortion Surgeon General Koop, in January 1989, sent a report on the psychological effects of abortion to President Reagan in which he concluded that women are not necessarily traumatized by the experience of abortion and that there were many women who believed that deciding to get an abortion was the best decision they had made in their lives (Judis 1989).

Ironically, liberals who had attempted to block Koop's nomination were now very pleased with his actions while the conservatives who had championed his nomination had become his strongest critics. When George H.W. Bush was elected to the presidency in 1988, Koop urged him to speak out on AIDS, but the president refused. The Bush administration began to shut him out of Cabinet meetings, and Koop resigned as surgeon general in 1989.

The *New York Times*, which had opposed Koop's nomination, declared in an editorial that Koop had left the position of surgeon general with a distinguished example of leadership. Dr. Koop also helped change people's views toward the office. The surgeon general became a lightning rod in the struggle over the nation's values and character and not a forgotten figurehead of the PHS, as was the case prior to Dr. Koop (Trafford, 1995).

Both liberals and conservatives had misjudged Koop. They had mistaken his old-fashioned Christian religious views, which coincided with certain right-wing conservative positions, as a sign that he was a radical conservative bent on taking on the liberals. They failed to realize that Koop had a unique perception of public service that allowed him to separate his professional conduct from his moral and political beliefs (Judis 1989). He had a high sense of professional honor that allowed him to speak as the chief officer of the PHS and not as a moralist ("Koop *de Grace*" 1989). Dr. Koop was guided by personal virtues of integrity, honesty, courage, and independence. These personal virtues were supplemented by public virtues of disinterestedness, tolerance, respect, and pragmatism (Bowman and Wall 1997). Koop reflected a democratic and moral model of leadership.

Following Dr. Koop, Antonia Novello served as surgeon general from 1990 to 1993. She became the first woman and the first Hispanic to serve in this position (Goldsmith 2002; Krucoff 1991). Compared to Dr. Koop, Dr. Novello's tenure as surgeon general was not very controversial, largely because she pretty much toed the Bush administration's line on most issues and explicitly avoided stating her personal views on abortion. She used her office to advocate for AIDS education, antismoking campaigns, and better health care for women, children, and minorities—hardly a controversial agenda (Cohen 1990). She called for more restraints on beer advertising (Brunelli 1991). She similarly called for a restraint on cigarette advertising and criticized Camel cigarette ads featuring the cartoon character Joe Cool. However, given the fact that the Office of the Surgeon General carries no power to enforce, marketers were not scared (Warner 1992a). However, she did raise public awareness about many issues related to public health.

Dr. Joycelyn Elders, who served as surgeon general (1993–94) during the first Clinton administration, was another major controversial figure. She had served as director of the Arkansas Department of Health under Governor Clinton during the late 1980s. In that position she had earned the reputation for being a progressive who had increased prenatal care for poor women and expanded HIV testing, mammography, and in-home care for the terminally ill (Motavalli 1994). She had also earned the reputation for being a controversial administrator who was outspoken. Thus, when President Clinton nominated her for the position of surgeon general, conservatives were upset because of her liberal position on issues. Many considered her unqualified and attacked her liberal policies during her confirmation hearings. Attacks on Dr. Elders were so intense that Sen. Carol Moseley-Braun (D-Illinois), the only black senator, charged that the conservative senators were engaging in character assassination ("Elders Confirmed for Surgeon General Post" 1993). The confirmation hearings lasted almost six months. Despite the opposition of the conservatives, she was confirmed by the Senate by a vote of 65 to 34, and she became the first black surgeon general of the United States ("Elders Confirmed for Surgeon General Post" 1993).

Dr. Elders' fifteen-month tenure as surgeon general was surrounded by controversies because of her outspokenness and frank discussions of many issues considered to be taboo for public discussion. She became a lightning rod for conservatives. She was a strong critic of the tobacco industry like her predecessor Dr. Koop. She publicly blasted the tobacco industry for targeting cigarette advertising at teenagers. She expressed support for medicinal use of marijuana and sale of the RU-486 abortion pill (Motavalli 1994). For her support of sex education starting as early as kindergarten, including contraceptive distribution in schools, she was called the "condom queen." She was also called a "mass murderer" for her support of abortion (Randolph 1994). It was not just her liberal position on issues but also her bluntness that angered many conservatives. For example, she told abortion foes to get over their "love affair" with the fetus (Duffy 1994).

She also angered many by suggesting that the link between drug legalization and its possible effect in reducing violent crime should be studied. When it was made clear that President Clinton not only was against the legalization of drugs but also not in favor of conducting a study of the issue, it did not deter her from suggesting that she should persuade a big foundation or a university to conduct the study ("Another Look: Legalizing Drugs" 1994).

The significant losses suffered by the Democratic Party in the Congressional elections of 1994 emboldened Republicans and conservatives, who started calling for her resignation. The Traditional Values Coalition mailed letters to several hundred thousand supporters, criticizing her for malicious attacks on heterosexuals and Christians, and urging Elders's resignation (Popkin 1994). Dr. Elders's public comment about masturbation on World AIDS Day at the United Nations was the final blow to her tenure as surgeon general. She stated that masturbation was a part of human sexuality and perhaps should be taught in school (Popkin 1994). President Clinton, under increased political pressure, finally dismissed Dr. Elders by demanding her resignation in December 1994. Her resignation was explained by Leon Panetta, the White House chief of staff, as the outcome of too many embarrassing incidents for the Clinton administration (Greenberg 1994).

To Dr. Elders's supporters, her firing demonstrated the triumph of politics and prejudice over common sense because surveys have shown that the majority of men and women engage in the practice of masturbation. To them, Joycelyn Elders will go down in history as a courageous surgeon general who was dismissed for speaking the truth ("Politics of Masturbation" 1994). They argued that she was made the sacrificial victim in light of the election defeats of 1994 ("Circle of Jerks" 1995). While politicians had decided that public talk on sexuality is inappropriate, to Dr. Elders the public dialogue on health-related issues must be a part of the surgeon general's duty and the bully pulpit was her instrument of power (Wilson 1997). According to Dr. Elders, the fact that she was very visible, high profile, and getting people's attention made her a real threat to the far right (Elders and Chanoff 1996).

Following the hasty departure of Dr. Joycelyn Elders, President Clinton nominated Henry W. Foster for the position of surgeon general. In his home state of Tennessee, Foster was well known for his program to promote teenage sexual abstinence and was honored by President George H.W. Bush for his work. He was an obstetrician/gynecologist and displayed a calm and professional manner (Greenberg 1995). The Foster nomination set off a controversy in the Senate during the hearing process as conservatives attacked the fact that he had performed about thirty-nine abortions during his thirty years of practice. The Clinton administration had overestimated the appeal of Foster's teen-abstinence message and had underestimated congressional Republicans' willingness to engage over abortion (Cohn 1995). The "vetting" process by the Clinton staff was uncoordinated and tardy (Borger 1995).The debate during the confirmation process had very little to do about Foster's qualifications, and he was called an abortionist by people opposed to his confirmation. In fact, the controversy over the Foster nomination again illustrated the politicization of the confirmation process ("Advise, Consent, Destroy" 1995; Carter 1994). Ultimately, Dr. Foster's supporters failed to muster the sixty votes needed to break the filibuster by Senator Gramm (R-Texas). Foster's nomination was dead and his ordeal in the Senate had lasted four months.

Dr. David Satcher served a four-year term from 1998 to 2002 as the sixteenth surgeon general of the United States. During most of this time he also served as the assistant secretary for health. In July 2001, Dr. Satcher released a report dealing with the promotion of sexual health and responsible sexual behavior. The country's major newspapers called the report balanced, courageous, and wise. The Bush administration, however, quickly distanced itself from the report, and the Christian Coalition of America charged that the report devalued the merits of remaining abstinent until marriage and called the report an affront to the values of people of faith (Keenan 2001). Politics again overshadowed a sound and balanced report.

The controversial tenure of C. Everett Koop, the forced resignation of Dr. Joycelyn Elders, and the failure of Dr. Henry Foster to win Senate confirmation demonstrate the clash of science and politics and how the position has become politicized. In fact, it threatened the very existence of the office as House Republicans tried to abolish the position. The new Bush administration elected to leave the position empty for almost a year rather than take on another confirmation fight, allowing the deputy surgeon general to serve as acting surgeon general during the period (Mullan 1997).

The above discussion illustrates not only the "politics" surrounding the office of the surgeon general, but also how recent surgeon generals have provided important leadership by using the visibility of the office to focus the public's attention on public health problems facing the country and to start a dialogue on policy alternatives. Both Dr. Koop and Dr. Elders used scientific knowledge to raise important public health concerns and policy questions. They tried to speak truth to power, that is, policymakers. Unfortunately, people in positions of power were not interested in listening to the truth. Both generated a great deal of controversy because scientific knowledge often got entangled with the politics of values. Dr. Elders articulated many of the same public health concerns that Dr. Koop had. However, she became embroiled in more intense controversy not only because of what she had to say but also because of how she said it. Bluntness and a lack of diplomacy made her role less effective by making her tenure in office very short.

Commissioner of the Food and Drug Administration

The Food and Drug Administration (FDA) has gone through significant changes over the last twenty five years. New scientific methods have led to the discovery of new therapies, and advances in manufacturing and testing methods have transformed the FDA from a small agency into a large agency with expanded responsibilities (Wechsler 2001). Between 1980 and 1989, Congress expanded the FDA's duties and responsibilities, and it was asked to do more with reduced resources. Thus the agency was demoralized due to downsizing and the antigovernment attitudes of the 1980s (Powledge 1992). The agency had to adjust to political change. The appointment of Dr. David Kessler as commissioner of the FDA in 1991 signaled a major shift in the agency's mode of operation.

David Kessler, during his six-year tenure at the FDA, turned out to be one of its most active and controversial leaders. He responded to the country's changing health needs and public health issues vigorously, for which he felt vilified by his detractors (Kessler 1996). As commissioner he took on many issues that generated a great deal of controversy and political heat. He cracked down on drug advertising and took silicone breast implants off the market. He responded to the AIDS epidemic by expanding agency resources devoted to regulation of critical therapies and by accelerating the review of critical therapies, that is, a "fast track" approval process for drugs that can benefit patients suffering from life-threatening illnesses (Wechsler 2001). He also instituted a quicker approval process for new drug applications, authorized external review of some new drugs by outside contractors, and accepted data from foreign studies in lieu of repeating studies in the United States, among other innovations (Powledge 1992).

The quicker drug approval process required hiring more reviewers and thus acquiring more resources. Since Congress was not about to authorize more funding, Kessler pulled off a major coup when he convinced the drug industry to pay user fees that would allow the FDA to hire more reviewers to speed up the new drug application review process. Congress passed the Prescription Drug User Fee Act (PDUFA) in 1992, requiring drug companies to pay user fees and allowing the FDA to use the revenue generated from such user fees to hire more reviewers and to support other agency functions (Wechsler 2001)

He also introduced sweeping food labeling reforms to simplify food labeling so consumers could be better informed about the content and nutrition value of foods they purchase. He also took on the food marketing community. However, political pressure forced him to back away from publicly endorsing new food label initiatives aimed at children (Warner 1992b).

Kessler's leadership of the FDA, above everything else, will be remembered the most for the battle he fought with the tobacco industry to assume regulatory authority over tobacco products and nicotine as a drug. Kessler, assisted by internal documents of tobacco companies obtained through a lawsuit, was able to demonstrate that tobacco companies had known for years that nicotine was addictive and that they were knowingly designing a product to deliver an addictive drug to consumers. Thus the tobacco product, in essence, was a vehicle for the delivery of nicotine. This helped establish the "intent" of the tobacco companies. Kessler and the FDA were also able to demonstrate that marketing and promotional practices of tobacco companies were deliberately aimed at youth. How to proceed further became a question of political strategy.

Congress in 1994 had gone Republican and that changed the political landscape of Congress. Congressman Henry Waxman (D-California), chairperson of the House Subcommittee on Health and the Environment and a strong political ally of Kessler and the FDA, was replaced by Tom Bliley (R-Virginia), who was more sympathetic to the tobacco companies. President Clinton in 1995 approved the FDA issuing new regulations of tobacco products. The proposed rules would have restricted the underage purchase of tobacco products, and prohibited billboard advertising near schools and all but the text-only ads in print publications geared toward youth. However, in a five to four vote, the United States Supreme Court ruled that Congress did not intend to place tobacco within the FDA's jurisdiction, even though it took pains to note that tobacco use among children and adolescents posed the single most significant threat to public health (Kessler 2002).

Despite this loss, there was also a major victory. Attorneys general of several states filed a class-action lawsuit against the tobacco companies on behalf of smokers who had suffered severe health problems because of their smoking addiction. The prospect of potential continuing lawsuits led to a historic multistate settlement between states and the tobacco industries, whereby tobacco companies agreed to pay billions of dollars to be distributed over time to individual states as partial compensation for expenditures associated with tobacco-related health problems.

Kessler, as commissioner of the FDA, was able to use his feisty style to leverage his reduced resources. He provided the FDA with a renewed sense of mission. He was able to sow fear among the regulated and to get their voluntary compliance (Powledge 1992). He made decisions based on good scientific information. However, it also brought him into conflict with powerful political forces. He stepped down as commissioner in 1996.

Director of the National Institutes of Health

Historically, the National Institutes of Health (NIH) has been characterized by a low-key managerial style—slow, deliberate, collegial, and inertia-bound. However, NIH went through a major transformation under the leadership of Dr. Bernadine Healy after she assumed the position of director in April 1991. She brought a flamboyant personal style that contrasted sharply with previous directors. For example, Dr. James Wyngaarden, who served as director of NIH from 1982 to 1989, hardly attracted any attention from outside the scientific community. The position of director was left vacant until 1991, during which time President George H.W. Bush sought a candidate acceptable to antiabortion groups (Greenberg 1992). Dr. Healy successfully navigated the political minefield at her confirmation hearings by indicating that while she was personally opposed to the administration's antiabortion restriction on fetal-tissue research, she would feel bound to obey government policy. During her tenure as director of the NIH, she demonstrated her willingness to disagree publicly with the administration on biomedical policy when she believed that scientific principles were at stake. She was blasted by some Republicans in Congress for her decision to support a federally funded survey of teenage sexual behavior. She was over-ruled by Louis Sullivan, secretary of HHS, who deemed the survey inappropriate. She also stood up to Rep. John Dingell (D-Michigan) over NIH's management of scientific misconduct (Palca 1991). Under her leadership, NIH drafted a strategic plan to guide NIH's biomedical research, and she had increased spending for women's health issues.

However, her bluntness made her a controversial figure. She alienated many members of Congress and made others angry by her backing of the Bush administration's ban on fetal-tissue research. Thus, when Bill Clinton was elected president, Healy was informed that she would not be asked to continue in the new administration, and she resigned in February 1993 (Cohen 1993). Her public skirmishes with members of Congress were key factors in her departure (Greenberg 1993). President Clinton in August 1993 nominated Harold Varmus, a Nobel Prize–winning biologist, as director of NIH. Despite some concerns raised about his lack of administrative experience and his dislike of political influence in setting research goals, his nomination was strongly supported by the biomedical research community, and he was confirmed by the Senate. He served as director of NIH for six years and left in December 1999. He left NIH in good fiscal shape (Harshall 1999). In fact, Varmus had Congress eating out of his hand, which helped boost NIH's budget from $10 billion to almost $16 billion during his tenure ("Harold Varmus" 1999).

After being without a permanent director for two years, the Bush administration finally nominated and the Senate confirmed Elias A. Zerhouni as director of NIH in 2002. His leadership will be tested by bitter political battles over issues such as genetic engineering, stem-cell research, cloning, and the inevitable clash between science and politics.

Director of the Centers for Disease Control and Prevention

The Centers for Disease Control and Prevention (CDC) is the world's most respected epidemiologic agency. The anthrax scare following the September 11 terrorist attacks and the prospect of bioterrorist attacks have placed the agency in the spotlight. The overall mission of the CDC essentially has remained the same—disease prevention through training, investigation, education, health promotion, and technology control. Traditionally the CDC has not been embroiled in political controversies, with the exception of the swine flu vaccine program fiasco in 1976, which resulted in a liability claim of about $84 million and the replacement of the director of CDC by the Carter administration. The Reagan administration injected politics into the

CDC's operation by refusing to let the chief of abortion surveillance testify before the Senate on the safety of abortion (Cotton 1990).

During the 1980s the CDC's slow response to the AIDS crisis generated a great deal of criticism. Some accused the CDC of overestimating the cost for treatment of AIDS patients, resulting in significant negative policy consequences (Green, Oppenheimer, and Wintfeld 1994). Others charged that politics was involved in the CDC's decisions about AIDS and that the CDC was concealing important information about AIDS from the public, leading to the further spread of AIDS rather than treatment and prevention. Critics argued that inexperienced leadership and ineffective health education undermined efforts to stop the spread of the disease (Kaliher 1998).

The CDC also became embroiled in a controversy over its handling of the anthrax attacks following the September 11 terrorist attacks. The resignation in March 2002 of Jeffrey Koplan, director of the CDC, was attributed to the criticism of the CDC's handling of the anthrax attacks and its failure to communicate with other public health officials and the public (McLellan 2002). The Bush administration, after a long delay, filled the position of director of the CDC when Dr. Julie Geberding assumed the post in July 2002. According to her, the CDC has made major progress in improving communication with other providers and indicated that the heightened focus on bioterrorism will require more coordination at the CDC (Piotrowski 2002b). In fact, President Bush has requested a $61 million increase in the 2004 budget for the CDC, with most of the agency's budget slated for bioterrorism preparedness and programs to prevent chronic diseases and AIDS (Mitchell 2003). Thus, Dr. Gerberding's leadership will be crucial in guiding and directing the agency's six thousand scientists to meet the challenges confronting public health in the twenty-first century.

There are also increasing charges by critics that public health policymaking under the Bush administration has been dominated by the President's political agenda. Several members of Congress have charged that federal scientific decisionmaking is being subverted by the political ideology of the Bush administration and that some scientific advisory committees whose recommendations are at odds with the president's political agenda have been terminated. For example, critics have charged that very qualified scientific members of the CDC's Advisory Committee on Childhood Lead Poisoning Prevention have been replaced with individuals who are openly associated with or are sympathetic to the views of the lead industry (Levin 2002).

How the new leaders of major public health agencies at the federal level manage the clash of science and politics will shape the course of future public health policies in the United States.

Public Health Leadership at State and Local Levels

State and local public health officials and professionals are facing new challenges in public health brought on by welfare reforms, escalating Medicaid costs, privatization, problems of the uninsured, and in preparing public health agencies to respond to a possible bioterrorism attack. Privatization of public health services at the local level is increasing. For example, a national survey of local health departments revealed that 73 percent had privatized public health services of some type. Such privatization practices are intimately related to divergent conceptions of public health and the role of local health departments (Keane, Marx, and Ricci 2001). Such privatization reflects a broader shift toward "managing" rather than directly providing public health services (Keane, Marx, Ricci, and Barron 2002). Another survey also revealed that 23.5 percent of local health departments had privatized at least one environmental health service (Keane, Marx, and Ricci 2002). The role of state and local public health systems will continue to evolve due to dynamic changes taking place in the health care system as a whole. How the public health system responds or adapts in response to financial and political stress and how well it educates the public about the value of public health will be crucial to its success (Smith 1998). Many states are already experimenting with different strategies for expanding health care access and at the same time trying to contain health care costs (Hanson 1993).

State governments are also beginning to receive an infusion of federal funds to improve public health infrastructure preparedness to defend against a possible bioterrorist attack. These funds will be used to improve infectious disease surveillance, communication capabilities, public health laboratories, and data collection and reporting abilities. Public health professionals will need to play a crucial role in the development of public health policies that meet these challenges. This in turn will require a strong leadership role by not only public health officials at state and local levels but also by public health professionals in general because nothing substitutes for strong leadership (Veninga 2001). Leaders will need to provide a clear sense of mission and purpose to the public health agencies.

The Institute of Medicine's (1988) report on the future of public health described the public health system as in disarray with little understanding or agreement about its mission. A 1994 content analysis of the mission statements of forty-two state health departments revealed that only 34 percent of state health departments specifically addressed organizational philosophy in their mission statements compared to 79 percent of business firms and 84 percent of hospitals. Similarly, only 41 percent of state health departments provided any indication of their organizational self-image, and 80 percent did not indicate in their mission statement how they wished to be viewed by those outside the organization (Duncan, Ginter, and Kreidel 1994).

In 1993 a survey was conducted of the public health officials of local health departments in six states to measure how effectively they perform the three core functions of public health—assessment, policy development, and assurance. The results indicated that local public health officials believed that they perform the core public health functions at only 56 percent effectiveness and perceived their performance as only 32 percent adequate (Barganier et al. 1994).

The Institute of Medicine's (1988) report criticized public health departments for not being on the cutting edge of public health policy formulation and recommended that every public health agency assume responsibility for the development of public health policies by promoting the use of scientific knowledge in public health decisionmaking and providing leadership in the development of public health policy.

As we discussed earlier in the chapter, there has been a historical lack of public health leadership in public health policy development, which has been attributed to the short tenure of many public health officials, the pervasive provider monopoly over health policy development, and the conflict between scientific and professional judgment on the one hand and the necessity of bargaining and compromises that are very much a part of the policymaking process in the political arena (Williams-Crowe and Aultman 1994). However, as Louis Rowitz (2001) reminds us, public health professionals are responsible for making our public health system work. To make the public health system work, it requires that public health officials develop necessary leadership skills to become important players in public health policy development. Interviews conducted with public health agency representatives responsible for legislative relations in several states suggested that to be effective, legislative policy entrepreneurs require a well-organized agency, a talented staff, clear communications, effective negotiations, and active and ongoing participation in the policymaking process (Williams-Crowe and Aultman 1994).

Public health professionals have been slow to develop strategies to demonstrate the usefulness of their scientific knowledge and skills to policymakers and the general public to compete successfully in a policymaking community driven by political dynamics (Institute of Medicine 1988). However, the last ten to fifteen years have witnessed several hopeful developments. There has been increased recognition that public health professionals must develop leadership skills that increase their ability to work with legislators. In a survey conducted by the CDC and the Public Health Foundation, of the seventy-eight management skills listed, the "ability to work with legislators" received the highest composite score among state health officials (Centers for Disease Control and Prevention 1992). Public health professionals need to develop not only managerial and leadership skills but also an ability to communicate and collaborate across many sectors of society (Kesler 2000). This is reflected in a survey of 620 public health administrators in which one-third of local health administrators thought that the media and the medical community had adversarial relations as a result of inaccurate reporting and relations between the two sides, which needed to be improved (Gellert, Higgins, Lowery, and Maxwell 1994). Thus leadership has become a central issue in public health (Mann 1997). Public health professionals must develop skills that allow them to become more effective players in public health policy development or risk becoming irrelevant (Nolan 1994).

It was in recognition of the need for leadership development skills among public health officials that in 1991 the Public Health Practice Program Office (PHPPO) of the CDC began to provide technical assistance and support for the establishment of state, regional, and national public health leadership institutes. This has led to the establishment of a network of such leadership institutes through collaboration between schools of public health and state public health departments throughout the country. Today there are several state and regional institutes. The National Public Health Leadership Development Network is a consortium of such institutes providing training in leadership development. Members of the consortium at its 1995 annual meeting began the process of identifying major areas of leadership practice. One of the areas identified was that of legislation and politics, recognizing the fact that the field of public health requires leaders to have competence to facilitate, negotiate, and collaborate in an increasingly competitive and contentious political environment (Wright et al. 2000). More than forty states now have access to a state or regional public health leadership program. Most leadership institutes are offered in cycles of one to two years in length with on-site and off-site meetings (Wright, Rowitz, and Merkle 2001).

The Public Health Leadership Institute (PHLI) is funded by the CDC. The PHLI program goals include strengthening public health leaders' skills, enhancing communication, developing a network of public health leaders, and expanding the understanding of public health leadership development. Its program is being offered by the Center for Creative Leadership and the University of North Carolina at Chapel Hill Kenan-Flagler Business School and School of Public Health ("Availability of Applications for the Public Health Leadership Institute" 2001).

In 1998 the Robert Wood Johnson Foundation in collaboration with the National Governors Association (NGA) and other partners established the state health leadership initiative program, which invites newly appointed state health officials to participate in a program designed to better prepare them to respond to many managerial and policy challenges, to enhance their ability to improve the effectiveness of their agency personnel, and to develop state health officials' leadership skills to become integral members of the state health policymaking team.

As the above discussion demonstrates, there is an increased recognition of the important role of leadership in public health policymaking as reflected in the establishment of public health leadership institutes and state public health leadership initiatives. This is a hopeful sign. However, most of such leadership training programs treat the political aspect as only one component of leadership among a long list of other managerial competencies as part of leadership development. They fail to recognize that leadership is inherently political in nature. Most such programs have also tended to focus on state and/or local public health officials. What also needs to be recognized is that not just public health officials but also professional associations of public health professionals need to play a leadership role in the development of public health policy if public health is to fulfill its mission.

Leadership and Professional Public Health Organizations

Many organizations of public health professionals provide training, serve as a forums for the exchange of ideas, and speak to the issues of public health concerns. They often serve as policy advocates trying to promote specific policy alternatives to address public health problems. Such professional organizations can play an important leadership role in making sure that the scientific knowledge base is used to inform policymaking and that the views of public health professionals are heard in the policymaking communities at all levels of government. While it is impossible to discuss all public health organizations, some of the most important ones are discussed below.

The American Public Health Association

The American Public Health Association (APHA) is the oldest and largest organization of public health professionals in the world. It has played a major leadership role in the professionalization of the field. It has more than 50,000 members from over fifty occupations. It is the most important voice on matters of public health, and for over 125 years it has tried to influence policies and priority setting ("About APHA" 2003). Its membership includes researchers, health service providers, health administrators, teachers, and other public health workers. It is highly interdisciplinary and represents over seventy-five academic disciplines. The annual meetings of the APHA are attended by over 10,000 members, representing a wide range of public health occupations and academic disciplines. For example, the November 1996 annual meeting of the APHA was attended by over thirteen thousand members from seventy-seven different disciplines in public health and related fields (Griffiths and McPherson 1997).

The APHA concerns itself with a broad range of issues that affect personal and environmental health. The Scientific and Professional Affairs unit of the APHA promotes evidence-based public health policy, practice, standards, and leadership. The APHA publishes a monthly newspaper, the *Nation's Health,* and a scholarly journal, the *American Journal of Public Health* ("About APHA" 2003).

The APHA relocated its headquarters from New York to Washington, DC, in 1969, and the association went through some dramatic changes during the 1970s, taking on a stronger advocacy role and becoming more visible. The association supported various legislations such as the Safe Drinking Water Act of 1975 and affirmative action. During the 1980s, when health budgets were slashed, the APHA became more active. It held its first national public health leadership conference in 1980. The association began to take policy positions on issues such as tobacco, alcohol, drugs, abortion, and Medicaid. Its members began to testify before congressional committees. In 1985, twenty members of the association were arrested during a demonstration against apartheid, and in 1986, the APHA led a demonstration at the Nevada Nuclear Test Site. During the 1990s, the APHA worked to promote a single-payer health care system ("APHA's Recent History Rich with Advocacy, Science" 1997). After the September 11 terrorist attacks and the anthrax scare, the APHA has worked to increase the public health budget to deal with the threat of bioterrorism.

In 1998, the APHA joined the CDC to launch the Public Health Innovation Project to help public health practitioners develop their skills and encourage them to share information about advances in the field ("APHA Launches Innovative Health Projects Network" 1998). In 2002 the APHA, in collaboration with the CDC and other partner organizations, launched a set of national public health performance standards that includes three assessment instruments designed to assess state public health systems, local public health systems, and local governing boards such as the board of health ("APHA and National Partner Organizations Celebrate Launch of National Public Health Performance Standards" 2002). That same year, the APHA also endorsed a set of principles that spells out ethical conduct for public health professionals and organizations ("APHA Adopts Code of Ethics for Public Health Profession" 2002).

Most important, in recognition of the need for a strong public health leadership to tackle the challenges confronting public health, the APHA started to offer leadership training beginning with the 1999 annual meeting ("APHA Leadership Training Benefits Entire Association" 2000). In 2003, the APHA started a leadership development and training program, made possible by a $178,000 grant from the W.K. Kellogg Foundation. The program consists of a two-year training period focused at the executive, governance, and staff levels, and includes training to develop skills in areas such as technology, advocacy, media relations, and writing ("American Public Health Association Begins Leadership Development . . ." 2003).

The Association of State and Territorial Health Officials

The Association of State and Territorial Health Officials (ASTHO) is a nonprofit organization that represents state and territorial health officials. Its mission is to influence public health policymaking and assure excellence in public health practice. It helps state health officials with the development and implementation of programs and policies that promote health and prevent diseases. ASTHO works to protect and improve the health of all people and communities. It involves itself in scientific, educational, legislative, and policy issues related to public health ("State Health Officials Named by H.H.S. Secretary . . ." 2002). The organization often conducts surveys of state public health officials on a wide range of issues. For example, in 1989, ASTHO did an extensive survey of state and territorial health officials to determine state efforts directed at prevention and control of tobacco use and presented suggestions for evaluating states' progress with subsequent surveys ("State Tobacco Prevention, Control Activities. . ." 1991).

The National Association of County and City Health Officials

The National Association of County and City Health Officials (NACCHO) was created in 1994 when the National Association of County Health Officials (NACHO) and the U.S. Conference of Local Health Officials were combined into one organization. NACCHO is a national nonprofit organization, and it represents local public health agencies including counties, cities, districts, and townships. In 2002, NACCHO expanded to include tribal public health agencies serving tribal communities on reservation lands. Today the organization has a membership of over one thousand local agencies. It serves as a national voice for local public health ("About NACCHO" 2003).

NACCHO provides educational, research, informational, and technical assistance to local health departments and facilitates partnerships among various government agencies to promote and strengthen public health. The association conducts studies to assess local health departments' capacity, develops strategies to help local health departments address problems of health disparities in communities, provides support for planning, management of resources, and training, fosters community collaboration, and provides support for pollution prevention. NACCHO, in partnership with the Robert Wood Johnson Foundation and W.K. Kellogg Foundation, implements the Turning Point Project, designed to develop a more effective public health infrastructure ("About NACCHO" 2003).

The National Association of Local Boards of Health

The National Association of Local Boards of Health (NALBOH) is a major voice for local boards of health on matters of national public health policies. It works closely with the CDC, NACCHO, ASTHO, APHA, and other public health-related organizations. It sponsors an annual national education and training conference for members of local health boards, develops and disseminates information and educational programs, and provides technical assistance ("About NALBOH" 2003).

The Public Health Foundation

The Public Health Foundation (PHF) is a nonprofit, national organization committed to supporting and advancing the efforts of federal, state, and local public health agencies to promote and protect public health. Its efforts are directed at strengthening and building the capacity and infrastructures of public health agencies through applied research, training, and technical assistance. It also provides information to public health agencies about health improvement planning, improving performance, and the understanding and appropriate use of data ("About Public Health Foundation" 2003).

The Association of Schools of Public Health

The Association of Schools of Public Health (ASPH) is a national organization that represents deans, faculty, and students of accredited schools of public health. It was established in 1953 to facilitate communication among the leaderships of schools of public health. It works with federal health agencies on projects designed to strengthen public health education and the public health profession. ASPH also maintains a data center. In collaboration with the U.S. Public Health Service, ASPH publishes *Health Reports*, a peer-reviewed journal that serves as a forum to which academicians and practitioners may submit their research on innovative public health programs and practices ("What is ASPH?" 2003).

The Society for Public Health Education

The Society for Public Health Education (SOPHE) is an independent professional association of health education professionals and students. The mission of the association is to promote health education, healthy behavior, healthy communities, a healthy environment, and to contribute to health education theory and research. Its efforts are directed at promoting public policies that are beneficial to health. The association offers two continuing education conferences annually ("Society for Public Health Education" 2003).

The American Association of Public Health Physicians

The American Association of Public Health Physicians (AAPHP) represents public health physicians and its mission is to promote public health, educate the public about the importance of public health physicians, and foster communication, education, and scholarship in public health. The association advocates public health preventive services, and serves as a voice of public health physicians to the American Medical Association (AMA), news media, the government and the general public ("American Association of Public Health Physicians" 2003).

The Association of Teachers of Preventive Medicine

The Association of Teachers of Preventive Medicine (ATPM) supports health promotion and disease prevention educators and researchers. Individual members of the association include physicians, nurses, public health professionals, and health services researchers. The association also includes institutional members such as academic departments and programs, health agencies, and schools of public health. ATPM develops curriculum, communication, and professional development tools for educators and researchers. The association publishes *American Journal of Preventive Medicine* ("About Us" 2003).

The American College of Preventive Medicine

The American College of Preventive Medicine (ACPM) is a national professional society of physicians committed to health promotion and disease prevention. It promotes the practice, teaching, and research of preventive medicine. ACPM works with governmental and nongovernmental agencies to strengthen the practice of preventive medicine ("What is ACPM?" 2003).

The American Association of Public Health Dentistry

The mission of The American Association of Public Health Dentistry (AAPHD) is to improve oral health. It promotes disease prevention, health promotion, and the education of public health professionals and decisionmakers about the importance of oral health to overall health ("About the AAPHD" 2003).

Leadership, Politics, and Public Health

In the field of health care, the importance of good leadership has become more evident as we enter the twenty-first century. Different types of leadership can produce different outcomes and affect how conflicts get resolved within the context of health care. Variables such as personality and style of a leader can influence health policy development (Firth-Cozens and Mowbray 2001). Two styles of leadership discussed most frequently in the literature are that of transactional and transformational leaders. A transactional leader uses power to achieve goals and policy objectives while the transformational leader motivates followers by engaging them intimately in the process of work to create an environment that allows followers to perform beyond expectations (Burns 1978).

Some view maintaining and building trust as an important ingredient of leadership (Lewis 2002). Others view good leadership to include risk-taking, inspiring a shared vision, empowerment, and building trust and teamwork while rigidity, poor relationships, low self-awareness, and a lack of open and reflective thinking are viewed as causes of leadership failure (Chaffee and Arthur 2002). Potentially good leaders fail because of their inability to create productive relationships (Kerfoot 2002). Thus there is a considerable variation in leadership roles, philosophies, and styles, and leaders are often portrayed as commanders, daredevils, zealots, healers, heroes, and technicians (Grazier 2002).

Unfortunately, a vast amount of the literature pertaining to the issue of leadership in the field of health care and public health deals with the leadership role in health care organizations and as a result is geared toward a management perspective. The literature often consists of a long laundry list of qualities, personality traits, and styles that successful or effective leaders are supposed to possess. Even when the literature on leadership acknowledges that the leadership process may sometimes be political in nature, the primary thrust of the literature is to suggest that the best leadership is somehow above politics. It ignores the reality that politics is a central and common element in all leadership (Weaver 2000). This is especially true of health care professionals who act in the capacity of public health officials at national, state, or local levels of government.

As we have discussed throughout this chapter, public health's focus on promoting the health of the population and community as a whole and preventing diseases requires public health officials to go beyond their scientific training and into the thicket of democratic politics (Beauchamp 2002), making it necessary for them to acquire and practice the skills of politics (Fox 2002). Since the mid-nineteenth century, public health officials in the United States—whether serving as commissioners, secretaries, or directors at different levels of government—have provided not just managerial and scientific roles, but also important leadership roles to agencies of the government when dealing with issues from sanitation to the prevention and spread of HIV/AIDS and use of tobacco (Mullan 2000). The same is true of the leaders of professional associations of public health professionals discussed in this chapter.

The challenges confronting public health leaders in the United States at the dawn of the twenty-first century are several. First, how to resist forces of private markets such as managed care and competition, and the welfare reforms brought on by budget deficits confronting the federal and state governments, overtaking community welfare. Second, how to counter electoral politics mobilizing a majority around politics of values based on religious moralism and fundamentalism that not only try to limit democratic discussion, that is, what can be said in educational programs about sex, abortion, and HIV/AIDS, but also try to undermine the formulation of effective public health policies (Beauchamp 2002). The prospect of bioterrorism will also require strong leadership to build effective partnerships between federal, state, and local public health officials and agencies (Parmet 2002).

As the discussion in this chapter has demonstrated, the clash of science and politics is inevitable in the practice of public health because trying to use the scientific knowledge base for the betterment of public health takes place in a political arena and not in a laboratory, and policymaking is governed by political forces. Issues of HIV/AIDS, abortion, drug addiction, needle exchange programs, physician-assisted suicide, homelessness, Medicaid, Medicare, and personal lifestyle-related and environmental-related causes of ill health touch a sensitive public nerve. Inevitably, public health practice becomes involved in the politics of the time and place, and public health practitioners, whether they like it or not, must be political players (Mullan 2000). Strong and effective leadership will be required on the part of public health professionals in bringing about effective actions in the interests of public health. The task of public health leadership will be how to build a consensus out of the conflicting health interests of the public, the economic interests of the health care industry, and the political interests of policymakers at all levels of government (Milio 1994). This may require public health officials and practitioners to be idealists like Don Quixote, pragmatic cynics like Machiavelli's Prince, and willing to ambush the public conscience and budget like Robin Hood to fulfill its mission of preventing diseases and promoting public health (Mullan 2000).

Study Questions

1. What is leadership? What are different approaches to the study of leadership?
2. Historically, public health professionals have not been major players in public health policy making at various levels of government. Why?
3. Describe some of the important public health leadership positions at the federal levels of government.
4. Write an essay in which you describe the role of the U.S. surgeon general. How has this position evolved?
5. With the leadership of Dr. C. Everett Koop and Dr. Joycelyn Elders as your reference point, write an essay in which you discuss the politics surrounding the surgeon general's role. What were the differences in leadership styles of the two surgeon generals?
6. Write an essay in which you discuss the leadership of David Kessler as commissioner of the Food and Drug Administration.
7. Discuss the role of public health leadership at state and local levels of government in the United States.

CHAPTER 3

The Politics of Public Health and Private Medicine

Aesculapius, the Greek father of medicine, had two quarrelsome daughters. Hygeia, the goddess of health, was known for preventing illness. Panacea, the goddess of cure, was known for treating illness. They began life as equals, but eventually the demand for Panacea's curative services grew so much that it exceeded her capacity to heal everyone. Consequently, the price for her services soon outstripped many people's ability to pay. (Smith 1994, 725)

Like the Greek mythology mentioned above, the curative and preventive models of health care have competed for preeminence in the American health care system. Since the second half of the twentieth century the curative model has dominated the American health care system while public health has often suffered a great deal of neglect. Even though the schism between public health and private medicine did not develop until the beginning of the twentieth century, two different approaches to explaining the human body were expressed centuries ago by Rene Descartes and Baruch Spinoza. Descartes viewed the human body as a self-contained, material machine. The Cartesian approach tried to explain how the human body works as an intricate machine, what causes it to malfunction, and what can be done to repair it. Spinoza in contrast, relying on Jewish tradition, espoused a more rational view that regards the human body as a complex and spiritual being, and the human body can be understood only in relation to unities larger than itself, that is, the whole of nature (Barglow 2002). Medicine in the sixteenth and seventeenth centuries, rather than taking a more integrative approach between these two approaches, adopted the Cartesian model. Today, more than four centuries later, the contradictions between these two approaches still remain unresolved (Barglow 2002).

This divergence between public health and private medicine, that is, medical care, poses a serious threat to America's ability to cope with the nation's health problems that cannot be resolved exclusively through the curative model (Institute of Medicine 2002b). The emphasis on the curative model of medicine has come at the cost of preventive medicine. Almost half of America's health care expenditures are spent on problems that are significantly influenced by individual behaviors such as substance abuse involving smoking, alcoholism, and illegal drug use, sexually transmitted diseases, and intentional and unintentional injuries (Shine 1998). Almost half of all deaths in America can be attributed to unhealthy lifestyles requiring major preventive efforts (Houston 1991). For example, one out of every five deaths in America is caused by smoking-related illnesses such as cancer, heart disease, and pulmonary diseases (Centers for Disease Control and Prevention 1997). Thousands of additional lives are lost annually in motor vehicle accidents because of failure to wear seat belts or driving under the influence of intoxicants. The leading cause of death among fifteen to thirty-four-year-old black men is homicide (Department of Health and Human Services 1986). Thus it is clear that we cannot ignore the important role played by public health in disease prevention and health promotion. Both the preventive and curative models of health care must work together in a complementary manner to help address America's health problems.

In this chapter we first analyze some of the major differences between public health and private medicine as they exist today. Next we examine the history of the relationship between public health and private medicine and identify factors that contributed to the development of the schism between the two. Finally we analyze efforts designed to create more cooperation and collaboration between public health and private medicine in the last ten to fifteen years. We conclude with a discussion of ways in which the gap between public health and private medicine can be bridged.

Differences Between Public Health and Private Medicine

Over one thousand years ago, understanding the physical and social dimensions of community life was considered an absolute necessity for Greek physicians to successfully treat the problems of individual life (Reiser 1996). In fact, in medical history, the roots of public health can be traced back to the ancient Sumerian civilization. Excavations have shown that this civilization possessed knowledge of sanitation because ancient houses were built with drains and cesspools. Egyptians and Hebrews had strict instructions related to hygiene (Houston 1991). However, centuries later, two separate disciplines and professions—public health and medicine—have emerged, with each focused and working separately on problems of health care. Donna Shalala, secretary of health and human services during the Clinton administration, once stated that "medicine and public health have operated as trains on parallel tracks—with windows facing in opposite directions, looking at different terrain" (quoted in Reiser 1996, 1430).

Public health has devoted itself to studying the characteristics of populations and communities to understand illnesses and disease within a community using the analytical tools of epidemiology, statistics, economics, and sociology. Medicine has focused its attention on the individual patient to cure illnesses and disease through the analytical tools of biochemistry, physiology, anatomy, pharmacology, immunology, and genetics, among other disciplines (Reiser 1996).

Professor emeritus Harvey Fineberg (1990), while dean of the Harvard University School of Public Health, outlined eleven important distinctions between medicine and public health. The first distinction, as mentioned above, is the fact that public health focuses on the population while medicine focuses on the individual. Second, public health emphasizes prevention and health promotion for the whole community while medicine emphasizes diagnosis and treatment of the individual patient. Third, the public health paradigm employs a variety of interventions aimed at the environment, human behavior, lifestyle, and medical care while the medical paradigm puts primary emphasis on medical care alone. Fourth, public health has multiple professional identities resulting in a diffused public image while medicine is a well-established profession with a sharp public image. Fifth, public health has a variable certification of specialties beyond the professional public health degree while medicine has a uniform system for certifying specialties beyond a professional medical degree. Sixth, public health lines of specialization are organized by analytical methods (epidemiology), setting and population (occupational health), substantive health problems (nutrition), and assessment and policy development skills while lines of specialization in medicine are organized by organ systems (cardiology), patient group (pediatrics), technical skills (radiology), and so forth. Seventh, even though biologic science is central to both, public health is stimulated by major threats to the health of the population and thus moves between laboratory and field while medicine is stimulated by the needs of patients and thus moves between laboratory and bedside. Eighth, in public health numeric science is an essential feature of analysis and training; in medicine numeric science is not as predominant in training. Ninth, social science is an integral part of public health while it tends to be an elective part of training in medicine. Tenth, in public health clinical science is peripheral to training while in medicine it is an essential part of training. Finally, public health operates on a public service ethics tempered by a concern for the individual. In contrast, medicine operates on a personal service ethic tempered by awareness of social responsibility.

Jonathan Mann (1997) has similarly pointed out important differences between medicine and public health with respect to focus, scope, priorities, skills and expertise, and organizational structures. Some of the differences he points out are the same ones mentioned by Professor Fineberg. However, he points to some additional differences between public health and medicine. Public health operates in an environment of government organizations, large public programs, and the public policy community. Medicine operates in private medical offices, clinics, hospitals, and a variety of other medical care facilities. Medicine is expected to provide individual care and treatment while public health is expected to protect the population against broader health threats—epidemic diseases and harmful environmental conditions such as unsafe water, air and chemical pollution, and the like.

Since doctors treat individual patients for specific illness, disease, or injury, patients need medical care only part of the time, that is, when they are ill. In contrast, since public health professionals monitor and diagnose the health concerns of entire communities and populations and promote healthy practices to keep the entire population healthy, communities need public health all the time. Some have argued that a high concentration of resources in high-tech medicine with relatively marginal effects on health for a few has come at the expense of low-tech community programs that have a higher effect on health for many. It is easier to generate political support and market demand for health services that have identifiable benefits for the payer than for services whose effects are difficult to quantify and are dispersed among many people (Weiss 1997). As a result, medicine has come to be identified with an objective and reductionist technocratic science while public health is identified with interest-group-oriented politics and policies (Brandt and Gardner 2000). However, others have argued that the medical profession and medical interest groups have tried to make medicine serve its own narrow economic and social interests. They point to the social control function performed by the medical profession and private medicine's neglect of important physical and social environmental influences on overall health (Brown 1979). Constituents of each group have at times expressed antagonism toward each other. For example, medical professionals often view public health as a field corrupted by politics and believe that public health is incapable of good medicine and science. Public health professionals at times have characterized medicine as a field dominated by arrogance, self-interest, and economic aggrandizement (Brandt and Gardner 2000).

Politically, one of the most important differences between public health and private medicine is that the delivery of private medical care on a day-to-day basis takes place largely outside the political arena. Such is not the case with public health. Practitioners of private medicine enjoy significant discretion over location, type, size, and other details of their medical practice. Overall, the practice of private medicine is largely immune from public accountability. In sharp contrast, since public health agencies and public health practitioners are located within government bureaucracies, they often get embroiled in political conflicts and controversies as we discussed in chapter 2 on leadership. Community-based public health activities evoke a public response, which is not the case with the treatment of individual patients in a private medical setting (Weiss 1997). In addition, public health professionals constantly find themselves involved in political struggle and competition for scarce resources with other government agencies. Public health professionals often rely more on the hope that the scientific merit of their case and the humanitarian nature of their work will carry the day during policymaking in legislative bodies. However, in the practice of private medicine, organized political interests such as the AMA can rely on a host of tools such as lobbying and campaign contributions to exert political pressure to have their interests and preferences prevail during the policymaking process (Weiss 1997).

Despite all the differences between public health and medicine, it is however important to remember that there is also a significant overlap between the two. Public health practice requires a solid biomedical basis and involves many medical practitioners. Both medical practice and public health practice operate in an environment that is influenced by law, public policy, and government. Also, the ultimate goal of both is the same—to improve health (Mann 1997).

History of the Relationship Between Medicine and Public Health

The history of the relationship between medicine and public health in the United States can be best characterized as one filled with apprehension and tension. Despite some early cooperation between the two fields during the nineteenth century, much of the twentieth century was marked by considerable conflict. The two complementary approaches to health care—curative and preventive—evolved into competitive approaches during the twentieth century as both of them developed separate and distinct identities. Economic factors played a major role in much of this conflict. Starting in the 1990s, there are hopeful signs of decreased tension and increased cooperation and collaboration between the two. In chapter 1 we discussed the evolution of public health services in the United States. In this chapter we largely focus on public health's interaction with private medicine and examine events and factors that help explain the changing nature of the relationship between the two.

The Nineteenth Century: Period of Ambivalence and Accommodation

Public health in the United States began more as an episodic and necessity-driven response to local threats caused by epidemic diseases such as plague, measles, scarlet and typhoid fever, influenza, and the like rather than as a rational, systematic, and nationally directed activity under a well-thought-out comprehensive plan (Fee and Brown 2002). For example, during the late eighteenth and early nineteenth centuries, yellow fever posed a major threat on the East Coast that helped raise awareness about public health and led to the establishment of local boards of health in several cities such as Philadelphia, Baltimore, Boston, New York, and Washington, DC. However, business and commercial interests strongly opposed such boards on the grounds that their regulations interfered with commercial activities and as a result health boards in cities such as New York and New Orleans were either stripped of their powers or disbanded (Fee and Brown 2002).

Quarantine was a method often used by the government to prevent the spread of diseases (Markel 1995; Lucaccini 1996). Public health's use of techniques such as quarantine, that is, forcible removal of people suffering from diseases from their homes to prevent the spread of disease and protect the general public, often met with stiff resistance. Attempts by government to introduce compulsory vaccination also met with strong opposition from religious groups and individuals (Lupton 1995). In fact, much of the history of public health in the nineteenth century is a history of the struggle over its own mandates. Public health authorities encountered opposition from religious groups and others who objected on moral grounds to state intervention in the areas of health and hygiene. At the same time, public health also met with opposition from business and commercial interests that objected to public health regulations on the grounds of privacy and property rights to protect their own economic interests (Starr 1982). The period of Jacksonian democracy during the presidency of Andrew Jackson (1828–36) coincided with the individualistic and localistic antigovernment, antiprofessional and often anti-intellectual values of the country (Fee and Brown 2002).

Three major public health activities during the 1800s were: (1) dealing with the threats of epidemic diseases such as plague, cholera, and smallpox; (2) improving environmental conditions by draining marshes, swamps, and standing water; and (3) imposing local protective regulations and interventions directed at filth, garbage, and other urban problems (Fee and Brown 2002). Health problems connected with poor hygiene and sanitation made controlling communicable diseases, improving sanitary conditions, and addressing nutrition concerns a top priority (Egan 1994). Health problems in urban America reached their height during the mid-1850s as mortality rates in cities such as New York, Boston, and Philadelphia rose dramatically as large numbers of immigrants resided in crowded and poorly ventilated tenements and workers of all ages worked long hours in sweatshops. This gave rise to the occupation and sanitary health movement representing a coalition of interest groups comprised of workers, journalists, politicians, reformers, and many professionals who pressed for reforms and changes in the name of public interest. The sanitary reform movement (Duffy 1990) in many major cities such as New York played a crucial role in improving conditions in the cities and reducing mortality rates (Brieger 1997). For example, a significant decline in mortality rates in Philadelphia between 1870 and 1930 has been credited to the municipal public health services (Condran, Williams, and Cheney 1997).

The relationship between public health and medicine during the better part of the nineteenth century can best be characterized as one of cooperation and accommodation. Many physicians were actively involved in the sanitary and public health reform movement along with some businessmen. Charles E. and Carroll Rosenberg (1968) have chronicled the important role played by John S. Griscom, M.D., and Robert M. Hartley, a businessman, in pioneering the public health movement in the city of New York. The authors attribute the involvement of both Griscom and Hartley in the public health movement to their spiritual dedication and an intense pietism widespread in their generation.

Eugene Link (1992), in his study of the humanitarian tradition in medicine from 1776 to 1976, classifies physicians into five groups. According to him, iatrocentrics were physicians who were not involved in social change and tended to favor the status quo. Sanitationists were those who favored government aid to maintain cleanliness but were reluctant to call on bureaucracy for fear that its involvement would lead to more social control of medicine through increased regulations. Some physicians were public health advocates who engaged in social criticism because they believed that an emphasis on sanitation alone was not sufficient to maintain public health. They were the public health physicians. The fourth group of physicians was made up of those who were outspoken social critics, but who kept their professional and social concerns totally separate. They were the ones who often dropped out of regular practice and joined a reform movement. Finally, the fifth group included those physicians who viewed citizenship duties as an integral part of their medical practice. Many physicians during the nineteenth century fit into several of these categories. There were certainly many physicians who were advocates for sanitary reforms and public health.

For example, during the nineteenth century, physicians constituted the largest group among public health professionals.

The first half of the nineteenth century is often called the heroic age in medicine because of the vigorous means employed, such as bloodletting, to treat diseases, especially fever (Mermann 2001). However, during the early part of the nineteenth century, in keeping with the antiprofessional and anti-intellectual values of the times, medicine was not regarded very highly. Physicians were relatively poor and occupied a lower social standing in the community. Politically they were powerless. They could neither set nor enforce standards for medical practice or for medical education. Internal fights also contributed to their political powerlessness. The public did not hold physicians in high esteem and was suspicious of political as well as professional elites (Ritchie and Israel 1995).

During most of the nineteenth century, American medical education was in disarray. In 1800 there were only four functioning medical colleges. However, a phenomenal growth in medical schools took place during the century. The number of medical schools increased to eighteen by 1825. Twenty-six new medical schools were founded between 1810 and 1840, while forty-seven more were established between 1840 and 1876. Between 1873 and 1890, during the great wave of immigration, 114 new medical schools were added. It is estimated that a total of over four hundred medical schools was founded between 1800 and 1900. Many of these schools were short-lived and many failed during the Civil War (Stevens 1971).

Part of the reason for the growth of proprietary schools was the abandonment of licensing regulations during the 1830s and 1840s. During the period of Jacksonian democracy, there was an attack on elitism at all levels in American society, including all professional fields, and there was a demand for the repeal of licensing laws and the withdrawal of state recognition from medical societies (Stevens 1971). By 1830, what was left were largely unenforceable licensing laws and a network of medical societies that were more interested in fighting quackery than raising their own standards (Stevens 1971). By 1850, only two states and Washington, DC, still had any medical school licensing laws.

The repeal of licensing laws led to rampant quackery (Mermann 2001). It was in this context that the American Medical Association (AMA) was founded in 1847 to improve medical education. However, the AMA remained largely ineffective and powerless until the end of the nineteenth century. During the first half of the nineteenth century, American medicine was a shifting collection of coexisting opinions and a broad spectrum of practitioners from different social backgrounds and of different intellectual attainment. Medical pluralism was the prevailing theme (Kaptchuk and Eisenberg

2001). It took many years before the medical profession was able to overcome many of these problems through a mixture of diplomacy, compromise, and "federalization," which helped heal major divisions within the profession (conventional practitioners, homeopaths, eclectics) and gave the medical profession a formidable power structure. The AMA also became a major political force (Ritchie and Israel 1995). During the second half of the nineteenth century, the AMA agitated for adequate vital statistics legislation and for expanding the role of the federal government in areas of public health. The AMA also assumed a leadership role in pushing for a federal department of health during the 1880s. However, the war with Spain and the Philippines overshadowed the AMA's attempt to secure national health legislation (Burrow 1963).

The Civil and the Spanish-American Wars encouraged the spread of industrialism, growth, and a concentration of cities that significantly affected the lives of citizens. It led to an upsurge in public health medicine and physicians' practice. Public health physicians discovered that they could not function without a social context. The American Public Health Association (APHA) was founded in 1872, and the association helped give public health measures and preventive medicine a major boost. In response to the APHA's campaign, state governments moved to establish their own official boards of health (Ritchie and Israel 1995). The close tie between public health and physicians is reflected by the fact that in 1897 the APHA boasted a membership of 568 members, of whom 452, or 80 percent, were physicians (Terris 1976). The fact that at the turn of the century physicians constituted up to 80 percent of the American Public Health Association's membership reflected its dominant position in the field of public health. Physicians welcomed the insights offered by public health practitioners about the environment, sanitation, and policies to control epidemics. Public health practitioners on their part appreciated the contributions made by physicians through original research that provided new knowledge about diseases (Brandt and Gardner 2000). Thus physicians played a major role in the early development of public health in the United States. For example, one of the physician reformers who helped broaden the concept of public health was Albert L. Gibson, chief of medical services of the navy. In a report he compiled for the AMA in 1882, he made a strong plea for putting preventive medicine ahead of palliative medicine. His report was very controversial within the medical profession (Link 1992).

The discovery of microbes in the closing years of the nineteenth century helped create a new regime of public health. The new science of bacteriology helped improve the status of medical professionals working in the field of public health. Public health, rather than relying on the old miasmic and contagionist model of disease causation, now relied on bacteriology to cite tangible reasons for infectious diseases. This helped legitimize public health as a "scientific" activity. However, the discovery of bacteria as the cause of major diseases also drew attention away from the broad social causes of diseases and ill health such as poverty, poor housing, and the like. The emphasis in public health shifted more to focusing on personal hygiene (Lupton 1995). The development of bacteriology not only changed the theory and practice of public health but also its relationship to medicine. As public health developed a more precise understanding of the sources and modes of transmission of infectious diseases and shifted its attention from the environment to focus on the individual, public health increasingly came to rely on the techniques of medicine. Private practitioners of medicine came to view such expansion of public health activities to incorporate more of medicine as usurpation of the medical profession's authority (Starr 1982).

During much of the nineteenth century, not only was there a great deal of overlap between medicine and public health, they also acted as allies. The sharper boundary that exists between medicine and public health today did not exist during much of the nineteenth century. However, the tacit alliance between public health and medicine in the nineteenth century was slowly giving way to a deepening fracture between them, beginning in the twentieth century. The seeds for this coming conflict were planted in the nineteenth century.

The Twentieth Century

1900 to 1920s: Period of Conflicts

The beginning of the twentieth century also witnessed an increasing and deepening fracture between medicine and public health. By the middle of the twentieth century this friction had often turned into an open hostility. During the early part of the twentieth century, as the medical profession became tightly organized, developed a separate identity, and became a powerful political force, it came to view an ambitious and increasingly independent public health profession as a threat to its own economic interests (Fee and Brown 2000).

Beginning in the twentieth century, medicine developed biologically grounded disciplines such as biochemistry, physiology, anatomy, pharmacology, immunology, and genetics to explore the functioning of the human body and diagnose and treat various illnesses and diseases. While private medicine focused its attention on the individual, public health focused its attention on the community. After World War I, public health and private medicine continued their own separate ways. Each developed a separate system of financial, social, educational, and professional support (Reiser 1996). Several factors contributed to the deepening rupture between public health and private medicine.

Factors that Contributed to Conflicts Between Public Health and Private Medicine

Rising political power of the AMA. As we have mentioned earlier, the AMA since its establishment in 1847 had largely remained ineffective during much of the nineteenth century. Its effectiveness in promoting political reform depended on its ability to correct its own organizational shortcomings and improve the image of the medical profession through medical educational reform. During the early 1900s the medical profession under the leadership of the AMA transformed itself and consolidated its power. In 1901, AMA members approved a revised constitution that not only introduced structural reforms but tied the AMA more closely to local medical societies (Burrow 1963). In 1913 the AMA expanded its membership requirements to include all members in good standing with state and local medical societies. This helped increase the AMA's membership from 8,401 in 1900 to 70,146 in 1910. By 1920 the AMA membership had increased to 83,338. The AMA also significantly enhanced its political machinery to become an important player in national politics on health-related issues (Burrow 1963). It also helped bring about reforms in state medical organizations. The AMA also played a crucial role in bringing about major medical education reforms, especially through its establishment of uniform educational standards for medical schools. This helped make medicine a respectable profession. These changes helped unify the medical profession and turn the AMA into a potent political force.

During the 1920s and early 1930s the Republicans controlled the White House, the Senate, and the House of Representatives. This led to the rise of a conservative, free market era and the decline of progressivism. Public health came under increased suspicion, and representatives of local private practitioners attacked federal, state, and local public health activities and programs as "socialized medicine" (Fee and Brown 2002).

Economic interests. During the late nineteenth and early twentieth centuries, the medical profession displayed a positive of view of state intervention when it suited its purposes. For example, when in the late nineteenth century physicians were seeking licensing protections, they welcomed state intervention and supported efforts to expand the regulatory powers of health departments. During the progressive era, the AMA not only supported but pushed for a cabinet-level department of health. Initially the AMA even supported the idea of compulsory health insurance. The medical profession supported government regulations and/or activities that were complementary to private practice, but it strongly opposed activities that the profession perceived as interfering in their business or when they perceived government activity as competing with private practice (Starr 1982). For example, the AMA and the medical profession fought vehemently against dispensaries, health centers, the Sheppard-Towner Act, and veterans health benefits. Over a period of time it also came to oppose compulsory health insurance

Dispensaries. Today the word dispensary is used to describe a place where drugs are stored and prescriptions are filled, that is, a pharmacy. However, centuries ago dispensaries referred to medical institutions that provided free medical care for the poor. Dispensaries were more like hospitals except that they had no inpatient beds. Only outpatient medical care was provided. At stated times physicians would visit the dispensary and dispense medical care. Dispensaries provided most of the medical care, and only nontrivial surgical cases were sent to hospitals. Dispensaries were much cheaper compared to hospitals (Davis and Warner 1918).

Dispensaries came about in the closing decades of the eighteenth century and grew rapidly throughout the nineteenth century. Taking care of many sick poor people who lived in unsanitary conditions in the urban areas fell to the dispensary physicians. They were the significant providers of medical care. The first American dispensary was founded in Philadelphia in 1786, followed by New York in 1791, Boston in 1796, and Baltimore in 1800. Their numbers had grown to twenty-nine in New York by 1877 and thirty-three in Philadelphia by 1877 (Rosenberg 1974). The number of patients treated by dispensaries also increased dramatically. For example, dispensaries in New York treated 134,069 patients in 1860, 180,000 in 1866, 213,000 in 1874, and 876,000 in 1900 (Rosenberg 1967).

Several motivations accounted for the rise of dispensaries. One of the primary motivations was a sense of stewardship, that is, a sense of duty and obligation to take care of the poor and sick. The second motivation was economic in nature. It was based on a mercantile contention that maintaining the health of the poor would not only save tax dollars spent on almshouses or hospital care for chronically ill workers, but it would help the economy by helping to maintain the labor force at peak efficiency. The third motivation was the idea that dispensaries would serve as schools of clinical medicine, which were badly needed (Rosenberg 1974). Many elite physicians saw working at a dispensary as a stepping-stone in their career. Dispensaries were also ideologically consistent with most Americans' views about the responsibilities and functions of government. Based on the values of Christian benevolence and community-oriented social intervention, the American public viewed dispensaries as a necessary response designed to meet the needs of hardworking Americans (Rosenberg 1974). Dispensaries were essentially established as charities for the poor. They were often referred to as "medical soup kitchens" (Starr 1982).

However, by the early twentieth century dispensaries as viable independent institutions were dying, and most of them had disappeared by the 1920s. One of the reasons for this was that dispensaries had become marginal to the needs of the medical profession. With the rise of hospitals, hospital-centered internships and residency programs became a normal part of medical education, and elite physicians preferred hospital appointments just as an earlier generation of elite physicians had preferred a dispensary appointment (Rosenberg 1974).

The most important reason for the fall and disappearance of the dispensaries was that they came into conflict with the economic interests of private medical practitioners. By the late nineteenth century, dispensaries had lost much of their goodwill as well as appeal to elite doctors. While there was always some complaint about dispensaries competing with private physicians for a limited supply of paying patients, such criticism was often muted. During most of the mid and late nineteenth century, private physicians demonstrated a great deal of apprehension but certainly not open hostility toward dispensaries. However, following the Civil War, dispensaries came under strong attack from private medical practitioners as the supplier of ill-conceived charities for the unworthy poor. In many local communities, physician-sponsored reports generally concluded that a great portion of dispensary users was abusing the system because the users were financially capable of paying private physician's fees (Rosenberg 1974).

Many doctors felt put upon by the poor. Under increasing pressure from private practitioners, dispensaries began to hire social workers to investigate patients to make sure that they were truly impoverished, and in 1899 the state of New York passed a law that made it a misdemeanor to visit dispensaries under false pretenses (Starr 1982). In fact, the basic question discussed in most of the articles dealing with dispensaries at the time was how to keep people from getting treatment at the dispensary (Davis and Warner 1918). Claims that there were large numbers of people who could afford to pay for services of private physicians were often exaggerated. In fact, studies have shown that only a small percentage of dispensary patients were capable of paying for medical services (Davis and Warner 1918; Davis

1927). The opposition from private practitioners combined with reforms of medical education and the rise of the hospital as a center for medical practice brought about the demise of dispensaries. Ultimately, most dispensaries disappeared as freestanding institutions and others were absorbed as outpatient departments within modern hospitals.

Authority and activities of health boards. With respect to public health, the period of the early 1900s is referred to as the "golden age for public health" (Starr 1982). By the beginning of the twentieth century it had become very clear that many diseases were communicable in nature, and the development of vaccines led many communities on the East Coast to require their citizens to become immunized. In fact, in New York a leading public health figure, Hermann Biggs, argued that public health authorities could resort to any means necessary for the public good (Gorin 2001). Public health authorities frequently used police officers, zealous nurses, and physicians to go to the homes of those suspected of carrying disease for the purpose of immunization. In fact, police officers often held the arm of those who refused to be vaccinated while a city nurse administered the vaccine (Garrett 2000). However, the golden age of public health did not last very long.

Private practitioners demonstrated an ambivalent attitude toward expanding the role of public health. The development of state and local health boards was significantly influenced by the attitude of private practitioners. As we have mentioned earlier, private practitioners favored and supported public health activities that were complementary to their practice but strongly opposed those activities they perceived as being in competition with their economic interests. Thus the relationship between private practitioners and public health ranged from cooperation to resistance. Physicians welcomed state intervention when they were seeking licensing protection, and they even supported extending regulatory powers of health departments as long as health departments' activities did not interfere with their private practice.

A great example of cooperation and resistance between private practitioners and local health departments is provided by the city of New York. The city health department established a diagnostic bacteriology laboratory in 1892. The city made diagnostic tests available free of charge to physicians and doctors. The city health department also significantly cut the cost of serum by refining production techniques. The city began producing large quantities of tetanus serum offered as a rabies vaccine to people bitten by dogs. Such activities brought about a marked reduction in fatality rates from diphtheria and it received international acclaim. However, soon thereafter local manufacturing chemists and doctors began to denounce the health department's activities as "municipal socialism" and argued that such public health activities were an unfair competition with private business (Starr 1982). In April 1902, over one thousand doctors and druggists signed a petition urging the mayor to root out the commercialism of the city's health department. As a result of this pressure, later in the year the city health department ceased all outside sales of antitoxin while continuing to provide it free to physicians for the treatment of the poor (Starr 1982).

New York City also provides some excellent examples of the conflicts between private practitioners and the expanding role of public health. In 1897, under the leadership of Hermann Biggs, the health department proposed mandatory notification of all suspected cases of tuberculosis (Frieden, Lerner, and Rutherford 2000). The medical profession condemned this requirement, and the medical societies of New York and King Counties officially expressed their opposition to it (Terris 1976). The members of the New York Academy of Sciences called the new requirement "offensively dictatorial" and condemned the "aggressive tyrannies of the health board" (Fox 1975).

Between 1910 and 1920, many progressives argued for the creation of unified health centers in place of separate services for schoolchildren and programs for maternal and infant care. This came to be known as the health center movement. Private practitioners strongly opposed the health center movement despite the fact that the health centers were advocated as auxiliaries to private practice. For example, Hermann Biggs, head of the health department of the city of New York at the end of World War I, proposed building a network of health centers as a way to meet the needs of the rural areas for things such as hospitals, outpatient clinics, and laboratories, among others. These centers would offer private practitioners and their patients services such as x-rays, clinical consultations, and diagnostic tests. However, private practitioners saw this as a threat to their practice and argued that the proposed legislation gave too little power to the medical profession and too much power to county boards of supervisors and mayors of cities. The opposition from private practitioners doomed the legislation in the state legislature (Biggs 1921; Terris 1946; Terris 1976; Hunt 1921; Vaughan 1921).

Compulsory health insurance, the Sheppard-Towner Act, and veterans health. Following World War I, the AMA had become fearful of the expanding government influence over health care and medical practice and had become increasingly concerned over compulsory health insurance and other social experiments going on in Europe. Even though the AMA's leadership had earlier advocated compulsory health insurance, in 1920 the AMA officially denounced the compulsory health insurance proposal. Articles in the *Journal of American Medical Association* criticized the British health care system based on the idea of compulsory insurance (Burrow 1963).

During the 1920s another major confrontation between organized medicine and the government's role in public health took place over the passage of the Sheppard-Towner Act of 1921. Under the act, the federal government provided funds to states for maintenance and improvement of the health of mothers and children. Thus it established the first federal-state partnership for health services (Egan 1994). Like compulsory health insurance, the AMA saw this as a threat to the medical profession. The AMA campaigned actively against it (Terris 1976). Organized medicine denounced the Sheppard-Towner Act that provided health education to mothers by attacking it as "state medicine" (Meckel 1990). The AMA argued that this federal legislation threatened states' rights and claimed that maternal and infant mortality rates were not higher in the United States compared to other countries and that such rates could not be lowered through legislative action (Stevens 1971). The AMA expressed concern that the proposed law and its requirement of compliance in order to receive federal funds gave the federal government power over state public health problems (Burrow 1963). To record its opposition to compulsory health insurance as well as the Sheppard-Towner Act, the House of Delegates at the AMA's annual meeting in 1921 passed a resolution declaring its opposition to all forms of "state medicine" (Burrow 1963).

Despite opposition from the AMA, the Sheppard-Towner Act was passed in 1921 and was renewed in 1927 until 1929. However, the AMA ultimately did prevail, and under increasingly effective opposition mobilized by the AMA, efforts to further extend the Sheppard-Towner Act failed in 1931 and 1932. A federal-state program for maternal and children's health was reborn under the Social Security Act of 1935 (Stevens 1971).

Conflict between organized medicine and government also occurred over the passage of the World Veterans Act of 1924. The act allowed veterans of all military occupations and conflicts since 1897 with non–service-connected disabilities the use of all beds in veterans hospitals that veterans with service disabilities did not occupy. The AMA strongly condemned the act and argued that the law discriminated against private practitioners and denied patients the freedom of choosing their own physician (Burrow 1963).

As the above discussion has illustrated, during the early part of the 1900s significant conflicts arose between private practitioners and public health activities of the government. The underlying cause for many of these conflicts was economic self-interest. Private medicine saw the expanding government role in public health as a threat to its economic well-being. The attack on the Sheppard-Towner Act by the AMA, conservative physicians, and their political allies was part of a larger assault on public health and community provision of health services. For example, Sen. Reed Smoot (R-Utah) attacked the Public Health Service (PHS) for abusing the authority of state and local governments and claimed that the activities of the PHS were intended to "Russianize the United States" (Mullan 1989).

As Paul Starr (1982) has argued, public health suffered major political consequences from these attacks by private medicine and was relegated to a secondary status, and the golden age of public health crashed in the 1920s.

Educational reforms and the separation of medical and public health education. Another factor that contributed to furthering the estrangement between medicine and public health was educational reform of medical schools and establishment of separate schools of public health during the 1910s and 1920s.

The AMA had spent a considerable amount of time in the 1890s revising its constitution and organizational structure to strengthen itself and expand its membership. By 1903 the AMA had turned its attention medical education reform as its top priority. The AMA had come to realize that it could not successfully advance professional ethics or political reforms unless it first increased the level of medical training by raising the standards of medical education. In 1904 an editorial in the *Journal of the American Medical Association* called attention to the backward state of medical education in the United States compared to many other countries (Burrow 1963).

In the 1870s, William Welch, a well-respected researcher (who later went on to become the first dean of Johns Hopkins Medical School, established in 1893), had described American medical education as "simply horrible" (Stevens 1971). The proliferation of proprietary medical schools offered minimal education with practically no clinical or laboratory experience. This had led to an oversupply of incompetent physicians who were poorly trained, poorly paid, and held in low esteem by the public (Mermann 2001). To respond to this problem, in 1904 the AMA created a Council of Medical Education. The council's insistence on educational reforms led to the closing of twenty-nine marginal medical schools. By 1906 the AMA had launched a school-by-school survey, and in 1907 the council began classifying medical schools as worthy (A), acceptable (B), or hopeless (C) (Haller 1981). In 1908 the Carnegie Foundation for the Advancement of Teaching authorized a study of medical education in the United States. Abraham Flexner was assigned the task of carrying out this study (1981).

The Flexner Report of 1910 provided stinging criticisms of American medical education. The report argued that there was an overproduction of uneducated and poorly trained medical practitioners with disregard for public welfare, and that this overproduction was a result of the large number of commercial medical schools. The report argued for the adoption of uniform standards in medical schools and the need for teaching hospitals and clinical experience for medical students (Mermann 2001). Taking Johns Hopkins as the educational model for medical schools, the Flexner Report endorsed university education as a medical function, urged for the provision of a full-time staff, laboratory, and hospital facilities in order to combine teaching and research, and argued for raising standards of admission to medical schools and teaching (Stevens 1971). Flexner made an urgent plea to reduce the number of medical schools in the United States. The Flexner Report also argued that the "physician is a social instrument" and "medical school is a public service corporation" (Flexner 1910). Unfortunately, most discussions of the Flexner Report have tended to ignore this key point. Flexner saw public service as an important function of medicine.

The Flexner Report acted as a catalyst for the reforms already under way in the American medical educational system. The impact of the report was immediate. By 1915 the number of medical schools was reduced to ninety-two, and by 1920 the number was down to eighty-five (Stevens 1971). By 1933 the number of degree-granting institutions had dropped to sixty-six. Correspondingly, the number of medical students and graduates also declined significantly, addressing the problem of oversupply (Haller 1981). By 1932 almost all medical schools and state licensing boards required at least two years of college education (with some requiring three years or a college degree). Higher entrance requirements also led to increased standards for state licensing requirements. Thus by the 1930s the medical profession had successfully established an effective monopoly control of medical education (Stevens 1971). The organized medical profession controlled entry into the field through licensure and accreditation of medical schools and teaching hospitals, and it also controlled the practice and economics of medicine through its local medical societies (Brown 1979). By the late 1930s medicine had firmly established its status as a science (Stevens 1971).

It is important to note that not only government but foundations such as the Rockefeller and Carnegie played a major influential role in American medicine between 1910 and the 1930s. Their main influence was derived from their power of the purse. Between 1910 and 1030s, aside from billions of dollars spent by the government, foundations spent around $300 million for medical research and education. As mentioned before, the Carnegie Foundation was the one that authorized the Flexner study. The Rockefeller Foundation in 1901 founded the Rockefeller Institute for Medical Research, and by 1928 the Rockefeller Foundation had given gifts totaling $65 million to the institute. Initially the Rockefeller Foundation did not support medical research that examined the relationship between social factors, health, and diseases. During much of the 1910s the Rockefeller Institute focused its resources on subjects such as chemistry, biology, pathology, bacteriology, pharmacology, and experimental surgery in line with the emergence of a new science of medicine, that is, biological reductionism (Brown 1979). However, in 1916 the Rockefeller Foundation expressed its concern that sufficient attention was not being paid to environmental and social causes of disease. The Rockefeller Foundation advocated the establishment of separate schools of public health to remedy this problem (White 1991).

The Welch-Rose Report of 1915 has been viewed as the basis for the critical movement in the history of the institutional schism between public health and medicine because it led to the establishment of institutionalized public health education, that is, establishment of schools of public health supported by the Rockefeller Foundation (Fee and Acheson 1991). The report was authored by William Welch, founding dean of the Johns Hopkins School of Public Health, and Wycliffe Rose of the Rockefeller Foundation. The report focused more on research than practical education (Brandt and Gardner 2000). Some have blamed the Rockefeller Foundation's 1916 decision to support the establishment of schools of public health for creating the schism between public health and medicine and legitimizing the rift between medicine's laboratory investigation of the mechanisms of disease and public health's nonclinical concern with environmental and social influences on health and wellness (White 1991).

A year following the report, the Johns Hopkins School of Hygiene and Public Health was founded in 1916. By 1922, schools of public health were established at Columbia, Harvard, and Yale Universities. By 1999 there were twenty-nine schools of public health, enrolling around fifteen thousand students ("Changes in the Public Health System" 1999). Over the years, the types of students and training provided have also changed. In the beginning, students who enrolled in public health schools had already obtained a medical degree. However, in 1978, 69 percent of students enrolled in public health schools had only a bachelor's degree. Public health school training had evolved from a second degree for medical professionals to a primary public health degree with a focus on the six core disciplines of biostatistics, epidemiology, health services administration, health education, behavioral science, and environmental science ("Changes in Public Health System" 1999).

These schools of public health guarded their independence from medical schools and public health bureaucracies (Fee and Brown 2000). The discipline of public health came to focus on the analytical tools of mathematics, statistics, sociology, economics, and epidemiology for studying the characteristics of populations and communities that cause illness and finding the best ways to prevent illness and epidemics. Medicine came to rely on biologically grounded disciplines such as biochemistry, physiology, anatomy, pharmacology, and immunology for studying the functioning of the human body and treating illnesses when they occur in individuals (Reiser 1996).

However, the curriculum of public schools did not become standardized as was the case with medical education. Thus, the schools of public health that were established were heterogeneous rather than homogeneous like medical schools, serving a variety of functions such as doing research into social, biological, and environmental causes of ill health and diseases and at the same time training future public health workers to work in federal, state, and local public health agencies (Brandt and Gardner 2000). In contrast, medical schools had managed to establish uniform educational standards, and medicine was able to establish a well-defined, coherent identity.

The separation of public health and clinical medicine ultimately contributed to the triumph of curative medicine, with its focus on cure rather than prevention (Gorin 2001). White (1991) has argued that this has resulted in two interrelated problems. One is the inability of public health to attract and retain the best minds in medicine. The second is the failure by most physicians to understand and appreciate the public health (population) perspective. He suggests four causes for this. First is the failure of public health to establish itself as a distinct and separate profession with a well-defined boundary. The second reason is the failure to establish epidemiology as the fundamental science of public health. The third reason is the failure to teach epidemiology and social science concepts in medicine. The fourth reason is the failure of medicine and public health to cooperate (White 1991).

The 1930s to 1950s

Between 1933 and 1938, as part of the Roosevelt administration's New Deal initiatives, several new federal agencies were created such as the Federal Emergency Relief Administration (FERA), the Works Progress Administration (WPA), and the Public Works Administration. All three agencies provided federal funds to state and local health departments (Fee and Brown 2002). The New Deal was a response to the Great Depression and it helped revive the social reform agenda of the progressive years (Starr 1982). One of the major social reforms was the passage of the Social Security Act of 1935, a pension program for retirees. It also provided federal funds for public health in general and for maternal and child health services specifically. Originally, the Roosevelt administration had thought about including health insurance as part of the Social Security Act. The AMA strongly opposed the idea of health insurance and it was dropped from the Social Security Act before it was sent to Congress. The election of 1938 brought about a resurgence of conservatives, and the idea of health insurance died with it (Burrow 1963; Starr 1982).

The election of Harry S. Truman to the presidency again revived the national health insurance idea as he asked Congress to adopt such a program. Again, the AMA vehemently opposed the plan and argued that such a health insurance plan would make doctors slaves (Poen 1979). The Republican takeover of Congress in 1946 made adoption of a health insurance plan all the more problematic. The AMA launched a successful campaign against the proposed national health insurance plan by arguing that national health insurance was socialized medicine and adoption of the plan would lead to a socialist state. National health insurance was again successfully killed (Kelley 1956). The AMA had successfully defeated national health insurance proposals three times during 1910 and the 1940s. The rising political influence of the medical profession was clearly evident during this time period (Garceau 1941).

Instead of the comprehensive health insurance plan proposed by President Truman, Congress passed the Hill-Burton Act of 1946. This bill was designed by the AMA. Under the bill, the national government made federal funds available for modernizing and constructing hospitals. As a result of this federal funding, by 1966 some forty-seven hundred hospitals were built or renovated. In addition, in accordance with the wishes of the AMA, these hospitals emphasized a high-tech approach to medicine (Garrett 2000). The Hill-Burton Act brought about a major change in the power structure in the American health care system. By 1960 the medical areas closely connected to public health, like family practice, infectious diseases, and medical social work and others, had dropped significantly in status and prestige, commanding lower pay. While public health itself did not become irrelevant, the fact of the matter was that there was very little profit to be made in activities such as epidemic prevention and control, venereal disease surveillance, and prenatal screening of poor women (Garrett 2000).

The United States' entry into World War II in 1941 raised new challenges for public health due to large population shifts, military camps, industrial hazards, and an increase in venereal diseases (Fee and Brown 2002). The United States Public Health Service formed a Center for Malaria Control in the War Areas. In 1946 this center was renamed the Communicable Disease Center ("History of CDC," 1996) and later the Centers for Disease Control and Prevention (CDC). The Public Health Service Act of 1944 gave PHS its mission and structure as the lead agency in fighting diseases through medical science. In effect, the federal government centralized responsibility for supply of health services and knowledge in the PHS with state governments as partners. At the same time, the federal government relinquished its control over personal health services to employers, unions, and not-for-profit as well as investor-owned insurance companies (Fox 1994). From the late 1940s to late 1950s, due to the resurgence of conservatism, the advent of the Cold War, and McCarthyism, public health leaders and anyone advocating expanded public health service came under attack and ran the risk of being denounced as socialist or communist. Public health measures such as fluoridation of water came under attack as foreign communist plots (Fee and Brown 2002).

The post–World War II era witnessed the rise of epidemiology, which significantly changed the knowledge and practice of public health. Epidemiology, with its use of multiple determinants of health problems and statistical inferences, offered new methods for establishing causality and risks of various chronic diseases. Public health became more receptive to the authority of biomedicine (Brandt and Gardner 2000). Parallel to this development was the fact that the postwar years also marked a great expansion of the federal government's support of medicine in the areas of medical research and mental health. The National Institute of Health became the National Institutes of Health (NIH) in 1948 and the National Science Foundation (NSF) was established in 1950. The NIH played a crucial role in advancing biomedical research through its grant program.

By the end of the 1950s the separation of public health and the medical profession was complete and it was reflected in the changed nature of membership of the APHA and the number of physicians working in state health agencies. In 1897, 80 percent of the APHA total members were physicians. However, in 1968, of the total APHA members, only 29 percent were physicians (Terris 1976). Similarly, fewer physicians worked in state public health agencies. According to the Institute of Medicine Report (1988), between 1977 and 1982 there was a 22.5 percent decline in the number of physicians working in state health agencies (Kahn 2003).

The 1960s to 1990s

The decades of economic expansion following World War II brought about a tremendous growth of American medicine and the United States established an enormous medical research establishment. Hospitals stocked with high-tech equipment became the center of medical practice. The medical workforce increased from 1.2 to 3.9 million, and national health care expenditures jumped from $12.7 billion to $71.6 billion between 1950 and 1970. Medical science came to symbolize a postwar version of progress without conflict. However, this vision of growth without conflict came to an end in the 1960s (Starr 1982).

The landslide victory of Lyndon Johnson over the conservative Republican candidate Barry Goldwater in the presidential election of 1964 was seen as a mandate for a liberal agenda. It brought renewed social and political activism and resulted in the establishment of new programs and policies in health care. Medical care was the central part of Lyndon Johnson's War on Poverty program. The passage of the Medicare and Medicaid programs provided the elderly and the poor access to health services (Fee and Brown 2002). However, if the AMA had its way, Medicare would never have become a reality (Cassil 1998). The AMA and other organized interests used the rhetoric of "socialized medicine" to launch a malicious attack against Medicare (Skidmore 1970; Marmor 1973; Wolinsky and Brune 1994). Medicare and Medicaid became reality as a result of a compromise crafted by Rep. Wilbur Mills (D-Arkansas), chair of the House Ways and Means Committee, between Democratic and Republican proposals. The Democratic plan for a compulsory health insurance program became Part A of Medicare. A Republican proposal for a government-subsidized voluntary insurance program to cover physicians' bills became Part B of Medicare. A proposal to provide expanded assistance to states to meet the medical needs of the poor became Medicaid. Another approach used to expand access to health care services to the poor was the program of neighborhood health centers designed to provide one-stop ambulatory health services in low-income communities (Starr 1982). These programs significantly expanded access to health care for the elderly and the poor.

By the early 1960s the AMA had become one of the richest and most powerful political forces in Washington, DC, and it was contributing significant sums of money to congressional campaigns to candidates it viewed as supportive of the AMA's position. But even before the 1960s, the AMA was more interested in protecting the economic interests of organized medicine and less concerned with protecting the public's health. During much of the 1930s and 1940s the AMA's journal ran cigarette advertisements to raise money. From the 1950s to 1980s, because it was politically expedient, organized medicine remained silent even though evidence was beginning to emerge demonstrating a link between smoking and lung cancer (Wolinsky and Brune 1994). In 2000 the AMA spent about $16.5 million for public advocacy efforts aimed at elected public officials. However, some critics have argued that in recent years the AMA's once-formidable clout on Capitol Hill has eroded. The AMA has also experienced a decline in its membership. According to some estimates, only about one-third of practicing physicians belonged to the AMA in 2001 (Romano 2001).

The 1970s witnessed the creation of the Environmental Protection Agency (EPA) and the Occupational Safety and Health Administration (OSHA).

Public health advocates focused on these agencies due to the clear health implications of the use of pesticides, air and water pollutants, pharmaceuticals, petrochemicals, and the like. Human behavior and lifestyles that include smoking, drinking, and drug abuse, among others, led to new chronic diseases such as cancer and heart attacks. This presented a unique challenge to public health—how to change individual behavior and encourage lifestyle changes designed to prevent such chronic diseases. At the same time, legionnaire's disease and the fiasco of the swine flu scare in 1976 and 1977 damaged the credibility of the U.S. public health system (Garrett 2000).

However, the liberal mandate of the Johnson years came to an end. The progressive wave of the 1960s and early 1970s crashed due to economic problems and political backlash, and an ideology of a largely unregulated market economy gained favor in public policies. Escalating health care costs reversed the trend of expanded medical care. The redistributive public policies of the 1960s gave way to the regulatory policies in the 1970s. The notion that the United States needed more medical care and that the medical profession and other voluntary associations were best suited to organize medical services came under heavy scrutiny. The talk turned to the "crisis" in the U.S. health care system. Health maintenance organizations (HMOs) were pushed by the Nixon administration as a cost-effective alternative for the delivery of health services. Professional Standard Review Organizations (PSROs) and Health System Agencies (HSAs) were established for the purpose of peer review of the utilization of medical services and health planning, respectively. Even the Carter administration showed reluctance to endorse national health insurance legislation, and health care reform and promotion of a broad public health agenda went into retreat (Fee and Brown 2002).

The Reagan administration assumed office in 1980 under the banner of free market supply-side economic rhetoric and set out to dismantle regulatory agencies and social programs. The new federalism of the Reagan administration resulted in a reduced amount of federal funds bundled into block grants to states. The result was the elimination or slashing of health programs for the poor. The Reagan administration's budget and tax cuts of 1981, 1982, and 1983 had a far-reaching impact on public health programs. Many public health programs targeted for the poor were transferred to the states, and funding for programs that remained at the federal level were slashed.

Three critical public health trends that developed during the Reagan years were an emergence of new contagious threats such as *E. coli* and HIV, a skyrocketing number of uninsured Americans, and a heightened sense of individual instead of community responsibility for disease (Garrett 2000). The Reagan revolution and the ascendancy of conservative political ideology brought about a major upheaval in the American health care system (Fee and Brown 2002).

Thus, it was not a surprise when the Institute of Medicine (1988) in its study of the future of public health concluded that the American public health system had fallen into disarray. According to the report, there was a total absence of a shared mission among public health agencies; nor was there a common definition of public health or an agreed-upon list of its duties among states and counties. In addition, the report also concluded that a great deal of tension existed between public health and organized medicine, and the relationship between the two had become fraught with confrontation and suspicion.

In 1990 the executive director of the APHA, Dr. William McBeath (1990), charged that the three Republican terms in the White House had led to a broad-scale retreat of government from public health and a neglect of support for public health infrastructure, and he blamed the Ford/Reagan/Bush years for the erosion of local public health support in the country. Three weeks before the 1992 elections, the Institute of Medicine (1992) issued a report in which it warned that the world was beset by a greater variety of microbial pathogens than ever before and that the United States was defenseless against the new microbial threats because the country lacked a comprehensive national system for detecting an outbreak of infectious diseases.

Health care became the number one issue in the presidential election of 1992, and it swept Bill Clinton to the presidency in 1992. This again revived hope for the establishment of a national health insurance. President Clinton in September 1993 proposed to Congress an overhaul of the U.S. health care system and a universal health insurance program in the form of the Health Security Act of 1993. However, the main focus of the proposed health care reform was cost containment, and most of the debate surrounding it neglected the topic of public health. Immediately a fierce debate ensued over the nature of the proposed reform among supporters and opponents. Many public health officials argued that public health agencies should exercise control over medicine in America, making hospitals, doctors, health insurance agencies, and the whole U.S. health care apparatus accountable to public health boards and citizens' committees (Navarro 1994).

Aggressive lobbying by the opponents of the Clinton proposal followed. The opposition to Clinton's reform proposal was led by the health insurance industry, which argued that the administration was going to force a nasty government medicine down the country's throat and it would create a system of rationed care of poor quality with patients having no freedom of choice (Garrett 2000). By the summer of 1994 the euphoria had faded as

President Clinton's proposal to overhaul the U.S. health care system and establish a national health insurance system met with the same fate as had all other previous efforts to establish a national health insurance—it died in Congress without ever coming to a vote. The Republicans gained control of both the House and the Senate in the congressional elections of 1994 and with it disappeared any hopes of a major overhaul of the U.S. health care system.

As Reiser (1996) has argued, by the 1990s the separation of public health and private medicine had become increasingly more dysfunctional because both had created their own separate financial, social, educational, and professional support bases that provided very little incentive for meaningful cooperation and engagement between the two. Downsizing, reinvention, market competition, and managed care had become the new buzzwords. Many argued that after over one hundred years of fighting, maybe it was time for public health and medicine to collaborate and work as partners (Lasker 1997).

The 1990s and Beyond: Inching Toward Cooperation and Collaboration

> There have been few incentives for collaboration and interaction between medicine and public health. Today, we are challenged by the drive to cut costs, and it is imperative for us to leave the status quo of separation behind and to begin again to work together. . . . Medicine and public health must reevaluate our relationship, because in today's complex, dollar-driven world, we can no longer accomplish our missions alone.
>
> Richard F. Corlin, M.D., opening remarks to the Cooperative Actions for Health Programs (CAHP) session at the Chicago, November, 1999, APHA Meeting. (quoted in Phillips 2000, 465)

As we enter a new century, there are hopeful signs that the competition, hostility, and antagonism of the past may be replaced by cooperation between medicine and public health (Lasker 1997). In 1993 the AMA and the APHA launched a joint Medicine-Public Health Initiative project to encourage cooperation between the two fields. This initiative has also received significant support from private foundations such as Josiah Macy Jr., and W.K. Kellogg, and public agencies such as the Agency for Health Care Policy and Research (AHCPR) and the CDC. The Robert Wood Johnson Foundation and AHCPR are providing grants for collaborative efforts between medicine and public health (Reiser 1996).

In the spring of 1994 the presidents and chief staff officers of the AMA and APHA began exploratory discussions focusing on the interaction of medicine and public health in education, research, and practice. Other medical and public health organizations joined in this effort at a later date. The purpose of these meetings was to explore ways for the two disciplines to collaborate and to develop an agenda for action. Seven areas of potential collaborations were identified: (1) involving local communities and lay leaders in development of clinical education and research activities; (2) incorporating into the educational curriculum teaching of each discipline's intellectual tools; (3) developing research approaches to synthesize the knowledge of both disciplines; (4) working together to develop a shared view of health and illness; (5) working to integrate health promotion, disease prevention, and clinical care in providing health care; (6) collaborating in developing better measures of health; and (7) developing networks to translate ideas into practice (Reiser 1997).

The result of this early discussion led to a call for the National Congress on Medicine and Public Health to be held in Chicago in March 1996 ("Medicine/Public Health Initiative Aims at Collaboration for Health" 1995). Over five hundred delegates representing all fifty states attended, including presidents and deans of academic health centers, medical, and public health schools; presidents of hospitals, state and local medical societies; state, public health associations; commissioners of state, county, and local health agencies; foundation officials; business leaders; and heads of federal government agencies. The purpose of the congress was to help develop conceptual and administrative structures that can help facilitate collaborative efforts between public health and medicine ("Medicine, Public Health to Come Together for Groundbreaking National Congress in March" 1996).

Funding for the conference was provided by the W.K. Kellogg Foundation, the Agency for Health Care Policy and Research, and the CDC (Reiser 1997). This congress was the first of its kind in history. The results of the conference have been encouraging. The Agency for Health Care Policy and Research awarded three grants that foster research collaboration among hospitals, cities, and public health departments. Collaborative activities were undertaken in many regions and states (Reiser 1997). Today, the Medicine-Public Health Initiative has spawned over five hundred examples of cooperative arrangements between physicians and public health professionals (Voelker 1997).

The Robert Wood Johnson Foundation in collaboration with the APHA and the AMA commissioned the New York Academy of Medicine to convene an interdisciplinary panel to write a monograph on the collaboration between public health and medicine (Reiser 1997). In 1997 the monograph titled *Medicine and Public Health: The Power of Collaboration* was published (Lasker 1997) and two hundred thousand copies were distributed to health care professionals nationwide. As a follow-up to this, the New York Academy of Medicine also issued a *Pocket Guide to Cases of Medicine and Public Health Collaboration* (1998), giving readers direct access to cases on which the 1997 monograph was based. The print version of the guide is no longer available. However, an electronic *Pocket Guide to Cases of Medicine and Public Health Collaboration* is available at http://cues.nyam.org/pubhlth/epg. This site allows users to search the database through multiple index terms and text of the case abstracts, and to connect to relevant parts of the monograph, and also engage in online networking.

One of the other outcomes of the Medicine/Public Health Initiative was the creation of the Cooperative Action for Health Program (CAHP). The project involves collaboration between state medical societies, public health associations, universities, state and local health departments, businesses, schools, and other professional organizations. By 1999, the Robert Wood Johnson Foundation had provided grants of $10,000 to $15,000 to nineteen collaborative projects in eighteen states. The CAHP collaborations have included projects such as a gun safety video for teenagers, pockets guides and websites on asthma management, and domestic violence screening and referral, among others (Phillips 2000).

Other forces are also bringing medicine and public health together. Cost considerations are forcing consolidation and creation of integrated systems of care. Managed care is also forcing medicine to become more active in traditional public health areas. The push for practice guidelines is forcing medicine to incorporate data sets such as immunization records (Phillips 2000). The September 11, 2001, terrorist attacks on the Twin Towers in New York and the Pentagon, and the anthrax attacks that followed, have raised the specter of potential bioterrorism attacks. This has focused attention on the need for strong collaboration between medicine and public health to effectively deal with such an attack. The chapter on the politics of bioterrorism and public health addresses issues raised by the threats of bioterrorism.

How genuine and fruitful the collaboration between medicine and public health is and how long it will last remains to be seen. Some are optimistic while others are more cautious. For example, Stephen C. Joseph, assistant secretary of defense for health affairs and former dean of the School of Public Health at the University of Minnesota, argues that the next couple of decades will be the second golden age of public health and that medicine and public health will be transformed into an ecological science ("Medicine, Public Health, and Environment: Panel Discussion" 1994). One advantage claimed for ecological analysis compared to more narrowly focused biomedical and behavioral studies is that ecological analysis takes an integrative and comprehensive approach to understand how biological, psychological, sociocultural, and physical environmental factors jointly affect health and well-being. The argument is that social ecology, that is, the dynamic relations between people and their surroundings, can be used to explain the origins of a number of health problems and it can help develop broad-based education, therapeutic, and policy interventions (Stokols 2000).

Others are more skeptical about trying to heal a schism that has developed between medicine and public health. For example, Kevin Finnegan, editor of *Issues*, argues that it will be difficult to heal this schism because many public health issues involve major conflicts over social values. Public health issues such as AIDS and environmental protection invariably introduce questions of values and not just science ("Medicine, Public Health, and Environment: Panel Discussion" 1994). Similarly, the resurgence of infectious diseases has the potential to create a further split between medicine and public health over questions such as compulsory measures, prevention, and behavior modification (Brandt 1988). Interest in collaboration has not succeeded in bridging the gulf between medicine and public health in the past. Traditionally, obstacles to the integration of medicine and public health have been institutional, theoretical, and sociocultural. Separate schools and educational training, and a social versus a reductionist view of disease combined with fundamental differences in power, resources, and prestige between the two disciplines have prevented the two disciplines from pursuing opportunities to achieve common goals. Unless both medicine and public health can develop a single vision of health, true collaboration is not likely to occur (Brandt and Gardner 2000).

The Politics of Public Health and Private Medicine

In this chapter we have examined the relationship between medicine and public health from a historical perspective. During the eighteenth century these two fields were not distinct and separate. In fact, despite some apprehension, there was a considerable amount of accommodation and cooperation between the two during much of the nineteenth century. However, during the period of 1900 to the 1920s, public health and medicine became separate and distinct fields marked by suspicion and at times open hostility. By the 1950s this separation was not only complete, but the curative model of private medicine had become dominant over the preventive model of public health. By the 1990s, separation between medicine and public health had become dysfunctional. Since the 1990s, attempts have been made to increase collaboration between the two through the Medicine/Public Health

Initiative launched in 1993. How genuine this collaboration is and how fruitful such collaboration is in protecting the public's health and addressing the nations' health problems remains to be seen. If the collaboration between medicine and public health is to bear fruit, it will require more than just goodwill and desire to cooperate.

According to two new reports issued by the Institute of Medicine, America's public health system is in need of a major overhaul. The first report, *The Future of the Public's Health in the 21st Century* (Institute of Medicine 2002a), which is a follow-up to a 1988 report, concludes that while some progress has been made over the last decade, the public health system remains in disarray. The second report, *Who Will Keep the Public Healthy? Educating Public Health Professionals for the 21st Century* (Institute of Medicine 2002b), recommends the overhaul of public health education. The report argues that a gradual decline in the number of public health professionals with medical degrees has contributed to further a divergence between medicine and public health, and that this divergence poses a serious obstacle to the country's ability to address health care problems that cannot be resolved through medical treatment (the curative model) alone. The report recommends that not only should medical students receive basic training in public health, but a substantial number of physicians should obtain a master's level training in public health. The need for physicians trained in preventive and public health medicine is also heightened by the prospect of bioterrorism (Malecki and Brumback 2003).

A major challenge confronting public health is how to reduce the competition and the often subtle-to-open hostility that has existed between public health and medicine and find ways to engage in endeavors that are more cooperative to improve the nation's health. The primary goals of medicine must be prevention, maintenance, and promotion of health, and the treatment and cure of disease and injuries to relieve pain and suffering (Peng 1999). The challenge is how to make these preventive and curative models complementary pillars of the nation's health care system. Both have an important role to play. If public health and medicine are to succeed in meeting these goals, it will require a close integration of public health and private medicine with respect not just to curriculum, training, and practice, but also an integration of the theoretical and scientific knowledge base and philosophy.

This will require physicians to take into consideration multiple determinants of health and illnesses such as individual, behavioral, environmental, social, and community-level factors in the practice of medicine. It will require that we measure medical progress not just by extending individual survival and microlevel health data, but rather by using population health (community/macrolevel health data) as the yardstick to measure medical progress (Callahan 1998). For this to occur, the medical profession must recognize the reciprocal relations and duties of the medical profession and the community ("The Mutual Relations of the Medical Profession and the Public" 1996).

The Hippocratic Oath is widely viewed in the United States and most other societies as an exemplary summary of the physician's role. However, as Sidel (1992) has argued, the duties detailed in the oath are limited to those that physicians owe to other physicians and those that physicians owe to their individual patients. Nothing in the oath spells out physicians' obligations to the broader society. The oath, revised in 1983, includes more general formulations of the original duties. The medical profession must incorporate and emphasize the public service role of physicians.

Whether such developments are realistic is open to debate in the context of market competition dominated by large corporations interested in profit and market shares (Beauchamp 1996); the trend toward increased invasion of commerce into medical care and the resulting clash of commercial and professional cultures (McArthur and Moore 1997); and the tradition of interest group politics in American democracy in which narrow parochial interests with money and power regularly defeat public policies designed to promote the broader public interest (Navarro 2003).

Study Questions

1. Discuss the similarities and differences between private medicine and public health in the United States with respect to their respective missions/goals, organization/structure, education training/skills, financial arrangements, and strategies.
2. Discuss the history of the relationship between private medicine and public health in the United States. What factors contributed to the increased schism between the two?
3. Discuss the role of dispensaries in the history of public health in the United States.
4. Discuss the attempts made in the last ten to fifteen years to improve relationships and increase cooperation between private medicine and public health. Are such efforts likely to succeed in the long run? Why or why not?
5. Discuss the ways to bridge the current gap that exists between private medicine and public health in the United States.

CHAPTER 4

The Politics of
Public Health and Law

> Public health law is often perceived as an arcane set of
> rules buried deep within indecipherable statute books and regulatory
> codes. It does not have to be this way. The law can be transformed to
> become an essential tool for creating the conditions for people to be
> healthy. (Gostin 2001, 1365)

Historically, discussion of the history of public health has ignored the role
of law in public health practice. Law was generally accorded a subordinate
role in public health practice, and the role of law in public health innovation
was deemphasized. The increased incidence of chronic disease led to expansion of the scientific basis of public health during the second half of the
twentieth century. Despite the fact that this created a renewed interest in
environmental factors and individual behavior in controlling chronic disease, law and regulations were viewed mainly as mechanisms for legitimizing the findings of scientific research rather than as important tools in
improving the health of the population. However, in recent years historians
have begun to revise the history of public health to demonstrate the centrality of law in the development of public health practice. This revisionist history has added legitimacy to the public health law reform movement (Fox
2001). Under this new conception of the public health profession, public
health practice is viewed as the result of ongoing sociopolitical negotiations
involving experts from many disciplines requiring better skills of negotiation and accommodation rather than advocacy (Fox 2001). Law and regulations have come to be viewed as important tools in achieving the goal of
improved public health.

In this chapter we examine the legal foundations of public health practice, shortcomings of the current public health laws, and efforts designed to
improve public health laws by encouraging states to adopt model public
health law. Next we analyze the role that public health law can play in protecting the public's health. Finally, we examine litigation as a strategy to
protect and improve public health.

Legal Foundations of Public Health Practice

Concern that current public health laws are inadequate to address challenges that confront public health has led to efforts designed to improve the legal foundation for public health practice. According to Moulton and Matthews (2001), the legal foundation for public health practice consists of three ingredients. One important ingredient comprises the legal authorities, which consist of constitutional and statutory laws, regulations, administrative rules, and case law that allow public health agencies to take specific actions. This requires continual evaluation and improvement of public health laws to meet new emerging public health threats. A second ingredient includes the skills necessary to apply the appropriate legal authorities. This requires training public health practitioners in law-related skills that allow them to interpret and adjudicate legal issues. The third ingredient is to provide access to knowledge about the impact of laws on the public's health and how best to translate these laws into effective public health interventions. This requires applied research.

Applied public health law is considered an essential element for improving the legal foundation of public health practice. According to Horton et al. (2002), public health law research needs to focus on pursuing answers to questions such as why an adoption of public health law becomes possible in some environments and not others, and what motivates policymakers to create or not create laws that address specific public health concerns. It is also important to communicate the results of public health law research to public health practitioners, lawmakers, and the public. Communication can help the findings of public health law research become public health policy or gain acceptance by policymakers who have the power to convert such findings into public health laws. A partnership between public health practitioners and lawyers can also help garner support of lawmakers for new public health laws (Horton et al. 2002).

Law is indispensable to protecting public health. Law played a major role in some of the biggest public health accomplishments of the twentieth century such as vaccination, fluoridation of drinking water, control of infectious diseases, motor vehicle safety, safer workplaces, and recognition of the health hazards of tobacco use, among others. The legal authority of public health activities must be dynamic, constantly updated, and public health professionals must be willing to use new legal tools in order to be effective and successful (Moulton et al. 2002).

The legal foundations of public health practice are found in the constitutional and statutory laws of the national and state governments. As we briefly discussed in chapter 1, most of the national government's public health powers are derived from its power to tax, spend, and regulate commerce. The Tenth Amendment to the U.S. Constitution reserves for states all powers that are not given to the national government nor denied to the states. One of the most important powers states enjoy is the police power to promote the general welfare of society, giving states authority in the area of public health and safety (Gostin 2000a).

Public health law consists of laws and regulations passed at federal, state, and local levels intended directly or indirectly to protect public health. Law is an important tool for accomplishing public health objectives simply because public health programs are entirely dependent on legislative authorization. It is through law that government can regulate behavior detrimental to public health. Yet at the same time, law also protects people from offensive and/or undesirable public health measures (Hodge 1997–98).

During colonial times, public health laws were limited primarily to controlling infection and the spread of communicable diseases. The compromise at the Constitutional Convention created a federal system of government that gave the national government limited, enumerated, but supreme powers and state governments broad sovereign powers via the Tenth Amendment. Over the years, the national government's intervention in public health became more pronounced as a result of the federal courts' broad interpretations of Congress's spending, taxing, and commerce powers, especially during the New Deal and the establishment of executive branch agencies by Congress to improve public health. These developments are discussed in chapter 1.

This expanding federal role in public health has often created a collision between national and state powers. Two of the most important constitutional questions that establish the validity of public health laws/regulations of the national or state governments are: (1) whether a particular level of government has the constitutional power to act to protect public health; and (2) whether the specific manner in which that particular government has acted violates or exceeds constitutional principles of individual rights (Hodge 1997–98). The federal courts, needless to say, have played a major role in addressing these questions. The federal courts at times interpreted the national government's power to protect health and safety more broadly, allowing the expansion of national power in public health areas. Yet at other times, federal courts have interpreted the national government's power more narrowly. For example, in 1995 the U.S. Supreme Court in its ruling in *United States v. Lopez* signaled a change in the court's view of balance of powers between the national and state governments. The Supreme Court in this case ruled that Congress had exceeded its commerce clause authority when it made gun possession within a school zone a federal crime and declared the congressional law unconstitutional by concluding that gun violence did not substantially affect interstate commerce. Similarly, in 1997, in *Printz v. United States*, the Supreme Court used the Tenth Amendment's reserved power doctrine to overturn a provision in the Brady Handgun Violence Prevention Act that directed state and local law enforcement officers to conduct a background check on prospective handgun buyers (Hodge 1997–98). Along that same line, the Rehnquist court has also leaned heavily toward protecting state autonomy with its reliance on the Eleventh Amendment, which grants states immunity from certain lawsuits in federal courts without their consent. This is known as the sovereign immunity doctrine, and the Rehnquist court has used this doctrine to limit Congress's power to authorize lawsuits against states (Hodge 1997–98).

Gostin (2000b) has argued that public health law has five essential characteristics. The first characteristic of public health law is that since health is indispensable not only to an individual but to the community as a whole, it is the responsibility of government to ensure conditions for people to be healthy. Second, public health is organized to provide aggregate health benefits to all people in a community, and thus public health law must reflect a population-based perspective. Third, public health law deals with the relationship between the state and the people, that is, the community at large. Public health law has to do with the effect of collective government action to protect the public health of the population, that is, benefits and burdens placed by government on different interests in society. Fourth, public health law deals with creating necessary organizational arrangements to provide necessary public health services. Finally, to protect public health it is sometimes necessary that public health law coerce individuals and businesses. However, Gostin (2000c) argues that coercive intervention by government can be justified in only three cases—to avert a risk of serious harm to other persons, to protect the welfare of incompetent persons, and to prevent risk to the person himself/herself. The government must justify the use of coercive intervention by demonstrating that there is a significant risk based on scientific evidence, that economic costs are reasonable, that human rights burdens are reasonable, and that costs, benefits, and burdens are fairly distributed.

According to Gostin "Public health law is the study of legal powers and duties of state to assure the conditions for people to be healthy (e.g., to identify, prevent, and ameliorate risks to health in the population) and the limitations on the power of the state to constrain the autonomy, privacy, liberty, proprietary, or other legally protected interests of individuals for the protection or promotion of community health" (Gostin 2000d, 4).

The government's attempt to promote or protect public health often creates conflict between governmental authority and individual autonomy, liberty, privacy, and property. Thus public health law creates a paradox. On the one hand it is the responsibility of government to act to promote the health of the people, which often requires strong measures to control health risks. On the other hand, government cannot excessively and unjustifiably invade individuals' rights in the name of community good. As a result, public health law must carefully address the question of whether a coercive government action would truly reduce aggregate health risk or whether less intrusive action might reduce those risks as well or better (Gostin 2000d). Courts have established some important principles with respect to constitutional limits on government authority. Courts have stated that even when the government uses its police power and acts within the limits of its substantive authority, both the federal and state governments must act within procedural limits, that is, government must use fair and due procedures when government actions affect constitutionally protected rights to life, liberty, and property (Wing 1999; Fleisher 1980).

Another limitation to public health law in democratic societies comes from the public itself. Elected local public officials might be reluctant to carry out measures that might be politically unpopular and could lead to loss of political support in the next election. As William Hobson wrote several decades ago:

> The history of community health development shows that no country has ever reached a high standard of health mainly because it possessed the necessary medical knowledge concerning the cause of disease; it requires in addition a people whose social development is such that they will persist in the necessary practical measures for the control of disease even in the absence of epidemics. . . . In many parts of the world today, lack of an efficient form of local self-government is the greatest bar to health progress . . . the local politicians elected to office are loath to carry out any measure which might cause them to lose favour in the eyes of the electorate, whilst the public health law, if it exists, is usually ignored. (Hobson 1963, 1–2)

Given the importance of public health law, Clute (1973) has argued that law should be accessible to public health professionals for several reasons. One reason is that public health professionals should know something about law in general so they become aware of how law can be used as a tool in the solution of health problems. Second, knowledge of certain details about some parts of the law can help public health professionals recognize problems for which they should seek legal advice. Third, current legal assistance available to public health professionals is inadequate because there are still few lawyers who specialize in public health law. Finally, law may have unforeseen and adverse side effects (Clute 1973). Of course, public health laws come in a variety of forms.

Scutchfield and Keck (1997) have argued that most public health laws today fall into one of eight categories. Environmental health laws deal with food, workplace safety, wastewater disposal, and air pollution. Laws and regulations requiring the reporting of diseases and injury (surveillance) enable public health officials to track disease, identify trends and disease outbreaks, and provide a basis for intervention. Laws dealing with vital statistics regarding birth and death records provide an important basis for a great deal of public health work, especially causes of death recorded on death certificates. Laws dealing with disease and injury control, such as preventing teenagers from drinking and smoking, focus on the prevention of diseases and injury at the community level. Laws dealing with involuntary testing provide a basis for determining disease prevalence in a given community. For example, in many communities food handlers are tested regularly to check for infections that might be spread through food preparation. Laws dealing with contact tracing, even though voluntary in nature, are often an effective way of controlling certain diseases such as tuberculosis and sexually transmitted diseases. Immunization and mandatory treatment laws can help control and/or eradicate diseases. However, in the United States some people are exempted due to religious objections. Finally, some public health laws impose personal restrictions, such as when public health officials restrict a person carrying bacteria from working as a food handler.

According to Levy (1999), the most important challenges that will affect public health law in the twenty-first century include the genetics revolution, access to quality care, access to reproductive care, alternative health care, population changes, reemergence of infectious diseases, information and communication evolution, tobacco use, violence, chemical hazards in the workplace, exports of hazards, and global public health issues such as global warming and depletion of the stratospheric ozone layer. The September 11, 2001, terrorist attacks and the anthrax scare that followed helped draw attention to the problems and shortcomings of the current public health laws and raised awareness about the need to revise and update laws to meet the new challenges facing the American public health system.

Shortcomings of Current Public Health Laws

In recent years, concerns have been raised that existing public health laws are so outdated that they have become an impediment to public health practice. For example, in its report *The Future of Public Health* (1988), the Institute of Medicine concluded that the country had lost sight of the mission of public health and allowed public health activities to fall into disarray. The report placed part of the blame for this problem on an obsolete and inadequate body of enabling laws and regulations. The report urged state governments to review their public health laws and make necessary revisions for the purpose of clearly delineating the basic authority and responsibility of public health agencies and boards and for supporting modern disease control measures to address public health problems such as AIDS, cancer, and heart disease. A new report issued by the Institute of Medicine (2002) entitled *The Future of the Public's Health in the 21st Century* concluded that although some progress had been made since its 1988 report, the U.S. public health system still remained in disarray. The report stated that many state public health laws were ineffective in advancing the public's health because they were outdated, inconsistent, and ambiguous, and recommended that a national commission develop recommendations for state public health law reforms.

Gostin (2001, 2002) has summarized three major criticisms of the current public health laws. One of the criticisms is that a great deal of public health law is antiquated because it was formulated in the late nineteenth and early twentieth centuries. These laws often do not reflect a contemporary scientific understanding of injury and disease, thereby reducing their effectiveness. Nor do these laws reflect legal norms for protecting individual rights. For example, many current public health laws do not reflect advances in public health practice and constitutional law and neglect important issues such as individual privacy and prohibition against discrimination.

The second major problem with current public health laws is the multiple layers of laws since laws in most states consist of successive layers of statutes and amendments built up over 100 years or more to deal with specific disease or health threats. Many states' disease-specific laws are ill-equipped to deal with emerging public health threats. The result is that many states have created several classes of communicable disease laws, each with different powers (Gostin 2001, 2002).

The third major criticism is that public health laws are highly fragmented not only within states but also among the states. The fifty states acting independently have created their health statutes over the years, creating tremendous variations among the states with respect to the structure, substance, and procedure for detecting, controlling, and preventing injury and disease. The variation is so great that it is almost impossible to categorize these laws and regulations (Gostin 2001, 2002).

In addition, many state public health laws do not clearly define the responsibilities and powers of public health agencies and officials. Some states do not clearly define the public health powers of local governments. Other states give broad discretionary powers to public health departments/boards without due process.

Public Health Law Reform Movement

The public scrutiny following the September 11 terrorist attacks and the anthrax scare that highlighted the shortcomings of the current public health laws also gave impetus to the public health reform movement spearheaded by the Center for Law and the Public's Health at Georgetown University and Johns Hopkins University under the leadership of Professor Lawrence Gostin. The hope is that public health law reform can help reinvigorate the public health system and become an important tool in creating conditions that make it possible for people to live healthy lives.

In fact, as far back as 1986, Gostin (1986) had argued that changes in medicine and constitutional law necessitated modification of public health law in the United States. He had recommended that legislative reforms remove artificial legislative distinctions between venereal and other communicable diseases, provide criteria for defining "public health necessity," provide strong confidentiality protections in collection and storage of public health information, and allow public health officials to select from a ranked series of less restrictive alternatives in handling public health problems. However, in his recent writings, Gostin has questioned the primacy of individual freedom and values of autonomy, privacy, and liberty and called for a balance between these values and values of partnerships, citizenship, and community (Gostin 2000d).

Gostin has recently argued that one of the main goals of public health law reform should be to clearly identify and define essential public health functions and establish clear mission statements that establish the purposes and goals of public health agencies (Gostin 2000d). He further argues that a model public health law should reflect three principles—duty, power, and restraint. In other words, the law should impose duties on government to promote health and well-being within a population; it should give public health authorities sufficient power to regulate individuals and businesses to achieve community health and security; and the law should restrain government from overreaching in the name of public health by providing sufficient substantive and procedural safeguards, protection against discrimination, and protection of privacy and security of information (Gostin 2000d).

Others have argued that efforts designed to strengthen the legal foundation of public health practice include (1) improving legal authorities, that is, constitutional and statutory laws, regulations, and administrative rules to enable public health agencies to take defined action; (2) improving skills to apply such legal authorities; and (3) improvement in information resources (Moulton and Matthews 2001).

In response to the call for modernization of state public health laws, the Centers for Disease Control and Prevention (CDC) created a new Public Health Law Program that cosponsors the Public Health Law Collaborative with partner organizations (Moulton and Matthews 2001). In April 2000 the Turning Point Public Health Statute Modernization Collaborative was formed with the support of the Robert Wood Johnson Foundation and the W.K. Kellogg Foundation for the purpose of transforming and strengthening the legal framework of the public health system by developing a model public health law. The goals of this collaborative are to conduct an analysis of current state public health laws, develop a model state public health law, disseminate the model law for possible state adoption, and evaluate how it is used. The collaborative is made up of a multidisciplinary group consisting of representatives from several states, national organizations, and government agencies.

In October 2000, with the support of the CDC, the Center for Law and the Public's Health was established at Georgetown University and Johns Hopkins University. The center has become the primary national resource on public health law. The center conducts research on public health law topics, works with public health leaders on public health law and policy issues, and drafts model public health laws ("Welcome to the Center for Law and the Public's Health" 2003). Similarly, in June 2003 the Public Health Law Association (PHLA) was launched to serve as a network for people interested in public health law for the purpose of sharing information and data (Krisberg 2003).

The Georgetown/Johns Hopkins Program on Law and Public Health put together a multidisciplinary panel of privacy, public health, and legislative experts to propose a model public health information privacy act. In 2001, as a result of this effort, the Center for Law and the Public's Health drafted and proposed the Model State Public Health Privacy Act (MSPHPA). The CDC recommended that state governments consider adopting the model legislation to strengthen the protection of public health data (Gostin, Hodge Jr., and Valdiserri 2001). The model act is designed to preserve the states' and local health departments' ability to act to protect the public's health and at the same time provide strong privacy safeguards for public health data. Current state public health laws dealing with public health information privacy are inconsistent, fragmented, and inadequate because of a wide variation among states with respect to the degree of privacy protections allowed and give varying rights to access to public health data. Many laws allow multiple exceptions to prohibition against disclosure. The model act applies to all protected health information (oral, written, electronic, and visual) held by public health agencies that relates to an individual's past, present, or future physical or mental health conditions. The act defines what constitutes "protected health information" and makes the acquisition and use of such data contingent upon legitimate public health purposes by regulating how public health agencies acquire, use, disclose, and store such information. It imposes stringent requirements to justify the acquisition of such data and strictly limits disclosure of such information for public health purposes without informed consent (Gostin, Hodge Jr., and Valdiserri 2001).

In 2001 the Center for Law and the Public's Health, in collaboration with the National Governors Association (NGA), the Association of State and Territorial Health Officials (ASTHO), the National Association of County and City Health Officials (NACCHO), and the National Association of Attorneys General (NAAG), proposed the Model State Emergency Health Powers Act (MSEHPA, www.publichealthlaw.net/index.html). The model act gives significant emergency powers to state governors and public health agencies at state and local levels to deal with public health emergencies following the 2001 terrorist attacks, the anthrax scare, and the potential of future bioterrorism. Tommy G. Thompson, Secretary of Health and Human Services (SHHS), enthusiastically endorsed the draft of the model act. Legislation inspired by the model act has been introduced in more than thirty states (Gostin, Sapsin, and Teret 2002). Twenty-two states have passed bills that draw some ideas from the model legislation (Serafini 2003).

However, the model act has become very controversial in those states and has been criticized by both liberals and libertarians. Most of the controversy has focused on recommendations by the authors that critics argue give higher priority to collective action in emergencies over that of protecting privacy and property. Fierce arguments have ensued in several states about the powers of state governments during health emergencies since many legislators, physicians, and hospital executives generally accord higher priority to protecting privacy and property (Colmers and Fox 2003). Critics object to the fact that the model act gives state governors the power to declare a public health emergency but fails to provide any objective criteria for deciding the existence of an emergency. They also oppose language in the model act that requires immunization, isolation, taking over of private health facilities, and conscripting of physicians (Colmers and Fox 2003).

The fear caused by SARS has generated a significant amount of heated discussion about the idea of quarantine. The model legislation proposes to give considerable power to state governments for quarantine purposes. Many people object to the idea of state governments having almost unlimited powers to confine people to a hospital or in their homes against their will. As a result of controversies surrounding the idea of quarantine, state governments have made very limited progress in strengthening their emergency powers to deal with the outbreak of disease (Serafini 2003). Richards and Rathburn (2003) argue that the MSEHPA is unnecessary, would undermine existing emergency preparedness laws, does not address necessary public health reforms, and raises unacceptable ethical issues. They argue that incremental reform and planning is the key to effective public health law.

The Turning Point Public Health Statute Modernization Collaborative began meeting in April 2002 with the purpose of developing a Model State Public Health Act (MSPHA). Initially the collaborative group spent a year on the development and assessment phase and conducted an informal survey of state public health deputy directors. Twenty-four states responded to the survey. Of those, 71 percent indicated that bills concerning the improvement of public health infrastructure at state and local levels had been introduced in the state legislatures since the 1990s. Thirteen percent of states indicated that their bills had failed to pass the legislature. Many of these initiatives were limited to specific or minimal refinement of the existing laws. Thirty-three percent of states indicated that attempts to develop comprehensive public health reform proposals had failed due to abandonment at the department level, rejection by the state or local constituency, or inactivity by the state legislature. Another 30 percent of the states indicated that they had not considered any comprehensive public health law reform proposals (Gostin and Hodge Jr. 2002). However, several states such as Nebraska, New Jersey, and Texas have continued to use a variety of different reform approaches to build a solid legal foundation for an effective public health system by aligning public health's legal authorities with the new mission and expectations (Baker et al. 2002).

Following this period of development and assessment, the collaborative began the work of drafting the model act and issued the first draft in 2002 and solicited comments. The model act's main focus is on public health administration and practice and does not cover distinct areas such as mental health, substance abuse, DUI laws, and tobacco control regulations (Erickson et al. 2002). Following a period of review of the comments and incorporating those comments, the collaborative issued the final draft of the Turning Point Model State Public Health Act (TPMSPHA) in September 2003. The collaborative does not advocate that the model act represents a mandate to the states, nor does it suggest that states copy and adopt it as a whole. Rather, the collaborative hopes that states would use the model act as a tool to assess their existing public health laws to identify what changes they deem necessary and adopt them.

The model act is divided into nine articles. The first article deals with the purposes and definitions of concepts such as public health, essential public health services, functions, and the like. The second article articulates the mission and functions of public health. The third article concerns the public health infrastructure. The fourth article deals with collaborations and relationships with public and private sector partners. The fifth article deals with public health authorities and powers. The sixth article addresses the topic of public health emergencies. Article seven addresses the issue of public health information privacy. The eighth article deals with administrative procedures, criminal and civil enforcement, and immunities. The ninth article contains miscellaneous provisions.

The model act is designed to help state and local governments modernize their public health laws. The act is very comprehensive and spells out legal language the states could use in their modernization efforts (Late 2003). However, how successful state governments are in modernizing their public health law remains to be seen in light of the politics surrounding a proper balance between values of government authority/power, and community good versus the values of individual autonomy, liberty, and property. The issue of quarantine has already generated heated debate in American politics. Recently, President Bush added SARS to the list of illnesses that could be subject to quarantine, and he issued an order giving federal authorities the power to quarantine or isolate people entering the United States. However, this directive has no impact on individuals already here, leaving the decision on quarantine to each state government (Serafini 2003). The public health laws of each state have evolved over many decades and they reflect the concerns, science, and politics of their specific time periods. Furthermore, state public health laws reflect an expression of constituency expectations (Gebbie 2000). Thus, efforts to modernize public health laws in each state will be influenced by local concerns, science, politics, and public expectations. Each state is likely to follow its own unique path to reform.

Law as a Tool to Protect the Public's Health

Aside from the challenge of updating antiquated, inconsistent, and overlapping state and local laws and regulations, public health professionals will also need to become more involved in the legislative and policymaking process and be willing to use law as an important tool to improve public health. One of the challenges confronting public health professionals is to help legislators and policymakers connect the dots between public policies and translate scientific knowledge into public health laws and policies. This requires a partnership based on shared objectives among legislators, public health officials, lawyers, and community organizations (Benjamin, Lopez, and Monson 2002). Finding partners and allies is necessary for success (Gregoire 2002).

Governments at all levels have passed laws to protect public health through the regulation of private markets and individual behavior. In fact, a thirty-year increase in longevity during the twentieth century was in large part the result of improvements in areas such as pure water, pure food, motor vehicle–related injuries, and the like through the passage of laws such as the Safe Drinking Water Act (1974), the Highway Safety Act (1966), and the Pure Food and Drug Act (1906), among others (Fielding et al. 2002). Translating scientific knowledge into laws to improve public health has been at the heart of much of the statutory authority of public health (Fielding et al. 2002). Since the late 1980s, public health advocates have used a variety of strategies such as promoting specific laws, ballot initiatives, and court litigation to advance public health policies. Because elected policymakers and not public health experts generally have the final word on public health policy, and elected public officials have an eye toward reelection, voter education also has to be an important part of this strategy to make policymakers act on issues they have been reluctant to act on (DeMarco and Schneider 2000). Laws can act as a tool to advance public health because not only can they deter people from living unhealthy lifestyles, they can also educate people and businesses and provide incentives for creating safe products and an environment conducive to protecting and promoting the public's health (Gostin 2000b). The critical question is whether the policymakers, that is, legislators, have the necessary information and incentives to act on public health issues (Hyman 2000). To achieve the desired public health outcomes, public health agencies may use a variety of legal mechanisms such as laws, regulations, public policies, contracts, and the like (Lazzarini and Elman 2002). It is also important to note that aside from specific public health laws, improvement in population health may also be achieved as a by-product of laws and regulations that have other primary purposes such as economic development, transportation, housing, and the like (Fox 2001).

In recent years the American Public Health Association (APHA) has become a more active player in promoting laws and legislation designed to improve public health at the national level ("APHA Promotes Public Health Legislation" 2001). This has led to the passage of several key laws designed to benefit public health. The Minority Health and Health Disparities Research and Education Act (MHHDREA) of 2000, also known as the Health Care Fairness Act, will create a new center for research on minority health and health disparities. The Children's Health Act of 2000 expands the research and treatment of childhood issues such as diabetes, asthma, autism, and lead poisoning. The Public Health Threats and Emergencies Relief Act

(PHTERA) of 2000, which is part of the Public Health Improvement Act (PHIA) of 2000, is a wide-ranging act designed to improve the core capacities of national, state, and local public health systems ("Legislation to Benefit Key Public Health Issues" 2001; Benjamin 2001).

In this section we discuss how public health professionals can use the law as a tool to protect and promote the public's health. We also discuss some of the limitations and obstacles they confront.

Land Use Planning, Zoning, and Public Health Law

Today an overwhelming majority of people in the United States live in cities and urban areas. The built-up environment in which people live can have a significant impact on public health. The connection between urban planning and public health is not new. This was clearly demonstrated in the middle of nineteenth century when the tremendous increase in urban population caused by industrialization also created major problems of sanitation, overcrowded conditions leading to the spread of infectious diseases, epidemics, and decreased life expectancy. Successful sanitation reforms and changes in the built-up environment resulted in dramatic improvements in public health in the United States (Perdue, Stone, and Gostin 2003). Industrialization also brought the realization that close proximity between business and residential areas was unhealthy. The housing reform movement and the reform movement designed to beautify the cities grew out of this realization. As a result, zoning ordinances took hold in the 1920s (Scott 1971; Nolan 1916). Zoning ordinances separated residential, business, and industrial uses of land. However, by the mid-twentieth century the connection between the built-up environment and public health weakened as infectious diseases were brought under control and the planning of cities came to be viewed more as a matter of esthetics and economics and not public health (Perdue, Stone, and Gostin 2003). This has led to the call for reestablishing the link between urban planning/land use and public health and the need for incorporating the public health perspective into urban planning. This public health perspective helps focus discussion on how land use, housing patterns, and the water, sanitary, and transportation infrastructure impact the public's health in urban areas (Northridge and Sclar 2003).

Urban planning is a process of guiding the development of a built-up environment. Urban planners need to understand how the physical configuration of land use, housing patterns, open space, and density influences public health. According to Perdue, Stone, and Gostin (2003), the current built-up environment does not promote a healthy lifestyle because many urban areas lack safe open spaces, safe playgrounds, and green spaces. The law can be an important tool in creating a built-up environment that protects and promotes the public's health, and public health practitioners need to be actively involved in policymaking regarding population density, land use configuration, transportation, building and housing codes, and environmental regulations (Perdue, Stone, and Gostin 2003).

Zoning and land use planning can be an effective tool in addressing problems of crime through better design of the physical environment. Sarasota, Florida, is currently using Crime Prevention through Environmental Design (CPTED) principles to guide revitalization efforts in its crime-ridden North Trail Area (Carter, Carter, and Dannenberg 2003). Similarly, zoning laws can be used to protect public health by regulating the location and density of alcohol, tobacco, and firearms retailers. Since the 1970s, public health research has demonstrated the validity of the assertion that even a relatively small increase in the availability of alcohol leads to increased alcohol consumption, which in turn is related to alcohol-related problems such as violence (Ashe et al. 2003). For example, in the 1980s several California communities took the lead in passing zoning and conditional use permits (CUP) regulations regarding the location and operation of alcohol outlets (Wittman and Hilton 1987). Along the same line, many state and local governments have passed laws regulating the retail sale practices of tobacco outlets, such as laws prohibiting sales to minors, requiring retail clerks to be of legal age to sell tobacco, and requiring tobacco outlets to be located away from areas frequented by children such as schools and playgrounds. Also, several California communities have used their land use authority to limit the location of firearms dealers to commercially zoned areas. Some have prohibited firearms dealers from locating near schools, day-care centers, and the like (Wittman and Hilton 1987).

The above discussion shows that local land use planning and zoning laws/ ordinances can be an important element of a comprehensive strategy to improve the public's health. Zoning laws determine various categories of land use. Zoning can be used to designate certain areas as appropriate for certain use and to determine appropriate densities. Since many public health concerns are location specific and location dependent, zoning and land use planning have substantial implications for public health (Maantay 2001).

However, implementation of a public health perspective in urban planning will require collaboration among planners, policymakers, and public health professionals. This is not easy because zoning has always been a tool of local politics, and compromise in policymaking becomes necessary because it involves a great deal of jockeying for power. In addition, since land ownership is an important property right, directing people in use of their private property for the public good is not easy. Nonetheless, opportunities do exist to use planning and zoning laws to address important public health issues and to improve public health (Sclar and Northridge 2001).

Drug Abuse and Public Health Law

There are many areas in which defining certain problems as public health problems can be advantageous in helping promote laws that can improve public health. For example, defining drug abuse as a public health problem can be beneficial. America's War on Drugs since the 1970s has been based on defining drug use as a criminal problem, and thus billions of dollars have been spent on law enforcement in areas such as stopping drug trafficking and incarceration of drug users. However, America's War on Drugs was not a well-planned public health initiative; it was a law enforcement initiative. Groups such as Partnership for a Drug-Free America and the U.S. Department of Education's (DOE) Drug-Free Schools and Communities Program and slogans such as "Just Say No" symbolized the war on drugs.

Throughout the nineteenth century drugs were largely unregulated in the United States. Public concern about drug abuse made an antidrug environment part of the Progressive reform agenda. In 1906, Congress passed the Pure Food and Drug Act. The law was intended to inform the purchaser whether certain drugs were present. It did not prevent the purchase of or limit the amount of drugs available (Musto 1990). Federal drug prohibition started in 1914 with the passage of the Harrison Narcotic Act, intended to address concerns about the cut-rate marketing of British opium in China that adversely affected China's purchasing power for American goods. Under this law, physicians who prescribed opiates to addicts were arrested, convicted, and sent to prison (London 1995). In 1920 the Eighteenth Amendment to the U.S. Constitution imposed a national prohibition on alcohol. Prohibition not only failed to live up to the expectation of an alcohol-free society, but created problems of a black market in alcohol, organized crime, and violence. In 1933 the Twenty-First Amendment to the U.S. Constitution repealed the Eighteenth Amendment, lifting the prohibition on alcohol. In 1937, Congress passed the Marijuana Tax Act banning the nonmedicinal use, untaxed sale, or possession of marijuana (London 1995). By 1988, American society had developed a "zero tolerance" policy.

However, many critics have charged that America's War on Drugs has been a major failure. For example, Judge James P. Gray (2001), a California trial judge, argues that the war on drugs is an abject failure. He suggests that drug-prohibition laws have failed to reduce the amount of drugs available in the United States, drug prohibition has made drugs more dangerous to drug users, drug enforcement has led to an erosion of civil liberties, and drug prohibition has stifled democratic debate over drug policy. Such a perspective has led others to argue that legalizing drugs may benefit public health (London 1995). Richard Bonnie (2001) argues that the United States' drug policy should be grounded in a public health framework with the objective of reducing the adverse social consequences of drug consumption. He further suggests that we need better science for making and evaluating drug policy, that is, better data on consumption, price of drugs on the illegal market, and the like to assess effectiveness of drug policies, and we need to increase our investment in treatment.

Defining drug abuse as a public health problem can help redirect some of the resources being spent on drug enforcement for treatment of drug users ("Rethinking America's War on Drugs . . ." 2001). In fact, according to a survey conducted by the Pew Research Center for the People & the Press, while most of the respondents wanted the government to continue to focus on arresting drug dealers and blocking the flow of drugs into the country, half of the respondents also said that drug use itself should be considered a disease, not a crime ("Rethinking America's War on Drugs . . ." 2001). Recent developments suggest that this may be happening. More and more states are passing alternative drug reform policies, including the adoption of initiatives on the medicinal use of marijuana, syringe exchanges, and alternatives to jails ("Drug Reforms Sweeping States in Recent Years" 2003). A report issued by the Drug Policy Alliance in September 2003 reported that between 1996 and 2002, 46 states passed more than 150 laws that made significant changes in existing drug policy. According to the same report, between 1996 and 2000, voters in seventeen states approved drug policy reform initiatives designed to legalize the medical use of marijuana (*State of the States: Drug Policy Reforms, 1996–2002* 2003).

Tobacco Use and Public Health Law

Smoking kills more people than AIDS, vehicular accidents, homicides, suicides, fires, alcohol, and illicit drugs combined every year in the United States (Heishman, Kozlowski, and Henningfield 1997). Approximately 440,000 people die of a smoking-attributable illness every year. About 8.6 million people in the United States have at least one serious illness caused by smoking. Chronic lung disease accounts for 73 percent and 50 percent of smoking-attributable conditions among current smokers and former smokers, respectively. The annual direct medical cost for treating smoke-attributable illness is estimated to be around $75 billion (Centers for Disease Control and Prevention 2003). Even war has not killed as many Americans as has smoking. World War II claimed fewer American lives in four years as cigarettes takes each year. Over a twelve-year period during the Vietnam War, 58,000 Americans were killed (White 1991). However, the scientific evidence linking smoking to a variety of ailments did not emerge until the 1950s.

Beginning in the 1950s, several epidemiological studies found that cigarette consumption significantly increased a person's chances of suffering from lung cancer, heart disease, and stroke (Gostin, Brandt, and Cleary 1991). In 1964, U.S. surgeon general Luther Perry's Committee on Smoking and Health released a report that concluded that smoking was causally related to lung cancer in men and probably in women as well and implicated smoking to other ailments. This was the first time that the surgeon general of the United States issued a formal report on the health hazards of smoking, and the report became a rallying cry for the campaign against tobacco (Parascandola 1997). This ultimately led Congress in 1965 to pass the Cigarette Labeling and Advertising Act (CLAA) requiring warning labels on all cigarette packages, which read, "Caution: Cigarette Smoking May Be Hazardous To Your Health." The Federal Trade Commission (FTC) required that all cigarette advertisements also contain the same warning. Congress also prohibited advertising of cigarettes on any medium of electronic communication after January 1, 1971 (Gostin, Brandt, and Cleary 1991).

In 1970 the CLAA was amended and the warning on cigarette packages was changed to read, "The Surgeon General Has Determined that Cigarette Smoking Is Dangerous to Your Health." By the late 1970s, concerns about smoking during pregnancy and fetal health risks had become prominent. Prenatal health messages were displayed on billboards, posters, advertisements, and product labels (Oaks 2001). In fact, the warning on cigarette packages was amended in 1984 to include warnings about the dangers of smoking during pregnancy. The Comprehensive Smoking Education Act of 1984 mandated including four warnings on a rotational basis and the warnings include specific reference to lung cancer, heart disease, emphysema, and pregnancy complications; the risk of fetal injury and low birth weight; and the benefits of quitting smoking (Gostin, Brandt, and Cleary 1991). The four current rotating cigarette warning labels are: (1) Quitting smoking now greatly reduces serious risks to your health; (2) Cigarette smoke contains carbon monoxide; (3) Smoking by pregnant woman may result in fetal injury, premature birth, and low birth weight; and (4) Smoking causes lung cancer, heart disease, emphysema, and may complicate pregnancy (White 1991). The 1984 act also required warnings to be placed in advertisements as well as on packages.

In May 1984, Surgeon General C. Everett Koop issued his first report on smoking, which was the strongest indictment of smoking since the 1964 report, and he became a crusader against smoking (Judis 1989). In 1988, Surgeon General Koop's report concluded that cigarettes and tobacco were addictive, that nicotine is the drug in tobacco that causes addiction, and that pharmacological and behavioral processes of tobacco addictions were similar to addiction to other drugs such as heroin and cocaine. The report also concluded that tobacco use met the three criteria for drug addiction—it is very compulsive, the nicotine in tobacco produces psychoactive and mood-altering effects, and nicotine in tobacco reinforces behavior that results in the continued intake of nicotine (U.S. Department of Health and Human Services 1988; Heishman, Kozlowski, and Henningfeld 1997).

President Clinton in 1995 approved the Food and Drug Administration's issuing of new regulations on tobacco products. In 1996 the FDA under the leadership of Commissioner David Kessler, M.D., issued rules to regulate access to tobacco products. These rules would have restricted the underage purchase of tobacco products and prohibited billboard advertising near schools, among other things. However, in a five-to-four vote, the U.S. Supreme Court ruled that Congress had not intended to put tobacco within the FDA's jurisdiction (Kessler 2002).

In 1998, Sen. John McCain (R-Arizona) introduced the Tobacco Control Act in the United States Senate, which was designed to curtail the production as well as the consumption of tobacco. The bill granted significant powers to the FDA commissioner. The bill's provision provided for escalating penalties should the tobacco industry fail to meet targets for reducing teenage smoking 60 percent in ten years, and it would have raised the price of cigarettes over a five-year period (Pertschuk 1998). However, the bill got bogged down in the Senate over the tobacco tax revenue (Gardner 1998). The bill was defeated due to opposition from Senate Republicans in June 1998 ("Death of the Tobacco Bill" 1998). A small group of tobacco corporations spent $40 million on advertising to engineer the defeat of the bill. The bill was defeated despite the fact that it had been approved by the Senate Commerce Committee with overwhelming bipartisan support, had strong Clinton administration support, and also had public support.

The defeat of the tobacco control bill demonstrated the limitations of using the political process to formulate public health policy and should serve as a reminder to public health professionals that public health policymaking operates in a highly charged environment of interest group politics. Future policy successes will require not just scientific evidence but political skills to navigate the murky waters of politics infested with a variety of economic self-interests in order to promote and protect the public's health. Critics have labeled antismoking policy advocacy as tyranny of public health (Sullum 1998b).

Violence, Firearms, and Public Health Law

The rate of murders committed using guns in the United States is 44.6 percent, which is ten times higher than Europe's average of 4.7 per million persons. In the United States, 48 percent of households possess some kind of gun compared to 16.2 percent of European households. Most European countries have strict national-level gun control laws under which guns must be registered and gun owners must be licensed. Potential gun purchasers must undergo a comprehensive background check and pass a gun safety exam. In fact, handguns are either outlawed or restricted so stringently that very few people own handguns in European countries (Carter 1997). In the United States, efforts to regulate guns have generated a significant amount of controversy and heated debate over the problem of firearm-related violence involving issues such as whether the problem of gun violence is exaggerated, whether gun control reduces crime, whether gun control is constitutional, and whether gun ownership is an effective means of self-defense (Kim 1999). The history of gun control in the United States is a history of battle between the National Rifle Association (NRA) and gun control advocates (Brown and Abel 2003).

There are roughly 192 million privately owned firearms in the United States (Cook and Ludwig 1997). In 1998, licensed firearm dealers sold around 4.4 million guns. Of these, 1.7 million were handguns (U.S. Department of Treasury 2000). In addition, 1 to 3 million guns change hands each year in the secondary market without a great deal of regulation (Cook and Ludwig 1997). In 1998, 30,708 Americans died by gunfire. Of these, 12,102 were victims of firearm homicides, 17,424 committed suicides with the use of firearms, and 866 were killed as a result of unintentional shootings (Corlin 2001). By comparison, 33,686 Americans were killed in combat during the Korean War and 58,198 Americans were killed in the combat during the Vietnam War (Department of Veterans Affairs 2001). Risk factors associated with firearm violence include alcohol and drug use, stormy relationships, hopelessness, and ready access to guns. One-quarter of the victims are fifteen to twenty-four-year-olds (Voelker 1995). Some have argued that violence among children and adolescents has become a major threat to public health and safety (Guetzloe 1999).

Firearm-related injuries and deaths incur huge financial costs. For example, in the city of Philadelphia in 1996, more than thirteen hundred people were hospitalized for gun injuries, 25 percent of whom died in hospitals. Hospital costs alone totaled $40 million in 1996, three-fourths of which were paid by taxpayers and hospitals, without reimbursements (Gunderson 1999). During 1996 in the state of Pennsylvania, Medicaid covered about

50 percent of gunshot victims' medical costs, and the average hospital bill for a victim of gun violence was $29,500 (Gunderson 1999). It is estimated that nationally the total cost, including medical treatment and lost productivity, for a fatally injured gunshot victim is around $374,000. American taxpayers pay approximately 85 percent of the medical costs of injuries related to gun violence (Gunderson 1999).

Many have come to view injuries and violence as an epidemic and a public health problem (Durant 1999; "Injuries, Violence Pose Public Health Epidemic" 1999) and called for treating violence as a public health problem (Sidel and Wesley Jr. 1995; Kates and Schaffer 1997; Diamond 1999; Heath 2002). Some have argued for integrating the public health perspective into reporting on violence (Stevens 1998) and others have called on bioethicists to make firearm-related violence a focal point of consideration in developing thoughtful arguments and practical policy recommendations (Turner 1997).

The 1979 surgeon general's report *Healthy People* for the first time publicly recognized violence as a public health concern at the federal level (U.S. Department of Health, Education, and Welfare 1979). The Institute of Medicine (1985) published a report examining how intentional and unintentional injuries in America had become a mounting public health threat. In 1995, Surgeon General C. Everett Koop convened a Surgeon General's Workshop on Violence and Public Health, which put a spotlight on violence as a public health concern (U.S. Department of Health and Human Services 1986).

By the 1990s, even the medical profession had begun to acknowledge the public health implications of firearm-related violence, and many had begun to argue that the dominant view that medicine's interests should concentrate on healing was to take too narrow a view of the doctor's role (Horton 2001) and that physicians can help reduce violence by discussing the dangers of firearms with their patients (Voelker 1995). In June 1992, former surgeon general Koop and George D. Lundberg, editor of the *Journal of the American Medical Association (JAMA)*, launched a public health campaign to control guns and reduce the toll of violence (Trafford 1992) because law enforcement alone had failed to curb violence (Dinsmoor 1992). In fact, beginning in 1995 the American Medical Association (AMA) began to issue an annual Report Card on Violence (McAfee 1996). Our discussion of violence in this section focuses mainly on firearm-related violence and its relationship to public health law.

Most Americans tend to view gun violence as largely a crime issue and thus the public policy focus has been on stricter laws and longer prison sentences. Some have advocated the use of criminal deterrence as a public health strategy. For example, Jonathan Shepherd (2001) has explored the possibility of using deterrence rather than punishment as an inducement to keep criminal behavior from involving physical harm, such as the use of deterrence to dissuade drunk driving. This strategy advocates that rather than trying to prevent violence through the negative goals of conviction and punishment, it is better to prevent violence through the positive aim of promoting health (Sidel and Wesley 1995; Winett 1998; Horton 2001; Shepherd 2001). One area where there has been an attempt to link violence to public health is to use gun control as a public health, child safety, and suicide prevention issue.

Several groups such as the Violence Policy Center and the HELP Network have joined together to advocate the idea of gun control as a public health issue. Similarly, the CDC is also promoting the public health aspect of gun violence and injuries (Anderson 1995). Since there is a firearm in over 40 percent of American households, one of the strategies is to push gun control as a child safety issue. Given the fact that there are an estimated 192 million firearms in private hands in the United States, another strategy is to emphasize the lack of regulation within the firearms industry and to view guns as consumer products that should be regulated like any other consumer product (Vernick and Teret 2000).

Today there are laws governing firearms at the federal, state, and local levels. Most of the laws governing guns in the United States deal with the use, sale, and possession of firearms. The 1934 National Firearms Act (NFA) made it difficult to obtain firearms that were perceived as especially lethal such as machine guns and short-barreled long guns, which were the chosen weapons of gangsters. The law imposed taxes on all aspects of the manufacture and distribution of such weapons and enforced a disclosure of the production and distribution system ("Gun Control Overview" 1999).

The federal Gun Control Act (GCA) of 1968 required persons selling firearms to obtain a license. Under the law, the sale of long guns (rifles and shotguns) is prohibited to anyone under the age of eighteen and the sale of handguns is prohibited to anyone under the age of twenty-one. The law prohibits the purchase and possession of firearms by certain categories of persons such as those convicted of certain crimes, fugitives from justice, persons judged to be mentally ill or committed to mental institutions, and illegal narcotics users or addicts (Jacobs and Potter 1995). In addition, the law also prohibits importation of handguns considered to be unsuitable for or readily adaptable for sporting use. This stopped importation of the so-called Saturday Night Special handguns (Vernick and Mair 2002). The law was vehemently opposed by the NRA. In fact, it transformed the NRA, whose traditional focus was on training sportsmen in gun safety, into a lobbying superpower devoting large amounts of resources to political fights against gun controls (Kendall 2003).

The Armor Piercing Ammunition Act (APAA) of 1986 prohibits the manufacture and importation of ammunition composed of certain metal substances, and the 1988 Undetectable Firearms Act bans the manufacture, import, possession, and transfer of firearms such as plastic guns that cannot be detected by security devices. In 1990, Congress passed the Gun-Free School Zone Act (GFSZA), which prohibited the possession of a firearm in a school zone, but it was ruled unconstitutional by the Supreme Court in 1995 in *United States v. Lopez* (Carney 1997; "Gun Control Overview" 1999).

The Reagan administration during the 1980s had been friendly to the interests of the NRA. However, the assassination attempt on President Reagan, in which the White House press secretary James S. Brady was shot by John W. Hinckley in 1981, generated a movement to regulate handguns. Congress in 1993 passed the Brady Handgun Violence Prevention Act (BHVPA), also known as the Brady Act, which went into effect in 1994. The law required a five-day waiting period for a background check before a person could purchase a handgun (Auster 1996). This bill was strongly opposed by the NRA and its passage represented a major defeat for the NRA.

The Violent Crime Control and Enforcement Act (VCCEA) of 1994 made it unlawful for a person to manufacture, transfer, or possess certain military-type semiautomatic assault weapons for a ten-year period. This law expired in September 2004 when Congress failed to renew it.

In 1997 the U.S. Supreme Court in *Printz v. U.S.* struck down the background check component of the 1993 Brady Handgun Violence Prevention Act on grounds of the Tenth Amendment and ruled that it usurped states' rights (Carney 1997). The Court, however did not address the other provisions of the act, leaving a voluntary background check system in place. In 1998 the treasury secretary and the attorney general announced that background checks on prospective handgun purchasers would be conducted in every state ("Gun Control Overview" 1999). Following this announcement, almost all states have voluntarily instituted background checks of would-be firearms purchasers. The federally required waiting period was eliminated as a result of a sunset provision in the Brady Act in December 1998. Currently, federally licensed firearms dealers are required to conduct an instant check of would-be gun buyers through a nationwide system maintained by the Federal Bureau of Investigation (FBI) (Ludwig and Cook 2000). This computerized national instant check system provides criminal background checks on all firearms purchasers, not just handgun purchasers. All firearms dealers and pawnshop brokers are required to conduct such an instant background check (Anders 1999).

Congress in 1997 also passed the Federal Domestic Violence Gun Act

(FDVGA), which prohibits persons convicted of a misdemeanor crime of domestic violence from possessing guns and ammunition.

By and large, with few exceptions such as VCCEA at the federal level, laws governing the design, manufacture, and marketing of firearms are absent in the United States. There are also some exceptions at the state level. For example, in 1997, the attorney general of Massachusetts used the consumer protection authority to issue new regulations, which require that all new handguns sold in the state contain a device to prevent a child from firing a gun, a tamper-resistant serial number, and a loaded-chamber indicator or magazine safety (Vernick and Mair 2002). In 2000, Maryland enacted into law the Responsible Gun Safety Act requiring changes in handgun design. The law mandates that handguns sold in Maryland must have a device built into the gun itself to prevent the handgun from discharging unless the safety is deactivated (Vernick and Mair 2002).

However, there is no comprehensive federal law or regulatory policy in this area. Advocates who view guns as a consumer product issue argue that what is needed is a comprehensive consumer-product-based regulation of firearms that would include standards for safe design, closer regulation of firearms that are particularly dangerous, surveillance and recall authority, government oversight of firearms dealers and distributors, responsible advertising practices, and no immunity from litigation for firearms manufacturers (Vernick and Teret 2000).

Another possibility is an outright ban on handguns. For example, recently the town of Morton Grove in Illinois passed an ordinance banning handguns. However, passing such ordinances by local governments is made difficult by the fact that thirty-three states have preemption laws precluding local governments from passing statutes that would be more restrictive than the firearms laws of their state. Illinois does not have such a preemption law (Anderson 1995).

Given the fact that firearms have enjoyed a privileged status in American society, the challenge facing public health professionals is to educate the general public about the health dangers of firearms and continue to persuade the policymaking community of the virtues of regulating firearms as consumer products to improve public health. Two factors are in its favor. One is the fact that public opinion polls seem to indicate that a strong majority of the general public supports government regulation of gun designs (Teret et al. 1998). The second is the fact that no federal court has ever struck down any gun law as a violation of the Second Amendment. In fact, laws completely banning handguns have passed constitutional muster. Thus it is unlikely that laws regulating the design, manufacture, and marketing of firearms will fail the constitutional test (Vernick and Teret 1993).

During the 1990s, public opinion also shifted in favor of meaningful gun control in the United States (Young et al. 1996; "For the First Time, a Majority in U.S. Favors Ban on Handguns" 1993). Laws such as the 1993 Brady Handgun Violence Prevention Act passed by Congress reflected this shift in public opinion.

Since the primary purpose of public health laws designed to regulate firearms is to reduce firearms-related violence and fatalities, the ultimate question is how effective are such laws and regulations. According to a study by the Centers for Disease Control and Prevention (CDC), between 1993 (when the 1993 Brady Handgun Violence Prevention Act was passed) and 1998, quarterly gun deaths declined 29 percent and quarterly gun injuries declined 47 percent. However, the study also reported that gunshots remained the second leading cause of death in the United States and that firearms-related injuries continue to be a major public health concern (Gotsch et al. 2001). Similarly, a report released by the Department of Justice in 2000 showed that the number of violent crimes committed with guns was 35 percent lower in 1999 compared to 1992 ("Government Figures Show Gun Crimes Down. . ." 2000). However, Ludwig and Cook (2000), after conducting an analysis of the relationship between homicide and suicide rates and the Brady Handgun Violence Prevention Act, found no evidence that the implementation of the Brady Act was associated with a reduction in homicide rates.

Thus it is difficult to demonstrate a direct causal link between public health laws regulating firearms and a decline in firearms-related deaths and injuries. The study by CDC also argued that factors that might have contributed to the decrease in both fatal and nonfatal firearms-related injuries could be the aging of the population, improvements in economic conditions, decline of the cocaine market, law enforcement, improvements in violence prevention programs, and legislative changes, among others. Thus, laws intended to regulate firearms could be simply one of many factors contributing to a decrease in firearms-related deaths and injuries (Gotsch et al. 2001).

Gun control advocates had predicted that the 1993 Brady Handgun Violence Prevention Act would create a more secure and safe society because it would prevent ineligible persons from purchasing handguns, and fewer dangerous persons possessing handguns would mean less danger to others. According to a survey by the Bureau of Alcohol, Tobacco, and Firearms (1995), 41,000 out of 441,545 applicants were prevented from purchasing handguns under the law during 1994. Many whose applications were denied either had a felony record, were fugitives from justice, were under indictment, were drug users, were illegal aliens, had mental defects, or had been dishonorably discharged. The Department of Justice (DOJ) in 2000 released a report that showed that between 1994 and 1999, of the 22.2 million people who applied to purchase a firearm, about 536,000 were rejected based on federal, state, or local laws ("Government Figures Show Gun Crimes Down. . ." 2000). Because of this, the law was declared a major success. However, it is unclear from the report whether the applications denied were due to "false positives" or "false hits," meaning denials were based on mistakes in name checks and other problems in databases and checking procedures. Rejected applicants may have possessed other guns or subsequently purchased firearms by submitting a false application to another federal firearms licensee. Furthermore, many dangerous criminals are likely to purchase firearms on the secondary market or obtain them by theft (Jacobs and Potter 1995).

As Jacobs and Potter (1995) have pointed out, there are many regulatory gaps in the 1993 Brady Handgun Violence Prevention Act that allow circumventing of the regulatory process. One of the problems is that practically anyone can obtain a federal license to sell firearms. The only way to deny an applicant a license is if the applicant is found to have provided untruthful or inaccurate information on their application. There is no reliable way to determine if the applicant has lied on their application. Second, under the act, the would-be purchaser of a handgun from a federal licensee is not required to provide fingerprints but simply proof of identity, and phony identification such as a bogus driver's license can be used to purchase a handgun. Third, the process can be circumvented by having a friend or a spouse purchase the firearm. Fourth, the act is not applicable in the secondary (resale) market (Jacobs and Potter 1995).

According to Cook and Ludwig (2003), federal gun control legislation in recent decades has had no statistically significant effect on reducing gun-related deaths, nor has the overall suicide rate declined due to gun control legislation. However, the 1993 Brady Handgun Violence Prevention Act and the 1998 revisions did have some positive effects. These gun laws did help undermine gunrunning operations, in which large quantities of guns were purchased in Southern states and transported for resale in Northern states. The law also helped improve criminal history records. Unregulated sales of firearms at gun shows continue to remain a major problem (Cook and Ludwig 2003).

Overall, the relationship between laws designed to regulate firearms and violence/injuries is a mixed one. Firearms laws seem to have produced some positive results. However, it is difficult to establish a clear causal link between the two.

Tort Litigation as a Public Health Strategy

The last three decades have witnessed a significant increase in the use of litigation as a tool to protect and advance public health. Litigation has been used to advance certain public policies in areas such as tobacco and gun violence, among others. Individuals and organizations concerned with public health have turned to litigation to advance their policy goals (Parmet and Daynard 2000). Public health advocates have pursued litigation as an alternative strategy often out of frustration with their inability to achieve desired policy goals through legislative arenas. In context, litigation can be viewed as a component of a broader public health strategy aimed at changing how public health policy is formulated (Jacobson and Soliman 2002).

Parmet and Daynard (2000) have categorized public health litigation into four types. One type of litigation occurs between private plaintiffs and private defendants. The second type of litigation involves public plaintiffs and private defendants. The best example of this type of litigation is that brought by state attorneys general against the tobacco companies. The third type of litigation involves private plaintiffs and public defendants. In such cases individuals claim that the government itself is damaging public health by violating its own laws. Much environmental litigation falls into this category. The fourth type of litigation involves public plaintiffs and public defendants. Such conflicts arise due to overlapping jurisdictions and authority among various public agencies. An example would include the Environmental Protection Agency (EPA) suing a local government to clean up its water supply. According to Parmet and Daynard (2000), the majority of public health litigation falls into the first category involving private plaintiffs and private defendants. However, the litigation most likely to achieve changes in public health policy involves litigations between public plaintiffs and private defendants because government officials are in a better position to speak on behalf of the public and better articulate public health goals.

Jacobson and Soliman (2002) have summarized the major arguments for and against the use of litigation as a public health strategy. Proponents argue that large damage awards in product liability litigations can deter harm by discouraging the introduction of dangerous products. Court rulings can bring about direct changes in public health policies that may have been blocked by other policymaking institutions. Litigation can also help educate the public and stimulate public debate that can bring about change. Sometimes just the threat of potential litigation may produce a policy change because of a defendant's desire to avoid a potential negative outcome in a court of law.

Opponents of litigation as a public health strategy argue that the use of courts to substitute for legislative policymaking is inappropriate because courts lack the ability to clearly define policy objectives, understand the policy implications of their decisions, and assess the economic impact of various policy alternatives. Opponents also argue that the use of litigation poses a threat to the separation of powers, and that such a strategy is anti-democratic (Jacobson and Soliman 2002). To opponents, public health litigation represents an inherently paternalistic attitude and is contrary to the prevailing individualistic and market ethos. In addition, opponents argue that the economic efficiency and efficacy of public health litigation is questionable. Others have questioned the adequacy of the deterrence achieved by tort litigation and argue that product liability laws often deter innovations (Parmet and Daynard 2000).

The proponents of litigation argue that the criticism that litigation strategy is antidemocratic is misplaced. The legislative process itself is anti-democratic because of interest group domination and structural faults that prevent the public will from becoming public policy. Furthermore, litigation may force the issue of regulation into the legislative agenda, generate publicity and debate, and help educate the public (Parmet and Daynard 2000).

What is clear is that the proper use of litigation, especially by public agencies/officials, requires a solid assessment of the legislative and physical environments, and sound judgment regarding when to use and when to avoid litigation to protect and promote public health (Bonta, Praeger, and Schlichtmann 2002). In the following section we examine the use of litigation as a public health strategy in the areas of tobacco and guns.

Tobacco Litigation

Many advocates of tobacco control have been dissatisfied with the failure of policymakers to enact and enforce tobacco control laws. This has led them to support tobacco litigation as a way to achieve public health policy goals. Supporters of the litigation strategy argue that it is reasonable to seek policy change through judicial processes because courts can be a powerful and effective vehicle for social and political change when elected representatives have failed to address pressing problems (Scheingold 1974; McCann 1994).

According to Jacobson and Warner (1999), civil litigations serve four functions: to compensate an injured victim for harm suffered due to wrong-doing by someone; to deter future wrongdoing by the perpetrator; to establish accountability on the part of the wrongdoer by assessing liability and awarding punitive damages; and to provide equitable remedies such as issuing an injunction when relief cannot be obtained through monetary damages. They also argue that when it comes to tobacco litigation, courts have performed a dual function. The first function has been to review challenges to government's regulatory actions to assure that a particular regulatory action is based on appropriate legislative authority and is constitutional. The second function is to provide a venue where injured litigants attempt to recover damages suffered from tobacco-related diseases (Jacobson and Warner 1999).

In the early 1950s, evidence was beginning to emerge linking cigarettes and lung cancer. This initiated a first wave of lawsuits against tobacco companies, which lasted from about the mid-1950s to the mid-1970s. During this period, lawsuits were largely based on issues of negligence and liability. The main argument of the plaintiffs was that tobacco companies were negligent in warning them against the risks and dangers of smoking and thus the tobacco companies should be held liable for smoking-related diseases suffered by the plaintiffs. However, in almost all of these cases the plaintiffs failed to convince juries and courts that smoking caused lung cancer in a significant number of people (White 1991). The tobacco industry successfully argued that the proof of causation between smoking and lung cancer was lacking, and since smokers voluntarily assumed the risks of smoking, the tobacco industry should not be held liable for diseases suffered by the plaintiffs (LaFrance 2000; Teret 1986).

The beginning of the 1980s witnessed a second wave of tobacco litigation. There were several reasons for this. One was the fact that by the 1980s, scientific evidence linking smoking to cancer was no longer in dispute. Second, product liability laws had expanded substantially in the 1970s in most jurisdictions to define a defective product as one containing a manufacturing flaw, a bad product design, or an inadequate warning. The third reason was that during the 1970s and 1980s, congressional laws and subsequent amendments had forced cigarette manufacturers to include a warning on the danger of smoking on cigarette packages. Warnings were not to be just a formality but must adequately convey to the consumer the nature and extent of a product's risks (White 1991). Thus most lawsuits during the second wave relied on product liability rules to argue that cigarettes were defective in design, manufacture, and warning. In most such cases the courts ruled that even though cigarettes were inherently dangerous, neither design nor manufacturing defects could form the basis for liability (Jacobson and Warner 1999).

The third wave of lawsuits, which began in the early 1990s, was different from the first two waves because many of the lawsuits were dominated by class actions, especially by state governments to recover Medicaid costs for tobacco-related illnesses under the doctrine of unjust enrichment. States argued that they were not suing on behalf of injured smokers, but that they were suing in their own right to recoup tobacco-related financial costs absorbed by their Medicaid program (Jacobson and Warner 1999). When David Kessler, commissioner of the Food and Drug Administration (FDA), obtained the internal documents of tobacco companies through a lawsuit, he was able to demonstrate that tobacco companies had known for years that nicotine was addictive and that they were knowingly designing a product to deliver an addictive drug to consumers. Thus the tobacco product, in essence, was a vehicle for the delivery of nicotine. This helped establish the "intent" of the tobacco companies. This revelation caused a major negative reaction in public attitudes toward the tobacco companies and put pressure on the industry to reach an accommodation to limit its liability exposure.

In the summer of 1997 the tobacco industry settled Medicaid-related lawsuits with the states of Mississippi and Florida by agreeing to pay $3 billion and $11 billion, respectively, over a twenty-five-year period. This was followed by settlements with Texas for $14 billion and Minnesota for $6 billion (Jacobson and Warner 1999). In 1998 the tobacco companies agreed to make payments to the other forty-six states in perpetuity. The first twenty-five years of payments would add up to over $200 billion dollars ("Saved by Smokers: The Tobacco Settlement" 2001). In addition, the tobacco industry agreed to restrictions on marketing and advertising to youth, bans on outdoor advertisements, and funding antismoking advertisements, among other things (Jacobson and Soliman 2002). The settlement is called the Master Settlement.

The Master Settlement has led many to argue that the class action litigation approach has been an appropriate strategy in this area because of the large number of potential plaintiffs, facts underlying the tobacco industry's long campaign of distortions, and that without class action many potential plaintiffs would not have any representation at all (Daynard and Gottlieb 2001). The current emphasis on public health in relation to smoking or other risky individual behaviors is not new. However, critics argue that past efforts by public health officials to regulate risky behaviors by individuals were designed mainly to wipe out communicable diseases. According to critics, current concerns tend to focus on issues that are mainly lifestyle choices and ought not to be public health concerns (Sullum 1998a).

It is clear that lawsuits brought by individual plaintiffs during the first two waves of lawsuits were not very successful. In fact, between 1954 and 1994, individuals filed 813 claims against tobacco companies. Only two of these cases were won by individual plaintiffs, and both times the decisions were reversed on appeal (LaFrance 2000). However, the story has been very different since 1998's Master Settlement. Of the cases decided since the 1998 Master Settlement, plaintiffs have been victorious in several lawsuits. Litigation against tobacco manufacturers has increased dramatically, and the industry has suffered significant financial losses (Jacobson and Soliman 2002).

The important question is whether the Master Settlement agreement has achieved its stated policy goals. Over the next twenty-five years, the total payment by tobacco companies is expected to reach close to $250 billion. At the time of the 1998 settlement there was a great deal of talk about how states would use the settlement money they had won for antismoking programs. The CDC has recommended that states should use about 20 percent to 25 percent of the money for wide-ranging tobacco control programs ("Saved by Smokers: The Tobacco Settlement" 2001).

According to a special report issued by Campaigns for Tobacco-Free Kids (2004), five years after the Master Settlement, most states had failed to keep their promise to use the settlement money to reduce harmful effects of tobacco, and the Master Settlement's marketing restrictions have done very little to reduce the tobacco companies' ability to market their products to children. According to the report, only four states (Maine, Delaware, Mississippi, and Arkansas) were funding tobacco prevention programs at the CDC's recommended levels while thirty-three states were spending less than half of the CDC's recommended minimum amount. The report concludes that the tobacco companies spend more in three weeks marketing their products than all fifty states spend over a whole year trying to prevent tobacco use.

The preliminary evidence suggests that the Master Settlement has failed overall to achieve most of its stated policy goals. The future success will depend on the ability of public health advocates to convince policymakers to allocate more settlement money for tobacco-control activities. However, in light of the fact that many state governments are facing financial hardship, policymakers are more likely to be tempted to spend the money to address more pressing political needs, such as education and budget deficits.

Firearms Litigation

In the absence of effective laws or regulations to address the problem of gun violence, public health advocates turned to product liability litigation as an alternative approach. For example, in *Kelley v. R.G. Industries*, a 1985 case involving a grocery store operator who was shot by a robber with a cheap handgun, Maryland's Supreme Court ruled that it was perfectly okay to hold manufacturers and marketers of Saturday Night Special handguns liable for injuries suffered by innocent persons because the manufacturers and marketers know or ought to know that the primary purpose of the product is for criminal activity. As a result of this ruling, the main defendant in this case, Rohm Gesellschaft Industries, the company that designed and marketed the guns, decided to discontinue exporting the Saturday Night Special to the United States because of its inability to obtain liability insurance (Teret 1986).

Two individual lawsuits against gun manufacturers made some initial headway during the 1990s. In 1993 a disgruntled former client used several firearms, including two semiautomatic assault weapons, to kill or injure fourteen people at a San Francisco law firm before killing himself. The survivors and relatives of some of the victims filed a lawsuit charging that Navegar, a Miami-based gun manufacturer, acted negligently by manufacturing and marketing assault weapons to the general public. The trial court granted the defendant's motion for a summary judgment. On appeal, the California Court of Appeals ruled against the defendant. Navegar appealed the ruling to the State Supreme Court, which reversed the earlier ruling and held that under a California statute, firearms products could not be deemed defective in design on the grounds that its benefits do not outweigh the risk of injury it creates (Vernick and Mair 2002).

In the case of *Hamilton v. Accu-Tek* in February 1999, a jury in New York found gun manufacturers liable for the indiscriminate marketing and negligent distribution of guns that make possible the criminal misuse of the gun. This was the first time that a federal district court jury had found manufacturers liable for negligent distribution. On appeal, the U.S. Court of Appeals for the Second Circuit certified two questions to the state's highest court, the New York Court of Appeals: (1) Whether the defendant owed the plaintiff a duty to exercise reasonable care in the marketing and distribution of the handgun it makes, and (2) whether the liability in the case can be apportioned on a market share basis. The New York Court of Appeals responded that this was an excessively broad application of liability theory, given the remoteness of injury claims and lack of direct casualty. Based on this answer, the U.S. Court of Appeals for the Second Circuit reversed the jury award and dismissed the case in 2001 (Jacobson and Soliman 2002).

The successful class action lawsuits against tobacco companies that resulted in the Master Settlement have encouraged many city and county governments to file similar lawsuits against gun manufacturers in cities such as Chicago, New York, Los Angeles, New Orleans, and Miami (Gibeaut 2000; Cohen and Grace 1998; "The Gun Lawsuits" 1999; "California Cities, Counties File Gun Suits" 1999). Local governments have primarily used three rationales in their lawsuits against gun manufacturers—product liability, public nuisance, and negligence claims. In September 1999 the Department of Housing and Urban Development (DHUD) threatened gun-makers with a possible class action lawsuit on behalf of thirty-two hundred public housing authorities to recoup the cost of providing security against gun-toting criminals. This was in part influenced by the Clinton administration's frustration with Congress, which in 1999 rejected all new federal gun control proposals by the president (Bai 1999; "Government v. Gun Makers" 1999).

The initial indications are not very promising regarding lawsuits filed by local governments against gun manufacturers. Lower courts have already dismissed several lawsuits brought by municipalities. Furthermore, many states have adopted laws banning local government lawsuits against gun manufacturers. Despite these setbacks, litigation can accomplish something positive if it can lead to negotiated settlements to avoid large litigation costs. For example, Smith and Wesson, one of the major gun-makers, settled a lawsuit with the city of Boston, agreeing to safety and design standards, including new sales and distribution practices for its products (Jacobson and Soliman 2002).

On the negative side, when it comes to lawsuits against gun manufacturers, plaintiffs face many difficult challenges because guns are legally manufactured and they function as intended. As gun manufacturers are often seen as far removed from the physical injury, it is not always easy to identify the manufacturer of a gun as being involved in an injury or death, and such cases raise several complex issues about liability theories (Vernick and Mair 2002).

Stephen Teret, director of the Johns Hopkins University's Center for Gun Policy and Research, has tried to shift the battle over gun control from a more polarizing debate over gun ownership to a debate over gun design and distribution. This strategy has the advantage of skirting some constitutional issues. He has argued for pushing gun manufacturers to produce child-proof and personalized smart guns that would use simple locks or other devices so that only authorized users can operate such firearms (Levine 1999).

While the advocates of gun control won some important battles in Congress during the Clinton administration with the passage of the Brady Handgun Violence Prevention Act in 1993 and the Violent Crime Control and Enforcement Act of 1994, it would be a mistake to underestimate the power of the NRA and the gun lobby. With the election of George W. Bush and Republican control of both houses of Congress, the influence of the gun lobby is on the rise again. Attorney General John Ashcroft has proposed shortening the length of time the Federal Bureau of Investigation (FBI) is required to keep records of background checks, from ninety days required under the Clinton administration to a single business day (Tumulty 2003).

Even more important, in April 2003 the U.S. House of Representatives by an overwhelming bipartisan vote (285 to 140) passed the Protection of Lawful Commerce in Arms Act (PLCAA). The bill prohibits civil liability action from being brought against manufacturers, distributors, dealers, or importers of firearms or ammunition for damages resulting from the misuse of their products by others. The bill does allow persons injured with defective or illegally sold guns to sue gun-makers and dealers for their injuries. The intent of the bill is to make the gun industry largely immune from lawsuits (Quindlen 2003).

The bill has fifty-five cosponsors in the Senate and is supported by Senate majority leader Bill Frist (R-Tennessee) and Senate minority leader Tom Daschle (D-South Dakota), reflecting bipartisan support. When the bill came up on the Senate floor for debate and a vote in March 2004, gun control advocates managed to add two amendments to the bill—one designed to extend the ban on assault weapons for another ten years and the second to require background checks of gun purchasers at gun shows. The acceptance of these two amendments to the bill changed the whole dynamics in the Senate. The Senate sponsors of the bill and the NRA, who were strongly opposed to the two amendments, suddenly reversed course and urged the supporters to vote against the bill. On Tuesday, March 2, 2004, the Senate of the United States by a vote of 90 to 8 defeated the measure designed to shield gun manufacturers and dealers from lawsuits (Stolberg 2004). The outcome left people on both sides dissatisfied and the issue is likely to be revived again in the future.

The Politics of Public Health and Law

The relationship between public health and law, ignored historically, is gaining prominence due to the renewed recognition of the centrality of law to public health practice. Law and regulations have come to be viewed as important tools in protecting and promoting the public's health. However, public health law often created a paradox because government attempts to promote or protect public health often creates conflict between government authority and individual autonomy, liberty, privacy, and property. On the one hand, it is the responsibility of government to act to promote the health of the people, which often requires strong measures to control health risks. On the other hand, government cannot excessively and unjustifiably invade individuals' rights in the name of community good.

Courts have played an important role in establishing constitutional limits on government authority. Courts have stated that when government uses its police power and acts within the limits of its substantive authority, it still must operate within procedural limits. For example, government must use fair and due procedures when government action affects constitutionally protected rights to life, liberty, and property. Another limitation to public health law in democratic societies comes from the public itself. Elected local public officials might be reluctant to carry out measures that might be politically unpopular and could lead to a loss of political support in the next election.

The terrorist attacks of September 11, 2001, and the anthrax scare that followed focused attention on the inconsistent, outdated, and fragmented state of public health laws at the state level, giving rise to the public health reform movement in an attempt to update and modernize public health laws to deal effectively with new emerging diseases and bioterrorism threats. However, reforms designed to give state governments more power and authority during public health emergencies, such as imposing quarantine, have also become embroiled in political controversies, reflecting the tension between government's authority to protect public health versus the right to liberty and privacy.

Law can be an important tool in protecting and promoting the public's health and public health advocates have at times successfully used scientific evidence to get policymakers to respond by passing laws and regulations designed to protect the public's health as demonstrated in our discussion of tobacco and firearms laws and regulations. However, public health advocates have also met with failures and frustrations as demonstrated by the defeat of the tobacco control bill in 1998.

Failures to promote public health objectives in the legislative arena have led many public health advocates to advocate the use of litigation as a public health strategy to promote such objectives. In this chapter we analyzed the use of litigation strategy in the areas of tobacco and gun controls. The results have been mixed. Litigation strategy has produced some important successes in the area of tobacco control. However, litigation as a public health strategy has had less success in the area of gun control.

Have tobacco and gun control laws and regulations produced positive public health outcomes? The evidence thus far is inconclusive. State governments have failed miserably in using money received as a result of the Master Settlement with the tobacco industry for antitobacco educational programs. Financially strapped state governments have found it politically more expedient to spend the money from the Master Settlement to help balance their budgets or use it in areas such as education rather than making tough choices arising from revenue shortfalls.

Similarly, the evidence is mixed with respect to gun control laws and regulations. For example, the waiting period and the background check requirements of the Brady Act have been credited for preventing dangerous persons from obtaining guns and for reducing gun-related homicides and suicides. However, some other evidence raises doubts about the actual positive impact of such laws.

Overall, it is reasonable to conclude that the use of law and litigation as strategies to protect public health has produced successes as well as fail-ures. What it demonstrates is how much the politics of the time and the relative influence of powerful economic interests shape public health law.

Study Questions

1. What role does law play in public health practice? What is the legal foundation of public health in the United States? Discuss the legal/constitutional foundations of federal, state, and local governments' roles in public health.
2. Discuss the role of courts in shaping public health laws in the United States. Cite examples of cases when appropriate.
3. According to Scutchfield and Keck, what are the different types/categories of public health laws? According to Levy, what are the most important challenges that will affect public health law in the twenty-first century?
4. What are the current shortcomings of public health laws in the United States? Discuss the public health law reform movement. Why are reforms of public health laws difficult to achieve?
5. Write an essay in which you discuss how law can be used as an important tool to protect and promote the public's health. Be sure to include in your discussion examples of accomplishments as well as limitations in the use of law as a tool in protecting and promoting the public's health.
6. Discuss the use of litigation as a strategy in protecting and promoting the public's health. Using examples of tobacco and firearms, discuss factors that help explain successes and failures of litigations as a public health strategy.

CHAPTER 5

The Politics of Science and Public Health

The focus on populations rather than individual patients is grounded not only in theory, but in the methods of scientific inquiry and the services offered by public health. The analytical methods and objectives of the primary sciences of public health—epidemiology and biostatistics—are directed toward understanding risk, injury, and disease within populations.
(Gostin 2000, 12–13)

The scientific revolution began during the period of what we now call "the Enlightenment." Following on the work of Bacon, Newton, Descartes, and so forth, the idea of science as an empirically and theoretically sound basis for knowledge challenged other bases for knowledge, such as tradition and religion (faith). As such, it became a basis for power. If you had scientific backing for something, appropriate information, then you had a strong argument for doing it. Consider the controversy over whether to teach evolution in the schools by itself, or replace it with a more faith-based version known as creationism, or teach both together as equally valid theories of the origin of the universe. The power of science can be seen by the fact that those who support the creationist view have adopted terms such as creation science to give it the same validity as evolution. More recent advocates have used the more neutrally sounding term, intelligent design.

Having science information on your side then becomes a battleground for policy disputes. And even when the science supports a particular position, other values based on moral codes may conflict with it and suggest alternative courses of action. Thus science related to policy disputes, which are in essence political disputes, itself becomes politically charged. This has certainly characterized public health issues.

Science and Public Health Research

The scientific basis for public health policy is founded upon five disciplines (Schneider 2000). The core discipline within the public health field is epidemiology, the study of disease patterns within human populations (and, where relevant, in animal populations). Epidemiologists search for causes of disease and seek to prevent their further spread.

For example, public health was and is heavily involved in understanding one of the most recent threats to public health, the West Nile virus. According to the Centers for Disease Control and Prevention (CDC) website, the West Nile virus first appeared in 1937 in Uganda, and in the 1950s its environmental background was established in Egypt. In 1957 the first human cases were observed in Israel, and the equine (horse) version was seen in France and Egypt in the 1960s. The first humans with the disease in the United States appeared in 1999, and the disease has been seen in horses and birds. The disease is spread by mosquitoes and by 2002 had been observed in humans in most of the United States (Centers for Disease Control and Prevention n.d.a).

Once the mechanism(s) for the spread of a disease such as the West Nile virus or legionnaire's disease or AIDS is understood, then treatment and preventive efforts can be undertaken. For example, the CDC website asks the public to report dead birds. It also recommends prevention against mosquito bites, such as using repellent or wearing long-sleeve shirts.

Related to epidemiology are **statistics** or **biostatistics** (Schneider 2000). Public health deals with populations rather than individuals and searches for differences between subgroups in a population. For example, there have been claims that some areas suffer higher rates of a particular type of cancer than would normally be found in a population (see the discussion in chapter 7). Such claims have been made by residents who feel they have been exposed to chemicals in the environment and by cigarette smokers. Biostatisticians would sample various population groups to see if such claims are merited.

The third scientific foundation of public health includes the **biomedical sciences.** This is particularly where public health merges with medicine (Schneider 2000). While public health is a much older discipline than the biomedical sciences, which have their origin in the eighteenth century, the biomedical sciences have demonstrated that bacteria, germs, and viruses are the causes of many diseases. For example, much research was conducted in the 1980s to discover the virus that causes AIDS.[1]

The fourth science of public health includes the **environmental health sciences** (Schneider 2000). The basic argument here is that environmental insults, largely from chemicals, may cause health problems. Apart from the strict development of ecology and environmental-related sciences, disciplines such as toxicology have also been important.

The final science includes the **social** and **behavioral sciences.** Epidemiologists have established linkages between human behaviors and diseases, particularly those of a chronic nature (as opposed to acute health problems, such as poisoning or toxins in the food supply such as *E. coli*). For example, smoking appears to be related to lung and other cancers. A diet high in certain kinds of fats is linked to cancers and heart disease. Violence, clearly a human behavior, has also become a concern of the public health community.

This rather large and variegated scientific basis for public health is hardly without controversy. Indeed, there is virtually no part of public health that is not confronted with conflicted claims. Certainly part of the reason for such conflicted claims is the nature of public health (see chapter 1): public health remedies often call for changes in behavior and can affect economic interests (Schneider 2000). Many of the controversies surrounding public health policy have focused on the validity and interpretation of the scientific basis for policy decisions.

The Evolution of Public Health Research

As noted, epidemiology is the most fundamental of public health sciences. While it is always helpful to fully understand the underlying mechanism(s) for a health or medical condition, it is not always necessary or possible to understand the cause to prevent the spread of disease. Public health policies based on some notion of epidemiology go back to ancient times. Two especially important historical figures are Hippocrates and John Snow.

Hippocrates (460–377 B.C.) is considered the "father" of medicine, and the oath that doctors take upon receiving their license to practice medicine is based on the ancient Hippocratic Oath. He wrote "On Airs, Waters and Places," a series of observations about the effect of environmental conditions on human health. For example, he wrote about how variations in water quality can lead to health problems (Hippocrates).

His most important contribution, apart from the founding of what was probably the world's first medical school, was to stress the importance of empirical science based on observation rather than on a belief that the gods were responsible for a person's health. For example, Hippocrates emphasized the importance of diet and exercise as a way of improving and maintaining one's health (British Broadcasting Company n.d.).

If Hippocrates is considered the "father" of the medical profession, John Snow is considered the "father" of epidemiology (Schneider 2000). Snow's claim to fame was his effort to stem cholera epidemics in nineteenth-century London. To understand the science of epidemiology as well as some of its strengths and weaknesses, it would be useful to consider this episode at some length.

Cholera is an intestinal bacterial infection that causes diarrhea in its victims and can lead to death. It is spread by contaminated water and food (Centers for Disease Control and Prevention n.d.b). At the time, there was no good explanation for how cholera spread, for evidently it did not spread by contact with an infected person (Goldstein and Goldstein 1978).

Snow, and others, (see Goldstein and Goldstein 1978) hypothesized that the cholera bacteria was transferred by water. He also noted after several years of observation that in the 1849 epidemic, some groups of people were infected with cholera and some were not. As Snow relates (see Goldstein and Goldstein 1978, 37–46), those who had drunk water from a pump on Broad Street were much more likely to become infected than those who had not. Snow had the handle from the Broad Street pump removed but, astonishingly to Snow, it did not result in a diminution of the epidemic, which had already peaked. What Snow found was that people who went to a coffee shop in the neighborhood were more likely to become infected than people who went to a brewery in the neighborhood. It turned out that the coffee shop used water from the Broad Street pump, but the brewery had its own water supply.

With another outbreak in the 1850s, Snow was able to conduct what amounted to a controlled scientific experiment (Goldstein and Goldstein 1978). A controlled experiment, the highest form of scientific evidence, occurs when all but one of the variables are the same for two different groups. In this case, two water companies served the same neighborhood. Snow's task was to see if there was a relationship between the water supplier and cholera infections. Through a simple chemical test, Snow was able to identify which families had which water supplier. He found that the death rates from cholera varied dramatically between the consumers of the two water suppliers. The overall death rate outside of this neighborhood was 59 per 10,000 houses. For the two companies, the death rates were 37 per 10,000 houses and 315 per 10,000 houses. Clearly there was something different about the second group (Goldstein and Goldstein 1978; see also Snow 1856). Snow even notes that a company that made use of water from the Thames had a much lower cholera death rate than the company studied on Broad Street. He attributes the difference to the fact that the third water company filtered its water before sending it to its customers.

This classic case study of John Snow and the Broad Street pump nicely illustrates how epidemiology works as well as the limits of epidemiology. As we noted earlier, epidemiology is the study of disease patterns among populations groups. Clearly there was a cholera epidemic, and Snow was imaginative and observant enough to notice the patterns. Once the transmission path of a disease is discovered, steps can be taken to retard or eliminate the epidemic.

Further, Snow's efforts made use of statistics. He gathered data and calculated death rates, showing that the death rates in one group were much higher than another. He provided explanations for why some got sick while others did not, even within the group using the same water supply. This is how epidemiology works.

Of course, Snow was not able to answer all questions. He could not establish the bacterium that caused cholera, but he could establish the relationship between contaminated water supplies and infections. Snow also does not do what modern statisticians do: establish more precisely the nature of the relationship and the statistical likelihood that an outbreak of a disease is related to a particular contaminant.

If Snow is considered the father of epidemiology, one of the first persons to demonstrate a linkage between a substance in the workplace and cancer was Percival Pott. Pott, working in the late eighteenth century, found an elevated rate of cancer of the scrotum among assistants of chimney sweeps. The assistants, young boys, often worked naked because of the heat. An important component of the pollution produced by chimneys is soot, which is now a well-established carcinogenic (cancer-causing) substance (Hall 1998; Hunter 1969).

We can see that Snow's and Pott's efforts underlie the work of epidemiologists. Many of the same questions and issues arise in the more contemporary debate over the linkage between smoking and lung cancer.

Epidemiology can take us only so far. It is vitally important to understand disease patterns. And epidemiological evidence can help find the source of a disease outbreak or an epidemic. Sanitation, one of the great victories of public health, was enabled by showing the relationship between, say, clean water and disease. But what is missing are the underlying explanations.

This is where the biomedical revolution comes in. One of the earliest uses of biomedicine came in the 1700s. Smallpox is/was one of the most feared diseases that particularly struck young people. One source describes smallpox in the eighteenth century as a killer disease the equivalent of cancer or heart disease in the twentieth century (Scott 1999). Those who contracted smallpox either died or were badly scarred.

Edward Jenner, a British physician, noticed that milkmaids did not contract the disease. He speculated that those who contracted cowpox, a similar disease, became immune to the smallpox virus. He experimented, beginning in 1796, by vaccinating subjects with cowpox. By 1800 the practice of vaccination against the dreaded disease had crossed the Atlantic to America. Eventually, with quality controls and wider availability of cowpox as the source material (that is, commercial production), smallpox became effectively extinct (or so we thought) by the 1970s, and smallpox vaccination ceased, partly because of the disappearance of the virus and partly because the reaction to the vaccine created more risks than the risk of contracting smallpox (Henderson 1997). While smallpox was one of the first biological weapons (see chapter 8), it has reappeared in the twenty-first century as a possible tool of bioterrorism.

Vaccination eventually became a tool of modern medicine and public health. The nineteenth-century French scientist Louis Pasteur, whose work led to several important developments in biomedical science, developed vaccines for, among other diseases, anthrax, another modern bioterrorism weapon. Vaccination has led to the demise of other diseases such as polio and chicken pox.

The first polio vaccine, developed by Dr. Jonas Salk, was tested in the 1950s in a nationwide experiment involving many of the nation's school-children. Using a classic controlled experiment design, the schoolchildren, who were volunteered by their parents, were divided into two groups. One group, the experimental group, was given the Salk vaccine; the other group, the control group, was given a placebo injection. Children were randomly chosen to be in one or the other group. The experiment was a double-blind experiment: neither those giving the series of injections nor those receiving them knew who was receiving which injections. Statistical analysis of the results of the experiment clearly showed that those receiving the vaccine were much less likely to contract polio than those given the placebo.[2]

Pasteur was also one of those who argued that living organisms (bacteria and viruses) were responsible for diseases. This laid the foundation for modern medicine. First, the idea that disease was a punishment from God was limited to a few fringe groups. Second, physicians eventually could begin to treat the causes of diseases through both typical public health measures (such as draining swamps that bred disease carriers such as mosquitoes) and then the development of powerful medicines, antibiotics such as penicillin, which could kill bacteria.

Another element in the development of the scientific bases of public health came from the social and behavioral sciences. This was the linkage between human lifestyle activities and illnesses. As modern medicine and public health measures got a handle on acute diseases, chronic maladies that developed over a period of time became the focus of research.

Highlights in this area included the linkage between smoking and specific cancers and between diet and exercise and heart disease. The linkage between heart disease and other factors was established in the famous Framingham study. This was a longitudinal (conducted over time) study that began in 1948 focusing on the residents of Framingham, Massachusetts. The study was carried out by what is now known as the National Heart,

Lung, and Blood Institute (NHLBI), part of the National Institutes of Health. In later years the study was continued jointly with Boston University (National Heart, Lung, and Blood Institute n.d.). The study began with a cohort of over five thousand people from the town, ages thirty to sixty-two. They were given an extensive series of tests and asked about their lifestyle, such as diet. Then investigators returned every two years and redid the tests. In 1971 a second generation of the study sample was included in the investigations. These were the children of the original cohort and their spouses. The result of the studies showed a number of factors related to the incidence of heart disease. These included "high blood pressure, high blood cholesterol, smoking, obesity, diabetes, and physical inactivity—as well as a great deal of valuable information on the effects of related factors such as blood triglyceride and HDL cholesterol levels, age, gender, and psychosocial issues" (National Heart, Lung, and Blood Institute n.d.). The long-term study also produced a substantial number of scientific papers, over one thousand, beginning in the 1950s (National Heart, Lung, and Blood Institute n.d.). More recently, investigators are searching for genetic markers for heart disease (National Heart, Lung, and Blood Institute n.d.).

A similar long-term study, the Nurses Health Study, began in 1976, with a second study begun in 1989. The study was originally designed to investigate the long-term effects of using oral contraceptives. It then morphed into a study that examined the risk factors for chronic diseases (see Brigham and Women's Hospital n.d.).

None of this research has been free of controversy, and we will spend some time considering these controversies in more detail.

Role of Science in the Formulation of Public Health Policies

A rational model of how public policy is made and how policy analysis is done assumes that there is an objective, scientific basis for making decisions. This is certainly the usual assumption for public health policies. Because public health policies have both positive and adverse effects, the minimum requirement is that those policies be based on the best available science. Thus if government is to close an enterprise, such as the Broad Street pump mentioned above, or restrict the use of some activity or substance, such as restrictions on the use of pesticides, that decision ought to be based on the best available scientific evidence, what might be called "regulatory science." Many public health conflicts are grounded in disputes over the nature of the scientific evidence, which invariably mask disagreements over policy issues, values, and interests.

If agency decisions are to be made on the basis of the best available scientific evidence, it stands to reason that agency policymakers must be able to call upon scientific experts. After all, expertise is an important source of bureaucratic power, and information is an important source of power (Rourke 1976).

Some expertise resides within agencies. Government employs a number of people trained in the sciences. A second source of expertise includes science advisory boards or committees (SACs). These committees are made up of scientists outside of government appointed to boards to advise agencies on science-related policy matters. Such boards are found in agencies with public health (as well as other) responsibilities, such as the various components of the National Institutes of Health, the Food and Drug Administration, the Environmental Protection Agency, the Occupational Safety and Health Administration, and so forth. There may be two hundred or more such committees (see "Scientific Advisory Committees" 2003).

Evaluation of Public Health Policies

How well has public health policy worked? What would be appropriate criteria for deciding the successes or failures of public health policies? One way to tell is to look at those cases in which the health of the population has improved by the presence or absence of disease and death. Another indicator might be to look at life expectancy. We shall use many of these.

Isaacs and Schroeder (2001) present a list of public health victories. These include the dramatic decrease in blood lead levels due to the elimination of lead gasoline and lead in such consumer products as paint and solder. A second public health victory was the decline in tooth decay due to fluoridation of the water supply. The third victory is the decline in auto fatalities due both to safer cars and tougher drunk driving laws. A fourth victory, though only a partial one according to the authors, is the decline in smoking. They also briefly mention the development of vaccines that have virtually eliminated childhood diseases such as polio and the mumps.

These and other successes are not just the product of technology development in the biomedical sciences. Rather, the successes are due to "social and behavioral change" (Isaacs and Schroeder 2001, 30). Four reasons underlie public health success stories: the credibility of the scientific evidence, passionate public health advocates, working with the media, and laws and regulations (Isaacs and Schroeder 2001).

Public health policies have experienced other successes, some of the rather broad sort. The development of sanitary policies, such as water treatment and sewage plants, the development of a safe water supply, and so forth are examples of broad-based public health policies.

There have also been successes in the environmental area (which we will consider at greater length in chapter 7). Easterbrook (1995, 1999), among others, has pointed to the increased quality of our air and water. Similar points are made by Davis (2002) and Vig and Kraft (1997).

We could also look at life expectancy figures. According to the report *Healthy People 2010* (Department of Health and Human Services 2000), life expectancy at birth for someone born in 1900 was less than fifty years for both males and females. By 2000 that figured had increased to over seventy years of age. Further, life expectancy for those at ages sixty-five and seventy-five continued to increase.

The Centers for Disease Control and Prevention (Centers for Disease Control and Prevention 1999) published a series of articles focusing on what they felt were ten of the most important public health achievements of the twentieth century. The ten achievements are: "immunizations, motor vehicle safety, workplace safety, control of infectious disease, declines in death from heart disease and stroke, safer and healthier food, healthier mothers and babies, family planning, fluoridation of drinking water, and tobacco as a health hazard" (Centers for Disease Control and Prevention 1999). The CDC argues that these triumphs added as much as twenty-five years to the life expectancy of the average American.

In short, while there is much work that needs to be done to improve the health of the public and improve public health policies, it is reasonably clear that public health policies have had their successes.

Of course, not everyone agrees with this assessment, and there have been some spectacular failures. Perhaps the most famous or notorious cases of public health failure is the swine flu case in 1976 (Broder 2002). Army recruits in New Jersey came down with a mysterious flu that CDC scientists thought resembled the devastating Spanish flu which, worldwide, led to an estimate of perhaps as many as 100 million deaths in the 1918–19 period. The decisionmaking became very alarmist at the possibility of a repeat of the earlier epidemic. Eventually, President Gerald Ford asked for funds to inoculate the entire population. Problems in producing the vaccine were enormous, and several people died from the vaccine. Some people who were administered the vaccine came down with the rare Guillain-Barre syndrome. Further, it turned out that of the five hundred Army recruits who came down with the flu, only one died, nor did the flu appear elsewhere. All told, the original $135 million that President Ford requested turned into some $400 million, with almost a fourth of that total being paid in damages (Broder 2002). Perhaps as important in the story of the swine flu epidemic is that dissenting views, which were available, were rarely heard above the cacophony of concern about the epidemic. A full hearing of the scientific evidence and views was never held.

While they argue that there have been many public health successes, some have pointed out that most of those came in the late nineteenth and early twentieth centuries (Bennett and DiLorenzo 2000). The latter part of the twentieth century saw public health focus more on social policy issues, and public health science became more political than science. Critics have argued that when public health professionals began to add new subjects to their curricula, such as "sociology, anthropology, and political science" (Bennett and DiLorenzo 2000, 3), their focus drifted away from disease to poverty, human rights, and issues of gun control.

Politics, Science, and Public Health Politics

Scientific Evidence and Realities of Politics

In the ideal, best-of-all-possible worlds, public health policy, any public policy for that matter, would be based on the best available scientific evidence. As we have noted, public health policy's scientific basis crosses many scientific disciplines, from basic biology and the biomedical sciences to the social and behavioral sciences. We have also seen that there have been some important and remarkable public health success stories. Yet the successes mentioned above have not come without struggle. For the most part, those struggles have involved politics. That is, even public health policies with a strong scientific basis can be opposed by those who would be adversely affected by it. It is true in public health as in other policy areas that the nature of the evidence is a crucial part, but only a part, of political and policy debates. Indeed, one definition of a policy analysis, certainly related to what we discuss in this chapter, is "strategically crafted argument" (Stone 2002, 8). This is not meant to necessarily accept the postmodern argument that there is no such thing as truth, only people's perspectives on it. It is to acknowledge that people may seek to construct evidence in ways that support their views.

Why the controversies? Part of the answer, which forms a major portion of this chapter, is the nature of scientific evidence. But another important part has to do with the impacts that public health policies have on affected interests. Many public health policies adversely affect some economic interest (Schneider 2000). Recall the discussion of John Snow and the Broad Street water pump. If Snow was correct, and that certainly appears to be the case, then the private owner of the accused water pump would have to close the pump and suffer economic harm. Tobacco companies resisted regulation of their product and opposed any evidence suggesting that tobacco consumption was harmful. We could go on and on.

The adverse economic impact of public health policies is nicely captured in the play *Enemy of the People*, by the nineteenth-century Norwegian playwright Henrik Ibsen (1981). Ibsen's satirical comedy concerns a Norwegian town famed for its healing waters. The medical officer for the baths, Dr. Thomas Stockmann, discovers that rather than making users better, the waters contained pollutants that made them sicker. After careful investigation, Dr. Stockmann said that some visitors came down with gastric and typhoid fever. His policy recommendation was to close down the baths. The mayor, his brother Peter, and the other leaders of the town opposed closing the baths because it would have a devastating affect on the town's economy. Dr. Stockmann soon becomes an "enemy of the people."

The image, or myth, of science is one of objectivity. Scientists are dispassionate observers seeking only facts and truth. The facts, the evidence, lead to the conclusions. Indeed, the power, the authority of scientists, is founded on this objective basis. Scientists seek truth and thus speak truth.

Politics is not necessarily about objective truth, though public policy is often rationalized as based upon evidence. Rather, public policy and public policy advocates are a function of a variety of factors, such as ideology and economic interests as well as evidence. Thus political power is an important component of public policymaking. Interests adversely affected by public policies or proposed public policies will seek to change those policies or prevent them from being enacted or implemented. In that sense the confluence of science and public policy can be described as "Speaking Truth to Power" (Wildavsky 1979), or perhaps more accurately, mixing truth and power (Rushefsky 1986).

Contradictory and Inconclusive Scientific Evidence

But there is another element to the debate over the use of scientific evidence: that evidence is not always perfectly clear. Further, some of the sciences that underlie public health policy present more problems than others. Epidemiology and the social/behavioral sciences are likely to produce more uncertain evidence than, say, biology.

Consider again John Snow and the Broad Street pump. Snow, as mentioned above, is considered the "father" of epidemiology and his studies of the nineteenth-century cholera epidemic in London are some of the first epidemiological studies. Yet Snow's research contained considerable uncertainties, and his policy recommendations affected economic interests.

In 1980 the Occupational Safety and Health Administration (OSHA) held hearings on its proposal to establish guidelines for determining when a chemical was a potential or established carcinogen (cancer-causing substance) that would require either regulation or banning (see Rushefsky 1986). One witness pointed directly to John Snow, the Broad Street pump, and the cholera epidemic. He noted that as a result of Snow's investigations, the pump was closed. Thus, this would seem to be a pretty simple success story. Yet the witness, Richard Bates, pointed out that had there been critics of such an intervention similar to those of modern regulatory policy, there would have been substantial criticism of the policy and Snow's studies because of gaps in the evidence:

> Many scientists would point out that it had not been conclusively demonstrated that the water was the cause of the disease. They would be troubled because of the lack of satisfactory theoretical knowledge to explain how the water could have caused the disease. Furthermore, other habits of those who had become ill had not been adequately investigated, so it would not be possible to rule out other causes of the disease. The scientists would have been correct. Others would have pointed out that some members of the community who drank from the Broad Street well had not succumbed to the cholera. Thus, even if there was something wrong with the water, there must be other factors involved, and if we could control these we would not have to be concerned about the water. These conclusions are also correct. Some who consume water from the Broad Street well would have objected to closing it because the taste of the water from other wells was not as agreeable. Finally, if the pump had been owned by an individual who sold the water, he would certainly have protested against closing down his business on the basis of inconclusive evidence of hazard. (Occupational Safety and Health Administration 1980, 5008 quoted in Rushefsky 1986, 7)

Bates's analysis captures much of the debates over public health policy. Conclusive proof is often demanded before an affected interest will admit that something the interest manufactures or sells ought to be regulated or banned. Conducting good epidemiological studies is not easy or simple (Davis 2000). Often the mechanism of causation is not known or well established or challenged. Further, affected interests can always ask the most difficult question: How do you know that this substance caused that illness? The years-long controversy over the hazards of smoking is a nice case in point: Take the Bates quote above and substitute lung cancer (and other illnesses) for cholera and tobacco for the Broad Street pump and little needs to be changed.

There are other uncertainties involved in regulatory science, some due to the nature of the problem and some due to the nature of the scientific enterprise. Let us consider the nature of the problem.

Relatively speaking, illnesses such as cholera are fairly simple because of their nature. They are acute diseases (that is, they appear a short time after exposure) and the trail from exposure to impact is thus relatively short. Even then, there are uncertainties. As the Bates quote points out, not everyone who drank from the Broad Street pump came down with cholera.

In general, public health and the biomedical sciences have had substantial successes in dealing with acute impacts. The troublesome problems are those that can be labeled chronic (see the discussion in Rushefsky 1986). Chronic illnesses, which more and more characterize advanced, industrial societies, are those that develop some time after exposure or only after continued exposure.

A particularly illuminating example of the problems of chronic illnesses is DES (diethylstilbestrol). DES is an estrogen (female sex hormone) administered to some 4 million women to prevent miscarriages in their pregnancies. One of the "side effects" of DES emerged only years later. The daughters of women who had taken DES came down with a rare cancer of the vagina (Davis 2002; DES Cancer Network n.d.). There may be as many as 10 million people born to women who took DES (DES Cancer Network).

This is clearly a much more complex problem than John Snow's cholera epidemic. It is virtually inconceivable that anyone could have thought of such an impact. Designing studies to discover such impacts would have been virtually impossible.

Smoking-related illnesses have many of the same characteristics of DES. For a long time the exact causal connection between smoking and lung cancer, heart disease, and stroke was not known.[3] As with cholera or DES, not everyone who smoked will get lung cancer, nor will everyone who gets lung cancer have smoked, though many will. Trying to establish the exact cause-and-effect has been difficult, and only in recent years have court suits against tobacco companies been successful. From our point of view, it is the chronic nature of the issue that is important. One does not get lung cancer immediately after smoking a cigarette. Cancer is a disease that can take decades to develop and after repeated exposures. While much lung cancer is preventable (do not start smoking), there is still no equivalent of a Broad Street pump.

Consider as a third example global climate warming, or the "greenhouse effect." While we consider this issue in more detail in chapter 7, we can make some preliminary statements now. There are considerable uncertainties surrounding the question of whether the climate is warming and whether man-made emissions are a significant contribution to that warming. If global warming will be a problem in the future, when would we have to begin remediating that problem? The costs of making changes to limit global climate warming are significant, but the benefits will occur sometime in the future (if at all). Global warming, like cancer, is a long-term, chronic issue, much more difficult to address.

Another characteristic of science also presents problems in making public health policy: the scientific basis for policy decisions is continually changing. This is because scientific research continues to evolve. Things that we thought were scientifically established at one point may be superseded by new developments. This is true of the "pure" sciences. Consider that we once thought that the sun revolves around the earth or that the earth was flat. While there are still many ways in which Newtonian physics explains the physical world, Einstein's thought experiments opened up new ways of thinking (see Kuhn 1970; see also Taubes 2001b).

Two more characteristics of regulatory science are important. First, there is often pressure on policymakers to make decisions, even if the scientific foundation is weak or not well developed. Second and related is the intermixing of science and politics.

The first problem can be illustrated by considering dietary recommendations, specifically dietary fat (Taubes 2001a). The recommendation from doctors and from the U.S. Department of Agriculture was to limit the consumption of dietary fat on the grounds that it was related to a high incidence of heart disease. Heart disease is the number one cause of death in the United States. The posited causal chain can be described as follows:

> The proposition, now 50 years old, that dietary fat is a bane to health is based chiefly on the fact that fat, specifically the hard, saturated fat found primarily in meat and dairy products, elevates blood cholesterol levels. This in turn raises the likelihood that cholesterol will clog arteries, a condition known as artherosclerosis, which then increases risk of coronary artery disease, heart attack, and untimely death. By the 1970s, each individual step of this chain from fat to cholesterol to heart disease had been demonstrated beyond reasonable doubt. But the veracity of the chain as a whole never has been proven. . . . To put it simply, the data remains ambiguous as to whether low-fat diets will benefit healthy Americans. Worse, the ubiquitous admonishments to reduce total fat intake have encouraged a shift to high-carbohydrate diets, which may be no better—and may even be worse—than high-fat diets. (Taubes 2001a)

Studies in the *New England Journal of Medicine*, by the American Heart Association, and other studies support this contention (Taubes 2001a). A congressional committee headed by South Dakota Democratic senator George McGovern originated this "anti-fat" dogma (Taubes 2001a).

Taubes (2001a) also provides us with a way of deciding how sound the scientific evidence is for policy decisions (or for the development of scientific knowledge for that matter) and it is worth quoting:

> To the outside observer, the challenge in making sense of any such long-running scientific controversy is to establish whether the skeptics are simply on the wrong side of the new paradigm, or whether their skepticism is well founded. In other words, is the science at issue based on sound scientific thinking and unambiguous data, or is it what Sir Francis Bacon for instance, would have called "wishful science," based on fancies, opinions and the exclusion of contrary evidence? Bacon offered one viable suggestion for differentiating the two: the test of time. Good science is rooted in reality, so it grows and develops and the evidence gets increasingly more compelling, whereas wishful science flourishes most under its first authors before "going downhill." (Taubes 2001a)

One reason why the dietary fat issue became complicated is that over time we learned that there are different types of dietary fats. There are the low-density lipoproteins, which do elevate blood serum cholesterol (hence the label "bad fats") and there are the high-density lipoproteins, which lower the risk of heart disease (the "good fats"). A low-fat diet recommendation is thus too simple; diets should contain the HDLs. Triglycerides are also related to heart problems. A broiled porterhouse steak contains a proportion (perhaps as much as 70 percent) of fat that will improve cholesterol levels. Further, if we substituted high-glycemic carbohydrates such as bread or potatoes for the steak, we might get less protection (Taubes 2001a).

A similar argument can be made about the dietary effects of salt intake (Taubes 1998). The basic proposition is that intake of salt raises blood pressure and elevated blood pressure leads to strokes. As with dietary fat, lowering consumption of salt can lead to an extended life. This analysis, again similar to his later article, presents many of the problems associated with the scientific basis of public health policy. "At its core, the salt controversy is a philosophical clash between the requirements of public health policy and the requirements of good sciences, between the need to act and the institutionalized skepticism required to develop a body of reliable knowledge" (Taubes 1998).

A further problem is that in public health, small benefits can have significant impacts on the health of the public. But epidemiology has difficulty detecting small benefits. There is polarization of researchers who tend to accept studies that agree with them (Taubes 2001a).

This leads us to consider several issues. How do we know if we have a good scientific basis for policy decisions? To what extent do other factors intrude on the decisionmaking process? Public health policy, any public policy, will be affected by factors other than just the scientific ones.

Rychetnik et al.'s (2002) review of criteria for evaluating research on public health suggests the complexity of the problem of relying on evaluation studies. There needs to be a specific and explicit theory of the intervention.[4] A distinction should be made between the inability of the study to detect outcomes and failure of the intervention, and theory failure and intervention failure. While the gold standard of research in this field is the randomized clinical trial (RCT), there are often barriers to conducting such trials, which include financial and time constraints. Thus other types of research designs are necessary. In sum, while evidence-based research is an important factor in making public health decisions, sometimes the evidence is lacking and our criteria for judging the quality of the evidence is limited (Rychetnik et al. 2002).

Politics cannot be divorced from public health policymakers. On the other hand, research can be used "more honestly and effectively to inform the politics of public health" (Collins and Coates 2000, 1389). Many public health policies are highly charged, but scientific research can enlighten the political debate if it is done honestly and presented honestly. Public health policies related to needle exchanges as a way to reduce the spread of HIV is a case in point.

Anderson (2000) addresses the question of how policymakers can "recognize 'sound' science and make good decisions. He notes that there is often conflict in the scientific studies. He also states the important difference between science and policy: "Science is based primarily on facts gained from studies and technical investigations. Policy, on the other hand, tends to be value-based and incorporates the wishes of the public, industry and special interests" (Anderson 2000).

Significantly, Anderson (2000) states that the public is somewhat precautionary (though this is not the term that he uses): take action even if available evidence may not be conclusive. On the other hand, affected interests demand overwhelming evidence, scientific certainty, before they are willing to take action that will have adverse economic impacts on them. The policymaker's role is to balance these various interests.

Further, science is much, perhaps even more, a developmental process as a body of knowledge (Anderson 2000). Over time a consensus may appear, though even then there will be researchers who dissent from the consensus.

Given the limitations of science and the demands of politics, how can policymakers distinguish good research, good science, from bad research, or what is sometimes called "junk science" (see below)? Anderson provides a kind of checklist to distinguish between good and bad science.

Some characteristics of sound science are:

- Comes from a credible source.
- Uses documented methodologies that produce verifiable results and conclusions.
- Carefully chooses statements of cause and effect.
- Clearly measures data reliability.
- Goes through peer review and publication.

Some characteristics of questionable science are:
- Shows bias.
- Has vested interests.
- Ignores or overlooks variables.
- Uses an inadequate sample size or biased sample collection methods.
- Bases conclusions on personal or anecdotal evidence.
- Contains statements of certainty.
- Confuses correlation with cause and effect. (Anderson 2000)

Science can assist public health policies in three ways (Gordis 1997). The first is to evaluate the impacts of proposed policies. The second is to evaluate public health policies that have been implemented. The third way is to help future policymaking by providing predictive information for policies that may be enacted in the future.

Bero et al. (2001) presents an interesting comparative case study of public health policymakers. The topic is workplace smoking restrictions to prevent the harmful effects from passive smoking (people who ingest smoke though they do not smoke themselves). The unusual nature of the case study is that, according to the authors, most such restrictions are done by state legislatures. Washington state and Maryland enacted such restrictions through regulation.

The different venue for policymaking is important for investigating how science is used. Legislative hearings tend to be dominated by personal views of what legislators think is correct and political considerations (views of constituents, campaign contributors, and so forth). Regulatory hearings are, by law, much more structured. Regulators, they continue, combine the expert and political roles. They may have expertise in the area, they have staff with expertise, or they can call on the scientific community through advisory committees. The political element is never gone because legislatures and interest groups hold them accountable (Bero et al. 2001). Further, regulators are mandated "to review the scientific basis of regulation, propose draft regulations, accept written public commentary and hold hearings on proposed regulations, consider all significant and relevant information, and then revise and finalize the regulation in light of the commentary received from interested persons" (Bero et al. 2001).

Bero et al. (2001) conducted a content analysis of hearings in the two states. They found that there were more arguments made supporting the workplace smoking regulations than against. However, nonscientific arguments outweighed in number scientific-based arguments. Further, the authors found that the supporters of the regulations were more likely to use scientific arguments, focusing largely on the amount of studies and the scientific evidence behind their support. Opponents of the regulations on the other hand were more likely, when addressing the scientific evidence, to point out problems with specific pieces of scientific evidence, "attacking the reliability, validity, and quality of the evidence base" (Bero et al. 2001). Opponents tended to question whether there was in fact a consensus on the issue; they emphasized the uncertainty of the evidence.

Opponents of the passive smoking regulations (largely the tobacco industry) moved in two ways (Bero et al. 2001). One was to fund research that supports their view (see Yach and Bialous 2001). Often research was not peer reviewed or used lower standards of peer review than found in the science literature and thus tended to be of relatively low quality.

Second, opponents of the regulation tended to use science in a strategic fashion (Bero et al. 2001; see also Stone 2002). By this they mean that opponents would ignore the entire body of the scientific evidence and focus on narrow aspects of individual pieces of research. This deconstruction of the science combined with the industry-funded research is tended, again, to create uncertainty. Further, the most devastating statement by those opposed to the public health initiatives is to ask whether there is proof that exposure to some substance led to a specific disease in a specific person. Given the nature of public health research, with its emphasis on groups and individuals, the answer is clearly no. If that is the case then, industry interests will argue, there is no point to regulating or banning a product. Uncertainty is relied upon as a barrier to public health policies, at least until the evidence becomes so overwhelming that opposition breaks down, as has pretty much happened with tobacco and CFCs.

Bennett and DiLorenzo (2000) argue, as mentioned above, that from the 1960s on, public health has essentially lost its way and that public health science, regulatory science, has become politicized. In their chapter on the politicization of science, where they critique a number of fairly prominent pieces of research, they conclude:

> We do not argue that *all* public health research is politicized. Our point is that ever since the public health movement was transformed into a political movement on behalf of various liberal causes during the 1960s, there have been many political activists in the public health movement who have become much more adept at public relations than at health science and that they routinely make claims regarding their published research that are simply not tenable. Consequently, we have been subjected to an endless stream of questionable public health "scares," from Alar to dioxin, asbestos, secondhand smoke, and electromagnetic fields, to name but a few examples. The unfortunate consequence is that because of the actions of a segment of the public health movement, the public is now warranted in being extremely skeptical of *all* claims made by public health researchers. (Bennett and DiLorenzo 2000, 114–15)

Of course, it could be argued that Bennett and DiLorenzo's critique is also politically based. The above quote suggests that the problem is "liberal" causes. Elsewhere, they argue that Medicare and Medicaid are socialistic programs. Indeed, much of their book is permeated with a libertarian, public choice critique of government programs. At one point they argue that public health bureaucrats are primarily interested in expanding their budgets and the scope of their activities. At another point they complain that, although most of the truly public health problems have been dealt with, we continue to graduate students from public health programs.

Milloy (2001) is an adjunct scholar at the Cato Institute, a commentator on Fox News, and runs the website JunkScience.com. Milloy's use of the term junk science suggests that he does not support many public health decisions and their scientific basis. His book *Junk Science Judo* contains a litany of decisions that he disagrees with. The aim of the book is to help the reader detect junk science.

His arguments, some of which are well founded, echo those of Bennett and DiLorenzo and others. He begins his book by asserting that there is a hidden agenda behind junk science and that is to help particular interests. His strong points are his discussion of the scientific method and the need to rely on a body of research that has been verified and replicated and subject to peer review, rather than a single study. He engages in a methodological critique of studies supporting decisions about dietary fat, links between coffee consumption and colon cancer, and so forth. Further, his discourse is not all one-sided, sometimes pointing out the weakness in industry-sponsored studies. His view of science is that it is strictly objective and wants a high degree of reliability.

However, Milloy and others (such as Efron 1984) have a particular view of science that may not be completely accurate. Milloy, Efron, and others contend that the heavy reliance of public health–type research on statistics suffers from two related problems. First, those relying on such studies tend to see the statistical associations obtained as indicating causation. Milloy tells us repeatedly that correlation is not causation. Indeed, he goes further and states that "Statistics Aren't Science" (Milloy 2001, 83), the title of one of his chapters. Further, he argues that unless we can establish the causal mechanism, the statistical association by itself is not sufficient grounds for taking action.

Milloy takes this argument to its logical extreme. As we saw earlier in this chapter, perhaps the most important science underlying public health is epidemiology, the study of disease patterns in populations. Milloy contends that because statistical studies are not scientific and do not present causal mechanism, then epidemiology rests on a shaky basis.

Milloy, Efron, and others also assert that the results of animal bioassay tests are not transferable to humans. This is because rats and mice are not people (though new studies based on the genome project have found that such animals share a genetic heritage with people, about a 90 percent similarity). People react differently than specially bred rats. Further, to get any kind of response from exposure to a substance requires administering a much higher dose of the substance than humans would consume. Milloy and Bennett and DiLorenzo also take issue with this, arguing that the high doses themselves overwhelm the body, and disease or illness is the result.

While there is some merit in these and other arguments, there are some problems with Milloy's and others' analyses. Perhaps the most important of all is Milloy's conception of science. Milloy's depiction of science is accurate as far it goes. But his call for certainty and knowing the underlying biological mechanism is dated.

Consider the discussion above of John Snow, the cholera epidemic in England, and the Broad Street pump. Recall Richard Bates's commentary about Snow's research and how it might be looked at in modern days. His comments perfectly mirror Milloy, Bennett and DiLorenzo, and Efron. Snow did not know the biological mechanism and he made use of statistics. Milloy criticizes the precautionary principle that environmentalists tend to embrace. If we were to accept Milloy's view of science and the weaknesses of epidemiology, the Broad Street pump would not have been closed (understanding that the cholera epidemic had begun to wane before Snow's discoveries). The precautionary approach amidst the lack of important information was the right one to take.

Additionally, the view of science that Milloy and others take is based on the writings of Francis Bacon and Descartes. This is not an unreasonable principle, nor is the insistence on getting proof. But the scientific enterprise has evolved beyond this simplistic view of science. Science has become less deterministic and more probabilistic (Rushefsky 1986).

> In the seventeenth century, Newton and his laws of motion so dominated scientific thinking that natural law was implicitly defined as one that made deterministic, causal predictions. By the nineteenth century, however, scientific theories that offered probabilistic and statistical predictions were quite acceptable. As Jacob Bronowski has emphasized, this progress required a revolution in scientific thinking. As a result, in the nineteenth and twentieth centuries natural science made major advances with the discovery of several probabilistic laws: Mendel's laws of heredity; the kinetic theory of gases developed by Maxwell, Calusius, and Boltzmann; and the laws of radioactive decay developed by Rutherford and Soddy, and by von Schweidler.
>
> This shift from a deterministic to probabilistic paradigm culminated in the formulation of Heisenberg's uncertainty principle, which states the limits to accuracy with which the physical measurements of subatomic particles can be made. No matter how sophisticated the instrumentation, there are inherent uncertainties in the measurements of position and/or momentum. Much of the research now being done in the natural sciences would not be possible without replacement of deterministic thinking with probabilistic thinking. (Behn and Vaupel 1982, 189–90)

In his chapter on epidemiology, Milloy presents an unintended example of the high, if not impossible, standard he would require to reach a decision. The pharmaceutical company Eli Lilly performed a clinical trial of raloxifene, an artificial estrogen. The trial, where a group of women took the drug and another group did not (were given a placebo), showed that there were considerably fewer incidences of breast cancer in the experimental group (given raloxifene). Indeed, although the experimental group was about twice the size of the control group, there were less than half the number of breast cancer occurrences in the experimental than in the control group.

Milloy correctly points out that the clinical trial did not establish a causal relationship because it did not eliminate other possible factors. But he also notes the most important flaw in such studies: "Why doesn't this study prove that raloxifene reduces breast cancer risk? *The researchers did not show that raloxifene actually prevented any breast cancers that would otherwise have occurred*" (Milloy 2001, 86, emphasis added).

This is virtually an impossible standard. Prove that something that would have occurred did not because of an intervention. This cannot be done. We cannot pick out the people likely to get breast cancer unless we can identify the specific gene or genes related to breast cancer (which in itself is a statistical statement). If we could establish the genetic linkage to the illness and we knew that every woman with the gene would get breast cancer, then perhaps we could do the kind of clinical trial demanded by Milloy. But as we are beginning to learn, having the genetic predisposition does not guarantee the appearance of the illness, because not all women with the "bad" gene or genes would get the disease. By Milloy's standards, under the best possible conditions, we could never provide sufficient scientific evidence that would permit a regulatory decision (in this case, permission to market the medicine).

For Milloy, the appropriate conclusion is to assert that epidemiology is not a science, and therefore decisions based on epidemiology are not justifiable. In addition, studies on animals, bioassays, that indicate possible carcinogenicity of a substance, are also junk science. This is because animals are not people, the test animals are given much higher doses than humans are exposed to, and the animal models are bred to be prone to cancer. So there is no point in doing any of this type of research or basing decisions on it.

While Milloy does not seem to have the same obvious political agenda as Bennett and Di Lorenzo, there are hints of it. In a chapter entitled "Know Your Friends," Milloy lists a number of organizations, websites, and people that readers can go to. While there is a bit of balance in the list, such as the Consumer Federation of America, Milloy's list includes the "usual suspects" of groups and people who oppose a stronger government role in this area: the American Council on Science and Health (which Milloy [2001, 177] describes as "a consumer education consortium"), the Competitive Enterprise Institute, and writers with the Cato, Hoover, and Hudson Institutes.

Milloy's work should not be simply dismissed because of the impossible standards set. He does make good points, for example about looking for measures of statistical significance. But his undermining of the entire public health enterprise suggests caution.

A third work criticizing the scientific basis for public health research is by Morrone and Lohner (2002). This is a much more balanced work than the previous two. But it takes an interesting twist on the issue of the validity of public health decisions. Their basic thesis is captured in the title: *Sound Science, Junk Policy*. It is not the science that is bad, but the judgments made by policymakers.

Their opening chapter on the nature of science is well worth reading. They begin by noting that "Junk science does not exist, because if science is not sound, it is not science" (Morrone and Lohner 2002, 1). They also point out that decisionmakers often have a fanciful view of what science can provide them. Morrone and Lohner say that decisionmakers (politicians and regulators) can solve policy disputes, can provide the right answers. But science and scientists often can only give uncertain, gray answers rather than black and white, yes-or-no answers. The scientific process takes time, with fits and starts, and is often subject to criticism. But Morrone and Lohner note that the media play up the results of single studies (say on diet), followed by stories of a subsequent, contradictory study. The media becomes confused, policymakers are confused, and the public who rely on the media for information become confused.

Significantly, Morrone and Lohner provide a useful corrective to writers such as Milloy and Efron. Recall that Milloy noted that statistics is not science and correlation is not causation. Consider the following quote from Morrone and Lohner (2002, emphasis added):

> The interpretation of scientific studies is another critical element of sound science. A good scientist never says something like, "Cigarettes cause lung cancer." Rather, the statement would be phrased, "There is evidence to suggest a significant relationship between cigarette smoking and lung cancer." This is an important distinction, and it helps society weed out questionable science and scientific studies. These seemingly ambiguous statements also frustrate society, in particular decision-makers and the courts, who are not satisfied with "significant relationships." The fact that good scientists will not make the cause-effect statement also *creates a loophole for critics of the studies in question to condemn science as unsound because there is not a definitive link*. This frustrates good scientists because one important characteristic of sound science is ultimately used against them to criticize their work.

Morrone's and Lohner's basic point is that much of the regulatory decisions, focusing primarily on environmental health issues, is not based on sound science, but politics. This leads them to a discussion of the regulatory process and interest groups (the term they actually use is nongovernmental organizations) or stakeholders. They distinguish between environmental and economic development interests. As examples of types of stakeholders, they mention think tanks, activist groups, and focused-interest groups. They then proceed to discuss examples of groups in each category. With the one exception of the Competitive Enterprise Institute, all of the groups mentioned are environmental groups. The problem is that these and other actors see the "acceptability" of the policy as the most important criteria rather than science. And the acceptability is societally determined (Morrone and Lohner 2002, 39).

Near the end of the book, they approach the question of what the true nature of public health problems is. To them, after a survey of domestic and global health problems, the major problems are ones of individual lifestyle. Thus public health policies that would influence lifestyle would be most appropriate. Education becomes an important public health policy tool. They write: "All of the approaches previously proposed have a common thread; they generally shift environmental policies from the collective population to the individual. Individual citizens would be responsible for controlling population, stopping nonpoint source pollution, driving less, consuming less, and taking better care of themselves. This is the key to effective policies—motivating individual citizens to participate in the protection of the environment (Morrone and Lohner 2002, 145).

Following the advice of Efron, Bennett and DiLorenzo, Milloy, and Morrone and Lohner would lead to a drastic diminution of the enterprise of public health and public health policies. So how do we address this?

First, we need to recognize that some of the arguments made by these critics, especially Milloy and Morrone and Lohner, have validity. But Efron, Bennet and Dilorenzo, and Milloy have a naive view of science. The assertion that the best available science should underlie public health decisions is hard to dispute. However, the nature of the scientific enterprise means that the call for certainty can never be met. Further, and here Morrone and Lohner make some good points, political demands often call for decisions to be made in the absence of complete certainty. The problem is that economic interests will be affected, and those interests will fight efforts that adversely affect them.

The case of smoking is illuminating here, almost a paradigm of these types of science-based disputes. One of the earliest studies of the linkage between smoking and lung cancer came in 1900, when the statistical linkage was made (remember, Milloy tells us that statistics is not science and correlation is not causation) (Report of the Advisory Committee to the Surgeon General 1964). In 1930, illness and death related to smoking was noted. The 1964 report noted that many of the chemical substances within tobacco were tested in animals (the bioassays that Milloy decries). For obvious reasons, human testing was not done. The Advisory Committee (1964) writes: "Therefore, the main evidence of the effects of smoking and other uses of tobacco upon the health of human beings has been secured through clinical and pathological observations of conditions occurring in men, women and children in the course of their lives and by the application of epidemiological and statistical methods by which a vast array of information has been assembled and analyzed" (Report of the Advisory Committee to the Surgeon General 1964, 19).

The advisory committee mentions two types of epidemiological studies, retrospective and prospective, that have been used. Together the bioassays and epidemiological studies convinced a number of health societies worldwide of the adverse health effects of smoking. The first cigarette package warnings were mandated in 1964. Thus the type of evidence used to require a warning label was precisely the type of evidence that Milloy and Efron would reject. Milloy's current concern is the Environmental Protection Agency (EPA) labeling secondary or passive smoking a health danger.

Over time, the case that smoking was hazardous to the user's health became significantly stronger. Eventually, advances in biology and chemistry were able to show the mechanism by which tobacco product constituents cause cancer as well as the addictive properties of nicotine.

Further, there is evidence that smoking adversely affects pregnancy and not just while a woman is pregnant, but also if the woman smokes before getting pregnant. The following is a list of such health problems: "Fertility problems; Low birthweight; Foetal, neonatal and perinatal mortality; Sudden Infant Death Syndrome; Ectopic pregnancy; and Spontaneous abortion" (Hacker 1998).

As controversial as some of the issues related to science and public health are, the biggest controversy has been over tobacco and health. The tobacco industry claimed for a long time that there was no scientific basis for regulating the use of tobacco. Indeed, as we now know, the tobacco industry in 1993 began to declare studies by the EPA and other agencies as junk science. Philip Morris worked with other industries that were or might be subject to such regulation to undermine the scientific basis of public health policy (see Org and Glantz 2001).

Others pointed to a large body of evidence that supported the health impacts of tobacco (for a summary, see the various reports of the surgeon general of the United States). Health advocates accused the tobacco industry of promoting studies that were favorable to them and hiding studies that were unfavorable. A considerable amount of litigation against the tobacco industry by smokers who had lung cancer almost always went down to defeat.

This changed in the mid-1990s thanks largely to one man, Jeffrey Wigand. Wigand went to work for the tobacco company Brown & Williamson in 1988 as vice president for research and development (Kleiner 2000). Wigand knew that tobacco was addictive and that at least one of the chemicals in tobacco smoke was implicated as a carcinogen, particularly one that smelled good. Wigand said that he wanted to have the additive taken out, but Brown & Williamson refused. Wigand was fired in 1993. In 1994, Wigand was approached by a producer for the CBS newsmagazine show *60 Minutes*. He agreed to tell his story, including how Brown & Williamson manipulated scientific evidence. The story was taped, but pressure applied by Brown and Williamson on CBS led them to show a censored version. This story eventually got out and Wigand was able to tell his story fully (Kleiner 2000), including testifying in court trials. A movie was made of this story, *The Insider*, with Russell Crowe as Wigand.

Additionally, the various suits in state courts eventually produced what became known as the Brown & Williamson papers (Hurt and Robertson 1998). The papers, which involve the entire tobacco industry, show that the industry knew of the addictive feature of nicotine and that tobacco causes illnesses, especially lung cancer, as far back as the 1950s. The industry engaged in a concerted effort to question the validity of the mounting scientific evidence (Hurt and Robertson 1998; see also Glantz et al. 1996).

Indeed, this is the other end of the debate over scientific evidence and public health. Economic interests try to manipulate the science and public opinion about the possible dangers of environmental pollution (Davis 2002; see also Rampton and Stauber 2001). In the debate over the health effects of asbestos, over sixty scientific articles had been published by 1960. Of the sixty-three articles, eleven were funded or sponsored by industry interests (Rampton and Stauber 2001). "The 11 industry studies were unanimous in denying that asbestos caused lung cancer and minimizing the seriousness of asbestosis—a position diametrically opposite to the conclusions reached in the nonindustry [medical school and hospital] studies" (Rampton and Stauber 2001, 86).

Another example is the issue of environmental exposures to lead and how long and difficult it was to get acceptance of the problem because of industry denial and opposition (Davis 2002; Rampton and Stauber 2001). The tobacco (and other) industry influences the publication process by hiring scientists to write articles favoring their viewpoint (Rampton and Stauber 2001). Sometimes articles or reviews fail to fully acknowledge the affiliation of the authors. A review of an environmental book in the *New England Journal of Medicine* by a doctor did not indicate that the reviewer worked for W.R. Grace, a chemical manufacturer (Rampton and Stauber 2001).

The tobacco industry funds institutes and scientists, and their studies supported the industry position (Yach and Bialous 2001). One example is John D. Graham, who was director of the Harvard Center for Risk Analysis. The center received money from Philip Morris and other tobacco companies and has done work on passive smoking. In 2001, Graham was nominated to head the Office of Information and Regulatory Affairs (OIRA). This office, within the Office of Management and Budget, oversees the writing of regulations by agencies such as EPA and FDA. The OIRA website describes Dr. Graham as follows:

John D. Graham, Administrator
OMB's Office of Information and Regulatory Affairs

John D. Graham, PhD, is serving for President Bush as Administrator, Office of Information and Regulatory Affairs, Office of Management and Budget. His responsibilities include coordination of regulatory review, paperwork reduction, statistical policy and information policy in the Federal government.

Prior to joining the Bush Administration, Dr. Graham founded and led the Harvard Center for Risk Analysis from 1990 to 2001. Dr. Graham is on leave from the faculty of the Harvard School of Public Health, where he taught graduate students the methods of risk analysis and cost-benefit analysis.

Dr. Graham earned his BA from Wake Forest University, his MA from Duke University and his Ph.D. from Carnegie-Mellon University. He served as a pre-doctoral fellow at the Brookings Institution and as a post-doctoral fellow at the Harvard School of Public Health. Dr. Graham has written seven books and more than 100 scientific articles and is best known for his scholarship on automotive safety and environmental policy. He was born and raised in Pittsburgh, Pennsylvania and is an avid golfer and bridge player. (Office of Management and Budget n.d.)

Not surprisingly, nowhere in this biography is there a mention of the connection between the center Graham directed and the tobacco company.

Does affiliation matter? In an interesting study conducted in the 1980s, Lynn (1983) found that scientists do have ideological perspectives and that they are linked to job affiliation. Those working in industry were more likely to accept the industry view on science-based issues while those working for government were more likely to accept a government view. Those in academia tended to be more in the middle. There appears to be a relationship between the funding of research and the outcome of that research (Rampton and Stauber 2001). Consider the following quote:

In 1996, journalists Dan Fagin and Marianne Lavelle reviewed recent studies published in major scientific journals regarding the safety of four chemicals: the herbicides alachlor and atrazine, formaldehyde, and perchlorethylene, the carcinogenic solvent used for dry-cleaning clothes. When non-industry scientists did the studies, 60 percent returned results *unfavorable* to the chemicals involved, whereas industry-funded scientists came back with *favorable* results 74 percent of the time. (Rampton and Stauber 2001, 219)

Difficulties and Complexities of Risk Assessment

Many of the issues and complexities discussed above can be found in risk assessment. Many of the decisions that agencies such as the Food and Drug Administration and the Environmental Protection Agency make are based on risk assessments. Even decisions about the threats raised by bioterrorism (see chapter 8) are ultimately based on risk assessment.

Let us begin by defining what is meant by risk assessment and then describing the process. For definitional purposes, we use the 1983 report of the National Academy of Sciences, *Risk Assessment in the Federal Government* (Commission on Life Sciences 1983). The report defines risk assessment as "the characterization of the potential adverse health effects of human exposures to environmental hazards" (Commission on Life Sciences 1983, 18). A broader term is risk management, defined as "the process of evaluating alternative regulatory actions and selecting among them" (Commission on Life Sciences 1983, 18).

There are four steps to risk assessment, as indicated in Figure 5.1 (Environmental Protection Agency 1991; Commission on Life Sciences 1983; Schierow 1994). The first phase is hazard identification. At this stage, some environmental substance is identified as a possible threat to human health. This has generally meant chemicals but can also refer to tobacco smoke (both first and secondhand) and biological agents (such as smallpox or anthrax). The basis for such a characterization is generally animal tests (bioassays) and epidemiological studies.

The second phase is exposure assessment. Some measure of how many people are exposed to the substance and how great the exposure is is important because a highly toxic substance may not pose a threat to human health if there is little or no exposure to it. Epidemiological studies are important here.

The third step focuses on the assessment of doses and responses. While there are practical difficulties in all these steps (see Rushefsky 1986), dose-response assessment may be the most problematic. Epidemiological studies generally do not find sufficient gradations of exposure to a substance, so bioassays become increasingly important. The animal models are given different doses and then a dose-response curve is extrapolated from the data. But there are generally only a few data points and there is controversy over the shape of the dose-response curve. For example, some argue that there is no threshold of exposure to a substance. That is, there is no safe level of exposure. Others argue that such thresholds do exist (see Rushefsky 1986; Schierow 1994).

Figure 5.1   **The Four-Step Risk Assessment Process**

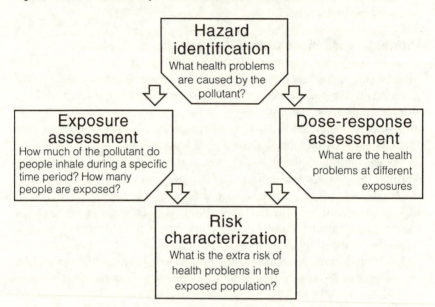

Source: Environmental Protection Agency (1991).

The fourth step is risk characterization. Based on the previous steps, the analyst will state what the health risk to the population is from exposure to the substance. Of course, the final decision on whether to ban a substance, limit or regulate its use, or do nothing is up to a regulatory agency leadership.

There is another important step in this process, risk communication (Agency for Toxic Substances and Disease Registry n.d.; see also Gray and Ropeik 2002). Risk communication is the process of informing the public about the nature and extent of some threat to human health. For example, if a regulatory agency decides that limiting exposure to a substance is necessary, it should state what the limits are and the possible threats. One important example of risk communications are the warnings on cigarette packs. The warnings state that smoking can lead to various health problems, and then the decision about smoking is left to the individual.

Another example of risk communication, though not necessarily a good one, came in February 2003. Tom Ridge, secretary of the new Department of Homeland Security (DHS), issued a code orange alert of the threat of a possible attack against the United States (both home and abroad). The communication suggested that the population buy supplies of food and water sufficient for three days and duct tape and plastic sheeting to seal off windows. The threat created a certain amount of panic as stores were stripped of their stocks of duct tape and plastic sheeting. The department and the Bush administration were criticized for unduly creating a disturbance. Some have argued that the threats from chemical and biological warfare have been greatly overstated (Easterbrook 2003).

Risk perception is an important component of risk management policy.[5] People act on their perceptions, even if not grounded in good data. The general public seems to be concerned particularly about risks that are unknown, uncontrollable, and dreaded (Gray and Ropeik 2002; Rushefsky 1989 [and the literature cited therein]; and Schneider 2000). Gray and Ropeik argue that the Bush administration, especially Attorney General John Ashcroft, unduly frightened the public by overemphasizing risks (Gray and Ropeik 2002).

> However, Ashcroft, knowing that how he handled the announcement [of the arrest in June 2002 of a suspected terrorist who had possible plans for setting off a radiological device] could make people either more or less afraid, dramatically described dirty bombs as weapons of mass destruction, when in fact such devices are really only dangerous in the immediate vicinity of their detonation, as nearly every scientist and most press reports said the next day. When he was contradicted by the scientific community, his trust level almost certainly fell in the eyes of some. And among those who heard only his description of dirty bombs, he raised public fear of these weapons such that should a device go off in the future, it may well be harder for the public to keep their fears in perspective. (Gray and Ropeik 2002, 113)

Of course, risk assessment and related activities are also open to the same charge of unduly scaring the public. This is the burden of Milloy's (2001) work. If one accepts the criticisms that Milloy makes, risk assessment is an impossible project, should not be done, and certainly should not be believed or relied upon. Nevertheless, government agencies continue to rely on risk assessments and related aspects of regulatory science in making their decisions.

Scientific Evidence and Morality Politics

If the scientific basis for public health decisions, what we have called regulatory science, is questioned in some of the issues considered above, consider what might be called "morality politics." These are policy issues that directly address closely held values. Scientific evidence that addresses issues of morality politics become even more permeated with politics and value issues than the kinds of issues discussed in the previous section.

What kinds of public health issues involve morality politics? Examples of such issues include sex education, AIDS prevention, needle-exchange programs, and the impact of abortions. Politically, the United States has often been described as being in a culture war (Hunter 1991; Lindaman and Haider-Markel 2002; Walsh 2001). The basic idea behind the culture war thesis is that polarizing disagreement exists over certain public policy issues that are fundamentally about values (for a critique of the culture wars thesis, see Fiorina, Pope, and Abrams 2004; Mouw and Sobel 2001). From our standpoint, the culture wars come into play when values, generally religious and politically based, override scientific evidence. Here we look at two examples.

The first example is needle exchange. An important path of transmission of the human immunodeficiency virus (HIV) is through multiple uses of needles employed in intravenous drug use, responsible for about one-third of new cases in the United States ("Syringe Exchange Proves Effective" 2002). And someone who contracts HIV can transmit it to other people through sexual contact. Therefore, it would stand to reason that there are several ways to prevent the spread of HIV and its transition to AIDS (acquired immunodeficiency syndrome). One way is to educate the public on safe sex (that is, the use of condoms). Another way is encourage the disposal of needles used to inject drugs. Both methods have scientific backing but also face political resistance from some segments of society. Most of those involved in such programs are illegal drug users.

As of June 2000, there were 154 such programs in the United States, most of them located in the Western portion of the country ("Needle-Exchange Programs Are Slowly . . ." 2002). The federal government has authority under 1998 legislation to fund such programs, assuming the evidence supports the efficacy of the program. In addition, a number of states conduct such programs (Maginnis 2000).

According to much of the research, needle exchange programs are effective in reducing the spread of HIV. For example, according to a 2002 study, intravenous drug users participating in a needle exchange program were only one-sixth as likely to contract HIV as users who did not participate in such programs ("Syringe Exchange Proves Effective" 2002).

There are two arguments made against such programs. One argument is that the data behind such studies is faulty. For example, the Family Research Council (FRC) argues that participants in needle exchange program studies are not randomly assigned to the experiments (needle exchange) and control group. Thus, there may be some important systematic differences among the two groups that account for the finding. Further, the FRC argues that those in needle exchange programs actually had higher rates of contracting HIV than those who did not. Finally, FRC cites data that those participating in needle exchange programs continued to share needles (Maginnis 2000).

Here one can see the interplay of science and ideology/values. To put it in terms that we have discussed above, there appears to be a correlation between participation in the program and HIV infection. The issue of causation, however, is more problematic. One interpretation of the data is that the programs lead to higher HIV infections. This is the stance of groups such as the Family Research Council. Another explanation for the correlation is that those participating in needle exchange programs were already at a much higher risk of contracting AIDS. The former interpretation has been used to oppose such programs (Schecter 2002).

There is a moral aspect to the opposition to needle exchange programs as well. That opposition is one that strongly opposes the use of illegal drugs and argues that needle exchange programs condone if not encourage drug use. Indeed, one should look at many of the criticisms of science-based policy (regulatory science) as a surrogate battle over the values that underlie the policy.

Consider another public health issue that involves morality: sex education. There are a number of reasons why public education should include sex education. First, there is the general view that appropriate and accurate knowledge leads to the kinds of behaviors that society approves of. While societal views have changed on out-of-wedlock, especially teen, births, the stigma is not nearly as great as it used to be,[6] and society in general would like to see a decrease in teenage sex and teenage parenting. Sex education is one way to do this.

Such a view by itself creates controversy. Sex education could be provided within the family or by the person's religious group. Should the public sector be involved?

And if the public sector is involved, then what should be the nature of the curriculum? Some groups support the idea of abstinence-only education. That is, sex education should teach that sex outside of marriage is wrong. One place where this controversy comes in is welfare reform. When Congress reformed the welfare system in 1996, it included grants to states to help them reduce teenage pregnancy. The George W. Bush administration sought funds for abstinence-only education. Groups such as the Family Research Council support this proposal. Groups such as Planned Parenthood oppose it (Wetzstein 2002). Planned Parenthood believes that teaching about the use of contraceptives is also important. But groups such as the Family Research Council argue that teaching about contraception is essentially condoning teenage sex.

There are two scientific questions related to the issue of sex education. First, how effective is abstinence-only education? The second question is, how effective are other programs? It should come as no surprise that groups that believe in abstinence-only education assert that it is effective and other programs do not work. Groups that believe in the other programs take the opposite position.

Tamara Kreinin (2002), president of the Sexuality Information and Education Council of the United States (SIECUS), argues that there are no studies supporting the effectiveness of abstinence education and that there are studies, evaluations, supporting the effectiveness of programs that focus on both abstinence and contraception.

The George W. Bush administration has taken the conservative stand and made changes in its website. For example, the CDC website used to say that teaching about contraceptives, particularly condoms, did not lead to increased sexual activity. Similarly, where the National Cancer Institute website had a statement that there was no relationship between abortion and breast cancer, that had been changed to read that the evidence is inconclusive (Clymer 2002).

The impact of the abortion debate can be seen even in scientific conferences. In February 2003 the National Cancer Institute held a conference looking at the relationship between abortion and breast cancer. Pro-choice groups argue that there is sufficient scientific evidence against the hypothesis that women who had abortions had a higher risk of breast cancer than women who did not have an abortion. A 1997 Danish study found no such relationship, and this report is considered to be of extremely high quality. The American Cancer Society also maintains that there is no relationship between breast cancer and abortion (Zifner 2003). A recent study did indeed establish that there was no linkage between breast cancer and abortion (Altman 2004).

The Politics of Science and Public Health

"Using science to inform public action to improve public health has been the critical foundation to what is now the statutory base for public health" (Fielding et al. 2002, 23). Or, "Get your facts first, and then you can distort them as much as you please" (Mark Twain, quoted in Faigman 1999, 172). Public health policy rests on a foundation of scientific developments. The science is both the body of knowledge that has accumulated over a period of time and the process by which science operates. Conflicts over public health policy are often seen at the level of the quality (and, to some extent, the quantity) of the evidence. Battles over science are effectively surrogates for battles over policy decisions that affect important societal values and interests.

Regulatory agencies have available to them technical experts within their agency and also make use of outside experts through scientific advisory boards (such as EPA and FDA) and through more informal scientific advisory committees. Regulated interests or stakeholders (Faigman 1999) also have experts available to them. In protecting their interests, stakeholders have distorted the scientific basis of public health decisions. This is most apparent in the case of the tobacco industry. But sometimes administrations can shape evidence to suit their values.

This çan be seen in the case of the Reagan administration, which sought to shape guidelines concerning the determination of whether chemical substances caused cancer (see Rushefsky 1986; see also Rushefsky 1984). This may also be the case for the George W. Bush administration.

The administration has suggested that agencies need to do more analysis focusing on risks, benefits, and costs (Skrzycki 2003). This is the latest stage in attempts by presidents, going back to the Carter administration (Rushefsky 1986) to control the writing of regulations (see Nathan 1983; Teifer 1994). The concern that some have about the use of science by the Bush administration can be seen in two events. In February 2003 the Association of Reproductive Health Professionals sent a petition to the Department of Health and Human Services asking the department to not let religious and ideological views color its decisions. The petition, "Preserving Core Values in Science," was signed by over twenty groups (most involved with reproductive issues). The petition lists several incidents by the Bush administration suggesting that values and interests were prevailing over scientific evidence.[7]

For example, members of scientific advisory committees are being asked questions that relate to their beliefs on issues such as the death penalty and their vote in the 2000 presidential election rather than on their scientific credentials (Zitner 2002). Consider the following:

> On Dec. 10 [2002], the Food and Drug Administration rejected a nominee for an advisory board who is known for his support of human cloning in medical research.
>
> Also recently, HHS Secretary Tommy G. Thompson's staff rejected a nominee to a board of the National Institute for Occupational Safety and Health who supports federal rules to curtail repetitive stress injuries in the workplace.
>
> The nominees had been chosen by officials within the FDA and occupational health agency but were then rejected by more senior officials. No specific reasons were given, but Bush opposes human cloning and last year signed a rollback of Clinton-era rules designed to limit repetitive stress injuries.

Those rejections followed incidents this fall in which public health advocates and Democratic lawmakers alleged that the administration had placed people sympathetic to industry on two panels at the Centers for Disease Control and Prevention. One panel advises CDC officials on the prevention of lead poisoning in children. The other makes recommendations on issues ranging from environmental toxins to bioterrorism preparations. (Zitner 2002; see also Weiss 2003)

Apart from pressure that interests, stakeholders, may place on the quality of the science, industry also funds a considerable amount of scientific research. That funding, as in the tobacco case, can distort findings. In other cases it may mean that industry-funded studies of pharmaceuticals often find results that favor the company (see the discussion in "Funding Can Taint Findings [Editorial]" 2003).

Of course, much of the problem is due to the uncertainty that marks regulatory science in the public health area. The more uncertainty, the more other considerations, such as values and interests, play a role. The uncertainty allows the "massaging" of data (Faigman 1999, 178). Nor are the risks that agencies focus on always the most important (Sunstein 2002). The costs and benefits of regulations should be considered in an unbiased manner. There is a tendency to focus on the more publicized risks and ignore the more important ones. Comparative risk assessment, as Morrone and Lohner (2002) argue, can help us focus on what is most risky (see also Environmental Protection Agency 1987). At the same time, we must not let interests undermine an entire field (epidemiology) to protect those interests.

Science has something of an exalted role in our society. Having the science on your side is almost as good as having God on your side. That makes the scientific basis of public health the target of disputes. But if we recall the story of John Snow and the Broad Street Pump, we can learn the appropriate use of science in policymaking.

Notes

1. For a discussion of the early years of AIDS research, see Shilts (1987).

2. This is mentioned in some detail because one of the coauthors (Rushefsky) participated in the experiment. He was in the control (placebo) group, but did not contract polio.

3. Part of the reason that the causal connection was not known is that the tobacco industry discouraged such research or hid it.

4. For a discussion of program theory, see Pressman and Wildavsky 1984, Thompson 1981, and Weiss 1972.

5. For a discussion of the origins of the risk perception literature, see Rushefsky 1989.

6. For example, if a high school girl became pregnant, she had to leave school. The

problem with this approach is that the teenager often never returned to school, and high school dropouts do not do well in the job market. Now there are programs that allow teenage moms to stay in school, including providing day care for the babies.

7. There have also been accusations about the distortion or hiding of evidence by the Bush administration in areas other than public health. See Noah (2004).

Study Questions

1. The underlying issue of this chapter is the relationship of science and politics. To what extent should science be the basis for making public health policy decisions? What are some of the constraints in doing this? To what extent should political considerations play a role?
2. Public health policy relies on certain fundamental sciences such as epidemiology as the basis for making decisions. What are the strengths and weaknesses of using epidemiology for making public health policy decisions?
3. How much evidence is necessary before a public health policy decision should be made? Does the answer matter when the problem is an acute one, such as an epidemic, or a more chronic one, such as exposure to mercury in fish?
4. Is the precautionary principle a good basis for making public health policy decisions? If not, what criteria or principles would you use?
5. Where do you stand on the idea of junk science? Do those who push this idea have a valid point or is junk science merely a means to prevent regulation of industry groups?
6. Is public health research politicized? If so, what changes should be made to make it less politicized?

CHAPTER 6

The Politics of Genetics and Public Health

In addition to the potential for discrimination, mandatory genetic regulation of Tourette's threatens the very promises of personal autonomy, freedom, and responsibility guaranteed in a democratic society. If society believes that genetics is a reliable indicator of behavior and treats individuals differently according to their genetic predispositions, then the issue of personal responsibility is eradicated. Criminal defendants may soon be able to introduce evidence showing a deficiency of serotonin in their brains, biologically predisposing them toward violent behavior, which could be used to mitigate punishment. (Yen 2003, 53)

The closest to an accepted definition of public health was provided by the Institute of Medicine (IOM): "what we as a society do collectively to assure the conditions in which people can be healthy" (Institute of Medicine 1988, 1). The IOM also described the three core functions of public health as assessment, policy development, and assurance. Within those core functions are ten essential services (Table 6.1).

Schneider (2000, 6) elaborates on this definition. Public health seeks to find out what health problems exist, why they exist, and then find remedies for them. Diagnosing problems is essentially the assessment function. The treatment plan is equivalent to policy development. Actually delivering the treatment is the assurance function.

Given these definitions and core functions, where does genetics fit in? It is becoming increasingly clear that much, though not all, human disease has a genetic component. It is also clear that genetic traits are found in populations and passed to subsequent generations.

Many of the major advances in human health in the nineteenth and twentieth centuries were based on public health interventions. These include improved public sanitation, immunizations, and increased safety of the food supply. The next major public health advances in the twenty-first century

Table 6.1

The Ten Essential Public Health Services

Assessment
1. Monitor health status to identify community health problems
2. Diagnose and investigate health problems and health hazards in the community

Policy development
3. Inform, educate, and empower people about health issues
4. Mobilize community partnerships to identify and solve health problems
5. Develop policies and plans that support individual and community health efforts

Assurance
6. Enforce laws and regulations that protect health and ensure safety
7. Link people to needed personal health services and assure the provision of health care when otherwise unavailable
8. Assure a competent public health and personal health care workforce
9. Evaluate effectiveness, accessibility, and the quality of personal and population-based health services

Serving all functions
10. Research for new insights and innovative solutions to health problems

Source: Institute of Medicine (2003, 99).

will be related to advances in the genetic sciences. It is to this subject that we now turn.

Developments in Genetic Science

The idea that characteristics of humans are inherited goes back to ancient Greece and the writings of Plato, Aristotle, and Hippocrates (Omenn 2000). Over the centuries, animal husbandry was based on the idea that traits could be handed down to subsequent generations. Farmers bred animals for their most desirable traits. However, the importance of the biological sciences to agriculture was unappreciated for most of this time.

The invention of the microscope and the discovery of sperm by van Leeuwenhoek in the 1600s then led to reports about medical conditions that could be inherited. An 1814 book by Joseph Adams presaged the twentieth and twenty-first-century focus on genetic counseling (Omenn 2000).

Work by Francis Galton strongly suggested the role of inheritance and, unfortunately, an emphasis on eugenics to rid the population of undesirable traits. At the same time, the German monk Gregor Mendel had been work-ing on a series of experiments that clearly showed that physical traits in peas were inherited (Cooper 2001; Omenn 2000; Patel and Rushefsky 2002). Mendel's work laid the foundation for the genetic sciences, and the laws of Mendelian genetics have formed the basis for much research. The first time the linkage between genes and specific diseases was made was in a 1902 paper by Sir Archibald Garrod (Omenn 2000). Research in genetics contin-ued in the twentieth century. By 1944, two scientists demonstrated that DNA was the hereditary material.

The biggest scientific breakthrough came in 1954. Watson and Crick (and Rosalind Franklin) suggested a model for DNA, the double helix. This be-came the basis for further genetic research. DNA itself was discovered in 1957 and the structure of DNA, made up of a sequence of four proteins, was discovered two years later (Patel and Rushefsky 2002). The implications of genetic research were profound and important: genetic research in fruit flies, viruses, and bacteria progressively revealed a universal molecular basis for human genetics and for evolution (Omenn 2000, 29).

The Human Genome Project

The genome is essentially the structure of DNA. It is the specific sequence of the four proteins that make up the DNA of difference species. Genomic research attempts to discover this structure in various species.

For humans the effort began in 1988 (Fink and Collins 2000; National Human Genome Research Institute n.d.; Patel and Rushefsky 2002). The Human Genome Project (HGP) began in 1988 with funding by the National Institutes of Health and other groups and eventually the U.S. Department of Energy. The original goal of the project was to map out the human genome by 2005, an effort that would cost about $3 billion (Patel and Rushefsky 2002). In 1998 a private corporation, Celera, announced that it would try to map out the human genome before the publicly funded group would, and the race was on. In 2000, Celera and the publicly funded groups announced to great fanfare that they had successfully completed the mission. The an-nouncement was a bit premature, though it created a media sensation. The actual completion of the mapping occurred in 2003 (National Human Ge-nome Research Institute n.d.).

The importance of genetic research and the human genome project to medicine, biology, and public health was obvious. Scientists would be able to link human disorders to genetic makeup. The mapping of the human genome would then facilitate finding the specific gene or genes respon-sible for the disorder. Then, in the most ambitious part of the entire prize, doctors would be able to repair or otherwise disable the accused genes. Disorders might be prevented, alleviated, retarded, or reversed. The potential is enormous.[1]

The genetics revolution created new fields of study. The overriding name for these new fields of study is **public health genetics**, defined as "the application of advances in genetics and molecular biotechnology to improve public health and prevent disease" (Khoury, Burke, and Thomson 2000b, 5). A related term is **community genetics**, combining the community and science aspects of genetics with the service portion involving public sector interventions (Khoury, Burke, and Thomson 2000b).

As was explained in chapter 5, the major science underlying the field of public health is epidemiology. Epidemiology is the study of disease patterns in populations, both human and animal (and sometimes the combination of both).[2] If scientists can establish a genetic basis or at least a genetic linkage to disease, then this becomes critical information in preventing disease in human populations and in the surveillance function. This then leads to the establishment of the field known as **genetic epidemiology**. The obvious definition is examining the role of genetics in diseases in human populations (Khoury, Burke, and Thomson 2000b, 9; Watkins and Jaako 2000). The purpose of genetic epidemiology is to examine whether genetics has a role in a particular disease and what the extent of that role is (Watkins and Jaako 2000). Genetics may play no role. There may be a single gene responsible for the disease. A number of genes may interact to produce a disease. And there is interaction between genetic makeup and environmental influences (Watkins and Jaako 2000).

A related field is **molecular epidemiology**. This brings together a number of different fields, such as statistics and medicine, to examine the interaction of environmental and genetic factors at the molecular level to human diseases (Dorman and Mattison 2000).

Yet another related new scientific field connects directly to the human genome project. This is **human genome epidemiology**, which focuses on the genetic variations and their impact on human disease (Khoury, Burke, and Thomson 2000b).

At least six other fields arise from genetic research and are encompassed in public health genetics. One such field is **ecogenetics** (Omenn 2000). This is a field that looks at variations in susceptibility to environmental insults (such as those discussed in chapter 8) and seeks a genetic explanation. Some subsections of the population may be genetically predisposed to the harmful effects of exposure to specific substances.[3] Testing for genetic susceptibility is known as **genetic toxicology** (Omenn 2000).

A controversial area of study is **behavioral genetics**, which searches for genetic sources of unhealthy behaviors such as smoking and other addictions (Omenn 2000). There may also be genetic components to mental illnesses, such as depression, as well.

Two new fields relate genetics to information (Austin and Peyser 2000). **Statistical genetics** has proven particularly useful in the human genome project. Statistics is an important component of epidemiology and will be crucial in examining the interaction of genetic and environmental factors as well as discerning single-gene disorders and multiple-gene disorders. **Bioinformatics** combines advances in computer sciences with molecular biology.

A final field that emerges from genetic research and public health is **pharmacogenetics**. This is a field that examines genetic-based reactions to pharmaceutical therapies (Austin and Peyser 2000). This is a critical field because it will enable doctors and researchers to individualize such therapies to the genetic makeup of patients and, hopefully, reduce harmful side effects of drugs.

Genetics will thus be useful in a variety of ways related to public health. It can help track diseases, including new ones, and help identify those diseases that have become resistant to antibiotics. It can similarly help in the development of new therapies as well as prevention ("Public Health Genetics Crucial to Treatment, Expert Says" 2000).

Genetic Testing and Screening

> About one in 20 live-born infants is expected to have a single-gene disorder or a condition with an important genetic component by age 25 years, about 1 in 33 will have a major birth defect, and a similar proportion will have a significant developmental disability. These infants will account for a disproportionate fraction of premature deaths, pediatric hospitalizations, and health care costs. Many of these conditions or their complications can be reduced by timely and effective primary prevention practices.... (Botto and Mastroiacovo 2000, 123)

As noted in the Institute of Medicine reports (1988, 2003), surveillance is an important public health function. Surveillance is discovering whether there are health conditions in society that might warrant a public health response. The earliest example of surveillance for birth defects was the thalidomide episode. Thalidomide was a drug prescribed for pregnant women to alleviate the nausea that often accompanies pregnancy. Unfortunately, it resulted in a large number of children born with very severe birth defects, largely to the limbs. Most of the problems occurred in Europe, because the

U.S. Food and Drug Administration (FDA) refused to approve its use in the United States. Beginning in the early 1960s, its use was banned in the United States and the rest of the world (Botto and Mastroiacovo 2000).

One of the most important areas relating genetics and public health is in testing and screening. The two terms are essentially indistinguishable (Wilfond and Thomson 2000). Screening tends to refer to preliminary testing as well as examining genetic issues in populations that are asymptomatic (Wilfond and Thomson 2000). Many of the tests discussed below are diagnostic in nature. Therapies for remedying problems found through screening/testing are not always available, a problem discussed below.

In a sense, genetic screening has been around for a while. When doctors take a family history and ask about the incidence of, say, cancer or heart disease in a family, there is implicit in this type of question the heritable basis of disease. Doing genetic tests is much more recent.

One of the earliest genetic screens was for phenylketonouria (PKU) in newborns, which began in the 1950s (Pass 2000; Wilfond and Thomson 2000). Indeed, newborn screening and PKU screening in particular has served as a model for wider population screening (Khoury, McCabe, and McCabe 2003).

PKU is a genetic metabolic disorder based on the deficiency or absence of an enzyme used to produce a particular amino acid. This deficiency or absence leads to mental retardation (Children's PKU Network n.d.). Once PKU has been identified during a pregnancy, then the newborn is placed on a special diet that can prevent retardation. The gene is recessive, so that both parents must possess it for the disorder to be expressed. The Children's PKU Network estimates that one in fifteen thousand U.S. newborns will have the gene (Children's PKU Network n.d.).

PKU was the first genetic screening test because the test itself is fairly simple. Additionally, President John F. Kennedy had a mentally retarded sister and was interested in the issue of mental retardation (Pass 2000). During the 1960s, most of the states mandated PKU testing (Wilfond and Thomson 2000). Hypothyroidism is the only other condition for which screening is mandated (Khoury, McCabe, and McCabe 2003; Pass 2000). All told, there are nine disorders that can be screened for and for which treatment is available (see Khoury, McCabe, and McCabe 2003).

Screens for other disorders were developed. These include hemophilia and related disorders (Soucie, Rickes, and Evatt 2000), cystic fibrosis (Farrell et al 2000), sickle cell disease (Olney 2000), and human immunodeficiency virus (HIV). The National Electronic Library for Health, part of the British National Health Service, lists twenty-six tests for antenatal screening and another seventeen tests for newborn screening (National Electronic Library

Table 6.2

Antenatal and Newborn Screens

Screens employed by the British Department of Health	Screens not employed by the British Department of Health
Anaemia	asymptomatic bacteriuria in pregnancy
congenital cataract	biliary atresia
congenital heart disease	biotinidase deficiency
congenital hypothyroidism	chlamydia
congenital malformations	congenital adrenal hyperplasia
cryptorchidism (neonatal)	cystic fibrosis (neonatal)
cystic fibrosis	cytomegalovirus
diabetes	Duchenne muscular dystrophy
Down syndrome	foetomaternal alloimmune thrombocytopenia
foetal anomalies	fragile X
haemoglobinopathy and sickle cell disease	herpes simplex virus infection
haemolytic disease of the newborn	high blood pressure
hepatitis B	HTLV
HIV	MCAD and other inborn errors of metabolism
impaired hearing (neonatal)	neonatal alloimmune thrombocytopenia
neural tube defect	neuroblastoma
phenylketonuria	group B streptococcal infection
preeclampsia	thrombophilia
rubella	toxoplasmosis
syphilis	
Tay-Sachs disease	

Source: National Electronic Library for Health (n.d.), www.nelh.nhs.uk/screening/vbls.html.

for Health n.d.). Table 6.2 lists the screens. Of the forty-three tests, the Department of Health provides screening for twenty-one.

One of the more controversial areas was screening for HIV-1 antibodies, which began in the late 1980s. Unlike some of the screens, such as for PKU, HIV-1 screening was done more for public health purposes than for the specific health of the individual baby. There are no vaccines or cures for AIDS, which HIV would lead to, and at the time there were no appropriate medications that would either alleviate the symptoms of AIDS or retard the progression of HIV to AIDS. HIV screening was useful primarily in the early years for examining the spread of the epidemic. Happily, with biomedical advances, therapies are now available for newborns identified as having AIDS (Pass 2000).

This raises the very important public health question of how such information is used. As indicated above, if there are no available therapies, then the question of the prevalence of the disease or disorder is present, though this information provides no assistance to the newborn or the family. A second use is where such therapies are available, as with PKU or HIV. A third use is in genetic counseling.

While we consider genetic counseling in more detail below, in the case of newborn screening, genetic counseling can take various forms. First, the parent(s) are generally, though not always,[4] informed of the results and the problem unearthed by the genetic test. This helps them prepare for the problems that occur as the child grows. A second use of genetic counseling for parents is the possible termination of the pregnancy. If the child is likely to be severely physically or mentally disabled, the parents may decide to abort the pregnancy. Of course, this raises highly emotional issues related to abortion and the right to life and the right to choose. The third possible use is to counsel parents about further efforts at reproduction. Knowing the odds of having a baby with a genetic disorder might lead parents to decide not to have any more children.

Genetic testing and screening also occurs in children and newborns. Here the human genome project has been very useful. Cancer is a set of diseases that has a genetic basis, though it is likely that it is the interaction of genetic makeup, lifestyle (diet, obesity, and smoking, for example), and environment that results in the expression of many cancers.

Biomedical scientists have begun to identify the specific gene or genes that make a person highly susceptible to specific cancers. Doctors and families have known for a long time that cancer tends to occur in families, so that it seemed likely there would be a genetic basis for the diseases. This has indeed proven to be the case.

One area where there has been considerable research is in breast cancer, the most common form of cancer among women (Coughlin and Burke 2000). Studies have shown that mutations in two specific genes (BRCA1 and BRCA2) make women more susceptible to the cancer. This appears to be true even if the family history indicates little breast cancer (see Reynolds 2003). While the incidence of breast cancer seems to be increasing, there are some things that young women with the genetic mutations can do to decrease the probability of the appearance of the cancer (Reynolds 2003). These include exercise, keeping weight in normal ranges, and, apparently, pregnancy.

Colorectal cancer is another fairly common cancer that has some genetic relationship. However, unlike breast cancer, there does not appear to be a single gene or mutation that scientists can point to (Coughlin and Burke 2000).

Lung cancer, another prevalent disease, is more difficult to trace to a specific gene or set of genes. The obvious reason is that smoking is strongly

related to lung cancer, as are exposures to environmental or external substances (Coughlin and Burke 2000). Nevertheless, there does seem to be
some impact of smoking on genes. Complicating the possibility of establishing the causes of lung cancer is that some genetic changes appear to be
caused by the lung cancer rather than causing the cancer itself (Coughlin
and Burke 2000).

Prostate cancer appears to have several genetic linkages. As with breast
cancer in women, males with BRCA1 and BRCA2 mutations have an elevated probability of contracting prostate cancer. But there are other possible genetic contenders. Because of the complex genetic linkages, screening
programs are not very effective (Coughlin and Burke 2000).

A comprehensive review of genes and cancer concludes that much more
research needs to be done, especially on the linkage between genetic makeup
and environmental exposures, as well as the possibility that clusters of genetic mutations are involved (Coughlin and Burke 2000).

While cancer is a much-dreaded disease, there are other issue diseases that
might have a genetic component, especially infectious diseases (McNicholl et
al. 2000). Three of the most significant infectious diseases are tuberculosis
(TB), HIV, and malaria, and their threats seem to be increasing (McNicholl
et al. 2000; see also Garrett 2000). Some genes, host genes, may increase
susceptibility to these diseases while others may provide resistance to them.
Research in this area is cutting edge, and while the knowledge base is
increasing, it is very limited (McNicholl et al. 2000). As an example of the
varied impact of genetic makeup, two genes or sets of genes increase susceptibility to either coming down with malaria or dying from it, while
eight genes or sets of genes appear to increase resistance (McNicholl et al.
2000, 176–77).

McNicholl et al. (2000) point out the public health implications of genetics and infectious diseases. They note that pharmacogenetics can help in the
prescription of certain drugs rather than others for those with malaria. They
also point out that ecogenetics may be helpful in reducing exposure to infectious diseases, and in examining the interaction of genetics and environmental (including lifestyle) factors.

More to the point, the growing research on genetics and infectious diseases impacts various aspects of public health programs. These include surveillance, applied research, infrastructure and planning, and prevention and
control. Surveillance is examining the existence of the disease in a given
population and death rates associated with it. If research shows that people
with certain genetic makeups, or genotypes, are more susceptible to a particular infectious disease, then focusing on these risk-based groups would
be warranted. Drugs are being developed to alleviate (therapies) or prevent

(vaccines) disease based on genetic makeup. This is the highest priority of applied research (McNicholl et al. 2000).

Genetic differences, even small ones, may have marked differences in susceptibility to disorders. For example, the CD24 gene appears to be important in the occurrence of multiple sclerosis (MS), and very minor differences in the gene can double the susceptibility to the disorder as well as increase its severity ("Gene Differences May Alter Susceptibility to Multiple Sclerosis" 2003).

Infrastructure from a public health standpoint refers to having the labs and research in place, and then training people to use this information. Prevention and control often involves educating the population as to what can be done to reduce the incidence of a particular disease (McNicholl et al. 2000; see also Centers for Disease Control 1998, 2002).

The workplace is another area where genetics and health has proven important. We can distinguish among genetic monitoring, genetic screening, and information from medical records (Schulte and DeBord 2000). Genetic monitoring looks at a person's genetic makeup to see if it has changed over a period of time. This is essentially what is done with biological monitoring, discussed in chapter 8. Any changes might indicate exposure to some substance. The basic idea is to prevent health problems in the workplace (Schulte and DeBord 2000).

A related activity is genetic screening. The purpose of genetic screening is to see whether a current or future employee might be susceptible to a health problem due to exposure to a substance found in the workplace. Neither genetic screening nor monitoring is yet widely used because the research is recent and the current tests have not been validated yet. Both screening and monitoring have public policy implications, not just in the workplace, that we will explore below.

Effectiveness of Genetic Testing

Some screening and testing has been done for years, though the sophistication of genetic testing has increased dramatically in recent years. By 1995 some 80,000 tests were being conducted (Watson 2000). Testing and screening need to be evaluated on the basis of different types of validity (Khoury, Burke, and Thomson 2000b).[5]

One type of validity is analytic validity. Analytical validity asks the question of the effectiveness of the test or screen in discovering the genotype in the tested individual. The genotype can be defined as

> the "internally coded, inheritable information" carried by all living organisms. This stored information is used as a "blueprint" or set of instructions

for building and maintaining a living creature. These instructions are found within almost all cells (the "internal" part), they are written in a coded language (the genetic code), they are copied at the time of cell division or reproduction and are passed from one generation to the next ("inheritable"). These instructions are intimately involved with all aspects of the life of a cell or an organism. They control everything from the formation of protein macromolecules, to the regulation of metabolism and synthesis. (Blamire 2000)

This means that the genotype is the genetic makeup where one would look for particular genes or a set of genes or chromosomes, such as BRCA1, that might indicate a susceptibility to a particular disease (breast cancer in this case). Analytic validity asks about things like the predictive nature of the test or the sensitivity of the test (Khoury, Burke, and Thomson 2005).

A second type of validity is clinical and focuses on the phenotype. Phenotype is defined as "the 'outward, physical manifestation' of the organism. These are the physical parts, the sum of the atoms, molecules, macromolecules, cells, structures, metabolism, energy utilization, tissues, organs, reflexes and behaviors; anything that is part of the observable structure, function or behavior of a living organism" (Blamire 2000). Thus clinical validity looks for the outward characteristics of an organism. Phenotypes include things like eye and hair color as well as the presence or absence of a disease and are not necessarily linked to genotype. While we have discussed the genetic linkages to disease, it is also clear that much human disease is not linked to one's genetic makeup (genotype). Therefore, clinical validity asks whether this connection has been made. Included in clinical validity is "predictive values" (Khoury, Burke, and Thomson 2000b, 12); that is, clinical validity asks how well the test or screen predicts the expression of an underlying genetic problem.

The third type of evaluation is clinical utility (Khoury, Burke, and Thomson 2000b). This asks about the benefits that might accrue from testing and intervention (see, for example, the discussion above about PKU screening) as well as the risks and costs of such testing and evaluation.

Cost-effectiveness analysis is helpful in determining whether to undertake genetic testing and which tests to use (Goldie and Levin 2001). Cost-effectiveness analysis focuses on three aspects in guiding public policy decisions regarding genetic testing. They are "the target population, the prevalence of the mutation, and gene penetrance" (Goldie and Levin 2001). Clearly the tests work best when there is a close correspondence between the genetic background (genotype) and the expression of the disorder (phenotype) (Goldie and Levin 2001).

Public health is also concerned about quality assurance issues related to screening and testing (Khoury, Burke, and Thomson 2000b). There should be standards and guidelines for the tests as well as the laboratories conducting them. This includes certification of the laboratories.

Legislation passed in 1988 (the Clinical Laboratory Amendments) requires the establishment of the analytical validity of new tests. Clinical and scientific validity is not required. Further, tests developed in-house by laboratories are not subject to rigorous government evaluations. The Food and Drug Administration has limited regulatory authority in this area (Watson 2000).

Genetic Profiling

Genetic screening and testing on populations can be used to look at variations of disease and illness within a population, help develop targeted therapies for dealing with the disease or illness, and identify target populations. For example, in September 2003, scientists from the University of California at Los Angeles (UCLA) announced that they had found two different forms of leprosy based on genetic differences ("UCLA Study Uses Genetic Profiling to Distinguish Types of Leprosy" 2003). The implications of the study are both specific and general. First, the genetic profiling allows better targeting of a therapy, given the two different types of leprosy. Second, from a more general perspective, it provides a mechanism for distinguishing among infectious diseases. According to one of the scientists in the study, such genetic profiling can differentiate between those who have the symptoms of the common cold and those who may be the subject of a bioterrorism attack, say anthrax (see chapter 8). That would enable doctors and public health officials, in the case of the latter, to take appropriate action quicker. The same kind of tailoring treatment to individuals with leprosy can be done with other diseases, such as breast cancer.

Genetic profiling can also be used on a predictive basis. That is, based on a person's or population's genetic makeup, the susceptibility to a particular disease or illness can be projected.

Population screening will change the practice of medicine, creating the new field of "genomic medicine" (Khoury, McCabe, and McCabe 2003, 50). Previous types of screening focused on finding people who have genetic disorders prior to the appearance of the disease, such as PKU screening, using prenatal screening to decrease the occurrence of a disease order in future generations (for example, Tay-Sachs disease among certain Jewish populations), and discovering those who might be carriers of defective genes.

The new work in genomic medicine will have more far-reaching impacts.

By identifying those who are at risk or susceptible, preventive efforts can be undertaken (such as diet), detection would be earlier, treatment more effective, and the screening would become more precise (Khoury, McCabe, and McCabe 2003). Genetic screening can also play a role in outreach activities. That is, those from susceptible populations who have not undergone screening or testing or treatment might be contacted.

As a result of the work done on population screening and testing and genetic profiling and some of the issues raised by such research (see the discussion below), a set of principles has been developed to guide the testing process (Table 6.3).

The Politics of Genetics and Development of Public Health Policies

Genetic research, the human genome project, and the development of genomic medicine have implications that range far beyond advances in the biomedical sciences and the practice of medicine. They also raise very important societal and public health issues that have been categorized as ethical, legal, and social issues (with the acronym of ELSI). It is to these issues that we devote the remainder of the chapter.

Privacy and Confidentiality of Genetic Information

One very important set of issues deals with the privacy and confidentiality of genetic information. This is partly because the possibility exists that discrimination might occur, but also because genetic information has implications beyond the individual person. Genetic makeup is shared with parents, siblings, and other relatives. So if a particular genetic disorder or mutation is found in one person, it is possible that that person's relatives may have the same disorder or mutation.

One way to look at this is through the window of HIV/AIDS. If a person is tested for HIV and the test is positive, and assuming that it is not a false positive, then there are clear implications for the infected person. That person will need treatment (a regimen of drugs) to prevent progression of HIV to AIDS. But because AIDS is an infectious disease, via the exchange of bodily fluids, such as sexual transmission, blood transfusion (much rarer these days), or needle exchange, the infected person contracted HIV from somebody. And because a person with HIV is asymptomatic, then he or she might have passed the disease on to someone else. From a public health standpoint then, officials would like to find out how the person was infected and by whom and also to notify others who had contact

Table 6.3

Principles of Population Screening as Applied to Genetic Susceptibility to Disease: Public Health Assessment

- The disease or condition should be an important public health burden to the target population in terms of illness, disability, or death.
- The prevalence of the genetic trait in the target population and the burden of disease attributable to it should be known.
- The natural history of the condition, from susceptibility to latent disease to overt disease, should be adequately understood.

Evaluation of tests and interventions
- Data should be available on the positive and negative predictive values of the test with respect to a disease or condition in the target population.
- The safety and effectiveness of the test and accompanying interventions should be established.

Policy development and screening implementation
- Consensus regarding the appropriateness of screening and interventions for people with positive and negative test results should be based on scientific evidence.
- Screening should be acceptable to the target population.
- Facilities should be available for adequate surveillance, prevention, treatment, education, counseling, and social support.
- Screening should be a continual process, including pilot programs, evaluation of laboratory quality and health services, evaluation of the effect of screening, and provisions for changes on the basis of new evidence.
- The cost effectiveness of screening should be established.
- Screening and interventions should be available to the target population.
- There should be safeguards to ensure that informed consent is obtained and the privacy of those tested is respected; that there is no coercion or manipulation, and that those tested are protected against stigmatization and discrimination.

Source: Muin J. Khoury, Linda L. McCabe, and Edward R.B. McCabe, "Genomic Medicine: Population Screening in the Age of Genome Medicine," *New England Journal of Medicine* vol. 348, no. 1 (January 2, 2003): 50–58. Copyright © 2003 Massachusetts Medical Society. Reprinted with permission. All rights reserved.

with the infected person so that they could be tested for HIV and stop the disease from spreading.

Staying with our HIV example, because of the stigma attached to contracting HIV, a person is unlikely to volunteer for testing if his or her name becomes public. So privacy and confidentiality are important.

One other aspect of privacy is important. While genetic testing and screening have seen remarkable advances, responding to the results have in many cases not advanced so far. That is, while in some cases there are available therapies for some genetic-based disorders (PKU being the first example), in many cases there is not. So knowing that one has a genetic predisposition to a disorder can adversely affect the individual if there is no remedy. Further, there is a privacy right not to know one's genetic makeup (Krumm 2002).

One interesting personal and political issue relates to genetic testing. There are no laws that require that both parents consent to genetic testing of the fetus. So, in the event that the father might have a genetic predisposition to a particular disease, say Huntington's disease, the mother might want the father tested. The father might not want the test, because if it were positive, then he would know he had it also and there may be no treatment for the disease. However, the practice among clinical laboratories in the United States requires dual consent on their own. This type of agreement is one decided by the medical professions and is not subject to the usual procedures of the public sector (see "Roundtable: The Politics of Genetic Testing" 1996).

Informed Consent

Informed consent raises some of the most troubling historical issues in biomedical sciences. The infamous Tuskegee experiments is the major example of the problems that can be raised from medical experimentation. The Tuskegee experiments, conducted by the U.S. Public Health Service, sought to investigate the course of the disease syphilis in those who were affected by it. The researchers chose some four hundred African-American males from a relatively poor county in Alabama who were infected with the disease. They were not told that they were research subjects, and blacks were thought to be more susceptible to the infection. They were given regular checkups and treated for other diseases, as well as a meal, but were not told that they had syphilis. Nor were they treated with the appropriate cure, penicillin, when it became available. The forty-year "study" ended in 1972, when it broke in the media. In 1997 the federal government formally apologized for the study ("Remembering Tuskegee" 2002).

Informed consent issues, at the heart of the Tuskegee experiments, play a different role in genetic related areas. Genetic testing and screening are very simple processes that do not pose a health risk to the patient, as was clearly the case with the victims of the Tuskegee experiment and is also true with other medical procedures (Press and Clayton 2000). Experimental cancer treatments carry grave risks. There are also risks associated with gene therapy (repairing mutated genes) (see Patel and Rushefsky 2002). But that is the not the case here.

What is at issue is the information itself.

> It [genetic testing] can disclose potential health risks that may be unalter-
> able and may lead to a process of self-stigmatization. It tells about risks
> that might not occur for years or decades, if ever; individuals with no
> current health problems may upon receiving genetic information, label
> themselves as somehow ill. It provides information whose psychological
> safety and medical usefulness depend on the comprehension of probabil-
> ity and risk information. Finally, it gives one person information that may
> have exactly equal relevance for relatives who did not ask for this infor-
> mation. (Press and Clayton 2000, 506)

Informed consent procedures that currently exist are not terribly helpful (Press and Clayton 2000). Patients often did not read the forms and
frequently did not understand what they were consenting to.[6] One reason
for the problem is that the language of the forms is likely beyond the com-
prehension of many patients. A second reason is that doctors may not have
sufficient communications skills to explain informed consent issues to their
patients or may not themselves be well informed about this (Press and
Clayton 2000).

One area where patients are likely to have a problem, indicated by the
above quote, is the notion of risk and probability that attach to findings of
genetic tests. Risk is the chance that something, such as an adverse event
based on genetic background, might occur. Probability is the likelihood that
it will occur.

There are barriers to effective communications. For example, African-
Americans familiar with the Tuskegee experiment may be less likely to participate in medical studies. There is also the sociological distance between
researcher/practitioner and patient that affects the dynamics of the informed
consent process. The patient may also be impressed with the possibility of
the value of the information (Press and Clayton 2000). On the other hand,
the requirement for informed consent may lead to liability issues and thus
reluctance on the part of the researcher/doctor to provide full support.

Many of these factors play a role in prenatal screening (Press and Clayton
2000). Press and Clayton use as one of their case studies screening for maternal serum alpha-fetoprotein (MSAFP), essentially defects in neural tubes.
This an important test because the overwhelming majority of pregnant women
do not know they have the problem. The American College of Obstetricians
and Gynecologists sent a warning to its members that they might be subject
to liability suits if the tests were not offered. This resulted in physicians
pressing their patients to take the test, but not necessarily explaining it well
(Press and Clayton 2000).

A related issue is newborn screening (Press and Clayton 2000). Clearly the subjects of the screenings, the newborns, cannot give their consent.[7] In most cases the mandatory newborn screens, such as for PKU, are not accompanied with informed consent procedures (with some religious exceptions). The reasons for this are time, convenience, and what appears to be the obvious effectiveness of newborn screens.

Most of the disorders requiring mandatory testing are relatively rare (Press and Clayton 2000). Further, there are consequences of screening, including a very high rate of false-positive test results (results showing a disorder when there actually is not). More testing is being required and psychological harm can occur among the parents. Testing may also result in some discrimination issues for those who are carriers of particular genes.

An equally troubling issue is genetic testing on stored tissue samples or using medical records. The combination of new genetic testing abilities and information capabilities create issues of privacy and consent. Patients often sign fairly general consent forms, but those forms do not convey the research use to which the records or tissue samples would be put (Press and Clayton 2000).

Consent also plays an issue in epidemiological research. Recall that epidemiology is the study of disease patterns in populations. It is, as we have noted before, one of the major scientific underpinnings of public health. Further, both epidemiology and public health are concerned about disease patterns and health among populations and not, at least directly, individuals. This raises the question of the needs of society versus the privacy rights of individuals (Wedeen 2000).

Rules that protect the privacy of subjects in clinical research are well defined (Wedeen 2000). There must be a committee (institutional review board or IRB) at the researcher's institution that reviews proposed research to make sure that subjects are not harmed. There must be informed consent, and those most vulnerable, such as children, the disabled, the elderly, or prisoners, should have enhanced protections. Few of these protections are available in epidemiological studies. If there is no harm done to the subject (for example, resulting in discrimination) and if there is a benefit to society at large, then consent may be waived. But it is the researchers who make this decision, and there may be conflicts of interest (Wedeen 2000). Considering such things as the Tuskegee experiments, IRBs were developed as a way to avoid these kinds of unethical research activities. The history of the nonuse of consent goes back to eighteenth-century England and includes eugenics theories and practices, including those adopted by the Nazis in Germany. The revulsion against Nazi practices led to national and international efforts focusing on ethical guidelines for research (Wedeen 2000).

One problem in trying to obtain consent from a population rather than on an individual basis is that obtaining consent is expensive, and refusals undermine the conclusions of the study (Wedeen 2000). Another issue is that epidemiologists do not have the kinds of ethical codes that physicians have, and there is sometimes a thin line between clinical practice (where patients agree or consent to treatment) and research. Even in medical research and public health, the autonomy of the individual should be supreme (Wedeen 2000).

Discrimination Based on Genetic Information

> Genetic testing is not only a medical procedure. It is also a way of creating social categories. As a basic principle, we believe that people should be evaluated on their individual merits and abilities, and not based on stereotypes and predictions about their future performance of health status. In most cases, genetic testing can only reveal information about probabilities, not absolute certainties. We believe that individuals should not be judged based on stereotypes and assumptions about what people in their class or status are like. (Council for Responsible Genetics 2001, 4–5)

The advancement of genetic research and its application in the biomedical sciences have created the possibility for discrimination against people based on their genetic background. Such discrimination could be seen in several different ways (Hellman 2003).

One has to do with insurance. In the absence of a national system of health insurance, insurance is not mandatory, and insurance companies may use various methods to reduce their costs. One such method is the use of experience rating. Under experience rating, insurance premiums are based on an applicant's past medical history. The concern is that if an insurance company becomes aware of an applicant's genetic background and there is some genetic predisposition for the disorder, the company may either set premiums at a prohibitive rate or deny the applicant the insurance. This would leave the applicant vulnerable to perhaps catastrophic health care costs.

A second, related, area of possible discrimination is life insurance. Insurers may be reluctant to provide life insurance benefits to someone with a genetic predisposition to a disease. The Council for Responsible Genetics (2001) notes that genetic predisposition to some cancers has been established. Their position notes that the association of life insurance companies (the American Council of Life Insurance [ACLI]) has already claimed that their member "insurance companies should be allowed to use information about cancer predisposition to assign risk categories in medical underwriting and possibly refuse to insure those individuals who carry these genes" (Council for Responsible Genetics 2001, 2).

A third place where genetic discrimination might occur is in the workplace. Again, assuming that genetic information is available to an employer, the employer might be hesitant to hire someone who might present high health care costs for the company sometime in the future. Perhaps it is not the employee but a covered member of the employee's family that has the genetic marker that indicates a predisposition to a disease. The worker might then be denied protection or a job. Another employment aspect is that workers might be denied certain jobs with higher pay if the worker has a genetic predisposition to a disease that might occur from exposure to something in the workplace.

Some of these aspects can be combined. Insurance companies are regulated by the states, with very little regulation on the part of the federal government. For example, employers may self-insure. This is the case with the authors' employer, Southwest Missouri State University (SMSU). Such employers are not subject to state regulation (and SMSU would not be because it is itself a state agency) under a U.S. Supreme Court interpretation of the Employees Retirement and Income Security Act (ERISA) of 1974. However, the federal government does very little regulating of these companies, an issue that has arisen in connection with something called enterprise liability (see Patel and Rushefsky 2002). There is therefore less protection against such discrimination with self-insured companies ("Roundtable: The Politics of Genetic Testing" 1996).

Genetic discrimination can be seen as a civil rights issue. For one thing, it is based on the value of equality (see Rushefsky 2002; Stone 2002). Second, as the quote that begins this section indicates, discrimination is based on group characteristics, in this case, those possessing a genetic predisposition to a disorder.

It should therefore come as little surprise that the American Civil Liberties Union (ACLU) has taken up the cause. The ACLU argues that workplace discrimination is a real and serious issue. The organization cites several pieces of information to support this position. First, surveys have shown that the percentage of employers using genetic information when hiring personnel rose from 1.5 percent of respondents in 1982 to 6 to 10 percent by 1997 (American Civil Liberties Union 2000; see also Krumm 2002). In one sense this should not be a surprise. There were few if any genetic tests that could be used in 1982 compared to 1997. The more recent availability of tests makes them more likely to be used. The ACLU also notes that in a survey of one thousand people who had genetic predispositions, approximately 22 percent stated that they had experienced some workplace discrimination based on that predisposition.

A fourth area where genetic discrimination might occur has to do with adoption and child custody issues (Hellman 2003). In the event that a family is undergoing separation, the courts might decide custody in a particular direction if one of the parties to the custody fight has a genetic predisposition, say, for breast cancer or Alzheimer's disease. Similarly, a person or couple might be denied adoption if the genetic makeup of one or both of the prospective parents is troublesome.

All of these issues are theoretical. How real are they? The Council for Responsible Genetics (CRG) claims that there have been almost five hundred cases of such discrimination. The advocacy group provides some cases or anecdotes of discrimination (Council for Responsible Genetics (2001). One case is a seven-year-old boy who is in fine health but has a genetic predisposition for heart disease. Though there is medication to reduce the risk of heart disease, the insurance company denies him insurance on the grounds that he has a preexisting condition. In a second case, a child has genetically based mental retardation. The insurance company argues that this is a preexisting condition and thus denies him coverage. In a third case, a woman's employer finds out that she has a genetic predisposition to Huntington's disease and fires her. In the fourth case, a woman is concerned that if she takes a genetic test to see if she has the BRCA1 or BRCA2 mutation, she would not be promoted in her firm.

These kinds of anecdotal cases raise important issues. First, as mentioned above, there is a difference between genotype and phenotype. To recall, the genotype is the genetic background, while the phenotype is the expression of the disorder. Discrimination on the basis of genotype is difficult to justify (and for advocates of national health insurance, any kind of discrimination is hard to justify). Insurance, after all, is supposed to financially protect someone who becomes ill. Further, with a few exceptions, the genetic makeup is insufficient by itself to cause the disease. It does make the risk of having the disorder increase. This kind of genetic determinism (see also Lin-Fu and Lloyd-Puryear 2000) is not based on science. Further, genetic testing in some cases may not be entirely reliable (Krumm 2002).

Another argument about genetic discrimination and genetic determinism affects the way we look at physical and behavioral disorders. If we continue to assert that much of these disorders are genetically linked, then it would follow that appropriate remedies (if there are any) are biomedical (including genetic). The Council for Responsible Genetics (2001) argues, on the other hand, that many of these disorders stem from societal issues, including environmental causes (see chapter 7) and issues of access to services (see below).

Krumm (2002) argues that genetic testing by employers should be prohibited for a variety of reasons. First, there are other ways to gain the benefits of such testing. One example she provides is subsidizing the test, encouraging workers to take it without mandating the test. The second reason is that limiting the scope of information gathered from genetic testing is impractical. Third, obtaining voluntary consent for such testing is not necessarily obtaining informed consent. For example, the results of such tests become available to government agencies. Finally, as mentioned earlier, genetic testing impacts more than just the individual. The employee shares a genetic makeup with members of his or her family. Krumm concludes that federal legislation is necessary because without it mandatory workplace testing will become common.

Hellman (2003) argues that despite the anecdotal stories,[8] there is little empirical evidence to suggest that there is genetic discrimination in the workplace or by insurance companies. Indeed, she raises some intriguing questions about the topic. For example, is genetic discrimination different from other kinds of discrimination? One concern is that by raising the fear of genetic discrimination and that genetic discrimination is different from other kinds, we also assert genetic determinism. Her carefully reasoned argument suggests a limited role for genetic discrimination.

The American Association of Health Plans (AAHP) (2002) argues that new legislation is not needed. This organization asserts that federal legislation is sufficiently adequate to the task. AAHP also states that discrimination on account of genetic makeup should be prohibited, but the legislation should be carefully drawn so that it does not inhibit research in this cutting-edge area of biomedical sciences. Begley (2004) argues that there is no evidence that genetic discrimination has occurred and that at best proposed legislation protects against a theoretical rather than an actual risk.

One interesting application is brought up by Yen (2003). Her law review article focuses on a behavioral disorder, Tourette's syndrome (which her husband has) and whether there should be mandatory testing for it and other behavioral problems. She begins her article by considering the movie *Gattaca*. The movie is based on the notion of genetic determinism. That is, all health and behavioral/mental disorders have a genetic basis, and getting rid of the genetic defects would rid society of disorders. Therefore, the futuristic society pictured in the movie engages in genetic screening and testing.

A state might mandate testing for Tourette's syndrome in several ways. It might do so as a condition of obtaining a driver's license on the grounds that the involuntary movements typical of some suffering from the disorder would create a safety hazard for themselves as well as for others. A state might require testing as a condition for marriage so that both parties to the union would be aware of possible reproductive consequences. Testing might be required for adoptions so that adoptive parents would know about possible problems as well as problems that the parents themselves might have. States might mandate testing in employment (dealing with safety as well as social issues) and prisons (to segregate those prisoners who have a genetic propensity for violence) (Yen 2003) .

Yen concludes that mandatory testing for Tourette's syndrome is not justified. There is no compelling state interest, there are privacy concerns, and there is little risk to public safety and health. She also notes that engaging in this type of mandatory testing is "scapegoat genetics" (Yen 2003, 52). Society might arbitrarily decide that some kinds of behavior are dangerous or unwanted, and this can lead to discrimination. Such mandatory regulation also violates important values of a democratic society (see opening quote).

Policy Related to Genetic Discrimination

Legislation and other political action relating to privacy and discrimination in regard to genetic testing is spotty at best. No specific piece of federal legislation addresses these issues, though there are some pieces of legislation and action that touch upon these concerns ("Genetics Privacy and Legislation" n.d.). An analysis of proposed federal legislation by the National Cancer Advisory Board (2001) lists one House of Representatives resolution, seven proposal bills in the Senate, and three in the House. None have been acted upon.

In February 2000, President Bill Clinton issued Executive Order 13145 limiting the ability of federal agencies to make use of genetic information in regard to employment decisions (such as hiring or promotions). The executive order was careful to specify what was meant by genetic information:

> In general, protected genetic information means:
> (A) information about an individual's genetic tests;
> (B) information about the genetic tests of an individual's family members; or
> (C) information about the occurrence of a disease, or medical condition or disorder in family members of the individual. (White House 2000)

The order prohibits agencies from ordering employees or prospective employees to take genetic tests and forbids agencies from making personnel decisions based on genetic predisposition for a disorder (although there are some exceptions) (Genetics Privacy and Legislation n.d.). Note the privacy concerns in the executive order: it limits information about family members as well as about the employee or prospective employee.

From 2001 through 2003, seven pieces of legislation were introduced in the U.S. Congress, five in the Senate and two in the House of Representatives. One bill passed in late 2003.

One of the earliest proposals came in 1995, the Genetic Privacy and Non-Discrimination Act of 1995 (HR 2690 IH) introduced in the House of Representatives. As with the other proposals, this one sought to prevent discrimination on the basis of genetic information on the part of employers and insurers, and establish the rights of individuals and the conditions under which genetic information could be disclosed ("Genetic Privacy and Non-discrimination Act" 1995). The exceptions listed in the proposal were for identification of individuals or bodies in the course of criminal investigations, by court order, for establishing paternity, or, in the case of a blood relative, to help with medical diagnoses.

In 2002, two congressional Democrats, Sen. Tom Daschle of South Dakota and Rep. Louise Slaughter of New York, reintroduced the Genetic Non-Discrimination in Health Insurance and Employment Act, though it did not pass. The legislation would have prohibited insurers from using genetic (predictive) information in decisions on whether to insure or rate individuals and would likewise have prohibited workplace discrimination. The legislation, had it passed, included these provisions:

- Covers all health insurance programs, including those regulated by the federal government, state-regulated plans and the individual market;
- Prohibits insurers from restricting enrollment or changing premiums on the basis of predictive genetic information or genetic services;
- Bans health plans and insurers from requesting or requiring that an individual take a genetic test, or reveal the results of such a test;
- Prohibits health plans and insurers from pursuing or being provided information on predictive genetic information or genetic services;
- Covers employers, employment agencies, labor organizations and training programs;
- Prevents discrimination in hiring, compensation, and other personnel processes;
- Prohibits employers from requiring or requesting disclosure of predictive genetic information and allows genetic testing only to monitor the adverse effects of hazardous workplace exposures; and
- Requires predictive information possessed by an employer to be confidentially maintained and disclosed only to the employee upon request, or to researchers (under the "Common Rule"). (National Organization of Rare Disorders 2002)

In October 2003 the Senate passed a bill, the Genetic Information Non-Discrimination Act (S. 1053). The bill, which was approved unanimously, prohibits the use of genetic information in employment decisions. A companion, though stricter, bill has been proposed in the House of Representatives ("Senate Passes Genetic Discrimination Bill" 2003).

While there is no federal legislation specifically addressing genetic issues, there are several pieces of legislation that could be used to protect the privacy of genetic information ("Genetics Privacy and Legislation" n.d.). One such act is the Americans with Disabilities Act (ADA), passed in 1990. The ADA prohibits discrimination against people with disabilities and genetic susceptibility to a disorder as has been defined as such under the ADA. However, the legislation and regulatory rulings protect only those who show symptoms of the disorder and not those who may be carriers or are currently asymptomatic ("Genetics Privacy and Legislation" n.d.; Krumm 2002).

A second and more recent relevant legislation is the Health Insurance Portability and Accountability Act of 1996 (HIPAA) ("Genetics Privacy and Legislation" n.d.).[9] HIPAA limits the ability of insurers to limit or deny coverage. There is a twelve-month limit on exclusions of preexisting conditions (and then depending on the previous status of the employee), and the legislation states that genetic background is not to be considered a preexisting condition that could cause the limited exclusion. Regulations issued by the federal government in December 2002 to implement HIPAA, while not addressing genetic issues, do provide privacy protection of medical information.

An interesting possible application of a federal law to genetic privacy issues is the Civil Rights Act of 1964, particularly Title VII ("Genetics Privacy and Legislation" n.d.). Under Title VII, employers are prohibited from discriminating against someone on account of race, and if there is a genetic issue related to race and disease, then it might be covered.

As often happens, the federal government tends to trail the states as innovators in domestic policy. The same is true with policy areas touching upon genetic technology. The problem with the states taking the initiative is that you get a patchwork of legislation, with some states not addressing the issue and no state addressing all the issues. Table 6.4 shows the activities that states have taken in the area of genetic privacy. Issues associated with genetic privacy include informed consent (whether the patient has given permission for the use of the information or even the obtaining of the information in the first place) as well as access of the patient to the information obtained. Adding to that is the growing computerization of medical information (medical infomatics) that would also allow greater use of the information.

Table 6.4

States with Genetic Privacy Laws

State	Personal access to genetic information required	Informed consent required to				Define as personal property		
		Perform/ require genetic test	Obtain/access genetic information	Retain genetic information	Disclose genetic information	Genetic information	DNA samples	Specific penalties for genetic privacy violations
Alabama								
Alaska								
Arizona		✓						
Arkansas					✓			
California					✓			✓
Colorado					✓	✓		✓
Connecticut					✓			
Delaware	✓		✓	✓	✓			✓
Florida		✓			✓	✓		✓
Georgia		✓			✓	✓		✓
Hawaii					✓			
Idaho								
Illinois					✓	✓		✓
Indiana								
Iowa								
Kansas								
Kentucky								
Louisiana				✓	✓			✓
Maine					✓			
Maryland							✓	
Massachusetts	✓							

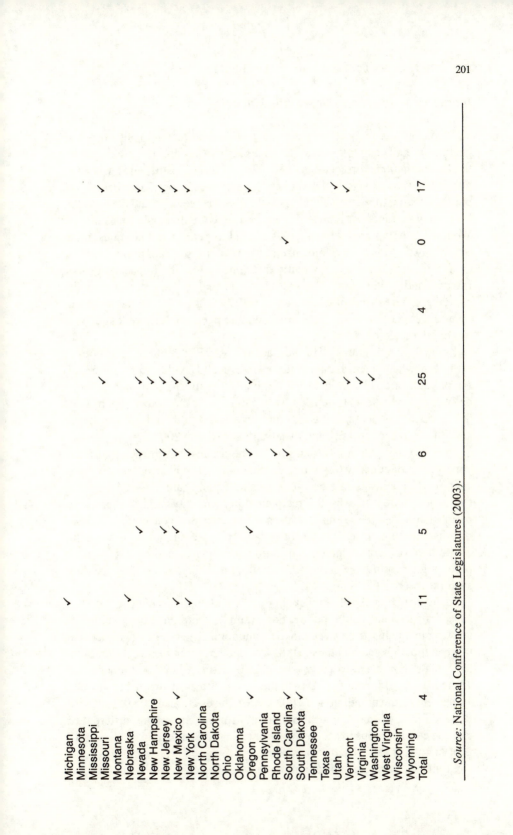

Source: National Conference of State Legislatures (2003).

Inequality and Access to Genetic Technologies

This chapter has focused on the impact of genetic technologies on public health. We have suggested that advancements in genetic research, such as the human genome project, have led to new disciplines in fields related to public health. We have looked at how genetic technologies can benefit the public's health, through such things as newborn screenings and the possibility of new therapies of human disease and individualized pharmaceuticals. We have also explored ethical issues related to genetic technologies, relating to privacy, autonomy, informed consent, and discrimination.

In this section we take a slightly different look at the impact of genetic research and public health. The focus is on inequality and access. Inequality can take different meanings. It can mean treating people in the same circumstances the same way. It also means that people in different situations might be treated differently.

Stone (2002, 39) quotes Harold Lasswell's 1958 definition of politics as "who gets what, when, and how." Likewise, recall David Easton's (1953, iii) famous definition of politics as the "authoritative allocation of values." Both definitions indicate that debates over public policy are very much about "Distributions—whether of goods and services, wealth and income, health and illness, or opportunity and disadvantage" (Stone 2002, 39).

In a very enlightening discussion, Stone argues that there are different conceptions of equality (eight by her reckoning). The most elementary conception of equality is that everyone gets an equal share.[10] One set of conceptions is based on who the recipients are. Equality might be based on membership, rank, or group affiliation. A second set of conceptions is based on what the item or items to be shared are. Here we might look at the value of the item or items. Finally, conceptions of equality can be based on the process for making decisions. Competition, a lottery, and voting are three such processes.

There is a fair amount of inequality in the United States in many different aspects of life and public policy. For example, there have been studies of growing inequality from an economic standpoint. The gap in wages between those at the high end and those at the low end has, with the exception of the late 1990s, continued to grow (see Ip 2004; Rushefsky 2002, chapter 2). There is a fair amount of poverty in the United States, estimated at just over 12 percent of the population in 2002 (U.S. Census Bureau 2003). Likewise, there are inequalities in education and in achievement among different racial and ethnic groups in society (see, for example, Jencks and Phillips 1998; and Thernstrom and Thernstrom 2003).

Similarly, there are substantial inequalities in health care. One aspect of inequality is access to health insurance. In 2002 an estimated 15.2 percent of the U.S. population did not have health insurance, representing an estimated 43.6 million people (Holahan and Wang 2004; Mills and Bhandari 2003). Studies have shown that people who lack health insurance are less likely to visit a doctor, less likely to obtain needed medications, and more likely to use hospital emergency rooms (a very expensive delivery care system) than people who have insurance (see Patel and Rushefsky 2002, chapter 5 and, in general, the *Journal of Health Care for the Poor and Underserved*).

But access to services by itself is insufficient (Lin-Fu and Lloyd-Puryear 2000). Many health care debates focus on access, such as lack of health insurance. Such arguments imply that if only health insurance were available, then those without insurance would automatically have access to care. The great equation is thus insurance coverage = access = health care.

However, just because one has insurance does not mean that the services are available. Not only do the services have to be available, they have to be "culturally appropriate and acceptable, particularly to racial and ethnic minorities, in addition to being accessible and affordable" (Lin-Fu and Lloyd-Puryear 2000, 274). The public must also be literate and informed about genetics and health care (Lin-Fu and Lloyd-Puryear 2000).

To take one example of the problems mentioned by Stone and Lin-Fu/ Lloyd-Puryear, there are variations among the states in newborn screening, though this is not necessarily related to insurance issues. Goldberg (2000) tells the story of two newborns, both with hereditary disease affecting their metabolic systems. One child was born in Massachusetts, which had just expanded its newborn screening program. His disorder was discovered, he was appropriately treated, and was growing normally.

The other child had the misfortune to be born in Texas, which did not routinely screen for his metabolic disease. As a result, his disorder was left untreated and "When he was 19 months old, Bryce's blood sugar levels suddenly plunged, he had massive seizures and fell into a coma. Brain damage left him unable to walk or talk" (Goldberg 2000).

Newborn screening programs present a classic dilemma of public health policy (Goldberg 2000). Both children's metabolic disorder is relatively rare. Therefore, public officials have to decide whether to spend the limited amount of public funds on the rare disorder or on something else. The result is wide disparities in newborn screening. Goldberg (2000) quotes one physician who very cogently points out the implications of this issue: "It's a very difficult situation to have a child who may be born across the street from another child and yet have a very different screening experience."

Further, the disparities are not necessarily due to the relative infrequency of occurrence of the disorder (Goldberg 2000). Some states screen for a disorder in which the incidence is 1 in 60,000, while others do not screen for a disorder (sickle-cell anemia) in which the occurrence is one hundred times more likely (1 in 600). Moreover, the costs of the tests are relatively cheap, $20 to $50 per newborn child, but if a disorder is missed or not screened for, the costs easily exceed $100,000 (Goldberg 2000).

One way to make genetic services available is to develop a genetic services infrastructure (Lin-Fu and Lloyd-Puryear 2000). This would include a literacy program and a development program. The development program would help the health care system incorporate genetic medicine into services under appropriate guidelines. Training of professionals is necessary, especially for those involved with genetic counseling as well as for family practitioners. Because much human disorder has some genetic component, therefore there should be a linkage between researchers and practitioners in the various fields, and not just medically trained practitioners, but others such as social workers (Lin-Fu and Lloyd Puryear 2000). Genetics researchers should also be linked with public health officials at all levels of government.

It should come as little surprise that not much of this has happened. The American health care system has not been carefully planned, but evolved out of a series of public and private decisions made during the twentieth century (and earlier) (see Starr 1984). One health policy scholar aptly describes our health care system as having developed accidentally (Reagan 1999).

There are three barriers specific to genetic services (Lin-Fu and Lloyd-Puryear 2000). The first is the knowledge base of the American people about genetic services. Not surprising, the level of information about genetic services (such as screening and testing) is very low.

A 2001 study by LTG Associates (Roeber, Les, and Massad 2001) addressed questions related to genetic literacy: what information is available, when is the information available, and how do people find the information. They conducted a thorough search of available information on the web, in conferences, in journals, in newspapers and magazines, in government sources, and so forth. The biggest gap in their literature search was on the third question, how people find information. The second question relates to things such as cultural factors (see below).

One interesting though not surprising finding is that as research in a particular area, such as genetics, progresses, the information is filtered through providers. That is, there is a kind of "hierarchical model" (Roeber, Les, and Massad 2001, 18) in which the provider gets the education and training and passes the information on to patients (though direct-to-consumer pharmaceutical advertiseing somewhat undermines this model). The implication of this is that patients are at the mercy of providers, and those without regular providers or regular care, largely the uninsured, are less likely to have access to available information.

The public health approach, based on the study of populations, is fraught with all kinds of equality-related problems (Roeber, Les, and Massad 2001). Some groups may be tainted due to their particular genetic problems, such as African-Americans and sickle-cell anemia or European Jews and Tay-Sachs disease.

Various ethnic minority groups may be especially difficult to reach for historic reasons. We have already mentioned the Tuskegee syphilis experiments. Some in the African-American community have become distrustful of government health efforts because of this past experience. Some have also expressed reservations about the gap between spiritual and scientific values (Roeber, Les, and Massad 2001, 57).

The second barrier is health insurance. Here issues can be raised about discrimination, but from an equality standpoint, the more important concern is lack of health insurance. Certain segments of the population are less likely to have insurance, and thus access to biomedical services, including genetic (Lin-Fu and Lloyd-Puryear 2001). The groups include those who are minorities, those who are foreign-born, those below or near the poverty line, and those with little education.

A sizable proportion of the population is also underinsured; that is, they have some insurance but it is inadequate (Lin-Fu and Lloyd-Puryear 2001). A significant number of children have no health insurance, and the State Children's Health Insurance Program (SCHIP) does an inadequate job of covering children who have special health needs, and it does not cover most screening tests. "Genetic services may therefore not be *affordable* even to those with health insurance" (Lin-Fu and Lloyd-Puryear 2001, 280; emphasis in the original). Further, the fiscal problems that the states have been experiencing have led to budget-cutting efforts, some aimed at Medicaid and SCHIP.

There are also ethnocultural barriers to access to genetic services (Lin-Fu and Lloyd-Puryear 2000). Culture affects how people look at their health, at health care, how they behave, and so forth. Providers rarely take this cultural view into account (Lin-Fu and Lloyd-Puryear 2000). "Nor are many [providers] aware that the health system itself is a cultural system designed and administered according to the mainstream culture" (Lin-Fu and Lloyd-Puryear 2000, 280).

For example, we earlier considered the notion that there is a genetic basis for many diseases. However, some cultures may have different ideas about how disease and defects are caused. Different segments of the population may have different ideas about things such as disabilities and childbirth. Finally, there may be differences in how cultures interact with providers (Lin-Fu and Lloyd-Puryear 2000). Some groups might expect that providers as authority figures would give clear information and orders, yet much genetic counseling tends to be "nondirective" and difficult for some to understand (Lin-Fu and Lloyd-Puryear 2000, 281.)

In addition to these kinds of cultural barriers, there are also language issues (Lin-Fu and Lloyd-Puryear 2000). A sizable portion of the population speaks a language other than English, and this proportion is growing. According to the U.S. Census Bureau, in 1980 11 percent of the population spoke a language other than English at home; by 1990 the percentage had risen to 14 percent; and in 2000 the figure was 18 percent (some 47 million people). Spanish was the most common other language, though there were also a sizable number of Asian languages spoken. The Census Bureau report also noted that most of these people said that they spoke English well (Shin and Bruno 2003). Language barriers make communicating about complex subjects such as genetics and genetic counseling and screening more difficult. The language barrier may require that family members sit in on meetings. Because genetic issues invariably have implications for those family members, very sensitive issues can cause problems related to privacy (Lin-Fu and Lloyd-Puryear 2000).

The health care system is not well prepared to deal with language and cultural competency issues. There are no requirements for licensing, few if any appropriately trained interpreters, and few minorities involved in genetics research (with the exception of those from Asian backgrounds). Beyond this, minority communities have little input into genetic research and treatment (Lin-Fu and Lloyd-Puryear 2000).

There is another aspect related to genetic research and minority communities. Genetic-based research has sometimes had a eugenics tone. Some have argued that the human population needs to be cleansed of those with weak genetic makeups. The controversy over *The Bell Curve* (Herrnstein and Murray 1994), which argued that differences in intelligence and therefore life outcomes are largely (though not entirely) based on genetics, illustrates why there might be some reluctance among minorities to take advantage of genetic services (Patel and Rushefsky 2002).

The Politics of Genetics and Public Health

The genetics revolution and genomic medicine have the potential for revolutionizing public health. They fit in very easily with the core functions of public health as set forth by the Institute of Medicine (2003; see also Khoury

1996). They have led to the creation of new fields of study within the larger field of public health and medicine, such as genetic epidemiology and pharmacogenetics.

To date, however, the penetration of genetics into the practice of public health has been relatively small. Much of this is due to recent scientific developments, particularly of the human genome, though some public health genetics-based activities, such as newborn screening, have a much longer history. This can be demonstrated by an unscientific survey of four publications.

One is the health policy journal *Health Affairs*. A search by the authors of the *Health Affairs* archive using the keyword "genetics" found ten items, seven of which were articles (the other three either mentioned grants or were letters to the editor). Their special issue on public health (November–December 2002) contained no articles dealing with genetics.

One of the major public health texts (Schneider 2000) covers genetic issues in nine pages. Gostin's (2000) magisterial treatment of the law of public health basically ignores the topic. The recent report of the Institute of Medicine (2003) makes only passing reference to genetic issues.

This is not to say that the medical and public health communities have not thought about genetics. There is a considerable literature. Ethical, legal, and social issues (ELSI) are discussed at the U.S. Department of Energy website (doegenomes.org).

While the promise of genetics and public health is great, there are also dangers lurking. Genetic screening and counseling raise important privacy and confidentiality issues and are tainted by unethical public health "experiments." There is also the danger of genetic determinism or reductionism. This is the idea that genetics are responsible for everything from disease to behavioral disorders (Petersen and Bunton 2002). Outgrowths of this were the eugenics movement and the misinterpretations of heredity found in *The Bell Curve* (Herrnstein and Murray 1994).

Related to this is what might be called "Promethean determinism" (Petersen 1998, 61). This is the view that through progress in science and technology we can improve defects in humans. This can come either by fixing the bad genes through genetic therapy or focusing on germ cells to prevent the inheritance of a disorder. This fits into an ideal that we can perfect humans by correcting what is wrong with them from a biological standpoint.

This also relates to issues surrounding homosexuality. There has been some speculation that the tendency toward homosexuality is genetically based. If that is the case, then the way to "correct" homosexuality would be through gene therapy (Petersen 1998; Petersen and Bunton 2002).

There is much room for growth in this area. The interaction of genetics, environment, and lifestyle is one area that needs further study. More training, both ethical and scientific, of researchers and practitioners is needed. The twenty-first century will undoubtedly see a transformation of public health brought on by the genetics revolution.

Notes

1. Other elements to genetic-based research present controversies not related to public health issues. These include cloning and stem-cell research. For a discussion of these issues, see Patel and Rushefsky (2002).

2. As an example of the interaction of human and animal epidemiological studies, consider the outbreak in 2003 and 2004 of avian flu in Vietnam, South Korea, and Japan (with a potential for spreading into Taiwan). The disease is apparently spread via exposure to feces from poultry. See Kuo 2004.

3. The genetic explanation should not be seen as a way to discount the health impacts of environmental insults. The reality is that there is an interaction between genetics and environment.

4. In the case of HIV testing, the screens were done after identifiable markers of the newborn were eliminated. These "blinded" studies were the product of the newness of the epidemic, the stigma attached to those with HIV or AIDS, and the unavailability of therapies. This is beginning to change as the therapies have become available. See the discussion in Pass (2000, 388–89).

5. Validity issues are typical of the field of evaluation research and are important in the biomedical and social sciences. For a discussion of validity issues in the evaluation of testing results, see Rossi, Lipsey, and Freeman (2004).

6. A similar phenomenon is likely occurring with the privacy regulations implemented in 2003 under the Health Insurance Portability and Accountability Act of 1996. Patients have to sign forms stating what their privacy rights are in regard to their medical information. The chances that patients carefully scrutinize and understand what they are signing are pretty small.

7. A somewhat analogous issue is prenatal screening. The fetus or unborn child has clearly not given consent.

8. For a discussion of the role of anecdotes in making public policy regarding managed care, see Rochefort (1998).

9. For a discussion of the politics of HIPAA, see Rushefsky and Patel (1998).

10. To make her distinctions of the different kinds of equality more vibrant, she uses an example of bringing a chocolate cake to her public policy class, and then goes into an extended discussion of how the cake might be sliced and distributed.

Study Questions

1. The basic question underlying this chapter is the role of genetics in health issues. How important is genetic makeup in causing health problems? What other factors might play a role in causing health problems?

2. To what extent should genetic screening be used as part of the job

interview process? To what extent should genetic screening be used in decisionmaking by health plans?

3. To what extent should genetic screening be used by prospective parents during pregnancy? Should prospective parents be able to use the results of genetic screening to determine whether to continue a pregnancy?

4. What kinds of privacy issues does genetic screening raise? What kinds of laws, if any, are needed to protect our privacy?

5. Should the states (and/or the federal government) pass legislation banning discrimination based on genetic makeup?

CHAPTER 7

The Politics of Environment and Public Health

Science and policy are two symbiotic cultures that would prefer to live independently but are resigned to an uneasy, if reciprocal, coexistence. Scientists are forever asking for additional studies and the public funds to carry them out. Policymakers are always seeking to meet the public's demands for increased safety with limited knowledge, short timetables, and declining budgets. Science proceeds slowly and incrementally. Policy may change erratically and apparently illogically. And when it comes to environmental causes of disease, science can rarely provide a crucial experiment, unambiguous data, or convergence from all the experimental domains that are relevant to the policy issue. (Krimsky 2000, 171)

There are many reasons why one should pay attention to the quality of our environment. The environment is, ultimately, the source of sustenance for humans. We depend on the availability and quality of environmental resources for air, water, food, energy, and materials to build homes and offices (essentially transforming the "natural" environment into the "built" environment). Wise use of environmental resources is necessary to sustain human populations and population growth. We might view the environment as intrinsically important. It benefits humans to have at least some areas left undeveloped and closer to their pristine nature.

The environment is also important for human health. To generalize, we will argue in this chapter that the environment and the politics of the environment and public health revolve around three ideas. First, as we saw in chapter 5 in the story about John Snow and the Broad Street pump, disease can be spread through untreated water supplies. A poor quality of environmental resources can adversely affect the health of humans. Second, a number of important diseases have their origins in human activity on the environment. Here we can talk about such things as AIDS, SARS, the West

Nile virus, and the potential impacts of stratospheric ozone depletion and global climate warming. Third, some have argued that humans have put substances in the environment that harm human health. These include chemicals (arsenic, lead), hormone disrupters, and cigarette products (passive smoking). While all the three factors have engendered controversy of the kind discussed in chapter 5, the second and especially the third have been particularly troublesome.

Lifestyle versus Environmental Factors in Public Health

Perhaps the most controversial and political of all issues related to the environment and public health is the relative contribution of various factors to human health. In general, we can attribute human illness and disease to four factors. The first, discussed in chapter 7, is genetic makeup. As we learn more about human genetic makeup through such scientific advances as the genome project (Patel and Rushefsky 2002), we are discovering that people have a genetic disposition toward certain diseases, such as Parkinson's disease, cancer, or heart disease.

Another explanation is the lifestyle factor, which we discuss below. This explanation suggests that behaviors of people lead to illnesses and disease. These lifestyle factors include smoking, eating, and exercise habits.

A third explanation is the environmental one. This one suggests that exposure to environmental insults leads to disease and illness. This can include passive or secondhand smoking, exposure to chemicals, and human transformation of the environment. This explanation is the major subject of this chapter.

There is, of course, a fourth factor. Human illness and disease are likely the result of the interaction of genetics, lifestyle, and environment. One important question for public health is to figure out the importance of each factor. A study in the health policy journal *Health Affairs* focused on premature deaths, a smaller category than overall deaths. The researchers found that "genetic predispositions account for 30 percent of premature deaths; social circumstances, 15 percent; environmental exposures, 5 percent; behavioral patterns, 40 percent; and shortfalls in medical care, 10 percent" (Longman 2003; McGinnis, Williams-Russo, and Knickman 2002). Premature deaths are a function of the interaction of all these factors (Longman 2003; McGinnis, Williams-Russo, and Knickman 2002).

Further, the study is limited in focusing only on deaths, or premature deaths. The focus on deaths is understandable. Death records, particularly in the United States, are of especially good quality. The cause(s) are noted on death certificates. However, disease and illness, morbidity, does not have the same high quality of records. Because not everyone in the United States has health insurance, such people suffering from diseases and illnesses are less likely to seek medical assistance until the disease or illness progresses. Even then, it is very difficult to pick up patterns of illness. This has become an important public health issue in regard to a possible bioterrorism attack (see chapter 8).

There is yet another consideration. We mentioned briefly above that human activity can change the environment in ways that produce illness, disease, and premature deaths. Morse (2003) argues that epidemics (he is writing in the context of the SARS epidemic, but his reference is to the development of epidemics in general) are not random occurrences. The viruses that cause SARS and Ebola, for example, occur in nature. They become human epidemics when humans come into contact with the virus or the virus carrier. The contact occurs when populations move into previously uninhabited areas. Additionally, human activities such as agriculture and clear-cutting forests cause the contacts.

On occasion scientists have organized to push the "public health agenda or an environmental risk hypothesis" (Krimsky 2000, 172). Three examples he gives are the dangers of radiation from nuclear testing, new developments dealing with genetic engineering research (in the 1970s), and the dangers posed by chlorofluorocarbons (CFCs) going to the stratospheric ozone layer. Most of the time scientists were behind rather than ahead of public policy developments.

In looking at the linkage between our environment and human health, we are drawn back to much of the discussion in chapter 5 on the scientific basis for public health decisions. There, we looked at such fields as epidemiology, toxicology, benefit-cost analysis, and risk assessment underlying such decisions. Much of the very heated debate focuses on the level of scientific certainty available to decisionmakers.

We can trace out two positions at polar extremes to each other. At one end are those who are **risk tolerant**, willing to wait until convincing scientific proof is evident. Such a person is willing to risk potential harm, is likely to be dubious about such potential harm, awaiting further evidence and unwilling to pay the costs of change for dubious benefits. Also, some people are willing to take risks because they consider short-term satisfaction/gratification worth the risk of some long-term potential harm.

At the other extreme are those who are **risk averse**. Such people are unwilling to wait for further information and doubt that complete scientific uncertainty is even possible. They are unwilling to accept the risks and willing to pay the costs of change. This risk aversiveness has become part of the modern environmental movement under the rubric of the

precautionary principle (see, for example, the readings in Raffensperger and Tickner 1999a). While there is no one accepted version or definition of this principle, the following definition, contained in the Rio Declaration on Environment and Development and adopted by the United Nations in 1992, captures the core elements of the principle: "Where there are threats of serious or irreversible damage, lack of scientific certainty shall not be used as a reason for postponing cost-effective measures to prevent environmental degradation" (quoted in Cranor 1999, 75).

The precautionary principle has been adopted in international agreements and in domestic legislation. At the international level, the precautionary principle can be found in the 1987 North Sea Ministerial Declarations (to protect the North Sea ecosystem), the Convention for the Protection of the Marine Environment of the North Sea (1992), the 1996 London Protocol, the 1992 Rio Declaration, the 1995 United Nations Agreement on the Conservation and Management of Straddling Stocks and Highly Migratory Fish Stocks, and the 1993 treaty creating the European Union (Santillo, Johnston, and Stringer 1999, 41–45).

At the domestic level, the National Environmental Protection Act (NEPA) embodies at least some of the ideas of the precautionary principle. The act, passed in 1969 and signed on January 1, 1970, by President Nixon (to symbolize the 1970s as the environmental decade), requires that environmental impacts be assessed before actions are taken involving federal agencies or recipients of federal funds (Rosenbaum 1977).

Other examples include the Delaney Clause adopted in 1958 as an amendment to the Food, Drug and Cosmetic Act (forbids suspected carcinogens from being added to the food supply), the Clean Water Act, and the Occupational Safety and Health Act. The most interesting use of the precautionary principle by the United States actually bridges domestic and international arenas. The International Joint Commission (Canada and the United States) agreed to end emissions of toxic substances into the Great Lakes. More than half of the states have adopted some version of the precautionary principle in their environmental legislation. Finally, some elements of the corporate sector have endorsed and/or used the precautionary principle (Raffensperger and Tickner 1999b). Some actions taken during the 2001–03 period suggest we are seeing changes in the use of NEPA and the requirements for environmental impact statements (see, for example, "Environmentalists Claim Bush Administration Is Undermining the National Environmental Policy Act" 2002).

In a sense, the precautionary principle was adopted by the George W. Bush administration in its 2002 National Security Strategy. The strategy called for preemptive strikes against countries that potentially posed a threat to the United States (National Security Council 2002). In its one implementation, the United States attacked Iraq, stating that it had weapons of mass destruction, that it aided terrorists, and that the weapons of mass destruction might be sold or given to terrorists. The failure to find such weapons, at least as of August 2004, suggests some of the problems with the principle. But Secretary of Defense Donald Rumsfeld captured the problem of uncertainty and, implicitly, the need to act even without complete certainty. Slate.com, an online magazine, took some of Rumsfeld's words and turned them into poetry:

The Unknown
>As we know,
>There are known knowns.
>There are things we know we know.
>We also know
>There are known unknowns.
>That is to say
>We know there are some things
>We do not know.
>But there are also unknown unknowns,
>The ones we don't know
>We don't know.
>—*February 12, 2002, Department of Defense news briefing* (Seely 2003)

Given all the unknowns, the Bush administration essentially asserted a risk averse position, though in the environmental area, the administration took a risk tolerant position.

The precautionary principle might seem like antiscience. Rather, it recognizes the limitations in the ability of the scientific enterprise to answer the kinds of questions needed for regulatory decisions. One of the important things that the precautionary principle does is to shift the burden of proof. Normally, a regulatory agency seeking to restrict or ban a substance has the burden of proof to show that the substance causes harm. Risk assessment is one mechanism to do so. Under the precautionary principle, the burden is on the manufacturer or user to demonstrate that the substance does not cause harm (Cranor 1999).

This is a very difficult thing to do. In statistics courses we learn that it is virtually impossible to prove a negative. Let us go back to the Bush administration, Iraq, and weapons of mass destruction. In the weeks and months before the attacks, the Bush administration demanded that Iraqi president Saddam Hussein prove that Iraq no longer had weapons of mass destruction. Hussein claimed they no longer existed, and United Nations weapons inspectors found nothing. Defense Secretary Rumsfeld then stated at a press conference that "absence of evidence does not mean the evidence is absent" (quoted in Cornwell 2002).

One way of understanding the precautionary principle is to, again, turn to statistics. Science and medicine make use of hypothesis testing. Take the case of medicine and the possibility that a woman has breast cancer or a man has prostate cancer. Tests are taken, but the tests are imperfect (there is uncertainty). Based on years of experience, doctors know that a particular test, say the PSA test for prostate cancer, will give correct answers most, but not all, of the time. Most of the time, if the test comes back negative, the patient does not have prostate cancer. Most of the time, if the test comes back positive, the patient does have cancer. But sometimes a negative test is wrong and the patient does have cancer. Sometimes the positive test is wrong and the patient does not have cancer.

In statistical terms we are referring to Type I (false negative) and Type II (false positive) errors (see Barrett and Raffensperger 1999; Schettler, Barrett and Raffensperger 2002). This is the uncertainty that we have been talking about. In comparing what they call mechanistic (traditional) science with precautionary science, mechanistic science tries to minimize Type I errors whereas precautionary science tries to minimize Type II errors (Barrett and Raffensperger 1999). "[I]t is better to claim there is an effect when there is none than to falsely claim there is no effect" (Barrett and Raffensperger 1999, 117).

Another way of looking at the precautionary principle is to consider the concept of "burden of proof." In criminal cases the burden of proof for deciding guilt or innocence, which is on the prosecution, is "beyond a reasonable doubt." After all, the justice system can impose severe penalties, from fines to imprisonment to the ultimate of sentences, capital punishment. Civil cases, however, have a looser standard. Juries are instructed to decide between plaintiff and defendant on the basis of the "weight-of-the-evidence." There might be some doubt, the evidence presented by the plaintiff may not be absolutely certain, but on the whole the evidence supports the assertions of the plaintiff. Given the above, it is not surprising that the precautionary principle supports the weight-of-the-evidence standard (see Barrett and Raffensperger 1999; Cranor 1999).

Cranor (1999, 82) notes that there are various reasons why environmental policy is so controversial:

1. Some are epistemic, having to do with the difficulty of acquiring knowledge and information about the health effects of substances because of the nature of the thing being assessed.

2. Some have to do with asymmetric acquisition of knowledge about substances because those who develop them tend to focus on their benefits and perhaps less on their potential harms.
3. Some have to do with the politics of chemical regulation—small, well-organized groups have considerable advantage over nonexistent or much less well-organized groups.
4. Some have to do with the conventions and internal mandates of research science that tend to focus less on preventing false negatives than on preventing false positives.

We should also point out that pollution has costs that need to be understood. In particular, if environmental pollution causes illnesses in children that are preventable, there are very real costs associated with it. Estimates can be made of what might be called the "environmentally attributable fraction" (EAF) (Massey and Ackerman 2003, 10) of illnesses due to exposure to environmental pollutants. One study focused on Massachusetts and found that the cost from diseases such as cancer, asthma, neurobehavioral disorders (such as autism and attention deficit hyperactivity disorder), lead exposure, and birth defects attributable to environmental pollutants comes to a little over $1 billion (in direct and indirect costs). The authors then extrapolate that to the country as a whole, reasoning that Massachusetts has about 2 percent of the country's population, and argue that estimated costs to the country as a whole could be as high as $50 billion. They also argue that these do not include costs such as the agony experienced by parents and so forth. While the study has its methodological limitations, largely because the data is not as good as it might be, it does give an indication of the boundaries of the costs (Massey and Ackerman 2003). The importance of this study is that if there are costs to remediating environmental pollution, there are also benefits to preventing of illness.

Environmental Degradation and Threats to Health

Having examined the theoretical basis for making policy decisions regarding the relationship of environment and health, we now turn to exploring the more specific threats. It should be mentioned that there are those opposed both to the theoretical arguments made above and to the specific linkages addressed in this section. We will explore those criticisms in this section.

If anyone should be given credit for the focus on environment and health, indeed on the focus on the environment as an important policy area, that person would be Rachel Carson (1962). Her book *Silent Spring* eloquently attacked the ever-growing presence of synthetic pesticides, such as DDT and other organophosphates. She linked them to reproductive problems in wildlife, especially birds (hence the title of her book), and to cancer. She thus anticipated the endocrine disruptor hypothesis discussed below. Carson's book was heavily attacked as unsubstantiated by science. Yet its influence remains.

Chemicals

One potential threat to human health is from chemicals in the environment. Here we are not, generally, talking about naturally occurring chemicals. Rather, we are examining human exposures to man-made chemicals released in the environment. Indeed, much of the discussion of environment and human health focuses on these kinds of chemicals. In the discussion below, we concentrate on three heavy metals as examples of both health and environmental issues and the politics that surround them.

One important piece of information in this area concerns the levels of such chemicals found in humans. For the most part this is a relatively recent area of research. The best source of data here is the National Center for Environmental Health (NCEH), a part of the Centers for Disease Control and Prevention (CDC) within the U.S. Department of Health and Human Services (DHHS).

In 2003 the NCEH issued a report entitled "Second National Report on Human Exposure to Environmental Chemicals." The report is an analysis of the 1999–2000 National Health and Nutrition Examination Survey (NHANES). The survey looked at levels of 116 chemicals in the blood and urine of those participating in the survey. The report makes two important caveats. One is that levels of human exposures are not the same as levels of the chemical in the environment. Second, and most important, the report cautions that it is not saying anything about the health effects of the exposures. The report points out that the ability to detect human exposures has increased dramatically; smaller and smaller levels can be detected. However, while a few chemicals have been well studied for their effects on humans, lead being the most prominent example, much more research needs to be done. The chemicals examined include dioxins, herbicides, phytoestrogens, and organochlorine pesticides, among other classes of chemicals.

One set of chemicals, among the best studied, are the heavy metals. Among the heavy metals, one of the most important from our perspective is lead. Lead is a fairly ubiquitous chemical that has been put to a wide variety of uses. Some of them include as an additive in gasoline, in paint, in pencils, batteries, and solders. Many of these uses have been phased out, for example, in gasoline and paint, though exposures remain. As a result of the phasing out of some of these uses, blood lead levels have decreased.

Lead can have very deleterious effects on human health. According to the report, lead has been labeled as a probable human carcinogen (cancer-causing agent). It can cause damage to central nervous systems, and there is the possibility that it can adversely affect female reproductive systems. Lead has also been associated with diminished intelligence and behavioral problems (National Center for Environmental Health 2003).

Controversy over the impacts of lead exposure has been one of the longest running debates in this field. Concerns about the effects of lead were noted in the first century of the first millennium (Markowitz and Rosner 2002b). Concern in the United States was seen as early as 1908. Lead became a major issue in 1923 when it was first used as an additive in gasoline for the nascent automobile industry. Some have argued that the various industries involved denied that lead posed a threat to human health and applied pressure to prevent regulations that would require elimination of lead additives (see Montague 1999; Markowitz and Rosner 2002b; Davis 2002).

Lomborg agrees that the toxicity of lead is a pretty settled issue. However, he also noted that primarily because of the elimination of lead from gasoline, lead concentrations in the air have declined considerably and, more important, levels of lead in the blood of humans, especially children, have declined dramatically. He cites a report by the Environmental Protection Agency (EPA) that estimates that because of these declines, an estimated twenty-two thousand deaths per year have been averted. Lomborg (2001, 171) continues, "It is also estimated that in the U.S., children will on average avoid losing up to three IQ-points with lower lead levels and that 45,000 fewer retarded children will be born. Finally, about 12 million fewer men will get hypertension." The NCEH (2003) report noted that higher levels of lead in the blood were found among refugees and immigrants, those in lower socioeconomic groups, and children in urban areas. Recently, high levels of lead were found in the drinking water supply of Washington, DC (see Nakamura and Leonning 2004).

A second important heavy metal is cadmium, used in a wide variety of industries and products, such as plastics and batteries. It can be absorbed through smoking and can contaminate the air and water as well as food supplies. Low-level chronic exposure to cadmium can lead to kidney damage and bone disorders in children. Large-scale acute exposures can adversely affect the lungs. Cadmium has been assessed as a human carcinogen and can have reproductive and genetic effects (National Center for Environmental Health 2003, 13–14). Again, the NCEH notes that blood and urine sample levels are below government criteria for exposure (in this case, set by the Occupational

Safety and Health Administration). The report also states that at this time the available scientific evidence does not indicate whether there is cause for concern. Lomborg (2001) points out that concentrations of cadmium (and other pollutants such as DDT and PCBs) in coastal waters have fallen over the years.

One last heavy metal will be discussed here, mainly because of the controversy that policy in this area has generated. That metal is arsenic. At high, acute doses, arsenic can cause skin and blood problems, diarrhea, and other gastrointestinal effects. At lower, long-term levels, arsenic exposure has been linked to metabolic and skin problems, and bladder and lung cancers.

The EPA had been working on a revised arsenic standard since the early 1990s under a congressional mandate. A 1996 review by a subcommittee of the National Academy of Sciences found that arsenic in drinking water was linked to bladder, skin, and lung cancer. The committee also determined that the existing Environmental Protection Agency maximum contaminant level (MCL) standard for arsenic (50 parts per billion [ppb]) was too high (Committee on Toxicology 2001).

In January 2001, shortly before it left office, the Clinton administration proposed an MCL level of 10 ppb based on a series of risk assessments. The 10 ppb was the same standard set by many European countries as well as the World Health Organization.

The newly inaugurated Bush administration suspended the proposed standard and instead sought to keep it at the current 50 ppb. The new administration suggested that the proposed arsenic standard might not be supported by the scientific evidence (Corn 2003; Jehl 2001). EPA administrator Christie Whitman suggested that there was no scientific basis for establishing a 10 ppb level. Further, Whitman argued that in some states, such as New Mexico, there were high levels of naturally occurring arsenic in the water supply, and requiring all states to meet the standard would create very high compliance costs for some water systems (Corn 2003). This raised an uproar in the environmental community and in Congress.

In July 2001 the U.S. House of Representatives voted to sustain the Clinton administration standard (Jehl 2001). Party politics was important here. The House leadership, under Republican control, sought to support the Republican president. However, a small but sufficient number of Republicans voted with the Democrats on the arsenic standard.

Electoral politics apparently played a role in the Bush administration's stance. Karl Rove, the president's political adviser, noted that Bush came close to carrying New Mexico in the 2000 elections. A decision that favored New Mexico, he apparently reasoned, would help the president's reelection campaign in 2004. Bush's communications director Karen Hughes thought this was a bad policy (Corn 2003; Frum 2003).

The Bush administration, preferring a 20 ppb standard, asked the National Academy of Sciences to review the evidence. In September 2001, the report from the academy supported the Clinton standard; indeed, it even suggested that a much lower standard, 3 ppb, be imposed (Committee on Toxicology 2001; Seelye 2001). The next month, EPA administrator Whitman announced that the 10 ppb standard would be kept, and the president signed legislation including the new standard. The deadline for compliance, which applies largely to electrical utilities, is 2006. Environmental groups such as the Natural Resources Defense Council supported the even lower standard (see "Christie Whitman . . ." 2001).[1]

As noted, the levels of many chemicals have been found to be below government criteria. Even if so, there are still reasons for concern. First, data about long-term exposure in humans is very sketchy. Second, having measurable amounts of so many chemicals in humans is itself cause for concern. And third, there have been few studies of the interactive or synergistic effect of the presence of all these chemicals. In other words, the question of what affect some or many of these chemicals is having on humans is virtually impossible to research. Consider the controversy over the legitimacy and meaning of animal testing of a single chemical or of epidemiological studies of exposure to a single chemical. If these are controversial, then synergetic studies would be even more so.

Issues such as lead and arsenic demonstrate that there is a linkage between science policy and politics. The George W. Bush administration has been accused of trying to manipulate the scientific evidence to support its policies. We use the example of lead and children to examine this issue.

First, it is important to note the issue of children and environmental health. Two aspects of children make them an especially important concern for the impacts of environmental pollutants. First, children are smaller than adults. They may receive the same exposure to a pollutant, but because their bodies are smaller, the impacts are likely to be greater; their body burdens are likely to be higher than those of adults. Second, and related, children are developing, growing. Exposure to chemicals is especially worrisome in fetuses. This can also enhance the impact of environmental insults. Additionally, because children have many years of life left to them, they are susceptible to illnesses that require long periods to develop, such as cancer (WHO European Centre for Environment and Health 1999).

According to the National Center for Environmental Health, over four hundred thousand young children in the United States have elevated levels of lead in their blood. The recommended level is ten micrograms of lead per deciliter of blood. Many of these children are from low-income neighborhoods and tend to be disproportionately minority (National Center for Environmental Health n.d.). The major sources of lead in these young children are lead in paint and dust in housing that is in a poor state of repair. Even though paints containing lead were banned in the late 1970s, some 24 million households still have the paint and/or the dust (National Center for Environmental Health n.d.).

An important controversy was whether the recommended maximum level should be lowered to five micrograms of lead. That is, there is research suggesting that cognitive problems are associated with levels as low as five micrograms (Committee on Government Reform, Minority Staff, 2003).[2]

As with many scientific issues, the government forms advisory committees to provide guidance. Within the Centers for Disease Control and Prevention, the relevant group was the Advisory Committee on Childhood Lead Poisoning Prevention. In 2002 the issue was about to be addressed. However, the secretary of health and human services, Tommy Thompson, rejected two scientists who advocated the lower limits and replaced them with scientists who have close ties to the lead industry (Committee on Government Reform, Minority Report 2003). Because science provides legitimacy for regulatory decisions, having science advisory committees support a particular decision gives great weight to that decision (which is not to say that the science should be the only basis for making a decision). By appointing members to such committees who support one limit versus another, the administration was in a sense "fixing" the evidence to produce the result it wanted.

Endocrine Disruptors

In the mid-1990s, a new (or renewed) controversy over environmental health erupted. The precipitating incident was the publication of a book entitled *Our Stolen Future* (Colborn, Dumanoski, and Myers 1997). In many ways the charges contained in this book represented the most serious indictment of the impact of the environment on human health. The authors (and others) contended that the future of mankind was literally at stake. *Our Stolen Future* ought to be considered a successor to Rachel Carson's *Silent Spring*. Carson wrote about how persistent pesticides would lead to reproductive problems among wildlife, especially birds, hence the title of her book. Colborn et al. extended this idea to humans.

The book itself, as the subtitle indicates, reads like a detective story, focusing especially on how Theo Colborn became concerned about disruptors. Colborn and his coauthors argued that human absorption of synthetic chemicals would result in adverse outcomes, such as reproductive difficulties and cancer. One of the important points made by the authors is that we should look beyond cancer to other disorders. They argue that the great emphasis put on cancer and testing for carcinogenic substances (see, for example, Rushefsky 1986; and Lichter and Rothman 1999) missed these other problems, especially reproductive and sexual development issues. The tests for cancer were not, they argued, applicable to hormone disruptors.

Their recommendations included actions that individuals and governments could take. They suggested that individuals know what is in the water supply, choose clean food, and avoid unnecessary exposure to chemicals, such as pesticides (including washing hands frequently).

Their policy recommendations follow the Montreal Protocol, established in 1987, dealing with chlorofluorocarbons and the ozone layer:

- Shift the burden of proof to chemical manufacturers.
- Emphasize prevention of exposure.
- Set standards that protect the most vulnerable, namely children and the unborn.
- Consider the interaction among compounds, not just the effects of each chemical individually.
- Take account of cumulative exposure from air, water, food, and other sources.
- Amend trade secret laws to make it possible for people to protect themselves against undesired exposure while preserving any real need for confidentiality.
- Require companies selling products, especially food but also consumer goods and other potential sources of exposure, to monitor their products for contamination.
- Broaden the concept of the Toxic Release Inventory.
- Require notice and full disclosure when pesticides are used in settings where the public might encounter them.
- Reform health data systems so they provide the information needed to make sound and protective policies. (Colborn, Dumanoski, and Myers 1997, 219–22)

The authors called for more research on the extent of exposure, the response to the chemicals, the impact of the chemicals on the environment, and the conditions under which government should intervene. Finally, the authors called for changes in the use of chemicals in products and in the environment.

The Children's Environmental Health Network (CEHN), in briefing materials presented in a congressional forum in 1997, noted that there were a number of lines of research that supported the hypothesis that exposure to chemicals was creating havoc with both animal and human endocrine systems (Children's Environmental Health Network 1997). One research path focused on cell biology. They noted that research indicated that persistent chemicals (i.e., those that remained in the environment for long periods of time) could become attached to hormone receptors and either enhance the functions of those receptors or inhibit them. A second line of research concentrated on wildlife biology. Such research has found reproductive failures in fish and birds. The third major line of research is laboratory studies. To provide a feel for the conclusions CEHN drew from the research, consider the following paragraph (Children's Environmental Health Network 1997):

> Experiments in the laboratory have confirmed the wildlife observations. For instance, studies of exposure during fetal life of male animals have shown reversed gonadal sex in turtle eggs exposed to PCBs, altered sexual behavior and gonadal development in rats exposed to low doses of dioxins, and marked feminization of rats exposed to the common fungicide vinclozolin. In multiple studies of female animals, many of these chemicals have promoted breast development and increased breast tumor rates. In female primates, PCB exposure impaired reproductive capacity, and dioxin exposure at doses similar to human burdens reduces fertility and causes severe endometriosis.

The fact sheet then turned to human effects. CEHN argued that these findings warranted concern about human effects. The fact sheet mentioned several findings suggestive of an endocrine disruptor effect. These included declines in sperm count and increases in other male sexual organ problems, such as cancer and undescended testicles. The fact sheet stated that there seemed to be a relationship between exposure to DDT and shortened periods of breast feedings by mothers. CEHN suggested there might be a relationship between elevated breast cancer rates and exposure to such chemicals.

Our Stolen Future was both controversial and influential. It challenged a number of assumptions in research and posed a serious threat to the chemical industry. For example, the National Center for Environmental Health 2003 report mentioned earlier looked at levels of various chemicals in the human body. This would be one piece of evidence to support the endocrine disruptor hypothesis. If there are some levels of these chemicals, and there are interactions among those chemicals, it might be inferred that they would impact humans in some way.

The American Council on Science and Health (ACSH), an industry-sponsored group, did not see it that way. In a report prepared as a response to the NCEH study, ACSH argued that our ability to detect smaller and smaller amounts of these chemicals in humans has grown dramatically. But just because there are these trace amounts, it does not follow that they will adversely affect human health. The levels of these chemicals have for the most part declined and are below levels at which human harm would occur (Kamrin 2003).

An earlier, 1999, study took great exception to the endocrine disruptor hypothesis (American Council on Science and Health 1999a). The study contended that there were two factors creating concern about disruptors: the ability to detect trace levels of the chemicals in humans and the environment, and irrational fear of the substances.

ACSH made the following points. First, there is evidence that high levels of some of these chemicals can adversely affect wildlife. However, human exposure is much lower. This point should impact risk analyses. Second, the council argued that there is no consistent scientific linkage between these chemicals in the environment and cancer in human breasts or prostates.

Third, the council asserted that humans are exposed to naturally occurring plant estrogens at much higher levels than synthetic chemicals found in the environment. Fourth, the council noted a decline of concentration levels of these chemicals in the environment. Fifth, some of the studies that supported "the endocrine disruptor hypothesis have been retracted, are not reproducible, or have not been reproduced" (American Council on Science and Health 1999a, 5–6). Finally, epidemiological evidence also does not support the hypothesis. The controversy continues.

The U.S. Environmental Protection Agency (EPA) focused on endocrine disruptors during the Clinton administration (indeed, Vice President Al Gore wrote the foreword to *Our Stolen Future*). In 1996, the EPA formed an advisory group, the Endocrine Disruptor Screening and Testing Advisory Committee (EDSTAC), made up of representatives from a wide range of groups. The purpose of the group was to develop a consensus on the issue of human effects that might lay the basis for congressional legislation (Environmental Protection Agency n.d.a). The committee issued its final report in 1998. Interestingly, the EPA website where the report is located notes that the report is now outdated.

In response to concern about endocrine disruption, legislation was passed in the mid-1990s requiring implementation of a screening program. The two pieces of legislation were the 1996 amendments to the Safe Drinking Water Act and the Food Quality Protection Act, also passed in 1996. Under the legislation, the screening was to have begun by 1999, and the EPA was to report on the program's progress by the summer of 2000.

The EDSTAC report noted that these two pieces of legislation were placed on top of an already existing structure of relevant legislation: the Federal Food, Drug and Cosmetic Act; the Federal Insecticide, Fungicide, and Rodenticide Act; the Clean Water Act; the Safe Drinking Water Act; and the Toxic Substances Control Act (Endocrine Disruptor Screening and Testing Advisory Committee 1998).

The committee report reviewed the chemicals covered under the various acts. The number was and is quite daunting. An inventory by the EPA found some seventy-five thousand chemicals covered by the Toxic Substances Control Act. Under the Federal Insecticide, Fungicide and Rodenticide Act were myriad pesticides that required registration or reregistration. The screening of these chemicals took substantial periods of time; resources were thin and the pace was slow.

The EDSTAC report recommended testing based on setting priorities of chemicals to consider. The report noted that the available evidence was slim, because the vast majority of possible chemicals had never been tested for endocrine disruption effects.

After the advisory committee completed its work, the EPA formed a new, narrower committee, the Standardization and Validation Task Force, again with fairly widespread representation, to evaluate the methods for testing for endocrine disruption. Currently the EPA has a National Advisory Council for Environmental Policy and Technology. A subcommittee of the advisory council, the Endocrine Disruptor Methods Validation Subcommittee, has replaced the task force (Environmental Protection Agency n.d.b). The EPA is partnering with a task force of the Organization for Economic Cooperation and Development to validate screening methods.

Additionally, a National Academy of Sciences 2000 report evaluated the scientific evidence supporting the endocrine disruptor hypothesis (Commission on Life Sciences 2000). The report referred to endocrine disruptors as "hormonally active agents" (HAAs). The National Research Council was asked by Congress, the Centers for Disease Control and Prevention, the Interior Department, and the Environmental Protection Agency to investigate this area.

The committee charged with the task focused on the following areas: "reproductive changes, developmental defects, neurobehavioral abnormalities, immunologic deficits, carcinogenesis, and ecologic effects of compounds" (Commission on Life Sciences 2000, 2). The committee noted considerable difficulties in undertaking its task. For example, the report noted that there were questions as to whether sperm counts were really in decline. Because of the complexity of these issues, causality was not clear. That is, even if an effect was found, say, reproductive problems in wildlife, the cause of those problems were uncertain. Other difficulties included how to weigh different kinds of evidence, such as experiments, epidemiological studies, extrapolating results, and so forth.

Nevertheless, there were important areas of consensus among the members of the committee. For example, the committee found that there was a correlation, and sometimes a direct connection, between prenatal exposure to polychlorinated biphenyls and development problems such as shorter gestation, lower birth weights, and memory and IQ deficiencies.

The report noted, again, the difficulties in undertaking this kind of research: "Understanding the relationships between exposure, absorption, disposition, metabolism, excretion, and response is important for predicting whether exposure to an agent will be harmful" (Commission on Life Sciences 2000, 8).

The report also stated that there are differences in the effect of exposures to HAAs in adults and children and the prenatal environment. These had to be considered also. The basic recommendation in all areas studied was for more and better research, especially research over long periods of time.

There is research that is supportive of the endocrine disruptor hypothesis. In a review of the literature, Rogan and Ragan (2003) find that laboratory and wildlife studies have found endocrine disruption, or signaling as they call it, at high doses. However, humans are exposed to much lower doses and so the hypothesis remains unclear. They conclude that though the evidence for human effects is weak, the hypothesis is founded on a sound scientific foundation and the potential threat posed by endocrine disruptors should be of concern.

Powers (2003) found that synthetic hormones— found in freshwater, from hormone therapy and birth control pills— have a feminizing effect on male fish. He pointed out that the levels used in the test (in Lake Ontario) were close to the concentrations of the hormone found in contaminated surface waters. Inability or difficulties in reproduction were found. Another study reviewed by Powers linked pesticides with decreased human sperm quality. Powers noted that in both cases, water treatment fails to remove the suspect chemicals. He argued that water supplies are "cocktails of small amounts" of these and other chemicals, often from commonplace sources that have been little studied (Powers 2003, 11).

The Hollywood Connection

No discussion of the issue of health and the environment can be complete without considering one particular set of events and the depiction of those events. This set of events was the movie *Erin Brockovich*, and the chemical was hexavalent chromium.[3]

The movie is based on a real-life story. Erin Brockovich was a down-on-her-luck single mother looking for a job. She talked herself into a job as an assistant to a lawyer, Ed Masry. She came across some complaints made by families in Hinkley, California, about sickness in animals and family members. A major company in the area was Pacific Gas & Electric (PG&E), which had a compressor station. The company notified the state in 1987 that it had found levels of hexavalent chromium in the groundwater, which supplied the town's groundwater. The levels far exceeded the legal amounts set by the Environmental Protection Agency. The company apparently knew of the contamination as far back as 1965. By 1987, PG&E had bought up some 75 percent of the houses in the area.[4]

Brockovich investigated much on her own and found families in the area using groundwater who appeared to be suffering from elevated disease levels, such as cancer. Masry's law firm hooked up with a larger, more experienced law firm. Over six hundred plaintiffs were eventually included in the case. The end result was an arbitrated settlement, where PG&E paid the plaintiffs $333 million, stopped using hexavalent chromium, and cleaned up the contamination.

We have in this one case, *Anderson v. Pacific Gas & Electric*, almost all of the issues involved in trying to link environmental insults to human health. First, we have a substance, hexavalent chromium, that has been studied and subject to maximum level contaminant goals by federal and state agencies. Second, there is some epidemiological evidence linking the contaminant to human health. This is one of the tasks that Erin Brockovich accomplished. Third, the source for the contaminant is a company. There is evidence, developed by Brockovich and submitted as part of the court record, that the company knew about the contamination, had known for years, and tried to keep it quiet. The company also denied the ill-health effects. This fits in well with the narrative of environmentalists that can be found in such books as *Deceit and Denial* (Markowitz and Rosner 2002b), which has as its subtitle *The Deadly Politics of Industrial Pollution*. The victims tend to be lower class, so we have the class warfare issue. There is a prominent trial that is eventually settled.

What makes this case a bit unusual is that it was made into a very successful Hollywood movie. The movie may have had the twin effects of hurting the relatively slow path of science and regulatory progress on the one hand and, on the other, of creating pressure for the legislature to provide more resources to the state regulatory agency and speed up the process of setting new standards (Steinpress and Ward 2001).

Sometimes Hollywood and real life converge and have a mutually reinforcing, long-lasting impact (e.g., *The China Syndrome* and Three Mile Island). Although the current controversy is taxing the scientific and regulatory processes, *Erin Brockovich* has led to a better informed public and resulted in a flurry of legislative activity and funding. This is accelerating our scientific understanding of the occurrence and distribution of chromium, the development of realistic regulatory standards (MCLs), and more effective remedial technologies. We can only hope that the scientific and regulatory communities can stay ahead of the screenwriters and be better prepared for the media and public response when the next contaminant du jour hits the screen. (Steinpress and Ward 2001, 322)

Environmental Tobacco Smoke

One of the most controversial issues in this area is the impact of environmental tobacco smoke (ETS), also known as secondhand smoking or passive smoking. The hazards of smoking, a lifestyle issue, are well established. Even the tobacco companies finally admit this.[5] The Philip Morris USA website (www.pmusa.com/health_issues/default.asp) states that it accepts the scientific consensus of the hazards of smoking, which include lung cancer, emphysema, and heart disease. Further, the company agrees that smoking is addictive and that even low-tar cigarettes present health dangers.

Philip Morris USA is a bit more hesitant when it comes to environmental tobacco smoke. Its website states that public health officials have concluded that ETS does present health hazards and therefore appropriate action is warranted. The health hazards listed on the website include sudden infant death syndrome (SIDS), respiratory diseases in children, and heart disease and lung disease in adults.

The basic principle underlying ETS is that inhalation by a nonsmoker of smoke from a cigarette can cause similar health hazards as smoking the cigarette itself. Concern about the health hazards of ETS has led to extensive banning of smoking in public places. These include government buildings, schools, airports, and airplanes. Local governments have also banned smoking in shopping malls and restaurants; private businesses have also banned indoor smoking.[6]

Industry representatives have not been as willing to accept this. As an example, consider a study published in the *British Medical Journal* (Enstrom and Kabat 2003). The authors used data collected by the American Cancer Society of a cohort that was studied beginning in 1958.

They found no significant difference in heart disease, lung cancer, or other respiratory diseases between spouses of smokers and spouses of nonsmokers. They concluded that there was no causal relationship between smoking and health problems and that the effects of ETS are, at best, quite small.

The study created a considerable storm and was criticized in subsequent pages of the *British Medical Journal*. For example, Vaidya (2003) argued that prior to the 1990s, there was no ban on smoking in public facilities in

California. Therefore, even if spouses lived with nonsmokers, they would still have been exposed to ETS. Part of the problem was that some of the research was funded by the tobacco industry. But even the normally skeptical American Council on Science and Health acknowledged the health effects of ETS (American Council on Science and Health 1999b). The health effects noted by ACSH included irritation of respiratory tract, increased risk of respiratory illnesses among children, and aggravation of chronic respiratory diseases such as asthma among adults. The council argued that ETS is a weak human carcinogen and a weak factor in cardiology disease. The council appeared to support limiting exposure to smoking indoors.

The debate over ETS and what to do about it took place over several decades and amid mixed politics and science (Bayer and Colgrove 2002). Concern about ETS was expressed as early as 1971 by then U.S. surgeon general Jesse Steinfeld, and a 1972 report by the surgeon general laid out the first case against ETS. This led to the creation of a nonsmokers' movement that sought to ban ETS. Regulatory agencies began separating smoking and nonsmoking passengers in buses and airlines as early as 1973. In 1974, Connecticut became the first state to ban smoking in restaurants. The scientific studies began to accumulate (Bayer and Colgrove 2002).

The tobacco industry sought to stifle the antismoking movement. It funded scientists who suggested that the evidence showing negative health effects of passive smoking was weak. The industry also shifted gears and started touting the rights of smokers and the important values of liberty and limited government. In the end, the anti-ETS forces seemed to have the upper hand.

Global Warming

Global warming, also known as the greenhouse effect, is the heating of the atmosphere because of emissions of certain chemicals. These chemicals, which include carbon dioxide, methane and chlorofluorocarbons, can trap heat in the atmosphere and keep it from escaping. This is similar to what happens in greenhouses, where the heat is trapped inside, thus the phrase "greenhouse effect." Another contributor to global climate warming is tropical deforestation.

Greenhouse gases have two sources, natural and human. The natural sources are the more significant ones, but human contributions are important as well (see Environmental Protection Agency 1999; Easterbrook 1995). Carbon dioxide, mainly emissions from the burning of fossil fuels, is the major greenhouse gas. The bulk of these gaseous emissions emanates from developed countries, especially the United States (Rushefsky 2002).

While not without controversy, there is data that indicates a gradual overall warming of the earth's atmosphere. An important consensus source is the Intergovernmental Panel on Climate Change (IPCC). Its third report (2001) laid out the scientific data. According to the report, the earth's temperature increased by about 0.6 degrees Centigrade, with much of it coming in the latter part of the 1990s. The report found that snow cover and ice caps have shrunk, and that there were more frequent incidents of heavy precipitation in the late twentieth century.

Of course, while there is data that indicates what has been happening, two important issues need to be addressed. First, is there a linkage between the emissions of these gases and global climate change? The data is correlational or associational, and so the causal linkages are not entirely clear. Second, even if there is a linkage, how do we know what will happen in the future? One answer to this second question is that we can wait and see, a risk tolerant position. Another answer is that we can make use of the data that we do have on emissions and climate changes and other factors and develop computer models to make predictions. This latter solution is the one that has been used, and it is as controversial as the idea of global climate warming and human contributions to it.[7] The IPCC (2001) report asserted that computer models have become more refined over time, and the consensus appears to be strong that the phenomenon is taking place.

Leaving aside the controversy over global warming (see, for example, Lomborg 2001), our purpose is to consider what the possible health effects of global climate warming would be. A report from the U.S. Environmental Protection Agency (1997) sets out the possibilities. We should expect more heat-related health problems, including death. People suffering from cardiovascular and respiratory disease could find their conditions aggravated because of the increased air pollution. Infectious diseases might become more prevalent because more of the earth would have appropriate conditions for them. Increased frequency and intensity of storms might overrun storm sewers, resulting in more intestinal disorders.

In addition to these types of issues, we should examine federal policy toward other environmental and health issues. For example, assuming that global climate warming presents a serious set of problems, then perhaps government should become involved. If the problem is increasing emissions of greenhouse gases, then the logical solution is to reduce those emissions.

The private sector certainly can play a role here, through changes in industrial processes or moving away from fossil fuel–based transportation technologies. Indeed, this is beginning to happen, as hybrid automobiles are beginning to make an appearance and fuel cell technologies are being researched.

But this issue will likely require a much larger response than private markets can accomplish on their own. One first step was the negotiating of the Kyoto Protocol, agreed to by the international community with the assistance of the Clinton administration. The Kyoto Protocol contains a major problem: it calls for targeted reductions on the part of the developed nations but not on the part of developing countries (including such giants as India and the People's Republic of China). The Clinton administration never submitted the treaty to the Senate for confirmation.

During the 2000 presidential campaign, George W. Bush promised that he would try to limit carbon dioxiode emissions, though he rejected the Kyoto Protocol. As president, Bush emphasized the continued uncertainties of the scientific foundation of global warming as the reason for acting very cautiously. When he did decide on a policy, it had two parts. The first was to engage in an energetic research program on global warming.

The second was to change the terms of the debate. Instead of calling for reductions in emissions, the president called for reductions in emissions relative to the size of the economy. This is a critical difference for a couple of reasons. First, as the economy continues to grow, one would expect emissions of greenhouse gases to grow; the growth rate would slow but overall emissions would continue to increase. Second, the president was essentially calling for a more efficient economy, at least in terms of greenhouse gases. Third, the private sector is already responding and so actual policy decisions by the administration would be unnecessary (see Corn 2003, 111–16).

Congress has similarly declined to act. In 2003 a bipartisan bill sponsored by Arizona Republican John McCain and Connecticut Democrat Joseph Lieberman was rejected by the Senate. Senator McCain (2003) argued that, environmentally and economically, their bill made sense. He cited a study that suggested his bill would cost each American an average of $20 a year to implement, and another study suggesting that costs of global climate warming for the average American were $160 a year. He also noted that companies such as DuPont were realizing substantial savings from reducing greenhouse gas emissions. The bill was defeated in late October 2003, but supporters were pleased that they got as much support for the bill as they did (Lee and Revkin 2003).

Biological Agents

A report by the Institute of Medicine (2003) lists a number of factors that together have increased risks from infectious diseases. One factor is climate, which can impede or promote the transmission of diseases and the growth of infectious agents. A related factor is ecosystem changes. The report suggests that such changes, including climate changes, can make it easier for microbial agents to be transferred to new places. A third factor, again related to the previous two, is human behaviors. Population increases and economic development in previously sparsely populated areas can promote contacts with microbial agents. Other factors include technological developments, war, poverty, and crumbling public health infrastructures (on the latter, see Garrett 2000).

The case for the "ecological origins of new diseases" is strongly made by Walters (2003, 156; see also Mestel 2003). The human impact on the environment—demographically, agriculturally, and industrially—is responsible for a number of plagues that have relatively recently become noticeable. The plagues include HIV/AIDS, Lyme disease, SARS, the West Nile virus, hantavirus, and antibiotic resistance.

To take one of these plagues, Walters writes about one of the most interesting connections between the environment and infectious diseases, Lyme disease. Symptoms of Lyme disease include a rash, fatigue, joint pain, and muscle aches (Centers for Disease Control and Prevention n.d.). Transmitters of Lyme disease are ticks that picked up the disease from deer and mice in forests. Walters notes that lack of diversity of species within forests makes it easier for transmission. Theory and experimental evidence linked humans and the environment: "Acorns attract deer and mice, mice infect ticks, and infected ticks give people Lyme disease. People's health was linked to acorn production" (Walters 2003, 106).

Politics of Environmental Protection

National Government

Concern about the environment has a long history, going back to the early years of the twentieth century and the administration of President Theodore Roosevelt. The modern environmental movement has its origins in the 1960s and flowered in the 1970s. Rachel Carson's *Silent Spring* was one precipitator of this movement (Caulfield 1989). The legacy of environmental concern (Rosenbaum 1977) and the environmental movement was a series of laws and the development of an elaborate set of agencies.

While there was some modest legislation prior to this time, the symbol of environmental legislation was passage of the National Environmental Protection Act (NEPA) and its signing by President Richard Nixon on January 1, 1970. Other legislation quickly followed. Table 7.1 lists the major pieces of federal legislation related to environmental health. The legislation has produced a vast array of agencies. Table 7.2 lists some of the agencies involved in environmental health.

Table 7.1

Major Environmental Legislation

Year	Law
1969	National Environmental Policy Act
1970	Clean Air Act Amendments
	Occupational Safety and Heath Act
1972	Consumer Product Safety Act
	Federal Insecticide, Fungicide, and Rodenticide Act
	Federal Water Pollution Control Act (Clean Water Act)
	Noise Control Act
1973	Endangered Species Act
1974	Safe Drinking Water Act
	Clean Air Act Amendments
1975	Hazardous Materials Transportation Act
1976	Resource Conservation and Recovery Act
	Solid Waste Disposal Act
	Toxic Substances Control Act
1977	Clean Air Act Amendments
	Surface Mining Control and Reclamation Act
1980	Comprehensive Environmental Response,
	Compensation and Liability Act ("Superfund")
1984	Hazardous Materials and Solid Waste Amendments
1986	Safe Drinking Water Act Amendments
	Superfund Amendments and Reauthorization Act
1987	Clean Water Act Reauthorization
1990	Clean Air Act Amendments

A major player as a government actor is the Environmental Protection Agency (EPA). The EPA has perhaps the broadest responsibilities. It was created by executive order of President Nixon, combining agencies from several different departments (Whitaker 1976). Its responsibilities in the environmental health area include setting out advisories about possible human health and environment issues (risk assessments), children's health, research on exposure, health risk assessments, health effects, health risks, occupational health, health of seniors, and toxicity assessments (Environmental Protection Agency n.d.c).

A number of agencies within the federal Department of Health and Human Services (DHHS) play important roles in studying the linkage between the environment and human health and making regulatory decisions. The Food and Drug Administration (FDA) is the oldest of these agencies. Its origins begin with the Bureau of Chemistry in the Department of Agriculture. The agency itself was established by the Food and Drug Act of 1906, after a series of revelations and scandals about the quality of the American food supply. A major precipitator for the legislation was the publication of

Table 7.2

Major Executive Branch Agencies with Environmental Responsibilities

White House Office
Office of Management and Budget
Council on Environmental Quality
Department of Health and Human Services
Environmental Protection Agency
Department of Justice
Department of the Interior
Department of Agriculture
Department of Defense
Nuclear Regulatory Commission
Department of State
Department of Commerce
Department of Labor
Department of Housing and Urban Development
Department of Transportation
Department of Energy
Tennessee Valley Authority

Source: Kraft and Vig (2000).

Upton Sinclair's *The Jungle*, an exposé of the meatpacking industry (Hilts 2003).[8] The FDA regulates the safety of food products and animal feed, among others.

Another important agency is the Centers for Disease Control and Prevention. The CDC as well as the EPA is involved in epidemiological studies to detect the impact of environmental insults on human health. Some of what it does is undertake research through the National Center for Environmental Health. The National Center for Infectious Diseases tracks global epidemics, some of which stem from changes in the environment. The CDC website notes that one of its most important missions is to provide information for those who make health decisions. This includes health providers, state and local health departments, and federal agencies.

The Agency for Toxic Substances and Disease Registry (ATSDR) also plays a critical role in this area. According to its website (www. atsdr.cdc.gov/), the mission of the agency is to provide information and make decisions regarding exposures to toxic substances, such as asbestos. It provides information related to health assessments as well as educates the public and public officials about the hazards of various substances. Its mission includes several initiatives directly related to human health. These include information related to children's health, research on the linkage between fish consumed from the Great Lakes and human health, and human health and urban issues.

State and Local Governments

In the federal system that characterizes government in the United States, state and local governments play an important role in domestic policy. Public health, and particularly environmental health, is no exception. All states have health departments, and they focus at least partially on environmental health. To take the authors' home state (Missouri) as an example, the Missouri Department of Health and Senior Services (DHSS) has a strategic planning document that includes a section on the environment (Missouri Department of Health and Senior Services 2003). The department has a surveillance system that focuses on environmental hazards such as mercury and lead poisoning. DHSS's strategic plan calls for environmental management of hazardous substances. Two of its strategies are to respond to information from the public about possible exposures to hazardous substances and to assess exposure of humans to substances found at hazardous waste sites.

States also have agencies that focus directly on the environment. To use Missouri again as an example, the agency is the Department of Natural Resources (DNR). These state agencies have an important role in environmental protection. Much federal policy in the environmental area is implemented by the states and their agencies, such as Missouri's DNR. For example, states have the primary implementation responsibility for the quality of the nation's drinking water and air quality (Rabe 2000).

States are starting to develop the capacity to track environmental health trends in conjunction with the federal government (National Conference of State Legislatures [NCSL] 2003). For example, several federal agencies (EPA, CDC, and the National Aeronautics and Space Administration [NASA]) are collecting data on environmental health. The EPA is attempting to create a data exchange among federal and state agencies. The CDC has given grants to states to engage in biomonitoring (measurement of chemicals in humans).

Another area of interest is tracking health conditions related to environmental hazards. This is one of the oldest and most successful functions of public health agencies in regard to infectious diseases. In terms of chronic diseases, such as asthma, that might be related to environmental conditions, tracking is in a relatively primitive state. Some diseases, such as cancer, have much better tracking records. Developmental disease is another area where tracking is weak.

The NCSL summarizes a report by the Pew Environmental Commission about the weaknesses of state tracking systems:

- Currently, very few states have made any attempt to track autism, mental retardation, or cerebral palsy.
- Cancer registries in many states have been neglected for years. In some states that do collect data, resources are not available to perform analysis and respond to incidents such as cancer clusters.
- Many states have no birth defects tracking or their tracking attempts are inadequate. Birth defects are the leading cause of death among infants, and some birth defects, such as hypospadia, have increased dramatically during the past few decades.
- Twenty-one states do not have internal programs to specifically track asthma. It is nearly impossible to compare data between states since the quality and detail of the data vary tremendously. (National Conference of State Legislatures 2003, 4)

Some states have been quite aggressive in pursuing the linkage between the environment and human health. California is perhaps the best example of this. California's Environmental Protection Agency (CAL/EPA) has a set of programs devoted to children's health. In 1999 the state legislature passed the Children's Environmental Health Protection Act. Gray Davis, the state's governor, established a Children's Health Initiative in 2000. The programs include cleaning up hazardous waste sites near schools and monitoring the air in portable classrooms. Agencies within CAL/EPA include the Air Resources Board, the Department of Pesticide Regulation, the Department of Toxic Substances Control, the Integrated Waste Management Board, the State Water Resources Control Board, and the Office of Environmental Health Hazard Assessment (California Environmental Protection Agency n.d.).

Some states, and California is again a good example, may want to go further in environmental protection than the federal government. For example, in August 2003 the federal Environmental Protection Agency issued a rule revising the new source reviews. Under new source reviews, a corporate or utility facility that sought to upgrade its equipment would have to meet current clean air standards. The Bush administration argued that such a rule, mandated by the 1977 Clean Air Act amendments, inhibited such upgrades and, thereby, economic growth. The standard adopted by the EPA would be waived if emissions were not increased and the change was functionally equivalent to what was being changed (Environmental Protection Agency 2003a, 2003b).

State governments were concerned about the rule during the proceedings leading up to the announcement of the final regulations. The states and local governments were represented by two state association interest groups, the State and Territorial Program Administrators and the Association of Local Air Pollution Control Officials. In their announcement (2003a, 1) released the same day that the federal regulations were published, the two associations denounced the new rule, stating that it would "seriously erode public health and environmental protection and have detrimental impacts on air quality." Several months later the two associations published a menu of options that states could use that would provide greater protection than the federal standards (2003b, 2003c).

As noted above, the federal government has not taken active steps to remediate the problem of global warming. In the absence of federal action, a number of states have moved on their own. During the 2001–03 period, over half the states passed legislation addressing the issue. California, as is fairly common, led the way with a 2002 law strictly limiting carbon dioxide emissions. Other states are requiring their electrical utilities to use other sources of energy besides coal and oil. Of course, a problem that results from this is a wide disparity of policies across the country (Lee 2003).

Local public health agencies are at the front line of environmental health issues, as they are with many public health issues. To use our home city, Springfield, Missouri, as an example, the Springfield/Greene County Public Health Department has as one of its missions to monitor and control air pollution emissions within the city limits. It does this to enforce state and federal statutes. The local health department enforces the regulations for the Missouri Air Conservation Commission and the state Department of Natural Resources. The agency focuses on what the federal EPA defines as the major or "criteria" air pollutants: ozone, nitrogen oxides, volatile organic compounds, sulfur dioxide, carbon monoxide, and particulate matters (Springfield/Greene County Health Department n.d.).

An interesting example of action by a local government was the adoption of the precautionary principle as official policy by the San Francisco Board of Supervisors. The ordinance adopted by the board sets out the basic elements of the precautionary principle: anticipatory action, right to know, alternatives assessment, full cost-accounting, and participatory decision processes (San Francisco Government n.d.). Indeed, the city has an impressive array of environmental programs.

Social Ecology

A classic definition of politics has been provided by David Easton, who saw politics as the authoritative allocation of values (Easton 1953). Societies use some combination of markets and governments to allocate resources and values. When governments do the allocation, then it becomes authoritative. Much environmental policy involves an authoritative restriction of somebody's behavior.

Take for example the issue of passive smoking. As we discussed earlier, there is evidence, contentious as it might be, that exposure to tobacco smoke may have harmful health effects, particularly among those suffering from respiratory diseases, such as asthma. As a result of such concerns, a number of cities have passed ordinances either limiting or prohibiting smoking in restaurants. Federal legislation has similarly banned smoking on airplanes. While one can argue the health effects of such regulations, they do mean that those who would like to smoke on a plane or, especially, in a restaurant have to give up what is to them a pleasurable behavior. This type of example can multiplied many times. It is the heart of environmental policy.

This example makes it easy to see the definition of politics as authoritative allocation of values. Some people (smokers) are prohibited or limited in their behavior (smoking) because it may adversely affect another group of people. There is a value basis for these types of decisions.

The whole area of environment and health involves a consideration of values and efforts to affect those values. Paehlke (2000) notes that environmental policy involves a new range of values. For him these values include ecology, human health, and sustainability. The ecology value states that there are interrelationships and dependencies among all living creatures. Paehlke writes that human life and survival depend on plants, animals, the weather, and so on. So the filling of wetlands or the cutting down of tropical forests can have an effect on human survival.

The second core belief, most important for our purposes, is environmental health. That is, the value suggests we limit the impact of the environment on human health, for example, exposures to toxic substances. While there may be agreement on the importance of human health as a value, how to achieve it is quite contentious (Paehlke 2000).

The final value is sustainability. Sustainability is the capacity for humans and the environment we depend on to continue. This may be the most important value, as the other two (ecology and human health) depend on this last one (Paehlke 2000).

The values suggest that it is necessary to change the relationship between humans and their environment. We have the greatest capacity among all species to change the environment. Accepting the importance of these values means ascribing to them a status closer to the importance of the value of economic growth.

There are a number of different ways to look at values and the environment. For example, Ophuls (1977) argued that environmental considerations required a major change in our value system because environmental degradation and depletion of resources would lead to scarcity. Others also take a highly critical view of the relationship between humans and their environment.[9]

For example, one set of perspectives is known as social ecology. The basic idea behind social ecology is that smaller political systems are needed to create a more harmonious relationship between humans and their environment. It is a rather radical idea, involving some of the aspects of communitarianism (see Bookchin 1971; Clark 1999). Others suggest that the inherent nature of capitalism, particularly on a global scale, hurts the environment (see Warnock's 2003 review of *The Enemy of Nature*).

Similarly, the Green Party platform is a radical critique of mainstream politics and economics. The platform argues that the exploitation of humans is paralleled by the exploitation of the environment. Humans and their environment should be in a more harmonious relationship. Apart from changes in how humans make use of the environment, for example, relying much more on renewable energy technologies and phasing out synthetic chemicals, the platform also calls for much more grassroots democracy (Green Party USA n.d.)

It is not necessary to adopt the more extreme versions of environmentalism to understand that what we do to the environment does have some impact on human health. Such a perspective suggests that our values need to be reassessed. In particular, the value of human health, as described by Paehlke (2000), confronts the important value of economic growth.

As one example of how a change might be necessary, consider the terrible fires that afflicted Southern California in the fall of 2003. Over twenty people died, thousands of homes were decimated, and over half a million acres were burned. In conventional economic usage, the fires did not impede economic growth. On the other hand, the rebuilding of homes and communities will contribute to an increase in our gross domestic product. Similarly, degradation of the environment does not subtract from our normal understanding of economic growth. The costs of human harm from the environment (see the discussion above and Massey and Ackerman 2003) are not considered in normal measures of the economy.

A second example concerns the issue of how economists understand the costs of production. This also includes an understanding of social welfare economics and the role of government in society. A conventional view of the rationale for government intervention to protect the environment (see, for example, Siebert 1981) focuses on negative externalities. An externality is the "effect of one or more persons that emanates from the action of a different person or firm" (Samuelson 1964, 465). A negative externality is one in which the effect is harmful. An example of a negative externality is the buildup of chemical retardants used in children's clothing (especially sleepware) in human tissue. Another example is the use of fluorocarbons in air conditioning and refrigeration systems that deplete ozone from the stratosphere. The cost of cleaning up a waste disposal site or remediating human harms or the health costs of environmental pollution are not part of the private costs of manufacturing the product. There are, however, important social costs. The rationale then for government intervention is to capture some of those social costs. But note that in the normal calculations of economic activity, in the absence of pressure group or government intervention, private production does not directly consider these other costs.

A third example of values relates to benefit-cost analysis. There are several ways in which the standard benefit-cost analysis understates or neglects environmental human health concerns. First, as noted above, environmental pollution is not included in the normal costs of business. Indeed, there may not be any price or costs attached to these concerns. Therefore, the standard analysis suggests that these concerns be "carried along," though they will not appear in a quantitative benefit-cost analysis.

Second, benefit-cost analysis rightly accounts for the impact of time on benefits and costs. Those benefits and costs that appear earlier in a project will be weighted more heavily than those that appear later. Those later benefits and costs will be discounted because they accrue over a long period of time.

Consider the issue of global warming. Assuming that the phenomenon is real, the most serious impacts of global warming will occur fifty to one hundred years in the future. Action to forestall global warming (such as reducing the emissions of carbon dioxide) needs to be taken now. The costs are up front, the benefits are down the road. A standard benefit-cost analysis would likely result in a decision to not take any action. If we then added the issue that global warming might not be as serious as some suggest, then we can further discount the benefits by the probability of the effects occurring.

In short, the standard analysis and the values they rest on would not lead us to undertake actions to minimize human harm. It is the values that need change.

The Politics of Environment and Public Health

The linkage of environment and health is one of the most important issues on the public health agenda. Many of these, such as exposure to toxic substances and chronic diseases, are controversial and therefore political. Certainly some segments of the population, such as children, the elderly, and those suffering from chronic respiratory diseases are more vulnerable than others. As mentioned earlier, the impact of environmental changes on human health is but one of a number of causes of

POLITICS OF ENVIRONMENT AND PUBLIC HEALTH   241

human illness, not the most important, though not insignificant either. The scientific basis for the linkages that underlie the public health regulatory regime is subject to disagreements, often based on ideological, value, or interest conflicts. Establishing the health hazards of tobacco, both from directly inhaling cigarettes and from environmental tobacco smoke, is a case in point.

Not everyone agrees about the importance of the linkage of environment and health. Lichter and Rothman (1999), for example, argue that environmental cancer is a "political disease." Their review of the evidence suggests that there are significant disagreements between activists and scientists and that the media tend to rely on the activists. Lomborg (2001) likewise argues that most of the claims made about our worsening environment and its impact on human health, including the endocrine disruptor hypothesis, are overstated.

Most recently, consider the charges levied by Erin Brockovich and Ed Masry (2003). They asserted that there is a linkage between oil and gas operations and lymphoma and thyroid cancer in students who attended Beverly Hills High School. They cited testing that found elevated levels of benzene and methane, both suspected carcinogens.

In response, Umansky (2003) argued that the linkage does not in fact exist, and that the scientific claims asserted by Brockovich and Masry are weak. Umansky stated that the case that brought them fame, chromium-6 and Pacific Gas & Electric, is much less supported by the facts than the movie and the story conclude.

An impressive set of agencies has been established, beginning in the 1970s (though in the case of the Food and Drug Administration, going back to the early years of the twentieth century). These agencies can be found at all levels of government and are concerned with research, monitoring, prevention, and regulation. Despite suggestions that the linkage between environment and health is weak, there is evidence that the interaction of environment and genetics is important (see chapter 6; and Khoury, Burke, and Thomson 2000).

But more can be done, particularly at the local level. What is needed, and is going on to some extent, is an increased capacity of local communities to promote public health. We can see some of this in the monitoring activities of local public health agencies. We can see this in the movement by municipalities to ban smoking in public facilities, such as in government office buildings and restaurants.

The federal publication *Healthy People 2010* provides a series of indices for creating healthy communities. While the list is not as comprehensive as advocates of corrective action would like, it does provide a beginning basis for improving the health of communities.

Environmental Health

8–5   Increase the proportion of persons served by community water systems who receive a supply of drinking water that meets the regulations of the Safe Drinking Water Act.

8–11   Eliminate elevated blood lead levels in children.

8–12   Minimize the risks to human health and the environment posed by hazardous sites.

8–15   Increase recycling of municipal solid waste.

8–18   Increase the proportion of persons who live in homes tested for radon concentrations.

8–22   Increase the proportion of persons living in pre-1950s housing that has been tested for the presence of lead-based paint. (Office of Disease Prevention and Health Promotion 2001, 36)

Reducing the impact of the environment on healthy communities will require increasing the capacity of local public health agencies to act to produce healthy communities. Srinivasan, O'Fallon, and Dearry (2003) argue that what they call the "built environment" (1446) can have negative impacts on human physical (and mental) health, particularly on chronic diseases. While they note that these chronic diseases are the result of the combined effect of genetic and environmental variables, they also note that there are positive benefits from creating sustainable communities. They call for more research on the positive changes that could come from adding green spaces to urban communities, relying more on mass transportation, making use of less toxic materials, and so forth.

The healthy cities movement fits into this idea (see, for example, Tibbetts 2003). Local communities and their residents become more responsible for their health and look for ways in which to improve lifestyle and environmental influences on health. This also fits in nicely with the devolution movement in the United States, sometimes called the new federalism, a turning of power and responsibility from the federal to state and local governments. Local governments can work to bring in industries that are more environmentally conscious.

The Institute of Medicine notes what they call the "urban health penalty" (Institute of Medicine 2003, 54), which is the greater prevalence of health issues in urban than in suburban areas, at least some of which are attributable to the environment. They also note that the types of environmental problems we face now are different from the classic case of John Snow and cholera discussed in chapter 5. The environmental problems are both more global and local, and the health problems are more chronic than acute. Alleviating these problems will require action at all levels: international, national, state, and local.

Notes

1. Frum has a somewhat different take on the story. According to him, environmental groups pushed the Clinton administration to lower the standard. The Clinton administration then dallied around for years, issuing the new regulation just days before the George W. Bush administration would take office as a "nice little bomb" (2003, 37) for the new administration.

2. The report cited the following study: R. Canfield et al., "Intellectual Impairment in Children With Blood Lead Concentration Below 10," *New England Journal of Medicine* (April 17, 2003): 1517–26.

3. Note also similar controversial movies such as *A Civil Action* with John Travolta, and *The Insider* (about the tobacco industry), starring Al Pacino and Russell Crowe.

4. The material in these paragraphs is based on information from the website www.lawbuzz.com/famous_trials/erin_brockovich/erin_brockovich_ch1.htm#preface.

5. For a discussion of how the tobacco industry tried to manipulate the scientific basis for the hazards of smoking, see Glantz et al. 1996. For an examination of the politics and policymaking surrounding smoking, see Fritschler 1996.

6. The authors' hometown, Springfield, Missouri, has been wrestling with the ban. At one point it banned smoking in certain eateries, depending on the size of the facility and the extent that it served alcoholic beverages. The city council was much criticized for its confusing action.

7. To provide some perspective on how controversial the global climate warming issue is, consider a lawsuit filed in late 2003. The suit was filed by an author of an environmental science textbook that was rejected for use in the public schools by the Texas State School Board of Education. The book was rejected as being "anti-Christian" and "un-American" in part because it argued that there was a scientific consensus in support of global climate warming. The board apparently relied on critiques and testimony by Citizens for a Sound Economy and the Texas Public Policy Foundation, two conservative groups. The board, dominated by Republicans, voted to reject the book along party lines (all Republicans voted to reject the book and all Democrats voted to retain it). See Clarkson 2003.

8. Note how we have mentioned several writers or activists that helped spark policy change. Consider Rachel Carson and Erin Brockovich.

9. Stating the problem this way is itself a value judgment. It suggests that humans are separate from the environment in which they live. This can have profound effects on the view that one takes. From one perspective, humans are given dominion over the earth's natural resources. This can be viewed as a rationale in two ways, either as a responsibility for the quality of the environment or a license to exploit the environment. Another perspective suggests that humans are an intrusion on the environment, aliens, and have only deleterious effects on the environment.

Study Questions

1. How important to human health is the environment? How much focus should public health policy place on environmental factors as opposed to other factors such as lifestyle or genetics?

2. This chapter discusses the precautionary principle (as does chapter 5).

To what extent should public health policymakers rely on this principle in making decisions about possible environmental insults to health? How much evidence is necessary before policymakers should act?

3. One of the most intriguing debates in this area concerns endocrine disruptors. Much of the debate over environmental policy, scientific evidence, industry interests, and health is related to this very controversial area. Is the threat of endocrine disruptors serious enough to warrant public policy actions? Or is the whole debate overstated?

4. Another area of controversy concerns secondhand, passive, or environmental smoke. This has led many government authorities to ban smoking in restaurants, government buildings, and so forth. Do you support or not support such a ban? Does the evidence support or not support such bans? Where do you stand on the rights of people who smoke?

5. The ultimate environmental health issue is global warming. Some have argued that we can already see signs of global warming. Others argue that the threat is real but fairly far in the future (fifty or more years). Still others argue that the evidence does not support the hypothesis of global warming. If global warming is real, then we ought to act now to limit its effects. But those actions are costly in terms of money and lifestyle changes. How real do you see the threat of global warming to be? Should we take action now to reduce carbon dioxide emissions; or is this yet another example of overwrought environmentalism?

CHAPTER 8

The Politics of
Bioterrorism and Public Health

All these functions, in all tiers of public health from villages to global levels, required maintenance of a crucial social contract: the individual or country agrees to openly disclose information for the sake of the larger community. And in return public health authorities promise never to abuse their trust, maintaining discretion and protecting patient privacy.

But the fear of bioterrorism threatened to destroy that vital social contract, as it was not one shared by law enforcement or defense. The closer public health drew to the other two, the greater the danger that it would lose all trust and credibility in the eyes of the public it served.

(Garrett 2000, 548)

In the mid-1990s, novelist Tom Clancy published two books that, looking back from today's vantage point, seem rather prescient. In the earlier one, *Debt of Honor* (Clancy 1994), Japan (and India) attempts to defeat the United States economically. The effort fails. But at the end of the book, a Japanese pilot, disgraced by the failure of his country's plan, flies an airliner into the Capitol Building in Washington, DC, wiping out virtually the entire American government with the exception of Clancy's protagonist, Jack Ryan. Ryan, a former navy officer and Central Intelligence Agency (CIA) analyst/operative, was just appointed vice president of the United States. As a result of the devastating attack, Ryan ascends to the presidency, and it is his task to reconstitute a new government.

That task is the major concern of the sequel, *Executive Orders* (Clancy 1996). Apart from trying to rally the country from the terrorist attack and form the new government, Ryan and the country are faced with new challenges. This time the challenge stems from the Middle East, namely Iran, as well as other countries such as the People's Republic of China. The United States is seen as being very vulnerable, given its internal problems.

245

The leader of Iran hatches a bioterrorism plot against the United States. The Ebola virus is captured (Clancy is very detailed here as elsewhere in his writings) and then brought into the United States. Iranian agents unleash the virus in several places around the country through an aerosol mechanism.

Clancy has prophetically depicted much that concerned the United States in the early part of the twenty-first century. There has been great concern about the threat of biological warfare for some time. This was compounded by the terrorist attacks on the United States on September 11, 2001, when two commercial airliners were flown into the World Trade Center in New York City (where one of the coauthors was raised, and where his brother and older daughter work), a third was crashed into the Pentagon in Washington, DC, and a fourth crashed in Pennsylvania rather than complete its mission thanks to the intervention of passengers who were aware, via cell phone, of what had happened. This was followed later in the year by anthrax-coated envelopes sent through the mail in 2001 and ricin-laced mail sent in 2004.

Biological weapons were also known at some point to be in the possession of Iraqi leader Saddam Hussein. The possession by Iraq of weapons of mass destruction (WMD) as well as the refusal of Iraq to allow weapons inspectors to check for such weapons, was one of the prime reasons mentioned for the U.S.-led invasion of Iraq in 2003.[1]

These events form the backdrop for the topic of this chapter, bioterrorism. There is no one single definition of terrorism. Terrorism is a deliberate attack on civilians in order to accomplish a goal. The CIA defines terrorism as "premeditated, politically motivated violence perpetrated against noncombatant targets by subnational groups or clandestine agents, usually intended to influence an audience" (Central Intelligence Agency n.d.).[2] The Federal Bureau of Investigation (FBI) defines terrorism as "the unlawful use of force or violence against persons or property to intimidate or coerce a government, the civilian population, or any segment thereof, in furtherance of political or social objectives" (Federal Bureau of Investigation 1996, 3). Bioterrorism is therefore the use of biological weapons in such an attack. The purpose of a terrorist attack, particularly a bioterrorist attack, is not so much to inflict casualties, though that is certainly one purpose, as to strike fear in the target population, fear that may not be warranted by the attack.

This chapter begins by looking at the beginning of the use of bioterrorism. It then follows with a discussion of the major biological agents, the conditions under which such an attack is likely to be successful or unsuccessful, and the motivations of those who would engage in such an attack. The subsequent section looks at the U.S. effort at understanding bioterrorist attacks, including simulated attacks. The next section examines the public health implications of a bioterrorist attack, including the state of preparedness of the public health system. We conclude with some thoughts about bioterrorism and the future.

Bioterrorism in History

The use of biological weapons as agents of war goes back several millennia. As far back as the sixth century B.C., Assyrians may have been the first to use bioterrorism. They reportedly used a fungus, rye ergot, to poison the wells of their enemies. An Athenian leader may have done a similar thing about the same time (Biological Terrorism Response Manual n.d.; National Public Radio 2001).

The Middle Ages saw several uses of crude biological weapons. The incidents demonstrate that causing panic is as much the strength of these weapons as the casualties that might result from their use. In 1346 the Tartar army threw the bodies of people who had died of plague over the walls of a city it was laying siege to. A similar episode occurred in 1422 and again in 1710 by Russians in their war with Sweden.

During the French and Indian War in North America (1754–63), the British apparently provided blankets to Indian allies of the French. The blankets were infected with smallpox and quickly devastated the Native American population, which had not developed a natural immunity to the virus (Henderson et al. 2004b; Sidel and Levy 2003; Tucker 2001).

The modern use of biological weapons dates to World War I. The Germans were accused of infecting livestock with the infectious agent glanders, which appears to have resulted in a small number of fatalities. They were also accused of using biological agents in Britain, St. Petersburg, Russia, Italy, and in the United States (Biological Terrorism Response Manual n.d.; National Public Radio 2001).

Events leading up to World War II presented new opportunities for thinking about or using biological weapons. Much of this, though certainly not all, was done by the Japanese, particularly in their conquest of China (Biological Terrorism Response Manual n.d.; National Public Radio 2001). In 1931 the Japanese apparently attempted to infect a League of Nations (predecessor of the United Nations) commission that was looking into the Japanese invasion of Manchuria. The biological weapon was cholera, though the attempt was an utter failure. The next year the Japanese began an experimental program looking into the use of such weapons.

The effort became massive by 1936, when Unit 731 was formed. This was a laboratory complex that conducted both in-house and field experiments. The victims were Chinese and included the use of infected fleas. By

1940, plague, the dreaded disease of the Middle Ages, had appeared in China as a result of the Japanese occupation.

Investigations into biological weapons were not the purview of the Japanese (or the Germans) alone. In 1941–42 the British begin looking at anthrax as a weapon. In 1941 the United States opened its own program at Fort Detrick, Maryland, with some testing in Mississippi and Utah (Biological Terrorism Response Manual n.d.; Miller, Engelberg, and Broad 2001; National Public Radio 2001).

Following the war, the United States beefed up its biological weapons program, establishing a facility at Pine Bluffs, Arkansas, and expanding the operation at Fort Detrick. A lab was also set up at Plum Island, New York (Carroll 2004). A testing center was created in the early 1960s in Utah and the Pine Bluffs facility became a production and storehouse plant (Biological Terrorism Response Manual n.d.; Miller, Engelberg, and Broad 2001). In 1966 the army conducted a simulated bioterrorism attack in the subway system of New York, using a harmless biological agent.

Part of the rationale for the U.S. effort was the Cold War and the fear that the Soviet Union was developing such a program. Such a concern was not in the least appeased when the Soviet defense minister, Zhukov, stated in 1956 that such weapons would likely be used in the event of a war. CIA U-2 spy planes seemed to confirm that the Soviets did indeed have a biological weapons program (Biological Terrorism Response Manual n.d.; Miller, Engelberg, and Broad 2001).

In 1969 and 1970, President Richard M. Nixon issued an executive order ending the U.S. bioweapons research program for offensive purposes. Much of the rationale for this action was the belief within the Defense Department that biological weapons would not be needed, given the United States' advantage in nuclear weapons. In 1972 a number of countries, including Iraq, the Soviet Union, and the United States, signed the Biological and Toxic Weapons Convention. The convention sought to prohibit the possession or stockpiling of these weapons. Miller, Engelberg, and Broad (2001) observed that elements within the United States felt that the convention was too weak, and they kept up a defensive biological weapons program.

In some respects the skepticism about the convention was justified. The Soviet Union was indeed continuing its offensive weapons program. This was hinted at in 1979 when an explosion at a military base in Sverdlovsk released a form of anthrax, resulting in at least forty deaths and perhaps as many as one thousand. It was not until 1992, after the disintegration of the Soviet Union, that Russian president Boris Yeltsin admitted that the Soviet Union did have a very significant and well-developed biological weapons program (Biological Terrorism Response Manual n.d.; Miller, Engelberg, and Broad 2001).

Miller, Engelberg, and Broad (2001; see also Garrett 2000) began their work on biological weapons with a domestic event that took place in 1984. A cult, the Rajmeeshees, attempted to gain control over the local government in Wasco County, Oregon. The cult sought to get exceptions to local zoning ordinances so that they could expand their holdings. The local government refused. In retaliation, cult members apparently sprinkled *Salmonella* bacteria in the salad bars of a number of restaurants. The result was a number of cases of *Salmonella* poisoning.

There are several important points about this story (Garrett 2000). First, this was the first known bioterrorist attack within the United States (the British use of smallpox, mentioned above, does not count, because the country had not been established yet). Second, this first instance of such an attack was from a domestic source, not a foreign one. Third, the cult was not particularly sophisticated in its use of the bacteria and, so while there were some infections, there were no deaths. Fourth, the episode showed how easy it is to obtain biological agents.

The final two points of this episode relate directly to the capacity of the public health system to detect a biological attack. The team investigating the incidents consisted of members of the Oregon health department and the Center for Disease Control (CDC, later changed to Centers for Disease Control and Prevention, though the acronym remained the same). So this became a federal issue, with local, state, and federal authorities involved. Even then it took about a year for the team to determine the cause of the outbreak and trace it back to the cult.

This is a critical point about bioterrorism and public health. It is more difficult to determine the culprits in a bioterrorist attack than in a conventional one. And it is difficult perhaps to determine whether a biological attack even occurred, let alone find the culprits. The surveillance function of public health is critical.

And this brings us to the final point. The county did have a pretty good surveillance system (Garrett 2000), which was not true for all local governments. Without such a surveillance system, which means good reporting requirements and personnel capable of solving puzzles, the attack might have gone unnoticed. As Garrett (2000) points out, if the attack had gone undetected, the cult would be have been encouraged to escalate its efforts.

Japan also experienced a would-be terrorist attack in 1995, also by a cult group (Biological Terrorism Response Manual n.d.; Garrett 2000; Miller, Engelberg, and Broad 2001). The major event occurred on March 20, when a large number of subway riders in Japan were sickened during the morning commute. The perpetrators were the Aum Shinrikyo cult. The cult's purpose, apparently, was to hasten Armageddon, or the end of the world. The cult was a vast organization with thousands of members, and it had been stockpiling such weapons. They were even negotiating the purchase of nuclear weapons (Garrett 2000).

Biological weapons as well as the other two categories of weapons of mass destruction (WMD) became important in regard to Saddam Hussein's Iraq. Iraq had engaged in an eight-year war with Iran beginning in 1980 after the latter country had experienced its Islamic revolution and threatened to export it other countries, including Iraq with its large Shi'ia majority. The United States supported Iraq and sold it arms and provided it with intelligence (Phillips 2004). Militarily superior to the Iranians (with American and Soviet arms), Iraq was numerically inferior to the Iranians. At one point it employed poison gas against the Iranians. At another point it used poison gas to put down a rebellion by Kurds in the north (Purdum 2003).

The break with the United States came in the summer of 1990, when Iraq invaded its neighbor, Kuwait. The United States' response was to lead a coalition to remove Iraq from Kuwait as well as eliminate a threat to other countries in the region, such as Saudi Arabia. The American-led effort was successful, though the decision was made not to march to Iraq's capital of Baghdad and remove Hussein from office.

As part of the conditions for ending the war, Iraq agreed to give up its WMD programs and allow United Nations (UN) inspections. Over the next seven years Iraq alternately limited, prohibited, or allowed UN inspections. By the end of 1998, Iraq was refusing to allow any more such inspections.

The fear in the United States and elsewhere was that Iraq possessed biological (and chemical) weapons and was attempting to develop nuclear weapons. Without inspections, it was not clear what Iraqi capabilities were. According to Garrett (2000, 499):

> United Nations inspectors eventually concluded that Iraq had built an impressive biological armamentarium before the Desert Storm (1991) war, including about eight thousand pounds of anthrax, eight kilograms of concentrated botulinum toxin, and at least four other types of bacteria, five of viruses, and three other biotoxins. Just before the war broke out, the UN team concluded, Iraq had grown 340 liters of *Clostridium* for botulism toxin production. At numerous sites—particularly the Al Hakam Single-Cell Protein Plant, located a few miles south of Baghdad—stainless steel fermenters capable of holding 1,450 liters of biologicals were found.

United Nations inspectors found that some of the botulinum material had been transformed into weapons, but otherwise Iraq had been unable to accomplish much more along these lines. It was clear to the inspectors that the

Iraqis were trying to develop the capability, with the help of other countries, such as Libya (Garrett 2000, 501).

While the United States tried keeping the pressure on Iraq to allow inspectors and to discontinue its WMD programs, including missile strikes and considerations of war (Garrett 2000), it was the September 11, 2001, attacks that moved the United States to an offensive, preemptive stance.

Despite opposition from other countries, such as France, Germany, and Russia, the United States and Britain (with the support of and some aid from some other countries) launched an attack on Iraq in the spring of 2003. One of the reasons given for the attack was Iraq's possession of weapons of mass destruction, including biological weapons, the prior use of such weapons (against Iranians and Kurds as previously mentioned), the possibility that Iraq might transfer those weapons to terrorist groups such as al-Qaeda (the group that carried out the September 11 attacks), and possible links between Iraq and al-Qaeda (Daalder and Lindsay 2003; Purdum 2003).

The American military effort was a success, though the aftermath (rebuilding Iraq) has been somewhat shaky. Weapons of mass destruction have not been found and, indeed, may have been destroyed or had decayed by 1995 (Barry and Hosenball 2004).

Subsequent to the 9/11 attacks, there were two sets of biological threats in the United States. Beginning in September, 2001, letters containing weapons-grade anthrax were sent to various people, including the anchor of the NBC evening news Tom Brokaw, the son of a producer at ABC, two workers in Lake Worth, Florida, one of whom died, a letter sent to Senate Majority Leader Tom Daschle, postal workers, and so forth. In all, there were sixteen confirmed cases of anthrax and five suspected cases (Biological Terrorism Response Manual n.d.). No one has been arrested for sending these poisoned letters.

Then on February 2, 2004, a letter containing the biologic ricin was sent to the office of Senate Majority Leader Bill Frist. Senate office buildings were closed down for a couple of days while investigators looked to see if there was any other contamination. None was found, nor have the perpetrators been identified (Hulse 2004).

Potential Threats of Bioterrorism

Types/Forms of Biological Weapons

In general, biologics can be classified into three types (Kortepeter and Parker 1999). First are the pathogens, germs or viruses that cause disease. These include salmonella, anthrax, smallpox, and hemorrhagic fever (which includes Ebola, employed in Tom Clancy's *Executive Orders* mentioned above). Toxins are the second type. These include botulism and ricin. The third type include anticrop agents, such as rye stem rust and wheat stem rust (Kortepeter and Parker 1999). Kortepeter and Parker's analysis finds that anthrax and smallpox are the two agents likely to cause the most casualties in the event of a bioterrorism event. Both have high death rates, can be produced in large quantities, can be dispersed through aerosol transmission, and can survive for long periods of time (see also Henderson et al. 2004a, 2004b). They point out that the impact of the use of either agent is likely as much to be psychological, that is, causing panic, as the effects themselves. They also point out, and this is an invidious aspect of bioterrorism, that detection of the attack can be delayed for weeks. Plague is another pathogen that can have devastating consequences, as was the case in the Middle Ages, and there was a plague incident in India in the 1990s (Garrett 2000, 20–49; Henderson et al. 2004c).

The Centers for Disease Control and Prevention (CDC) lists three categories of bioterrorism agents. Category A agents are anthrax, botulism, plague, smallpox, tularemia, and viral hemorrhagic fevers. These are the most serious agents because they are either highly communicable or easily transmitted, mortality rates are high, and thus they have serious public health implications. They can also cause panic in the population. The CDC says that the public health system needs to be especially prepared for such an attack (Centers for Disease Control and Prevention n.d.).

Category B agents include brucellosis, food safety threats such as salmonella, glanders, Q fever, ricin toxin, staphylococcal enterotoxin B, typhus fever, viral encephalitis, and water safety threats. These are less serious threats with lower levels of mortality, and are less easy to spread than the Category A agents (Centers for Disease Control and Prevention n.d.).

Category C agents are potential threats such as hantavirus and Nipah virus. These are threats because they are easy to produce and disperse and could pose significant health threats (Centers for Disease Control and Prevention n.d.).

One other biological threat ought to be mentioned. The genetics revolution (see chapter 6) presents tremendous opportunities for harm. The ability to mix and match through gene splicing and recombinant DNA technologies, along with advances in the genome project, sets up the possibility for the creation of superbugs. These can be either pathogens that are enhanced or changed in some manner so that available vaccines or therapies become useless, or new pathogens that can be created (Miller, Engelberg, and Broad 2001). The nightmare possibilities are endless. Several novels have pictured how this might happen and the horrific results that would occur.

Miller, Engelberg, and Broad (2001) relate how Craig Venter, one of the founding fathers of the genome project, introduced President Bill Clinton to the book *The Cobra Event* (Preston 1998). The evildoer (to use President George W. Bush's term for bad guys) creates a new pathogen that combines smallpox with another virus that kills brain cells, resulting in a very violent and painful death. President Clinton wanted to find out whether, in Miller, Engelberg, and Broad's words, someone could "unleash an unstoppable plague with designer pathogens." The answer was that, in theory at least, this was feasible (2001, 226).

Two of the most serious threats are smallpox and anthrax. Tucker (2001) begins his book on smallpox with the following chilling description:

> In à maximum-security facility in Atlanta, the world's most dangerous prisoner sits in solitary confinement, awaiting execution. Wanted for the torture and death of millions of people, this mass murderer was captured in a global dragnet lasting more than a decade. Although the prisoner has been condemned to death, the jailers are debating whether or not to carry out the sentence. Some believe that studying the killer's methods could help to develop better defenses against such crimes, yet others fear that the prisoner could escape and wreak mayhem on an even greater scale. While the debate continues, the execution has been postponed.
>
> The world's most dangerous prisoner is the smallpox virus, and it is held inside two padlocked freezers in a secure room at the U.S. Centers of Disease Control and Prevention in Atlanta. (Tucker 2001, 10)

The smallpox virus and its relatives are thousands of years old, dating to the dawn of civilization. Tucker (2001) writes that perhaps the first evidence of a smallpox epidemic was in ancient Athens, about 430 B.C. Conquering nations brought smallpox to their new gains, such as Africa and the Western Hemisphere. The impact of the disease was so great that various countries looked to a variety of deities for aid. In the period before vaccinations, virtually entire populations would be exposed to the virus (Henderson et al. 2004b) Over time, exposed populations in countries with sizable populations developed resistance to smallpox exposure, but those newly exposed to it were devastated. Indeed, the first vaccines ever developed were aimed at smallpox, appearing as early as the early eighteenth century (Tucker 2001). Dr. Edward Jenner developed the first mass successful vaccine, injecting the related cowpox virus into subjects. Jenner found that those injected were immune from smallpox.

In the twentieth century a campaign was begun to eliminate smallpox, though by 1950 the disease had been conquered in the United States (Tucker 2001).

The CDC began a surveillance campaign in the 1940s to prevent the virus from entering this country. There were outbreaks in Canada, Great Britain, and Wales as late as the 1960s. Vaccination of the American population continued until 1972 and in the rest of the world until 1980 (Garrett 2000).

One major problem, indicated above, was that despite cooperation with world authorities on the eradication of smallpox, the Soviet Union maintained a supply of the virus (Tucker 2001; Garrett 2000). This was in violation of the Biological Weapons Convention, something the Russians did not admit until 1992 (Tucker 2001). Indeed, the Soviet Union tried to develop a "doomsday weapon" using smallpox. And there was concern about security issues of the stock in Russia (Tucker 2001). This is similar to problems seen with nuclear weapons and material in Russia and in some of the newly emergent countries of the former Soviet Union, such as Ukraine.

Questions arose as to whether the remaining smallpox virus stocks should be destroyed. Those who favored destruction argued that advances in genetics would permit scientists and doctors to be able to identify the virus if there were a future outbreak. Further, the smallpox vaccine, in the event of an outbreak, could be maintained without storing the virus itself. From our standpoint, the most important argument for destruction was a "moral suasion" one (Tucker 2001, 170–71). Retaining a virus anywhere would still keep alive the possibility of its use as a weapon of terror. Destroying the virus would signal to all, include rogue groups or countries, that use of smallpox as a weapon would be a crime against international law (Tucker 2001).

There were those, labeled by Tucker (Tucker 2001, 171) as "retentionists," who wanted to maintain at least some stock of the virus. One reason for doing this is that there might be an outbreak in the future. There were in Russia buried bodies infected with smallpox. There were also variants of smallpox in parts of Africa. The virus, the retentionists argued, would be needed for further study.

The retentionists argued that maintaining some of the virus would also allow continued research into the mechanism by which the infection worked and the response of humans to infection. Possessing the genetic structure, the DNA, was insufficient by itself for such studies (Tucker 2001, 171–72). There was also concern that if the inventory of the virus was destroyed, possible target countries would no longer consider it necessary to maintain stocks of the vaccine. Then if a new outbreak emerged, the major weapon against it would be missing.

This was the decision facing the Clinton administration. There was a lack of consensus on whether to destroy the remaining stocks, a debate that continued into the late 1990s. The president was increasingly concerned about terrorism after the 1993 attack on the World Trade Center in New York City, and even more concerned specifically about bioterrorism after the 1995 incident in Tokyo (Clarke 2004). A simulation of a smallpox attack on the United States showed that it would be hard to control (Tucker 2001). Indeed, an outbreak of smallpox is considered so serious that even a single case should be considered of great concern on the part of the international public health community (Henderson et al. 2004b).

In the event of a bioterrorist event involving smallpox, there are a number of strategies for limiting its spread. One is vaccination as a preventive measure. As noted, smallpox vaccination in the United States and elsewhere ended over thirty years ago. There is a question as to how long the immunity to smallpox lasts. There is concern that those who were immunized years ago may no longer have any protection, or weak protection at best. In the event of an outbreak, vaccination in the first days of exposure would drastically contain the spread (Lane and Goldstein 2003). Isolation of those exposed to the virus is another complementary containment strategy. Lane and Goldstein (2003) state that with the proper response, outbreaks of smallpox could be limited to about a month. Of course, this would follow once the outbreak has been properly identified.

There is also concern that the vaccination program itself might cause some deaths. One estimate is that vaccinating the entire population as a way to thwart a biological attack would result in the deaths of as many as five-hundred people. Because the likelihood of such an attack is small, some feel that the policy ought to be rejected (Lane and Goldstein 2003).

An alternate strategy might be to just vaccinate first responders, those most likely to come into early contact with the virus in the event of a biological attack. There are problems here also. There is a fair amount of turnover of first responders, so that would extend the subgroup that would need vaccination.

Another policy option might be to give citizens a choice of whether to get vaccinated. This would of course require that sufficient information be given to the population, including the likelihood of a bioterrorist event and chances of an adverse reaction to the vaccine itself (Lane and Goldstein 2003). The option that they recommend (2003) is actually the present course. This would involve vaccinating first responders only in the event of an outbreak, building up supplies of the vaccine, then ensuring that there is a continuous capacity to produce vaccine and training.

Necessary Conditions for a Successful and Major Bioterrorist Attack

Three conditions are necessary for a bioterrorist attack (Siegrist 1999). The first condition is that the target of the attack be vulnerable to such an attack.

Siegrist (1999) notes that the United States is indeed vulnerable to such an attack. Reducing vulnerability would require dealing with issues such as insufficient equipment (i.e., sensors) and lack of appropriate treatments for some biological attacks. This includes the lack of stockpiles of appropriate medications and the problem of short shelf lives of the medications. Further, there is limited emergency room capacity to take victims of such an attack.

The second necessary condition is the ability of a group or person to carry out such an attack (Siegrist 1999). Capability takes two forms. One is technical. This is the ability to fashion a biological agent into a weapon. During the anthrax events following the September 11, 2001, attacks, the question was raised as to whether the anthrax specimens were weapons-grade. If they were, then a fairly sophisticated operation was involved. Having said this, the technical features are not particularly complex (Siegrist 1999). The other kind of capability is institutional. As of 1999, some nineteen countries have such a capability. Siegrist (1999) writes that it is not clear whether terrorist groups can develop such weapons.

The third factor is the intent to carry out such an attack (Siegrist 1999). While we consider motivations below, we should briefly discuss asymmetric warfare (Smith, Corbin, and Hellman 2001). The United States emerged from the end of the Cold War as the world's sole superpower. No nation has the military capacity or budget to successfully challenge the United States on its own terms. The ability to carry out complex military operations, as seen in the first war with Iraq, in Afghanistan, and in the second war with Iraq demonstrated the capabilities of American technology, strategy, and personnel. National security strategies aim to keep the United States from being challenged. However, groups such as al-Qaeda are not likely to engage in a frontal, full-blown military assault against the United States. Rather, they are likely to engage in terrorist attacks where we are most vulnerable. In other words, they would use strategies that would bypass our strengths and attack us at our weaknesses. This is the notion of asymmetric warfare.

Stern (1999) suggests that, in general, the costs of engaging in a bioterrorist attack outweigh the benefits. For example, such an attack would lead to a government response against the group. Another issue is the health threat to the perpetrators.

However, Stern does note that there are conditions under which a group might choose to engage in such an attack.

> Candidates for successful use of biological weapons represent the intersection of three sets: groups that want to use these weapons despite formidable political risks; groups that can acquire the agent and a dissemination device (however crude); and groups whose organizational structure

enables them to deliver or disseminate the agent covertly. The intersection of these sets is small but growing, especially for low-technology attacks such as contaminating food or disseminating biological agents in an enclosed space [the Clancy scenario]. (Stern 1999, 517)

Motivations Behind a Bioterrorist Attack

Motivations for engaging in a bioterrorist attack, or any type of terrorist attack, vary. Also note that terrorist attacks do not have to involve weapons of mass destruction, which include chemical and radiological as well as biological weapons. As we have seen in 2004, more conventional explosives can be used in terrorist attacks, such as in Iraq, Spain, Morocco, and Turkey. Siegrist (1999, 507) wrote that, traditionally, terrorist attacks were used to "make a political statement." In the more recent period, terrorists have sought to cause as many casualties as possible and frighten an audience. Motivations can include political and/or religious reasons (Siegrist 1999).

Stern (1999) suggests a number of possible motivational factors. One is to get attention. She notes that a biological attack has characteristics that would especially provoke fear in a population. These include, for example, the invisible and indiscriminate nature of the attack.

A second motivational factor is economic terrorism. Biological agents could be used to attack the food supply or a particular corporation. She also says that an anthrax attack would cause economic havoc because of cleanup costs.

A third such factor is millenarianism. This is a belief that the world has to be cleansed of its sins and that a terrorist attack would be one way to accomplish this.

The fourth factor is what Stern (1999) calls premillennial tension. Stern was writing near the end of the twentieth century, and there was concern about a terrorist attack at the beginning of the new century/millennium, and that this would have some religious overtones.

The fifth factor would be to create chaos or for revenge. Stern (1999) notes that the organizer of the 1993 bombing of the World Trade Center was seeking revenge. She also specifically mentions Osama bin Laden in this connection.

A sixth motivation is what Stern (1999, 518) calls "mimicking God." In this case the terrorist is seeking to imitate the biblical plagues rained down upon Egypt. A seventh possible motivation is to show the technical capabilities of the terrorist organization. Finally, there is the copycat phenomenon (Stern 1999, 519). Once an attack is attempted, others may try to copy it or there might be pranks or hoaxes.

Propst (2002) distinguishes between "old" and "new" terrorists. The "old" terrorists sought to make changes in the political system (political motivation), help foster radical changes (a psychological motivation), or end perceived injustices in society (the mechanism for dealing-with-grievances motivation). "New" terrorists have the same categories of motivations, but the substance of those motivations is different. Rather than making changes in the political system, "new terrorists" seek to destroy it. Similarly, "new" terrorists do not seek to resolve injustices in society or the state, but to destroy it. The psychological motivation of "new" terrorists might be racist, or to create a new society. "Old" terrorists do have a religious motivation, but "new" terrorists might. This motivation might be to help move the world forward to an apocalypse or a messianic age.

An interesting empirical study about bioterrorism sought to understand the motivations for such an attack. Tucker's analysis (1999) looked at terrorism attacks from 1900 to 1999, two years prior to the 9/11 attacks, with a database of 415 incidents. Of those, 160 had criminal motivations, 219 were politically or ideologically motivated, and 38 were state-sponsored assassinations. Tucker's collection shows two spikes, one around 1986, with chemical weapons. The other, in 1998, was biological, largely anthrax. Tucker notes ominously that the targets for such attacks have evolved toward civilian targets and "symbolic buildings or organizations" (1999, 501). Some of the groups using biological terrorism included apocalyptic groups such as Aum Shinrikyo mentioned above, right-wing militia groups that were trying to destroy federal targets, and a left-wing group, the Weather Underground, which also wanted to attack federal targets. He concludes:

> In summary, the historical record suggests that future incidents of bioterrorism will probably involve hoaxes and relatively small-scale attacks, such as food contamination. Nevertheless, the diffusion of dual-use technologies relevant to the production of biological and toxin agents, and the potential availability of scientists and engineers formerly employed in sophisticated biological warfare programs such as those of the Soviet Union and South Africa, suggest that the technical barriers to mass-casualty terrorism are eroding. (Tucker 1999, 503)

Current Preparedness of the Public Health System to Deal with a Bioterrorist Attack

Perhaps the most important question we can ask is, "How prepared is the United States to respond in the event of a biological attack (or chemical, nuclear, or conventional attack)?" Certainly one of the major tasks the United States faces, one beyond the purview of this book, is preventing such an attack from occurring in the first place. This is not a task for public health. Public health has other tasks. One is detection of such an attack, or surveillance. A second is responding to the task. While improvements have been made since the September 11, 2001, attacks, much remains to be done.

A major issue concerning the ability of the United States to respond to a bioterrorist attack is that the system is highly fragmented (Versel 2001; Institute of Medicine 2003). A report of the Institute of Medicine (IOM) (1988), focusing on the system in general, found the public health care system in general to be in disarray. The follow-up report (Institute of Medicine 2003) found virtually no progress. Versel (2001) notes the elaborate and fragmented nature of the public health system in light of the possibility of a terrorist attack:

> The nation's emergency preparedness is fragmented among federal, state and local governments and private-sector organizations, including emergency medical services, law enforcement agencies, state National Guard unites, charities and religious groups.
>
> Now, with the advent of bioterrorism, there are new players in emergency response, including public health agencies, pharmaceutical companies, building inspectors and the Department of Defense. (Versel 2001, 2)

The editors of *The Lancet*, writing the month after the terrorist attacks, describe the U.S. public health system as "complacent, ill-focused, and overly bureaucratic" ("Bioterrorism: Safeguarding the Public's Health" 2001, 1283). Garrett (2000) describes public health capability has having collapsed. Her book, with the arresting title *Betrayal of Trust*, looks at public health around the world. But the U.S. public health care system faces similar problems. It is a foster child, the subject of neglect (see also Starr 1982).

Federal Level

After the September 11, 2001, terrorist attacks by al-Qaeda against the United States, investigations into the preparedness of the United States if other attacks took place were held by Congress and other bodies. While there had been some studies and commissions before 9/11, and some improvements in readiness had taken place, preparedness at the federal level was weak and needed much improvement (Waeckerle 2001).

A number of departments have some jurisdiction or responsibility in dealing with bioterrorism issues. These departments are Homeland Security, Justice,

Department of Defense, Veterans Affairs, Health and Human Services, Agriculture, and Energy (U.S. House Select Committee on Homeland Security 2004). Within Health and Human Services are several agencies that have specific responsibilities, including the Food and Drug Administration (FDA) and the Centers for Disease Control and Prevention (CDC). The Environmental Protection Agency is another agency with some responsibility in this area, as is, naturally, the Federal Emergency Management Agency (FEMA). In all there are more than twenty agencies at the federal level that have some responsibility in the event of a bioterrorist attack (General Accounting Office 2001).

There have been several attempts to deal with bioterrorism issues and terrorism issues in general. One is the "National Security Strategy to Combat Weapons of Mass Destruction" (White House 2002). This strategy has three components. The first is to defend and deter an attack through a counterproliferation strategy. The second is to engage in efforts to limit the availability of weapons of mass destructions, a nonproliferation strategy. The third is to develop the capability to respond to an attack, what the document calls "consequence management" (White House 2002). Democrats on the House Select Committee on Homeland Security criticized the strategy for its vagueness, for example, failing to identify the responsibilities of various agencies (U.S. House Select Committee on Homeland Security 2004; see also Crowley 2004).

Waeckerle described what he called a number of deficits in the response capability of the federal government. Some of these have been addressed, with more or less success, with the establishment of the Department of Homeland Security.

The first are command, control, and communications deficits. Waeckerle says that there is no overall authority, that there are many agencies that have some jurisdiction in the event of a bioterrorism attack. Further, because of the lack of a single command structure, communications among the agencies at the federal level as well as with state and local agencies is weak. The result is bureaucratic power struggles and an ineffective use of resources. As we will see below, the establishment of a Department of Homeland Security has only partially resolved some of these problems.

A second set of deficits is in regard to planning (Waeckerle 2001). What is meant by this is a lack of financing, training, and so forth at the local level, and a lack of coordination from the federal level on down. Further, there needs to be direction and support from the federal level to the state and local levels. Additionally, the U.S. Department of Health and Human Services was to have developed a nationwide plan for public emergencies by June 2003; as of February 2004, no such plan has been produced (U.S. House Select Committee on Homeland Security 2004).

As mentioned frequently throughout this book, one of the major tasks of any public health system is the detection of a threat to the public's health, in this case, a biological attack. And as we have noted in this chapter, one characteristic of a biological attack is that it might not be noticed for days. Thus surveillance is a critical function in the defense against and response to a biological attack. Waeckerle (2001) points out that the ability to detect an attack is limited because of lack of training of clinicians as well as a lack of appropriate technology to be able to discover an attack before it can be widely spread. Further, Waeckerle notes that many hospital and public health laboratories lack the capability of identifying such biological agents as anthrax. Even if they could, the possible demand might overwhelm them. Waeckerle (2001, 5) stated that "Congress must support public and private research for the development of real-time alerting and tracking surveillance systems with analytical capabilities as well as rapid and reliable diagnostic tests for bioagents."

Another deficit deals with investigations of a possible biological attack. Here Waeckerle as well others (see Garrett 2000 and Institute of Medicine 2003) noted the weakness in capacity and resources of the public health system. Again, lack of training, personnel, and other resources are to blame, and more funding is needed.

Waeckerle also looked at what he called management deficits. These include personnel deficits, such as the lack of training and education for first responders to a biological incident as well as other public health officials. Also included in management deficits are defects in the hospital system. This includes capacity, communications, and ability.

A third element of management deficits are medical treatment deficits. This refers to the lack of vaccines against many biological agents. There was also no strategy for stockpiling effective vaccines.

One legislative response to these problems came in 2002 with the passage of the Bioterrorism Act of 2002 (Public Health Security and Bioterrorism Preparedness Response Act of 2002). This act requires that the secretary of health and human services (DHHS) develop a national plan to prepare for and respond to a biological attack in coordination with state and local governments. This includes ensuring that state and local governments have the needed capabilities to respond to such an attack, including surveillance capability, trained workers, sufficient laboratory capacity, and effective communications. The act also calls for the development of a stock of medications, such as vaccines, in the event of an attack.

The legislation also establishes a new assistant secretary for public health emergency preparedness and the development of a National Disaster Medical System to coordinate the various activities of the federal government.

The legislation also called for improving the capabilities of the CDC to detect and respond to an attack.

Title II of the legislation focuses on biological agents themselves. The title calls for enhanced regulation of possible biological agents, including the registration of the agents themselves and those who could possess them. Title III concentrates on the safety of the food and drug supply, and Title IV on the safety of the water supply.

The Food and Drug Administration has issued regulations, many of them at the proposal stage, regarding many of these provisions. For example, in May 2003 a regulation covering food safety was proposed (Food and Drug Administration 2003).

One of its more important tasks is to ensure that there are sufficient supplies of appropriate vaccines in the event of an attack (Zoon 1999; see also Russell 1999). This includes an accelerated schedule for developing, testing, and improving new products. Writing prior to 9/11 and the anthrax attacks that followed shortly thereafter, Zoon (1999) provides a case study of the anthrax vaccine. There was only one such licensed vaccine, developed in 1970 and approved by an FDA review board in 1985. Zoon notes that new vaccines are being studied and tested with animals.

One problem that drug development raises is patent protection. In the fall of 2001, after the terrorist attacks, the Canadian government authorized a Canadian company to make ciprofloxacin, an antidote for anthrax. This would have violated the international patent on the drug held by the Bayer company. Rather than go along with this, Bayer donated large quantities of cipro, even in the event of an attack. The U.S. government purchased a sizable quantity of the drug at half price. The British scientific journal *The Lancet* denounced the U.S. government action in this case, as well as with AIDS. The editorial stated that in the event of a public health emergency, and AIDS certainly qualified, and the threat of an anthrax attack did as well, then the needs of public health should override the economic protections given to a company ("Patent Protection Versus Public Health" 2001).

In 2003, President Bush announced Project BioShield as part of his 2003 State of the Union Address (Gottron 2003). The problem the project was intended to address was the lack of suitable countermeasures in the event of a bioterrorist threat. Countermeasures include things like vaccines and antibiotics. In February 2004 the bioagent ricin was found in Senate Majority Leader Bill Frist's (R-Tennessee) office. There is no countermeasure to ricin. One assumption behind Project BioShield is that if there is a countermeasure, then terrorists might be deterred from making the attack ("Finish Project BioShield" 2004). In July 2004 President Bush signed legislation enabling Project BioShield (Branigin 2004).

One reason for this deficiency was the lack of a commercial market for the products. The proposal and the accompanying bill provided for increased funding and easier acquisition of the products. Review of the products would be accelerated and the government would provide a guaranteed market for the products (Gottron 2003).

Interestingly, the federal budget process has gotten in the way of accomplishing the project's goals. $5.6 billion was dedicated as part of the appropriations bill for the Department of Homeland Security in 2003, to be spent over the next ten years, with $890 million appropriated for fiscal year 2004. However, money cannot be spent unless it goes through the authorization process, which did not occur until July 2004 ("Finish Project BioShield" 2004).[3] As of December 2003, three companies that were working on an anthrax countermeasure were experiencing funding problems that were delaying development and experimentation (Barbaro 2003).

Another federal response to 9/11 was the creation in 2003 of a Department of Homeland Security (DHS). Originally President Bush opposed the creation of such a department, and the original impetus was from Congress. The president did create an Office of Homeland Security within the Executive Office of the President by executive order in October 2001, with former Pennsylvania governor Tom Ridge as its director. The problem with the office is that it had no authority, no programs or funds of its own (Clarke 2004). The Hart-Rudman Commission recommended a new agency in February 2001 that would be the focus of antiterrorism efforts (United States Commission on National Security in the 21st Century 2001). The president changed his mind, and in 2003 the Department of Homeland Security was established with Tom Ridge as its secretary.

The department itself was a considerable bureaucratic creation. It merged some twenty-two agencies and over 170,000 employees with a budget of almost $30 billion (Gorman 2004). And, some important functions that might be included in such a department were not, especially intelligence gathering and analysis (Clarke 2004).

How well has the new department worked? On its one-year anniversary in 2004, the record appears to be mixed (Gorman 2004). The department listed a number of what it considers successes, including two related to a possible bioterrorism attack: placing sensors in cities to help recognize an attack, and dispersing money to "first responders" (Gorman 2004).

Not all were quite as satisfied with the performance of the department. A 2004 report in *Time* magazine found that there was no strategy for dispersing homeland grant money, and that a disproportionate amount went to more rural areas and states that were unlikely to be at risk of an attack. This is apparently at least a function of congressional pressure to spread federal dollars around and make sure that all localities and states get a share. The problem is that much more seems to have gone to states such as Wyoming than to states such as California and New York (Ripley 2004).

Another line of criticism came from Democrats on the U.S. House Select Committee on Homeland Security (2004). Specifically, the report noted four important security gaps related to bioterrorism. The first concern was about the biological weapons that the Soviet Union had developed that had not been destroyed. The report was also concerned about the availability of former Soviet personnel who had worked on the secret bioterrorism project. The fear was that such weapons might be stolen by a terrorist group. The report noted that of the forty-nine sites that we knew about, only two had been fully secured and another two were the subject of enhanced security efforts (U.S. House Select Committee on Homeland Security 2004).

The second security gap was that organizations within the United States that dealt with potential biological agents were not fully secured, inventoried, or registered by the federal government. The report notes that the Bush administration had imposed on itself a November 2003 deadline, but had missed it.

Third, the report addressed the issue of countermeasures against a bioterrorist attack. It identified over fifty such measures, but to date only one is available. "No vaccine is available for botulinum toxin, bubonic plague or tularemia. Virtually nothing has been done to address the growing threat presented by bioengineered pathogens" (U.S. House Select Committee on Homeland Security 2004, vi).

Finally, the report looked at preparedness. It stated that there was no comprehensive plan in place and that the public health infrastructure is inadequate to the challenge posed by a bioterrorist attack. Most states do not have the laboratory facilities or workers for distributing vaccines. Furthermore, the vaccination program for smallpox has failed: "It targeted the vaccination of 500,000 emergency workers and ten million first responders, only 39,000 have been vaccinated" (U.S. House Select Committee on Homeland Security 2004, vi).

The minority members of the committee then made several policy recommendations to remedy these gaps. The first was to enhance the security of biological agents in the former Soviet Union. Second, the report recommends fully securing the stock of potential biological agents within the United States. Third, the report suggests moving beyond Project BioShield and developing, in conjunction with the private sector, vaccines and other countermeasures. The report suggests an effort akin to the Manhattan Project, which developed atomic weapons during World War II. The report recommends the speedy development of a comprehensive nationwide strategy for dealing with bioterrorist threats. This would be done with state and local agencies and the private sector (U.S. House Select Committee on Homeland Security 2004).

The report also noted that despite the urgency created by the 9/11 attacks and programs to distribute money, the ability of first responders to communicate was still limited and they did not have the needed equipment. Further, the report noted that there is at this time no way to know whether the United States is prepared to respond appropriately to a terrorist attack, whether bioterrorist or of another nature (U.S. House Select Committee on Homeland Security 2004).

State and Local Levels

While there have not been many bioterrorist attacks, there have been some. In the wake of such an attack, as was true for the 9/11 attacks, the bulk of the response to the attack will come first at the local and then state level. "These 'first responders' include firefighters, emergency medical service personnel, law enforcement officers, public health officials, health care workers (including doctors, nurses, and other medical professionals), and public works personnel" (General Accounting Office 2001, 2).

The breadth of services that would be provided is wide, and different from those responding to other types of threats. These include identifying that an outbreak has occurred, identifying the agent, and distributing vaccines and/or antibiotics. Providing medical services, both normal and emergency, and dealing with fatalities would also be necessary (General Accounting Office 2001).

In the aftermath of the 9/11 attacks and the anthrax attacks the next month, it became increasingly obvious that state and local governments were unprepared to respond effectively. In 2002 the federal government began distributing money to state and local agencies to increase their capacity to respond. This was done through two cooperative agreements between the federal government and the other levels, which ended in August 2003. How well did those agreements and funds work in enhancing preparedness?

The CDC had fourteen benchmarks to judge how well the program had worked. A report by the General Accounting Office (GAO), a staff agency of Congress, found mixed results. State and local agencies did create bioterrorism advisory committees, and health alert networks covered much of the population. Development of statewide and regional response plans were accomplished by only a few states. About half of the states reported that they had developed a system for assessing and reporting disease incidents (the surveillance function) as well as an interim plan for stockpiling vaccines and other needed medications. Again, problems related to budget issues hindered further accomplishments (General Accounting Office 2004). States also had designated a hospital preparedness coordinator and a hospital preparedness committee. Interestingly, the GAO reported that no state had a plan to deal with a sizable bioterrorism attack, one that would affect five hundred or more persons (General Accounting Office 2004).

The Trust for America's Health (2003) noted that in some areas considerable progress had been made. These three areas of improvement were in planning, communications, and in laboratories. However, it also noted six areas of concern. Perhaps most important was that state budgets for public health protections for bioterrorism were actually falling. This is a function of the fiscal crisis of the states that began in 2001 as well as the underinvestment in public health that has characterized the last several decades. Second, at least some of the federal money sent to the states had not been used. Third, the states were not prepared to stockpile vaccines and other medications. Fourth, local agencies were often left out of the preparations. Fifth, states and agencies were not prepared for threats, either natural or human. Finally, there was insufficient personnel to carry out needed tasks (Trust for America's Health 2003).

The report developed ten criteria for rating the states on preparedness to respond to a bioterrorist attack. These focus on funding, preparedness, and whether the states also had plans for dealing with SARS or a flu pandemic. Table 8.1 shows the ten indicators and how each of the states rates. Figure 8.1 shows the number of indicators each state had successfully achieved.

Staffing remains a major concern. For example, the report found that there were 300 *fewer* epidemiologists working in state agencies in 2002 than there were in 1992. Laboratories are inadequate in staff and equipment. Communication has improved, but coordination of agencies remains a serious concern (Trust for America's Health 2003).

The Trust report summarizes its findings:

> The fact that the majority of states have scores in the lower range depicts a trend: while states have achieved piecemeal progress, the full-scale effort to comprehensively fix the nation's public health system is falling short.
>
> The scores indicate that, despite the surge in federal funds, states are only modestly more prepared to respond to health emergencies than they were prior to 9/11. Overall, the preparedness effort has been severely compromised by the impact of state budget crises, the lack of priority placed on addressing underlying systemic problems and the failure to eliminate bureaucratic obstacles. (Trust for America's Health 2003, 6)

Table 8.1   **State Preparedness Scores**

States	Funding			Preparedness					Double Duty		Total / Score
	1 Spent or obligated at least 90% of FT 2000 Federal funds	2 Passed on at least 50% of Federal funds to local health department	3 State spending on public health increased or was maintained	4 Sufficient workers to distribute Strategic National Stockpile supplies	5 Has at least one BT Lab (Biosafety Level-3 Lab)	6 Has enough BT Labs to handle a public health emergency	7 No more than 3 counties without emergency alert capability	8 Has initial BT plan	9 Has pandemic flu plan	10 State-specific information about SARS was available during crisis	
Alabama	✓		✓		✓	✓	✓	✓			6
Alaska	✓				✓			✓			3
Arizona		✓			✓		✓	✓	✓		5
Arkansas							✓	✓			2
California	✓	✓	✓		✓			✓	✓	✓	7
Colorado	✓	✓	✓		✓			✓			5
Connecticut					✓		✓	✓		✓	4
Delaware	✓	✓			✓		✓	✓			5
District of Columbia		✓					✓	✓			3
Florida	✓	✓		✓	✓		✓	✓			7
Georgia					✓		✓	✓			3
Hawaii		✓					✓	✓		✓	4
Idaho					✓		✓	✓			3
Illinois	✓	✓		✓	✓			✓			5
Indiana		✓			✓			✓	✓		4
Iowa	✓				✓			✓			3
Kansas	✓				✓		✓				3
Kentucky							✓	✓			2
Louisiana	✓	✓	✓		✓		✓	✓			5
Maine	✓				✓			✓			3
Maryland	✓		✓		✓		✓	✓	✓	✓	7
Massachusetts		✓			✓			✓	✓	✓	5
Michigan	✓				✓			✓			3
Minnesota					✓		✓	✓	✓		5
Mississippi					✓			✓			2
Missouri	✓						✓	✓	✓		4
Montana					✓	✓		✓			3
Nebraska	✓	✓	✓		✓			✓		✓	6
Nevada		✓	✓		✓		✓	✓			5
New Hampshire		✓	✓		✓			✓	✓	✓	5
New Jersey		✓	✓				✓	✓	✓		5
New Mexico							✓	✓			2
New York	✓	✓	✓		✓		✓	✓			6
North Carolina	✓				✓		✓	✓		✓	5
North Dakota	✓				✓		✓	✓		✓	5
Ohio			✓		✓	✓		✓			4
Oklahoma	✓				✓			✓			3
Oregon		✓					✓	✓			3
Pennsylvania					✓		✓	✓			3
Rhode Island	✓	✓	✓		✓		✓	✓			6
South Carolina					✓		✓	✓	✓		4
South Dakota	✓	✓			✓			✓			4
Tennessee	✓		✓		✓		✓	✓	✓	✓	7
Texas		✓	✓		✓			✓			4
Utah	✓				✓	✓		✓			4
Vermont					✓		✓	✓			3
Virginia					✓	✓	✓	✓	✓		5
Washington	✓	✓			✓		✓	✓		✓	6
West Virginia		✓	✓		✓			✓			4
Wisconsin					✓			✓			2
Wyoming			✓		✓		✓	✓			4
	24	18	18	2	43	6	30	51	13	11	

Source: Trust for America's Health, *Ready or Not: Protecting the Public's Health in an Age of Bioterrorism,* http://healthyamericans.org/state/bioterror/Bioterror.pdf © 2003 Trust for America's Health. Reprinted with permission.

The Trust made a series of recommendations to improve these defects. These included making sure that public health agencies are prepared for all kinds of emergencies, not just a bioterrorism attack; that the federal government, Congress, and the CDC assure that the appropriated money to improve public health capabilities is being spent; and that the federal government

Figure 8.1   **State by State Preparedness Scores**

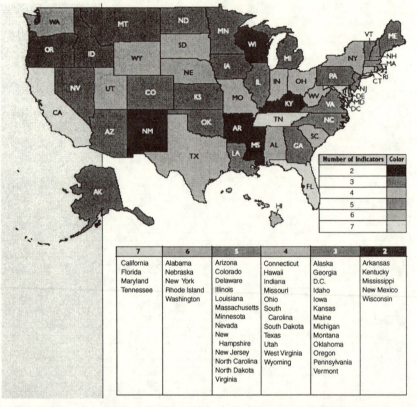

Number of Indicators	Color
2	
3	
4	
5	
6	
7	

7	6	5	4	3	2
California	Alabama	Arizona	Connecticut	Alaska	Arkansas
Florida	Nebraska	Colorado	Hawaii	Georgia	Kentucky
Maryland	New York	Delaware	Indiana	D.C.	Mississippi
Tennessee	Rhode Island	Illinois	Missouri	Idaho	New Mexico
	Washington	Louisiana	Ohio	Iowa	Wisconsin
		Massachusetts	South	Kansas	
		Minnesota	Carolina	Maine	
		Nevada	South Dakota	Michigan	
		New	Texas	Montana	
		Hampshire	Utah	Oklahoma	
		New Jersey	West Virginia	Oregon	
		North Carolina	Wyoming	Pennsylvania	
		North Dakota		Vermont	
		Virginia			

Source: Trust for America's Health, *Ready or Not: Protecting the Public's Health in an Age of Bioterrorism,* http://healthyamericans.org/state/bioterror/Bioterror.pdf © 2003 Trust for America's Health. Reprinted with permission.

should convene a summit with the states to develop a coordinated, national plan (Trust for America's Health 2003, 26–28).

War Game Exercises: Dark Winter 2001; Plague Attack, Denver, Colorado

In June 2001, a simulation, a war game, of a terrorist attack was conducted. The scenario was a smallpox outbreak that began in three states and spread to twenty-two other states as well as fifteen other countries. The results were not encouraging (McCarthy 2001). One important result of the exercise was that it took nine days before the attack was identified. Thus, limiting the outbreak was virtually impossible.

In July 2001, former senator Sam Nunn testified before Congress about the results of the exercise. Nunn discussed a number of problems exposed as a result of the exercise. These included:

- An attack on the United States with biological weapons could cause massive civilian casualties, breakdowns in essential institutions, disruption of democratic processes, civil disorder, loss of confidence in government, and reduced U.S. strategic flexibility.
- Government currently lacks adequate strategies, plans, and information systems to manage a crisis of this type or magnitude.
- Public health is now a major national security issue.
- Constructive media relationships become critical for all levels of government.
- Containing the spread of a contagious disease delivered as a bioweapon will present significant ethical, political, cultural, operational, and legal challenges. (Center for Strategic and International Studies 2001)

Other findings included the lack of sufficient vaccines, poor communication among the different levels of government and agencies, and hospitals and laboratories ill-equipped to deal with the massive outbreak (McCarthy 2001).

An earlier simulated exercise in Denver, Colorado, looked at what would happen if a plague bioterrorist attack occurred (Hoffman and Norton 2000). In this exercise the plague virus *Yersinia pestis* was released via an aerosol mechanism in three places in Denver. The participants were told of the incident three days after it happened. Hundreds of cases of plague occurred. The results were similar to the Dark Winter exercise: a fragmented public health care system, little coordination, and inadequate detection and treatment capabilities (Hoffman and Norton 2000; McCarthy 2001).[4]

Politics of Neglect: Problems and Shortcomings of the Current Public Health System

Lack of Comprehensive Strategy and Planning

The anthrax attacks in 2001 described above demonstrated some of the weaknesses of the public health system at the state and local levels. As of 2001, less than one-quarter of local public health departments had either a strategy or a plan for dealing with a bioterrorist event (Versel 2001). As noted above, the federal government has yet to develop a national strategy that would include all levels of government. Comprehensive planning does not yet exist.

Lack of Coordination Among Levels of Government and Agencies

The next two problems are related. The public health system is quite large and exists at all three levels of government. Prior to the 9/11 attacks there was little effort to coordinate what should be done in the event of an attack at any of those levels or even agencies between levels. Communication systems, as evidenced in the first responders' problems in New York City on September 11, were very inadequate, and so the response was ad hoc. Given the nature of the attack, including its unanticipated nature, this lack of communication and coordination is understandable. While there have been improvements, much yet remains to be done.

Fragmented Structure and Overlapping Jurisdictions

An important characteristic of American government is its fragmented structure. It exists in many policy areas (Rushefsky 2002). For example, there are myriad intelligence agencies in the federal government. These include the National Intelligence Council, the Central Intelligence Agency, the National Security Agency, the Defense Intelligence Agency, and the Federal Bureau of Investigation. Each military branch has its own intelligence agencies. The Departments of Homeland Security and Justice also have their own intelligence branches (Federation of American Scientists n.d.).

The same is true for the public health system, and particularly those agencies involved with bioterrorism threats. As we have seen, a large number of federal agencies have some bioterrorism response responsibility, plus there are the agencies in the fifty states and three territories as well as local public health agencies. It is thus not surprising that there is overlapping jurisdiction in this fragmented constellation of agencies and poor coordination that has taken a long time to correct. Even within the Department of Homeland Security there is confusion over who is in charge of training and grants for first responders (Crowley 2004).

Poorly Equipped Laboratory Facilities

Laboratories are a vital part of the public health system in the event of a biological attack. The labs must be able, in a timely manner, to identify a possible biological agent in the event of such an attack as well as recommend appropriate remedies. The United States has an abundance of clinical laboratories, most of them in physicians' offices or hospitals. There are also state labs and labs at the local level, although a majority of local public agencies do not have their own labs (Institute of Medicine 2003; Keck and Erme 2003).

Studies of the laboratories have found them to be inadequate in the face of a biological event. The Institute of Medicine (2003) and the General Accounting Office (2001) reported that when the West Nile virus outbreak took place in 1999 in New York, state and local labs were unable to deal with all the cases that came in. The CDC had to help. Ominously, if there had been a second outbreak of a disease around the country at the same time, the CDC labs would have been overwhelmed (General Accounting Office 2001; Institute of Medicine 2001). This occurred in a state that has a fairly well developed public health system. A major problem is the lack of trained staff. While efforts are being made to improve this diagnostic capability, much more needs to be done.

Inadequate Surveillance System

Surveillance means the ability to detect something. In general, the public health care system is supposed to detect the outbreak of diseases, such as SARS or West Nile virus. In the case of a bioterrorism attack, the public health system should be able to determine that an attack has occurred. A biological attack is considerably different from a conventional attack or a chemical or radiological attack; it is also more difficult to detect. As we have noted before, an attack, should one come, would likely not be noticed for several days, when people develop symptoms. Thus, while the probability of such an attack is low, detecting one would also be difficult.

As the Institute of Medicine (2003) report notes, the surveillance capability of the public health system is lacking. One reasoning is the fragmentation of authority mentioned above. As a result, there is no uniformity in tracking and cataloging outbreaks. The Institute of Medicine (2003, 127) describes the problem: states and local agencies "have not developed uniform data standards for data elements, collection procedures, storage and transmission."

The passage in 1996 of the Health Insurance Portability and Accountability Act (HIPAA) might have helped remedy this problem. It called for the development of standards and uniformity in the collection of information from medical records. However, state and local public health agencies are unsure what part of their data collection is covered by HIPAA (Institute of Medicine 2003).

Further, surveillance systems have developed in response to specific diseases. The result is the development of numerous data systems at the federal level (more than two hundred). This is compounded by the fact that those systems do not appear to match up well with state and local health systems (Institute of Medicine 2003).

Lack of Rapid Diagnostic Techniques

One problem demonstrated by the 2001 anthrax attacks was the inadequacy of the public health system to identify the agent. Laboratories were overwhelmed with real and fake threats. The protocols for identifying agents were limited. Equipment was in limited supply and outdated. Reagents were unavailable, and so forth (Conrad and Pearson 2003). Diagnostic tests need to be developed to more quickly identify bioterrorism agents (Margolskee 2003).

Insufficient Training

One important aspect is whether there is sufficient personnel to be able to carry out critical public health functions in the event of a bioterrorist event. The Institute of Medicine (IOM) report states that there are some 450,000 people in public health positions, plus others in private practice or nongovernmental positions. However, the report also states that the workforce is not well trained: "An estimated 80 percent of the current workforce lacks formal training in public health" (Institute of Medicine 2003, 116; Keck and Erme 2003).

The IOM report is referring to public health in general. When we move to bioterrorism threats, the lack of training is even more apparent (Trust for America's Health 2003). Given how recent the concern about bioterrorism is, the lack of training is understandable. Public health workers, physicians in general, emergency room physicians, and so forth have not been trained in any great numbers for the possibility of a biological event. The number of epidemiologists, those who by training would be able to scout a possible biological event, is lower than what is necessary.

Lack of Sufficient Stockpiling of Vaccines

A clear weakness in the public health system's ability to respond to a biological event is the lack of sufficient stock of vaccines and other medications. This has been seen in some of the simulations mentioned above. It is also the rationale behind Project BioShield, an effort that has barely begun.

Underfunded Public Health System

If there is one problem with the system that underlies all the others, it is funding. Garrett (2000) and others have argued that, overall, the public health system has been neglected and underfunded. The terrorist attacks of 9/11 have resulted in additional funding at the federal, state, and local levels. President Bush's budget proposal for fiscal year 2003 called for a total $37.7 billion on homeland defense, with $5.9 billion for defense against a bioterrorism attack. This amounts to an increase of 319 percent from the year before (Gerstenzang 2002). A lab at the University of Pittsburgh has become a regional center in the war against a bioterrorism attack. A similar new lab to be constructed in Fort Collins, Colorado, was called for in the Bush budget (Erickson 2002). Additional grant money from the National Institutes of Health for research aimed at bioterrorism has been approved (Southwick 2001).

In the two years following the 9/11 attacks, the federal government provided some $2 billion to the states to help them prepare for a bioterrorism attack. A study in 2003 found that despite the infusion of funds, the states remained unprepared (Patton 2003). The Trust for America's Health (2003) found that the public health system had been so severely underfunded during the 1990s (and before) that its capabilities had deteriorated. Federal spending in support of the public health infrastructure at the local and state levels has increased significantly. Most of the money came from grants from the CDC. The Trust report cited numerous surveys that found deficiencies in state and local infrastructure and capabilities, including reports from the Institute of Medicine (2003) and the General Accounting Office.

The Legal Challenge

Brownlee (2001) argues that the capabilities of the American health care system have improved dramatically since the great influenza outbreak in 1918, one that killed over six hundred thousand people in the United States and millions throughout the world. However, public health law has remained the same. Brownlee refers to a study of the public health laws in the states, conducted by Lawrence Gostin. Gostin finds them to be ancient and incoherent. Further, prior to 2000, not much thought was given to state public health law and a bioterrorist attack. Gostin's (2000) seminal work on public health law does not list bioterrorism in its index.

The reason for this patchwork state of public health laws is that they developed on a disease-specific basis. State health commissioners do not have the power to demand results from private labs or medical records, and thus the surveillance function is weakened.

Brownlee (2001) attributes much of this to recent concerns about privacy. Further, the federal Constitution, with its federal structure and division of powers between the federal and state governments, limits what the federal government can do. One example Brownlee (2001) points to is that the federal government has the primary responsibility for protecting the country from external enemies and threats, and the state and local governments for protecting its citizens from internal enemies and threats. However, a biological attack on the United States by an outside group would cross those jurisdictional boundaries.

As noted above, there have been some simulations of what would happen in the event of a biological attack. Brownlee mentions the exercise run in 2000 known as "topoff." From our standpoint, the most important finding was that no one appeared to be in charge at either the federal or state levels. The Dark Winter exercise found similar problems and conflicts between officials at different levels of government and between the public and private sector. Further, the fragmentation and inadequacies that characterize the public health system are also features of public health law (Gostin 2002). There are differences among the states, even among local units within states, in terms of what the powers of public health units are and what their responsibilities are.

What may be needed is a model public health law that states would adopt that would provide the authority and chain of commands. In October 2001, Lawrence Gostin, with the Center for Law and the Public's Health at the Georgetown University Law Center, produced such a bill, the Model State Emergency Health Powers Act, or MSEHPA, for the CDC, the National Governors Association, the National Conference of State Legislatures, the Association of State and Territorial Health Officials, the National Association of County and City Health Officials, and the National Association of Attorneys General. It was revised in December 2001 (Center for Law and the Public's Health 2001).

The preamble to the model legislation places the law in the context of the 9/11 attacks and government's primary responsibility for the security of its citizens. Threats such as terrorist attacks require a proportionate response to the crises they produce. Thus, the legislation would provide emergency powers to government. The preamble captures the flavor of what the model legislation would accomplish:

> The act requires the development of a comprehensive plan to provide a coordinated, appropriate response in the event of a public health emergency. It facilitates the early detection of a health emergency by authorizing the reporting and collection of data and records, and allows for immediate investigation by granting access to individuals' health information under specified circumstances. During a public health emergency, state and local officials are authorized to use any appropriate property as nec-

essary for the care, treatment, and housing of patients, and to destroy contaminated facilities or materials. They are also empowered to provide care, testing and treatment and vaccination to persons who are ill or have been exposed to a contagious disease, and to separate individuals from the population at large to interrupt disease transmission.

At the same time the Act recognizes that a state's ability to respond to a public health emergency must respect the dignity and rights of persons. The exercise of emergency health powers is designed to promote the common good. Emergency powers must be grounded in a thorough scientific understanding of public health threats and disease transmission. Guided by principles of justice, states have a duty to act with fairness and tolerance toward individuals and groups. The Act thus provides that, in the event of the exercise of emergency powers, the civil rights, liberties, and needs of exposed persons will be protected to the fullest extent possible consistent with the primary goal of controlling serious health threats.

Public health laws and our courts have traditionally balanced the common good with individual civil liberties. As Justice Harlan wrote in the seminal United States Supreme Court case of *Jacobson v. Massachusetts*, "the whole people covenants with each citizen, and each citizen with the whole people, that all shall be governed by certain laws for the 'common good.'" The Act strikes such a balance. It provides state officials with the ability to prevent, detect, manage, and contain emergency health threats without unduly interfering with civil rights and liberties. The Act seeks to ensure a strong, effective and timely response to public health emergencies, while fostering respect for individuals from all groups and backgrounds. (Center for Law and the Public's Health 2001, 6–7)

By the end of 2002, sixteen states had adopted some version of the model legislation (National Vaccine Information Center n.d.).

As Gostin (2002, 83) describes the model legislation, the focus is on the following five activities that we have addressed previously: "preparedness, surveillance, management of property, protection of persons, and public information and communication." The act requires that health care providers and others, such as pharmacists, coroners, and medical examiners, report cases that might be the result of a biological attack or an epidemic. It gives the governor the power to declare a state of emergency in the event of a biological event. The powers include the power to quarantine infected persons and to seize property as well as provide for compensation for the owners of the seized property. Additionally, mandatory vaccination is allowed, though there are exceptions for those who would suffer illnesses from the vaccination itself.

Gostin (2002), defending the model legislation, argues that both public health law as well as the public health system have suffered from antigovernment beliefs, thus leaving the United States more vulnerable than it need be to terrorist attacks. Gostin asserts what is essentially a communitarian viewpoint, that there needs to be a balance between individual rights and the needs of the larger society. Gostin (2002) notes that two types of libertarians have criticized the model legislation. One type is the personal libertarian. Their objection is to the compulsory powers given to public health units by the MSEHPA, such as quarantining or vaccinations. The seizure of property is also of concern. Economic libertarians object on the grounds that the legislation would interfere with economic activity. Gostin's response is the communitarian one. Given appropriate safeguards, sometimes liberty can be restricted. It is those protections and explicit objectives that provide protection against abuse of power.

In response to Gostin's defense of the model legislation, Annas (2002) argues that, while he agrees that state laws regarding public health need to be modernized, the real problem is the view that public health is a state rather than a federal issue. He notes that in the wake of the 2001 anthrax attacks following shortly upon the heels of the 9/11 attacks, the FBI took over the investigation. This is because a bioterrorism attack is a national security issue and not just a state or local one. For Annas, this is an opportunity to federalize public health in general.

Annas's second criticism is that public health law is paternalistic and instead should try to work with patients and providers as well as through physicians. Arbitrary treatment on the part of public health officials will reinforce the distrust the public already has of government.

Finally, Annas (2002) raises the question of democracy and public health. He notes that none of the organizations that sponsored the model legislation have endorsed it. Further, no state has adopted the legislation as proposed, but instead those that have adopted it have adapted it to their needs and views. Thus if one were interested in more uniformity in public health law, national legislation would be necessary. Annas (2002, 97) concludes, "Ultimately, public health must not rely on force but on persuasion, and not on blind trust but on trust based on transparency, accountability, democracy and human rights. There is plenty of time to draft and debate a twenty-first-century federal public health law that takes constitutional rights seriously, unites the public with its medical caretakers, treats medicine and public health as true partners, and moves us in the direction of global cooperation."

Brownlee (2001) raises the question of whether the American public would accept the shrinkage of privacy that would accompany such a law. She notes that the response to a biological attack would involve restrictions in movement, to contain the outbreak, and access to information and property. This is the age-old controversy of the value of security versus the value of free-dom or liberty that has marked much of American history. It is also involved in controversies over the USA Patriot Act, which gives law enforcement agencies more powers to investigate potential terrorist threats. Brownlee (2001) writes that in times of emergencies, extraordinary powers ought to be given to government, and chains of command should be already erected.

Bayer and Colgrove (2002) and Etzioni (2002) defend the model legisla-tion, or at least the idea behind it. Bayer and Colgrove write that public health law for most of the twentieth century had considerable teeth under the police power of the state. What led to changes and more concern about privacy and due process was the AIDS epidemic that began in the 1980s. There were issues related to reporting, quarantine, and testing. The result of debates was a view that civil liberties and public health were not antagonis-tic to each other. Bayer and Colgrove quote a principle that was developed out of this experience and coauthored by Gostin: "It may be useful to adopt the maxim that health policies and programs should be considered discrimi-natory and burdensome on human rights until proven otherwise" (Mann and Gostin, quoted in Bayer and Colgrove 2002, 99). Gostin, Bayer and Colgrove write, has attempted to balance the needs of the larger society, embodied in public health, with civil rights and liberties. What they see, however, is a deep philosophical and political chasm between these rights and public health perspectives and communities. They argue that both sides need to address the concerns of the other.

Etzioni (2002), one of the founders of communitarianism, argues for the importance of the public's interest. Etzioni argues that the 1960s saw exces-sive concern with individual rights to the detriment of the larger society, and this imbalance needs to be corrected. The problem, for Etzioni, is to ensure that the imbalance toward the other side does not occur. He does not believe that Gostin's model legislation represents such a threat.

Etzioni provides some criteria for deciding what this balance should be. One such criteria is that there be a "clear and present danger" (Etzioni 2002, 103).[5] This criteria has been used to suggest that the fundamental rights found in the Bill of Rights to the U.S. Constitution are not absolute. A bioterrorist attack would likely qualify as such a danger. The second crite-rion is that whatever public health measures are taken should be as volun-tary as possible. The third and related criterion is that the level of intrusion on the part of government be appropriate to the danger.

Gostin offers two other criteria (Etzioni 2002). The first is that whatever policy tools are employed to accomplish the task, they should be effective in meeting the needs. The other criterion is that there should be as equitable as possible an allocation of the burdens of whatever public health emergency efforts are necessary. Etzioni (2002) concludes that this issue has not been fully addressed. But overall, the public interest requires that society be given the tools to protect itself.

Future Challenges

> A comprehensive approach to bioterrorism requires concerted effort in three areas: prevention, including developing new and strengthening existing programs to secure pathogen stocks around the world; preparedness, including completing a comprehensive biodefense plan, strengthening and better targeting federal public health funding; and protection, developing the ability to defend our population through deploying drugs, vaccines and diagnostics required to combat infection and illness. (U.S. House Select Committee on Homeland Security 2004, 20)

The primary purpose of government is the protection of its citizens.[6] Public health is a part of the apparatus of protecting the health of the population as a whole. The threat of terrorism, embodied in the September 11, 2001, attacks, underlies the importance of security and public health. The threat of bioterrorism raises unique issues. The intent of a bioterrorism attack is to scare a population and cause panic. The surreptitious nature of such an attack makes it hard to defend against and difficult to respond to. The challenges are many. Biological weapons might be labeled the "poor man's atom bomb" (Miller, Engelberg, and Broad 2001, 316). As the United States became the world's only superpower following the demise of the Soviet Union, we also became a target for terrorists (Miller, Engelberg, and Broad 2001). After the September 11 attacks, the possibility of a bioterrorism attack grew.

The United States has developed an elaborate public health infrastructure. However, it might be overstating things to call it a system. The American public health system did not arise out of planning efforts, but like most things in this country, it grew piecemeal, in response to events, politics, and perceptions.

While the system is elaborate, it is currently insufficient for meeting the challenge of bioterrorism. Reports from the Institute of Medicine, the General Accounting Office, and the Trust for America's Health, among other groups and agencies, find massive gaps in training, funding, facilities, stockpiling, and communications. The effort to bolster the public health system has begun and has seen some modest results. Much more needs to be done if we are ever able to feel more comfortable about our ability to detect and respond to a threat.

We should also point out here another gap that makes detecting and responding to a biological event more difficult. This gap is insurance coverage. About 15 percent of the American population does not have health insurance. Many are people who work (see chapter 5 in Patel and Rushefsky 1999). This is a problem from a public health standpoint because people who lack insurance are less likely to have and see a doctor on a regular basis. When many of the uninsured do seek care, it is after symptoms have developed for a while. And for many of them, the primary care physician works in an emergency room.

This lack of insurance and the response to it undermines the surveillance function of public health. It means that people might be suffering from the symptoms of a biological attack for days before seeking treatment. And it means that emergency room personnel and their record systems must, to use the catchphrase of the failure to stop the 9/11 attacks, be able to "connect the dots." Without the training and systems, this is likely to be a significant weakness. Thus, some form of universal insurance would seem to be in the public interest on public health grounds.

Levy and Sidel (2003b) write that within public health is a set of values that are important regarding potential terrorism attacks. These include "promotion of health; prevention of disease, injury, disability and premature death; support of human rights and social justice; and visionary leadership by public health officials (Levy and Sidel 2003b, 17). Additionally, the American Public Health Association has issued a set of guidelines for addressing a terrorist threat (Table 8.2).

We return, as we began, to Tom Clancy. When we left President Jack Ryan, the United States had been the object of a bioterrorist attack, with the virus being Ebola. Work by the FBI and epidemiologists at the CDC found there were over 200 primary cases (that is, those initially infected by the attack) and over 3,000 cases of those subsequently infected. The epidemic seemed to be spreading via intimate contact and thus peaked in over a week or so. Eventually the epidemic died out. The country was saved, the transgressors were killed, including an arresting scene in which a cruise missile kills the Iranian leader on worldwide television, and Ryan won reelection in a later story.

Note that there were no stockpiles of vaccines to prevent the spread. Antiobiotics were not available. The epidemic did relatively little damage, except to the people who were infected, and ended on its own. We should be so lucky.

Should there be a real bioterrorist event of the magnitude that Clancy describes, we had best be prepared. Our public health system is not yet ready.

Table 8.2

Guiding Principles for a Public Health Response to Terrorism

In order to prevent future acts of terrorism and their adverse public health consequences, the public health community should support policies and programs that:

1. Address poverty, social injustice, and health disparities that may contribute to the development of terrorism;
2. Provide humanitarian assistance to, and protect the human rights of, the civilian populations that are directly or indirectly affected by terrorism;
3. Advocate the speedy end of the armed conflict in Afghanistan and promote nonviolent means of conflict resolution;
4. Strengthen the public health infrastructure (which includes workforce, laboratory and information systems) and other components of the public health system (including education, research, and the faith community) to increase the ability to identify, respond to, and prevent problems of public health importance, including the health aspects of terrorist attacks;
5. Ensure availability of, and accessibility to, health care, including medications and vaccines, for individuals exposed, infected, made ill, or injured in terrorist attacks;
6. Educate and inform health professionals and the public to better identify, respond to, and prevent the health consequences of terrorism, and promote the visibility and availability of health professionals in the communities they serve;
7. Address mental health needs of populations that are directly or indirectly affected by terrorism;
8. Assure the protection of the environment, the food and water supply, and the health and safety of rescue and recovery professionals;
9. Assure clarification of the roles, relationships, and responsibilities among public health agencies, law enforcement and first responders;
10. Prevent hate crimes and ethnic, racial, and religious discrimination, including profiling; promote cultural competence, diversity training, and dialogue among people; and protect human rights and civil liberties;
11. Advocate the immediate control and ultimate elimination of biological, chemical, and nuclear weapons; and
12. Build and sustain the public health capacity to develop systems to collect data about the health and mental health consequences of terrorism and other disasters on victims, responders, and communities, and develop uniform definitions and standardized data-classification systems of death and injury resulting from terrorism and other disasters.

Source: Levy and Sidel (2003b, 10).

Notes

1. This is neither the time nor the place to argue over the veracity of the claims. As of mid-2004, no weapons had been found, and there was evidence to suggest that whatever weapons of mass destruction Iraq possessed had been either rendered useless years ago or destroyed. See Nichols (2004) and Stevenson (2004).

2. The CIA definition is troublesome to some because it limits terrorist activities to groups outside of government. There have been examples of state-

sponsored terrorism, including by Iraq under Saddam Hussein against the Kurds in northern Iraq.

3. For a discussion of the budgeting process at the federal level and the difference between appropriations and authorizations, see Rubin 2000.

4. A "topoff" 2 simulation exercise was conducted in the spring of 2003. In this case, the event was a radiological one.

5. We should note here that *Clear and Present Danger* is also the title of a Tom Clancy book featuring Jack Ryan, one that predates his becoming president.

6. Security, the safety of the citizenry, is the oldest function of government and the primary reason why governments are formed. This is the argument put forth by Thomas Hobbes in *The Leviathan* (1651) and John Locke in *Two Treatises on Government* (1690).

Study Questions

1. How well prepared is the United States to prevent and respond to a bioterrorist attack? How well prepared are the various levels of government (federal, state, and local) to respond to such an attack?

2. What are the most important potential sources of a bioterrorist attack? What could we do to prevent such an attack?

3. An important issue in the ability of the United States to respond to a bioterrorist attack is fragmentation of government. What changes, if any, would you recommend to overcome this fragmentation?

4. Is the United States spending enough money on homeland security? Are we spending the money devoted to homeland security in the right places and in the right ways?

5. Another important issue is that preparing to respond to a bioterrorist attack requires planning. Planning and implementing plans often tread upon privacy, liberty, and property rights. Where should the balance be between community needs and civil liberties?

CHAPTER 9

Conclusion

> Public health is a bond—a trust—between government and its people. The society at large entrusts its government to oversee and protect the collective good health. And in return individuals agree to cooperate by providing tax monies, accepting vaccines, and abiding by the rules and guidelines laid out by government public health leaders. If either side betrays that trust the system collapses like a house of cards.
>
> (Garrett 2000, 584)

> The public health movement has become a victim of its own success. Each of its well-documented victories, in battles against diseases ranging from childhood maladies such as measles and mumps to scourges such as polio, tuberculosis and smallpox, has reduced the nation's sense of urgency.
>
> ("Costs of Complacency" 2004)

The mission of public health is to protect the community, however the community may be defined. The size of the community varies from local governments to states to the federal government to the global community. Public health agencies exist at all of these levels. The functions of public health are many and various. At a minimum they include surveillance, policy development, and treatment (Schneider 2000, 6). The successes of public health have enabled us to live longer, healthier lives. But we have also seen that, at least until recently, public health has had a secondary status in the health care system, had a nearly invisible presence, and been placed on a severely restricted diet of resources.

Curative versus Preventive Models of Health Care

One very important reason for both the complacency about public health and its secondary status has to do with what we talked about in chapters 1 and 3. To simplify a bit, the health care field is divided between two models, curative and preventive. Modern medicine embodies the curative model; with its elaborate technology, it has developed a preeminent place in the field. It emphasizes the treatment and cure of disease and is supported by medical research centers, biotechnology companies (including pharmaceutical companies), and significant amounts ofgovernment funding through the National Institutes of Health. Medical journals, almost by definition, are dominated by this field. Further, the curative model operates for the most part outside the public sector, and those involved in medicine have a fair amount of freedom from public scrutiny to engage in their profession.

Public health embodies the preventive model and focuses on populations and health prevention. There are fewer programs in public health than there are medical schools, fewer people work in the field, funding is much less. And, as many have pointed out (see "Cost of Complacency" 2004; Garrett 2000; Institute of Medicine 2003), the quality of the public health system has deteriorated. The public health system has suffered from neglect.

Part of the reason for neglect is that public health is a government function, with much of it carried out at the state and local level. State and local funding priorities have been in education and criminal justice and health care, meaning Medicaid. Little has been left for public health. Even with new infusions of funds from the federal government as a response to the 9/11 attacks, funding remains low. The fiscal crisis of the states, the big budget crunch, has meant that public health funding has to had to compete with scarce and, in some ways, fewer dollars.

Further, if we understand politics as involving conflicts of interests and values (Brown 1986), then public health finds itself in the middle of politics. Consider warning labels required on tobacco products or local ordinances forbidding smoking in public buildings. Or consider the emphasis on lifestyle factors in health and advice given about how to increase the quality of one's life. All of these involve value conflicts and require behavioral changes. Some affect industries in fairly drastic ways. Public health officials are often not the ones making the final decisions, but they can place these kinds of issues on the public agenda, lobby for them, and carry them out.

Another issue facing public health is a leadership one. If we are focusing on the politics of public health, it then stands to reason that public health professionals must engage in politics. Sometimes public health professionals proffer advice to policymakers. For example, political leaders may need advice on whether a potential flu epidemic requires extraordinary preventive measures. Health professionals have to deal with issues that strongly affect, as we mentioned above, values and interests. Some of the issues, such as HIV/AIDS, invoke strongly held values. Others, such as the threat of bioterrorism, require coordination between different levels of government in ways that are not seen enough.

Another important area of concern is law. Because public health involves government, it stands to reason that the functions of public health are set forth as well as limited by law. Public health can, on occasion, infringe on personal freedoms. This then brings in the judiciary to decide how much infringement in the name of the public interest is permissible. State public health laws need to be modernized as Gostin (2000, 2002) has argued. The threat of bioterrorism is one area where this can be readily seen.

Litigation, as we have discussed, has been one tool of public health. This can be seen in lawsuits against the tobacco industry and regulation of firearms. The former has been somewhat successful, with the settlement between the tobacco industry and the states. However, many states have used the money from the settlement to help meet their budget crunch and have done less than hoped in antitobacco campaigns. Gun control regulation has for the most part hit a wall of resistance from interest groups (notably the National Rifle Association) and the Second Amendment to the Constitution.

Perhaps the clearest example of the politics of public health comes in an area where we would normally think that politics has no place, science. The foundation science of public health is epidemiology. However, it and related fields, such as toxicology, are subject to critiques based on the uncertainty of the evidence. If public health decisions are to be made based on science, we want that scientific basis to be as strong as possible, especially when it involves economic loss on the part of some group. Criticizing the science underlying a policy, labeling it junk science as has been done, is a surrogate for attacking the policy itself. The more the attacks continue, the weaker it is to justify public health action, undermining community confidence in public health. This is seen most prominently in the environmental policy area. Stacking scientific advisory bodies to generate policy advice that one favors uses the aura of science to support policy in a way that undermines both science and policy. Mixing truth and power often produces a combustible concoction.

The genetics revolution offers both promise and concern for public health in the twenty-first century. The promise is of new methods for treating disease, both acute and chronic. New fields have arisen, such as pharmacogenetics, which can individualize a prescription to a particular genetic makeup. As we show in chapter 6, the genetics revolution has not yet had deep penetration into the public health field. But the potential is there. So are the concerns. The possibility of discrimination based on genetic makeup exists. There are issues related to genetic screening and counseling. Again, law becomes important to limit possible discrimination.

The terrorist attacks of September 11, 2001, and the anthrax scare that followed presented both problems and opportunities. Problems include the ability of public health at all levels to be able to respond to a bioterrorist attack. The results of simulations of bioterrorist attacks have been alarming. Weaknesses abound: in training, diagnostic capability, fragmentation of power, communications, and legal authority. Perhaps more than any other area we have discussed, the bioterrorism threat reveals the weaknesses of public health.

Reinvigorating Public Health

As happens sometimes, problems can be opportunities as well. The threat of terrorism has required a reevaluation and careful examination of public health in the United States. Additional funding, primarily from the federal government, has been forthcoming, and public health has a restored place in the health care system. The community focus of public health has once again become important. A reinvigorated public health system is now on the policy agenda.

That agenda is a crowded one. It is clear that the capacity of the public health system has to be increased. This means more personnel and more training. This includes more emphasis on public health in our medical schools and more public health programs. This implies a more equal status for public health with modern medicine. It means better diagnostic capabilities, such as laboratories. It means reexamining and modernizing public health law. It means more funding for public health at all levels. It means better communications among public health officials and agencies.

The 2003 Institute of Medicine report lists six areas for action and thirty-four recommendations. Many of those recommendations and findings were contained in their earlier report, published in 1988. Not enough change has taken place in the ensuing sixteen years. We have the opportunity to implement these and other recommendations to strengthen the public health system.

We would like to reinforce one important recommendation made by the Institute of Medicine. This is a recommendation for some type of universal health care. The results of our research for this book suggest that this is an important way in which the nation's health can be improved. Those lacking health care are more likely to suffer ill health because they do not have a regular source of care (see Patel and Rushefsky 1999). If the entire population were covered, then issues of genetic discrimination would not even come up. The nature of a bioterrorist attack also undergirds the support for universal health care. Such an attack might not be evident for several days to a week or more. Terrorist attack victims who have no health insurance might not seek care because they could not afford it. This might delay a response to such an attack. It is therefore, we believe, in the interest of the public at large that all be covered.

Politics and Public Health Policies

We have examined public health in the United States from a particular viewpoint, politics. We are not using politics in the sense of electoral politics. Rather, we see politics as involving issues of governance: who gets to make decisions and how those decisions are made. Government policymaking and the politics surrounding it are messy, involve lots of arguments, and have difficulty in resolving issues. The kinds of issues that surround public health are precisely those that intrude on interests and values. Even the distinction between public health, the preventive model, and medicine, based on a curative model, involves politics. Modern medicine has pushed public health aside. Conflict exists between individual rights and the needs of the individual community. The resolution of this basic dilemma of public health is the foundation for the politics of public health.

Study Questions

1. One important finding in this book is that the public health infrastructure is underfunded. That is, the authors believe that not enough money is budgeted for public health. Do you agree or disagree? Why?
2. The authors argue that some form of universal access to health insurance is vital to the country as a whole, though the nature of such access is not discussed. Chapters 6 (genetics) and 8 (bioterrorism) make this argument. Do you agree or disagree? Why?
3. Public health takes a community and preventive focus, whereas the prevailing model of health care is mainly individual and curative in focus. Where should the appropriate emphasis be between these two views? Why?

Chronology of Major
Public Health Laws and Events

1798   The Act for the Relief of Sick and Disabled Seamen established the United States Marine Hospital Service (USMHS). Twenty cents was deducted from the monthly wage of each merchant seaman to build or rent hospitals and pay for the medical care provided.

1813   The federal government passes a law encouraging the use of the smallpox vaccination.

1847   American Medical Association is founded to improve medical education and promote licensure laws to eliminate competition from homeopaths and other irregular practitioners of medicine. It also supported health reforms and development of public health boards at all levels of government.

1861   The United States Sanitary Commission is created to combat the unsanitary conditions faced by the soldiers in the Civil War.

1871   John Woodward is appointed as the first surgeon general (supervising surgeon).

1872   American Public Health Association was established, which ultimately led to the professionalization of public health.

1876   Louis Pasteur discovered the Germ Theory of Diseases.

1879   The National Board of Health was created. The power to enforce interstate quarantine laws was taken away from the Marine Hospital Service and given to the National Board of Health. However, the laws were given a legal life of only four years because of opposition from the Marine Hospital Service and health officers in the South.

1887   The first research facility, that is, the Hygiene Laboratory, is established at the Staten Island Marine Hospital.

1889   U.S. Public Health Commission. A regular corps of physicians is created.

1891   The Hygiene Laboratory moves to Washington, DC.

1902   A permanent Census Bureau is established in the federal government to collect vital statistics.

1904   The Council of Medical Education is created by the American Medical Association. The council engages in educational reform and begins ranking medical schools based upon their merit.

1906   Federal Food and Drug Act passed. The law was designed to supplement state control of food and encourage cooperative federal and state efforts to maintain an effective control of food in local, in interstate, or in foreign commerce.

1909   National Institute of Health created.

1910   First university degree in public health established, at the University of Michigan.

1910   The Flexner Report provides a critique of U.S. medical schools. The report leads to consolidation and improved standards in U.S. medical schools.

1911   *Journal of American Public Health Association* created.

1912   Name of the *Journal of the American Public Health Association* changed to *American Journal of Public Health*.

1912   The name of the U.S. Marine Hospital Service is changed by congressional law to United States Public Health Service (USPHS). It is authorized to study and investigate the diseases of man and their spread, and to publish information for the public.

1912   The Children's Bureau is established in the Department of Commerce and Labor (later the Department of Labor) in response to increased concern about child labor laws and the general welfare of children. Soon the bureau became involved in health related activities such as maternal and child welfare and infant mortality.

1912   The Progressive Party platform advocates a national health insurance system for the United States. The Democratic and Republican Party platforms of 1912 make no mention of social insurance.

1914   The Harrison Narcotic Act is passed by Congress. Under this law, physicians who prescribe opiates to addicts were to be arrested, convicted, and sent to prison.

1915   By this date all states as well as many of the large cities had established health departments.

1915   The Welch-Rose Report was released. It led to the establishment of institutionalized public health education.

1916   The Johns Hopkins School of Hygiene and Public Health founded.

1918   A Reserve Corps for temporary, peacetime duty is created within the Public Health Service.

1921   The Sheppard-Towner Act passed by Congress. The law provided grants-in-aid to states for maternal and child health programs for the purpose of reducing maternal and infant mortality.

1924   Congress passes the World Veterans Act, which allowed veterans who suffered from nonservice- related disabilities the use of all beds in veterans' hospitals that veterans with service disabilities did not occupy.

1930   Passage of the Parker Act allowed a larger number of regular and reserve officers to be commissioned. It made dentists, pharmacists, and sanitary engineers eligible for the Regular Corps.

1935   President Roosevelt includes national health insurance as part of the Social Security Act. However, it is dropped from the final legislation sent to Congress due to opposition from many groups.

1935   The Social Security Act is passed, creating the Social Security system.

1937   Marijuana Tax Act banned nonmedical, untaxed sale or possession of marijuana.

1937   The National Cancer Institute Act creates the National Cancer Institute.

1939   Public Health Service placed in the Federal Security Agency.

1944   Public Health Service Act passed. The law was designed to make the Public Health Service a tightly knit bureaucracy of career health professionals.

1946   The Hill-Burton Act (officially entitled the Hospital Survey and Construction Act) is passed by Congress. The law provides federal funds for construction of hospital and medical facilities. The law leads to a dramatic increase in the number of hospitals and medical facilities in the country.

1946   President Truman recommends a compulsory national health insurance. No action is taken.

1946   Communicable Disease Center (CDC) established.

1948   The National Heart Institute, the National Institute of Dental Research, and the National Institute of Biological Research created by Congress as part of the National Institute of Health. The National Institute of Health is renamed the National Institutes of Health (NIH).

1949   National Institute of Mental Health added to the NIH.

1950   National Science Foundation established.

1953   Federal Security Agency renamed Department of Health, Education and Welfare (DHEW).

1961   The Community Health Services and Facilities Act is passed by Congress. Under the law, the federal government provides large federal grants to stimulate and coordinate community health planning.

1964   Surgeon general releases first report concluding the negative health effects of smoking.

1965   Congress passes the Medicare Act, which becomes Title 18 of the Social Security Act. The law provides medical aid for the elderly.

1965   Congress passes the Medicaid Act, which becomes Title 19 of the Social Security Act. The law provides medical aid for the poor.

1965   Cigarette Labeling and Advertising Act (CLAC) requires warning labels on all cigarette packages, which read "Caution: Cigarette Smoking May Be Hazardous to Your Health."

1966   Comprehensive Health Planning and Public Health Service Amendments of 1966 are passed by Congress, designed to consolidate and coordinate the large number of separate programs operating at state and local levels.

1966   Education, Research, Training, and Demonstrations Act passed by Congress, intended to coordinate and integrate results of research conducted in teaching and research university establishments with clinical medicine.

1966   Highway Safety Act passed by Congress.

1968   The federal Gun Control Act (GCA) of 1968 requires persons selling firearms to obtain a license. Under the law, sale of long guns (rifles and shotguns) is prohibited to anyone under the age of eighteen and sale of handguns is prohibited to anyone under the age of twenty-one. The law also prohibits purchase and possession of firearms by certain categories of persons.

1969   President Nixon orders cessation of U.S. bioweapons program for offensive purposes.

1970   Communication Disease Center (CDC) renamed Center for Disease Control (CDC).

1970   President Nixon signs the National Environmental Protection Act, which requires that environmental impacts be assessed before actions are taken involving federal agencies or recipients of federal funds.

1972   Professional Standard Review Organization Act is passed. It creates Professional Standard Review Organizations to review physicians' decisions regarding patient care.

1972   Biological and Toxin Weapons Convention signed.

1973   Health Maintenance Organization Act passed by Congress during the Nixon administration to encourage development of health maintenance organizations (HMOs) as an alternate health delivery system to control rising health care costs.

1974   Congress passes Safe Drinking Water Act.

1975   The National Health Planning and Resources Development Act signed into law by President Ford. The law reflects dissatisfaction with previous efforts at health planning. The law creates around two hundred health systems agencies (HSAs) at local levels to influence the supply and distribution of health care facilities. The law allows local health system agencies to make planning decisions regarding expansion/construction of major health care facilities.

1977   President Carter proposes hospital cost containment legislation to contain rising hospital costs. The bill fails to pass Congress in 1977, 1978, and in 1979 due to strong opposition from hospital groups.

1978   President's Commission for the Study of Ethical Problems in Medicine and Biomedical and Behavioral Research is created, reflecting ethical concerns raised by advances in biomedical research.

1979   A separate Department of Education created out of DHEW, and DHEW is renamed the Department of Health and Human Services.

1979   The Carter administration proposes the creation of a national health insurance system. Several alternative bills are introduced in Congress. However, no bill passes.

1983   The Tax Equity and Fiscal Responsibility Act of 1982 goes into effect. The law introduces diagnostic related groupings (DRGs) as a way to control hospital costs for Medicare reimbursement. It replaces the retrospective payment system with a prospective payment system (PPS), under which the federal government would reimburse hospitals for services provided to Medicare patients on a fixed, flat fee per case basis within about 475 diagnostic groupings.

1983   The National Health Planning and Resources Development Act of 1975 is abolished. The law also abolishes PSROs. It mandates private peer review organizations (PROs) to continue monitoring of hospital services for Medicare.

1984   The surgeon general issues a report on the negative effects of secondhand smoke and suggests moving to a smokeless society.

1984   Cult in Oregon engages in bioterrorist attack in rural county.

1984   Comprehensive Smoking Education Act mandated, including putting four warnings on labels on a rotational basis, with the warnings including specific references to lung cancer, heart disease, emphysema, and pregnancy complications.

1986   Armor Piercing Ammunition Act prohibits the manufacture and importation of ammunition composed of certain metal substances.

1988   The Clinical Laboratory Amendments require the establishment of the analytical validity of new genetic tests.

1990   Congress passes the Americans with Disabilities Act, which prohibits discrimination against people with disabilities and genetic susceptibility to a disorder.

1990   Congress passes the Gun-Free School Zone Act, which prohibits possession of a firearm in a school zone.

1991   U.S.-led coalition repels Iraq from Kuwait. Iraq agrees though hinders weapons inspection.

1992   Russia admits it maintained bioweapons program.

1993   President Clinton introduces Health Security Act of 1993 in Congress. The law is designed to overhaul the U.S. health care system by creating a national health insurance system. Several other competing legislative proposals are introduced in Congress. None of the bills are voted on in Congress.

1993   Brady Handgun Violence Prevention Act (also known as the Brady Act) requires a five-day waiting period for a background check before a person can purchase a handgun.

1994   Violent Crime Control and Enforcement Act (VCCEA) of 1994 made it unlawful for a person to manufacture, transfer, or possess certain military-type semiautomatic assault weapons for a ten-year period.

1995   In *United States v. Lopez* the U.S. Supreme Court ruled that Congress exceeded its commerce clause authority when it made gun possession within a school zone a federal crime and declared the congressional law unconstitutional.

1997   Health Insurance Portability and Accountability Act passed by Congress.

1997   In *Printz v. United States*, the Supreme Court used the Tenth Amendment's reserved power doctrine to overturn a provision in the Brady Handgun Violence Prevention Act that directed state and local law enforcement officers to conduct background checks on prospective handgun buyers.

1997   Congress passes the Federal Domestic Violence Gun Act, which prohibits persons convicted of a misdemeanor crime of domestic violence from possessing guns and ammunition.

1998   Iraq throws out weapons inspectors.

1999   California passes the Children's Environmental Health Protection Act.

2000   The Minority Health and Health Disparities Research and Education Act of 2000, also known as the Health Care Fairness Act, passed by Congress to create a new center for research on minority health and health disparities.

2000   The Children Health Act expands research and treatment on childhood issues such as diabetes, asthma, autism, and lead poisoning, among others.

2000   The Public Health Threats and Emergencies Relief Act, which is part of the Public Health Improvement Act of 2000, is a wide-ranging act designed to improve the core capacities of national, state, and local public health systems.

2000   The Turning Point Public Health Statue Modernization Collaborative is formed with the support of the Robert Wood Johnson and W.K. Kellogg Foundation for the purpose of transforming and strengthening the legal framework of the public health system by developing a model public health law.

2000   The Center for Law and the Public's Health is established at Georgetown and Johns Hopkins Universities. The center has become the primary national resource on public health law. The center conducts research on public health law topics, works with public health leaders on public health law and policy issues, and drafts model public health laws.

2000   State of Maryland enacts the Responsible Gun Safety Act that requires changes in handgun design. The law requires that handguns sold in Maryland must have a device built into the gun itself to prevent the handgun from discharging unless the safety is deactivated.

2000   Public Health Improvement Act passed by Congress.

2000   President Bill Clinton issues Executive Order 13145, which limits the ability of federal agencies to make use of genetic information in regard to employment decisions.

2001   The Center for Law and the Public's Health drafts and proposes the Model State Public Health Privacy Act (MSPHPA). The CDC recommends to state governments that they consider adopting the model legislation to strengthen protection of public health data.

2001   The Center for Law and the Public's Health proposes the Model State Emergency Health Powers Act (MSEHPA) designed to give significant emergency powers to state governors and public health agencies at state and local levels to deal with public health emergencies following the 2001 terrorist attack, the anthrax scare, and facing the potential of future bioterrorism.

2001   Al-Qaeda terrorists hijack four airliners and crash two into the World Trade Center in New York City and one into the Pentagon. A fourth plane crashes in rural Pennsylvania. President Bush declares a war on terrorism.

2001   Anthrax is sent to various places by mail.

2001   Bioterrorism war game "Dark Winter."

2002   Public Health Security and Bioterrorism Preparedness Response Act is passed.

2003   The Turning Point Public Health Statute Modernization Collaborative issues a final draft of the Turning Point Model State Public Health Act (TPMSPHA) in September 2003. The collaborative hopes that states would use the model act as a tool to assess their existing public health laws to identify what changes they deem necessary and adopt those changes.

2003   Department of Homeland Security created.

2003   United States–led coalition attacks Iraq.

2003   President Bush announces Project BioShield.

2004   Ricin sent to Senate Majority Leader Bill Frist.

References

Foreword

Bunker, J.P. 1995. "Medicine Matters After All." *Journal of the Royal College of Physicians* 29: 105–12.

Bunker, J.P., H.S. Frazier, and F. Mosteller. 1994. "Improving Health: Measuring the Effects of Medical Care," *Milbank Memorial Quarterly* 2: 225–58.

Centers for Disease Control, National Center for Health Statistics. 2004. "Life Expectancy" (data are for United States in 2001). www.cdc.gov/nchs/fastats/lifexpec.htm. Table 27. "Life expectancy at birth, at 65 years of age, and at 75 years of age, according to race and sex: United States 1900–2001." www.cdc.gov/nchs/data/hus/tables/2003/03hus027.pdf.

———. 1993. "Public Health Is More Important Than Health Care." *Journal of Public Health Policy* 14, no. 3: 261–64.

Gordon, Larry J. 1997. "Enviromental Health and Protection." Chapter 21 in *Principles of Public Health Practice*, ed. F. Douglas Scutchfield and C. William Keck. Albany, NY: Delmar Publishers.

Gordon, Larry J., and Deborah R. McFarlane. 1996. "Public Health Practitioner Incubation Plight: Following the Money Trail." *Journal of Public Health Policy* (spring): 59–70.

Institute of Medicine. 1988. *The Future of Public Health.* Washington, DC: National Academy Press.

McFarlane, Deborah R., and Larry J. Gordon. 1992. "Teaching Health Policy and Politics in U.S. Schools of Public Health." *Journal of Public Health Policy* 13, no. 4 (winter): 428–34.

Preface

Patel, Kant, and Mark E. Rushefsky. 1999. *Health Care Politics and Policy in America*, 2d ed. Armonk, NY: M.E. Sharpe.

Patel, Kant, and Mark E. Rushefsky. 2002. *Health Care Policy in an Age of New Technologies*. Armonk, NY: M.E. Sharpe.

1: The Politics of Public Health in the United States

Allen, Arthur. 2002. "The Not-So-Crackpot Autism Theory." *New York Times Magazine* (November 10): 66–69.

Altman, Roberta. 1996. *Waking Up, Fighting Back: The Politics of Breast Cancer.* Boston: Little Brown.

"Americans Support Public Health Spending." 2000. *Nation's Health* 29, no. 11 (January): 32.

Anderson, Odin W. 1990. *Health Services as a Growth Enterprise in the United States Since 1875*, 2d ed. Ann Arbor, MI: Health Administration Press.

"APHA Promotes Public Health Legislation." 2001. *Nation's Health* 31, no. 7 (August): 2.

Bachman, Sara S. 1996. "Why Do States Privatize Mental Health Services?" *Journal of Health Politics, Policy, and Law* 21, no. 4 (winter): 807–24.

Ballam, Deborah A. 1994. "The Evolution of the Government-Business Relationship in the United States: Colonial Times to Present." *American Business Law Journal* 31, no. 4 (February): 553–640.

Bayer, Ronald. 1991. *Private Acts, Social Consequences: AIDS and the Politics of Public Health.* New Brunswick, NJ: Rutgers University Press.

Beauchamp, Dan. 2002. "The Law, the Market, and the Health of the Body Politics." *Hasting Center Report* 32, no. 4 (July–August): 44–47.

———. 1997. "Lifestyle, Public Health, and Paternalism." In *Debates and Dilemmas in Promoting Health: A Reader*, ed. Moyra Sidell, Linda Jones, Jeanne Katz, and Alyson Peberdy, 297–305. London: Macmillan.

Benjamin, Georges C. 2001. "Public Health Infrastructure: Creating a Solid Foundation." *Physician Executive* 27, no. 2 (March–April): 86–87.

Bloch, Harry. 1974. "Childhood in the Early Colonial Period." *Pediatrics* 54, no. 1 (July): 71–73.

Blueprint for a Healthy Community: A Guide for Local Health Departments. Washington, DC: National Association of County and City Health Officials.

Burris, Scott. 1997. "The Invisibility of Public Health: Population-Level Measures in a Politics of Market Individualism." *American Journal of Public Health* 87, no. 10 (October): 1607–10.

Cahill, Kevin M. 1991. *Imminent Peril: Public Health in a Declining Economy.* New York: Twentieth Century Fund Press.

Callahan, Daniel, ed. 2000. *Promoting Healthy Behavior: How Much Freedom? Whose Responsibility?* Washington, DC: Georgetown University Press.

Cantril, Albert H., and Susan Davis Cantril. 1999. *Reading Mixed Signals: Ambivalence in American Public Opinion About Government.* Washington, DC: Woodrow Wilson Center Press.

Casamayou, Maureen H. 2001. *The Politics of Breast Cancer.* Washington, DC: Georgetown University Press.

Cassedy, James H. 1962. *Charles V. Chapin and the Public Health Movement.* Cambridge, MA: Harvard University Press.

"CDC Report Finds Americans are Improving Their Health." 2001. *Medical Letters on the CDC and FDA* (October 7).

Centers for Disease Control and Prevention. 2002. "About CDC." www.cdc.gov/aboutcdc/htm.

Costanza, Angelo, ed. 1992. *The Politics of AIDS.* Shippensburg, PA: Shippensburg University Press.

Crum, Gary, and Peter Somani. 1992. "Hospital and Public Health Agency Relationships." *Hospital Topics* 70, no. 3 (summer): 4–6.

Cumming, Hugh S. 1921. "The United States Quarantine System During the Past

Fifty Years." In *A Half Century of Public Health*, ed. Mazyck P. Ravenel, 118–32. New York: American Public Health Association.

Dandoy, Suzanna. 1997. "The State Public Health Department." In *Principles of Public Health Practice*, ed. Douglas F. Scutchfield and William C. Keck, 68–86. Albany, NY: Delmar Publishers.

Dobbin, Frank. 1994. *Forging Industrial Policy: The United States, Britain, and France in the Railway Age*. Cambridge, England: Cambridge University Press.

Duffy, John. 1990. *The Sanitarians: A History of American Public Health*. Chicago: University of Illinois Press.

Duncan, Jack W., Peter M. Ginter, and Keith W. Kriedel. 1994. "A Sense of Direction in Public Organizations: An Analysis of Mission Statements in State Health Departments." *Administration & Society* 26, no. 1 (May): 11–17.

Etheridge, Elizabeth W. 1992. *Sentinel for Health: A History of the Centers for Disease Control*. Berkeley, CA: University of California Press.

Etzioni, Amitai. 1993. *The Spirit of Community: Rights, Responsibilities, and the Communitarian Agenda*. New York: Crown Publishers.

Fee, Elizabeth. 1997. "History and Development of Public Health." In *Principles of Public Health Practice*, ed. Douglas F. Scutchfield and William C. Keck, 10–30. Albany, NY: Delmar Publishers.

Fenn, Elizabeth A. 2001. *Pox Americana: The Great Smallpox Epidemic of 1775–1782*. New York: Hill and Wang.

Foreman, Christopher H., Jr. 1994. *Plagues, Products, and Politics: Emergent Public Health Hazards and National Policymaking*. Washington, DC: Brookings Institution.

Fox, Daniel M. 1994. "The Public Health Service and the Nation's Health Care in the Post–World War II Era." *Public Health Reports* 109, no. 6 (November–December): 725–27.

Garrett, Laurie. 2000. *Betrayal of Trust: The Collapse of Global Public Health*. New York: Hyperion.

Gist, Ginger L. 1998. "Learning from Experience." *Journal of Environmental Health* 61, no. 4 (November): 4.

Goldberg, Bruce W. 1998. "Managed Care and Public Health Departments: Who Is Responsible for the Health of the Population?" *Annual Review of Public Health* 19, no. 1: 527–37.

Gorham, Frederic P. 1921. "The History of Bacteriology and Its Contribution to Public Health Work." In *A Half Century of Public Health*, ed. Mazyck P. Ravenel, 66–93. New York: Arno Press, 1970.

Gostin, Lawrence O. 2000a. "Public Health Powers and Limits." *Journal of American Medical Association* 283, no. 22 (June 14): 2979–83.

———. 2000b. *Public Health Law: Power, Duty, Restraint*. Berkeley, CA: University of California Press.

Gostin, Lawrence O., James G. Hodge, and Ronald O. Valdiserri. 2001. "Informational Privacy and the Public's Health: The Model State Public Health Privacy Act." *American Journal of Public Health* 91, no. 9 (September): 1388–92.

"Health Care Priorities: Medicare Prescription Drug Benefit and Strengthening Public Health System Seen by Public as More Important Issues than Patients' Bill of Rights or Medicare Reform." *Health Care News* 2, no. 1 (January 7). www.Harrisinteractive.com.

Henig, Robin M. 1997. *The People's Health: A Memoir of Public Health and Its Evolution at Harvard*. Washington, DC: Joseph Henry Press.

Hinman, Alan R. 1990. "1889 To 1989: A Century of Health and Disease." *Public Health Reports* 105, no. 4 (July–August): 374–80.

Houston, Thomas P. 1991. "The Roots of Public Health." *Journal of Family Practice* 32, no. 3 (March): 2.

Institute for the Future. 2000. *Health and Health Care 2010: The Forecast, the Challenge*. San Francisco: Jossey-Bass Publishers.

Institute of Medicine. 2002. *The Future of the Public's Health in the 21st Century*. Washington, DC: National Academy Press.

———. 1988. *The Future of Public Health*. Washington, DC: National Academy Press.

Jimenez, Mary Ann. 1997. "Concepts of Health and National Health Care Policy: A View From American History." *Social Service Review* 71, no. 1 (March): 34–51.

Johnson, Haynes, and David Broder. 1996. *The System: The American Way of Politics at the Breaking Point*. Boston: Little, Brown.

Kluger, Jeffrey, David Bjerklie, Andrea Dorfman, and Andrew Goldstein. 2002. "A Public Mess." *Time* 159, no. 3 (January 21): 92–95.

Koop, C. Everett, and Harold M. Ginzberg. 1989. "The Revitalization of the Public Health Service Commissioned Corps." *Public Health Reports* 104, no. 2 (March–April): 105–10.

Koplan, Jeffrey P., and David W. Fleming. 2000. "Current and Future Public Health Challenges." *American Journal of Medical Association* 284, no. 13 (October 4): 1696–97.

Kotkin-Jaszi, Suzanne T. 2001. "State Public Health Departments and Changes in Federal Policies: Managed Care, Welfare Reform, and Privatization." *International Journal of Public Administration* 24, no. 6 (June): 511–20.

Lee, Philip R. 1994. "The Evolution of Public Health." *Journal of American Medical Association* 272, no. 17 (November 2): 1315.

"Legislation to Benefit Key Public Health Issues." 2001. *Nations' Health* 30, no. 11 (December): 1–2.

Levit, Katharine, Cynthia Smith, Cathy Cowans, Helen Lazenby, and Anne Martin. 2002. "Inflation Spurs Health Spending in 2000." *Health Affairs* 21, no. 1 (January–February): 172–81.

Lovelace, Kay. 2000. "External Collaboration and Performance: North Carolina Local Public Health Department." *Public Health Reports* 115, no. 4 (July): 350–57.

Markel, Howard. 1995. "A Gate to the City: The Baltimore Quarantine Station, 1918–28." *Public Health Reports* 110, no. 2 (March–April): 18–19.

McFarlane, Deborah R., and Kenneth J. Meier. 2001. *The Politics of Fertility Control: Family Planning and Abortion Politics in the American States*. New York: Chatham House.

"Medical Triumphs: This Century's Top Ten Public Health Achievements." *Consultant* 39, no. 9 (September): 2449.

Melosi, Martin V. 1999. *The Sanitary City: Urban Infrastructure in America from Colonial Times To the Present*. Baltimore: Johns Hopkins University Press.

Mermann, Alan C. 2000. *The Renaissance of American Medicine: A Century of New Learning and Caring*. New York: University Press of America.

Miller, Judith. 2002. "A Nation Challenged: Bioterrorism; Bush to Request a Major Increase in Bioterror Funds." *New York Times*, February 4, A1.

Milo, Nancy. 2000. *Public Health in the Market: Facing Managed Care, Lean Government, and Health Disparities*. Ann Arbor: University of Michigan.

Nathanson, Constance A. 1996. "Disease Prevention as Social Change: Toward a Theory of Public Health." *Population and Development Review* 22, no. 4 (December): 609–38.

National Institutes of Health. 2002. "NIH: An Overview." www.nih.gov.

Oaks, Laury. 2001. *Smoking and Pregnancy: The Politics of Fetal Protection*. New Brunswick, NJ: Rutgers University Press.

O'Connor, Karen. 1996. *No Neutral Ground? Abortion Politics in an Age of Absolutes*. Boulder, CO: Westview Press.

"Office of Public Health and Science, and National Institutes of Health, Office of the Director; Statement of Organization, Functions, and Delegation of Authority." 2000. *Federal Register* 65, no. 114 (June 13): 37136–37.

"Office of Public Health Preparedness: Organization, Functions, & Delegation of Authority." 2002. *Federal Register* 67, no. 10 (January 15): 1980.

"OSHA Facts." 2004. www.osha.gov.

Parascandola, John. 1995. "The First Edition of 'The Ship's Medicine Chest' 1881." *Public Health Reports* 110, no. 4 (July–August): 504–5.

Pear, Robert. 2002. "Traces of Terror: Legislation: Negotiators Reach Compromise on Measures to Strengthen Safeguards Against Bioterror." *New York Times*, May 22, A24.

"Public Health Achievements." 1999. *Nutrition Today*, 34, no. 3 (May): 103.

"Public Health: Costs of Complacency." 2004. *Governing: The Magazine of States and Localities* 17, no. 5 (February): 26–35.

Public Health Foundation. 2000. *Statewide Health Expenditures: A Pilot Study in Maryland*. Washington, DC: Public Health Foundation.

———. 1998. *Where Do the Dollars Go? Measuring Local Public Health Expenditures*. Washington, DC: Public Health Foundation.

———. 1997. *Measuring Expenditures for Personal Health Services Rendered by Public Health Departments*. Washington, DC: Public Health Foundation.

"Public Health Improvement Act of 2000." 2001. *Journal of Environmental Health* 63, no. 7 (March): 37.

Rawding, Nancy, and Martin Wasserman. 1997. "The Local Health Department." In *Principles of Public Health Practice*, ed. Douglas F. Scutchfield and William C. Keck, 87–100. Albany, NY: Delmar Publishers.

Robins, Leonard, and Charles Backstrom. 1994. "The Role of State Health Departments in Formulating Policy: A Survey on the Case of AIDS." *American Journal of Public Health* 84, no. 6 (June): 905–9.

Rosen, George. 1958. *A History of Public Health*. New York: MD Publications.

Savas, E.S. 1982. *Privatizing the Public Sector: How to Shrink Government*. Chatham, NY: Chatham House.

Scheiber, Harry N. 1997. "The People's Welfare: Law and Regulation in Nineteenth-Century America." *Yale Law Journal* 107, no. 3 (December): 823–61.

Schonick, William. 1993. "Public Health Agencies and Services: The Partnership Network." In *Introduction to Health Services*, 4th ed., ed. Stephen J. Williams and Paul R. Torrens. Albany, NY: Delmar Publishers.

Scutchfield, Douglas F., and William C. Keck. 1997. *Principles of Public Health Practice*. Albany, NY: Delmar Publishers.

Shilts, Randy. 1987. *And the Band Played On: Politics, People and the AIDS Epidemic*. New York: St. Martin's Press.

Snyder, Lynne P. 1994a. "A New Mandate for Public Health." *Public Health Reports* 109, no. 4 (July–August): 469–71.

————. 1994b. "Passage and Significance of the 1944 Public Health Service Act." *Public Health Reports* 109, no. 6 (November–December): 721–24.

Stabiner, Karen. 1997. *To Dance with the Devil: The New War on Breast Cancer*. New York: Delacorte Press.

Stolberg, Sheryl G. 2002. "The President's Budget Proposal: Health Spending: Buckets for Terrorism, But Less for Catalog of Ills." *New York Times*, February 5, A20.

Taylor, Allan. 2001. "Germ Colonies." *New Republic* (November 19): 41–42.

"Ten Great Public Health Achievements—United States, 1900–1999." 1999. *Morbidity and Mortality Weekly Report* 48, no. 12 (April 2): 241.

Thomas, Patricia. 2001. *Big Shot: Passion, Politics, and the Struggle for an AIDS Vaccine*. New York: Public Affairs.

U.S. Department of Health and Human Services. 2002. "The Office of the Surgeon General." www.surgeongeneral.gov/sgoffice.htm.

————. 2000. *Healthy People 2010: Understanding and Improving Health and Objectives for Improving Health*. Vol. 1. Washington, DC: U.S. Government Printing Office.

————. 1990. *Healthy People 2000: National Health Promotion and Disease Prevention Objectives*. Washington, DC: U.S. Government Printing Office.

U.S. Food and Drug Administration. 2002. "Protecting Consumers, Protecting Public Health." www.fda.gov.

U.S. Occupational Safety and Health Administration. 2002. "OSHA Facts." www.osha.gov.

Walker, M.E.M. 1930. *Pioneers of Public Health: The Story of Some Benefactors of the Human Race*. Freeport, NY: Books for Libraries Press.

Weiss, Lawrence D. 1997. *Private Medicine and Public Health: Profit, Politics, and Prejudice in the American Health Care Enterprise*. Boulder, CO: Westview Press.

Young, Quentin D. 1998. "Public Health: A Powerful Guide." *Journal of Health Care Finance* 25, no. 1 (fall): 1–3.

WHO Press Release. 2000. "WHO Issues New Healthy Life Expectancy Rankings." (June 4). www.who3.int/whosis.

Willever, Heather. 1994. "The Cadet Nurse Corps, 1943–1948." *Public Health Reports* 109, no. 3 (May–June): 455–57.

Wills, Garry. 1999. *A Necessary Evil: A History of American Distrust of Government*. New York: Simon & Schuster.

Winslow, Herbert H. 1977. *The New Public Health*. New York: Arno Press.

World Health Organization. 2000. "World Health Report 2000." who.int/whr/2001/archives/2000/en/statistics.htm.

2: Leadership, Politics, and Public Health

"About APHA." 2003. www.apha.org (accessed January 2, 2003).

"About NACCHO." 2003. www.NACCHO.org (accessed January 2, 2003).

"About NALBOH." 2003. www.nalboh.org (accessed January 2, 2003).

"About Public Health Foundation." 2003. www.phf.org (accessed January 2, 2003).

"About the AAPHD." 2003. www.aaphd.org (accessed January 2, 2003).

"About Us." 2003. www.atpm.org (accessed January 2, 2003).

"Advise, Consent, Destroy." 1995. *Economist* (US) 336, no. 7921 (July 1): 18.

"American Association of Public Health Physicians." 2003. www.aaphp.org (accessed January 2, 2003).

"American Public Health Association Begins Leadership Development, Training Program; W.K. Kellogg Foundation Supports Transition." 2003. *US Newswire*, January 22.

"Another Look: Legalizing Drugs." 1994. *Economist* (US) 330, no. 7847 (January 22): 26.

"APHA Adopts Code of Ethics for Public Health Profession." 2002. *Public Health Reports* 117, no. 3 (May–June): 299.

"APHA and National Partner Organizations Celebrate Launch of National Public Health Performance Standards." 2002. *US Newswire*, June 20.

"APHA Launches Innovative Health Projects Network." 1998. *Public Health Reports* 113, no. 1 (January–February): 11.

"APHA Leadership Training Benefits Entire Association." 2000. *Nation's Health* 30, no. 7 (August): 11.

"APHA's Recent History Rich with Advocacy, Science." 1997. *Nation's Health* 27, no. 9 (October): 1–2.

Asch-Goodkin, Judith. 2002. "Who's Minding the Store?" *Contemporary Pediatrics* 19, no. 4 (April): 14–15.

"Availability of Applications for the Public Health Leadership Institute." 2001. *Morbidity and Mortality Weekly Report* 50, no. 4 (February 2): 62.

Barganier, Clyde, Chinnadurai Devadason, Randy Caperton, Dennis McDonough, A.D. Miller, F. H. Young, Larry Gilbertson, and Arden Miller. 1994. "Public Health Core Functions—Alabama, Maryland, Mississippi, New Jersey, South Carolina, and Wisconsin, 1993." *Morbidity and Mortality Weekly Report* 43, no. 1 (January 14): 13–15.

Beaglehole, Robert, and Ruth Bonita. 2000. "Reinvigorating Public Health." *Lancet* 356, no. 9232 (September 2): 787–88.

Beauchamp, Dan. 2002. "The Law, the Market, and the Health of the Body Politics." *Hastings Center Report* 32, no. 4 (July–August): 44–47.

Bennis, Warren. 1996. *Organizing Genius: The Secrets of Creative Collaboration.* New York: Addison Wesley.

Borger, Gloria. 1995. "Looking Out for No. 1." *U.S. News & World Report* 118, no. 8 (February 27): 37.

Bowman, James S., and Brent Wall. 1997. "Koop as an Exemplar of Moral and Democratic Decision Making: An Axial Approach to Ethical Theory." *Administration & Society* 29, no. 3 (July): 251–76.

Brown, Richard E. 1997. "Leadership to Meet the Challenges to the Public's Health." *American Journal of Public Health* 87, no. 4 (April): 554–55.

Brunelli, Richard. 1991. "Novello Salvo Could Flatten Alcohol Ads: Surgeon General Meets Execs Dec. 14." *Mediaweek* 1, no. 43 (November 18): 2.

Burns, James M. 1978. *Leadership.* New York: Harper and Row.

Carlson, Margaret. 1989. "A Doctor Prescribes Hard Truth." *Time* 133, no. 17 (April 24): 82–84.

Carter, Stephen L. 1994. *The Confirmation Mess: Cleaning up the Federal Appointment Process.* New York: Basic Books.

Centers for Disease Control and Prevention. 1992. "Leadership Development Survey of State Health Officials—United States, 1988." *Morbidity and Mortality Weekly Report* 41, no. 3 (April 3): 221–23.

Chaffee, Mary W., and Donald C. Arthur. 2002. "Failure: Lessons for Health Care Leaders." *Nursing Economics* 20, no. 5 (September–October): 225–29.

"Circle of Jerks." 1995. *Nation* 260, no. 1 (January 2): 4.

Cohen, Charles E. 1990. "Butt Out: Guido Sarducci? Surgeon General Antonia Novello, Your Sister-in-Law, Wants Everyone to Quit Smoking." *People's Weekly* 34, no. 24 (December 17): 109–10.

Cohen, Jon. 1993. "Bernadine Healy Bows Out." *Science* 259, no. 5100 (March 5): 1388–89.

Cohn, Bob. 1995. "Foster Follies." *Newsweek* 125, no. 8 (February 20): 26–28.

Connolly, Ceci. 2002. "Leadership Void Slows Top Health Agencies." *Washington Post*, January 10, p. A01. www.washingtonpost.com.

Cotton, Paul. 1990. "CDC Nears Close of First Half-Century." *Journal of American Medical Association* 263, no. 19 (May 16): 2579–80.

Duffy, Michael. 1994. "Getting Out the Wrecking Ball." *Time* 144, no. 25 (December 19): 41.

Duncan, Jack W., Peter M. Ginter, and Keith W. Kreidel. 1994. "A Sense of Direction in Public Organizations: An Analysis of Mission Statements in State Health Departments." *Administration & Society* 26, no. 1 (May): 11–27.

"Elders Confirmed for Surgeon General Post." 1993. *Jet* 84, no. 22 (September 27): 34–35.

Elders, Joycelyn, and David Chanoff. 1996. *Joycelyn Elders, M.D.: From Sharecropper's Daughter to Surgeon General of the United States of America.* New York: William Morrow.

Fiedler, Fred E. 1967. *A Theory of Leadership Effectiveness.* New York: McGraw-Hill.

Fiedler, Fred E., and Martin M. Chemers. 1964. *Leadership and Effective Management.* Glenview, IL: Scott, Foresman.

Firth-Cozens, J., and D. Mowbray. 2001. "Leadership and the Quality of Care." *Quality in Health Care* 10, no. 4 (December): 3–7.

Fox, Daniel M. 2002. "The Politics of Policy Development in Public Health: Notes on Three Stories." *Journal of Public Health Management and Practice* 8, no. 1 (January): 65–67.

Gardner, John W. 1990. *On Leadership.* New York: Free Press.

Gellert, George A., Kathleen V. Higgins, Rosann M. Lowery, and Roberta M. Maxwell. 1994. "A National Survey of Public Health Officers' Interaction with the Media." *Journal of American Medical Association* 271, no. 16 (April 27): 1285–89.

Glanz, James. 2004. "Scientists Say Administration Distorts Fact." *New York Times,* February 19.

Glastris, Paul. 1987. "Warning: The Surgeon General May Be Good for Your Health." *Washington Monthly* 19, no. 13 (March): 13–18.

Goldsmith, Marsh F. 2002. "Antonia Novello, M.D." *Journal of American Medical Association* 288, no. 4 (July 24): 440.

Grazier, Kyle L. 2002. "Question of Leadership in Health Care" (editorial). *Journal of Healthcare Management* 47, no. 6 (November–December): 347.

Green, Jesse, Gerald M. Oppenheimer, and Neil Wintfeld. 1994. "The $174,000 Misunderstanding: Repercussion of Overestimating the Cost of AIDS." *Journal of Health Politics, Policy, and Law* 19, no. 1 (spring): 69–90.

Greenberg, Daniel S. 1995. "Nay on the Vote for Surgeon General." *Lancet* 346, no. 8966 (July): 41.

———. 1994. "Out Goes the Surgeon General." *Lancet* 344, no. 8939 (December 24): 1760.

———. 1993. "FDA's Kessler Stays, NIH's Healy Goes." *Lancet* 341, no. 8846 (March 13): 681–82.

———. 1992. "Making Waves at NIH." *Lancet* 339, no. 8789 (February 8): 353–54.

Griffiths, Sian, and Klim McPherson. 1997. "We Need Strong Public Health Leadership." *British Medical Journal* 314, no. 7081 (March 1): 685–86.

Hanson, Russell L. 1993. "Defining a Role for States in a Federal Health Care System." *American Behavioral Scientist* 36, no. 6 (July–August): 760–79.

"Harold Varmus." 1999. *U.S. News & World Report* 127, no. 15 (October 18): 18.

Harshall, Eliot. 1999. "Varmus to Leave NIH in December to Run Sloan-Kettering." *Science* 286, 5439 (October 15): 382.

"Independence of the U.S. Surgeon General." 1997. *Lancet* 350, no. 9090 (November 22): 1489.

Institute of Medicine. 1988. *The Future of Public Health*. Washington, DC: National Academy Press.

Jensen, John. 1997. "Before the Surgeon General: Marine Hospitals in Mid-19th-Century America." *Public Health Reports* 112, no. 6 (November–December): 525–27.

Judis, John B. 1989. "Nice Guys: An Officer and a Gentleman." *New Republic* 200, no. 19 (January 23): 19–22.

Kaliher, William B. 1998. "How Federal and State Policies Spread AIDS." *World and I* 13, no. 5 (May): 328–37.

Keane, Christopher, John Marx, and Edmund Ricci. 2001. "Privatization and the Scope of Public Health: A National Survey of Local Health Department Directors." *American Journal of Public Health* 91, no. 4 (April): 611.

———. 2002. "The Privatization of Environmental Health Services: A National Survey of Practices and Perspectives in Local Health Departments." *Public Health Reports* 117, no. 1 (January–February): 62–68.

Keane, Christopher, John Marx, Edmund Ricci, and Gerald Barron. 2002. "The Perceived Impact of Privatization on Local Health Departments." *American Journal of Public Health* 92, no. 7 (July): 178–80.

Keenan, James F. 2001. "Talking About Sex: The Surgeon General's Invitation to a Conversation." *America* 185, no. 4 (August 13): 17.

Kerfoot, Karlene. 2002. "In Your Corner' Leadership." *Pediatric Nursing* 28, no. 4 (July–August): 426–27.

———. 2000. "Leadership: Creating a Shared Destiny." *MEDSURG Nursing* 9, no. 6 (December): 323–24.

Kesler, John T. 2000. "Healthy Community and Civil Discourse: A Leadership Opportunity for Public Health Professionals." *Public Health Reports* (March–June): 238–42.

Kessler, David. 1996. "We've Fought the Good Fight." *Newsweek* 128, no. 24 (December 9): 28.

———. 2002. *A Question of Intent: A Great American Battle with a Deadly Industry*. New York: Public Affairs Press.

Koop, C. Everett. 1991. *The Memoirs of America's Family Doctor*. New York: Random House.

"Koop *de Grace*." 1989. *New Republic* 201, no. 17 (October 23): 7–9.

Kotchian, Sarah B. 1993. "Environmental Leadership in a Public Health Agency." *Journal of Environmental Health* 55, no. 5 (March): 60–61.

Krucoff, Carol. 1991. "Antonia Novello: A Dream Come True." *Saturday Evening Post* 263, no. 4 (May–June): 38–42.

Lashof, Joyce C. 1992. "Leadership, Community, Partnership." *Nation's Health* 22, no. 3 (March): 2.

Legnini, Mark W. 1994. "Developing Leaders vs. Training Administrators in the Health Services." *American Journal of Public Health* 84, no. 10 (October): 1569–71.

Levin, Arthur A. 2002. "Science Under Attack by the Bush Administration." *HealthFacts* 27, no. 11 (November): 4.

Levy, Barry S. 1998. "Creating the Future of Public Health: Values, Visions, and Leadership." *American Journal of Public Health* 88, no. 2 (February): 188–92.

Lewis, Donald C. 2002. "Trust Matters: New Direction in Health Care Leadership." *Healthcare Financial Management* 56, no: 9 (September): 110.

Likert, Rensis. 1977. *Past and Future Perspective on System 4*. Ann Arbor, MI: Rensis Likert.

———. 1961. *New Patterns of Management*. New York: McGraw-Hill.

Longest, Beaufort B., Jr. 1996. *Health Professionals in Management*. Stamford, CT: Appleton & Lange.

Loven, Jennifer. 2004. "Bush Replaces Members of Bioethics Panel." 2004. Associated Press, February 28.

MacPherson, Peter. 1995. "Is the Surgeon General Obsolete?" *H&HN: Hospitals and Health Networks* 69, no. 21 (November 5): 48.

Mann, Jonathan M. 1997. "Leadership as a Global Issue." *Lancet* 350, no. 9094 (December 20): 23.

McLellan, Faith. 2002. "CDC Chief Koplan Quits 'the Best Job in Public Health.'" *Lancet* 359, no. 9308 (March 2): 773.

Milio, Nancy. 1994. "Health, Health Care Reform, and the Care of Health." *American Behavioral Scientist* 38, no. 1 (September–October): 92–107.

Mitchell, Steve. 2003. "Bush's CDC Budget Focuses on Bioterrorism." *United Press International*, February 4.

Motavalli, Jim. 1994. "The Voice of Our Elders: The Outspoken Surgeon General Is Using Her 'Bully Pulpit' to Take on the Tobacco Companies." *E* 5, no. 5 (October): 10–13.

Mullan, Fitzhugh. 1997. "Federal Public Health, Semi-Reinvented." *American Journal of Public Health* 87, no. 1 (January): 21.

———. 2000. "Don Quixote, Machiavelli, and Robin Hood: Public Health Practice, Past and Present." *American Journal of Public Health* 90, no. 5 (May): 702–6.

National Association of County Health Officials and Centers for Disease Control. 1990. *National Profiles of Local Health Departments*. Washington, DC: National Association of County Health Officials.

Nerf, Matthew. 2002. "Senate Approves Appointment of Carmona to Surgeon General." *American Family Physician* 66, no. 4 (August): 549.

"New Surgeon General." 1938. *Time* 27, no. 14 (April 6): 50–52.

Nolan, Pat. 1994. "PH Leadership Institute Offers Key Skills to Professionals." *Nation's Health* 24, no. 6 (July): 8.

Palca, Joseph. 1991. "Bernadine Healy: A New Leadership Style at NIH." *Science* 253, no. 5024 (September 6): 1087–89.

Parascandola, John. 1997. "The Surgeon General and Smoking." *Public Health Reports* 112, no. 5 (September–October): 440–42.

Parmet, Wendy E. 2002. "After September 11: Rethinking Public Health Federalism." *Journal of Law, Medicine, and Ethics* 30, no. 2 (summer): 201–12.

Pear, Robert. 2004. "Taking Spin Out of Report that Made Bad into Good Health." *New York Times*, February 22.

Piotrowski, Julie. 2002a. "Public Health Priority No. 1: Three New Leaders Vow to Tackle Bioterror, Disease Prevention, and Health Education as Public Health Gains Heightened Attention." *Modern Health Care* 32, no. 6 (July): 6.

———. 2002b. "New Leader, New Mission: Heightened Focus on Bioterrorism Poses Unique Challenges for CDC's New Chief." *Modern Healthcare* 32, no. 7 (August 5): 16.

Pointer, Dennis D., and Julianne P. Sanchez. 1997. "Leadership in Public Health Practice." In *Principles of Public Health Practice*, ed. Douglas E. Scutchfield and William C. Keck, 111–30. Albany, NY: Delmar Publishers.

"Politics of Masturbation." 1994. *Lancet* 344, no. 8939 (December 24): 1714–15.

Popkin, James. 1994. "A Case of Too Much Candor." *U.S. News & World Report* 117, no. 24 (December 19): 31.

Powledge, Tabitha M. 1992. "The FDA's New Sheriff ." *Hastings Center Report* 22, no. 1 (January–February): 5.

Public Health Foundation and Centers for Disease Control. 1990. *Training Needs Assessment of Public Health Officials*. Washington, DC: Public Health Foundation.

Randolph, Laura B. 1994. "In the Eye of the Storm: Surgeon General Challenges the Status Quo." *Ebony* 49, no. 4 (February): 154–57.

Robertson, Peter J., and Shui-yan Tang. 1995. "The Role of Commitment in Collective Action: Comparing the Organizational Behavior and Rational Choice Perspective." *Public Administration Review* 55, no. 1 (January–February): 67–80.

Rowitz, Louis. 2001. *Public Health Leadership*. Gaithersburg, MD: Aspen Publishers.

Schultz, Stacey. 2001. "Missing in Action." *U.S. News & World Report* (November 19): 55.

"Senate Confirms Koop, 68–24." 1981. *New York Times*, November 7, A14.

Simendinger, Earl A. 1997. *The Challenge of Health Care Leadership: Executive Strategies for Managing Responsible Change*. Chicago: American Hospital Publishing.

Smith, David R. 1998. "Public Health and the Winds of Change." *Public Health Reports* 113, no. 2 (March–April): 160–61.

———. 1994. "Porches, Politics, and Public Health." *American Journal of Public Health* 84, no. 5 (May): 725–26.

Snyder, Lynne S. 1994. "Passage and Significance of the 1944 Public Health Service Act." *Public Health Reports* 109, no. 6 (November–December): 721–24.

"Society for Public Health Education." 2003. www.sophe.org (accessed January 2, 2003).

Sofalvi, Alan J. 1997. "Politics, Public Health, and the Surgeon General of the United States Public Health Service." *American Journal of Health Studies* 13, no. 1: 27–32.

"State Health Officials Named by H.H.S. Secretary Tommy Thompson to Council on Public Health Preparedness." 2002. *Ascribe Higher Education News Services*, August 23.

"State Tobacco Prevention, Control Activities: Results of 1989–1990 Association of State, Territorial Health Officials Survey—Final Report." 1991. *Journal of American Medical Association* 266, no. 22 (December 11): 3105–8.

Stivers, Camilla M. 1991. "The Politics of Public Health: The Dilemma of a Public Profession." In *Health Politics and Policy*, ed. Theodor J. Litman and Leonard S. Robins. Albany, NY: Delmar Publishers.

Trafford, A. 1995. "What Koop Wrought: Henry Foster and the Very Model of a Modern Surgeon General." *Washington Post*, February 19, C5.

Tucker, Robert. 1995. *Politics as Leadership*. Columbia: University of Missouri Press.

Upshaw, Vaughn M., William A. Sollecito, and Arnold D. Kaluzny. 2001. "Leadership in Public Health." In *Public Health Administration: Principles for Population-Based Management*, ed. Lloyd F. Novick and Glen P. Mays, 567–84. Gaithersburg, MD: Aspen Publishers.

Veninga, Robert. 2001. "Reclaiming Our Values." *Vital Speeches of the Day* 68, no. 5 (December 15): 155–57.

Vergano, Dan. 2004. "Bush's Changes to Advisory Process Draw Scientists' Ire." *USA Today*, February 19.

Warner, Fara. 1992a. "Novello Throws Down the Gauntlet." *Adweek's Marketing Week* 33, no. 11 (March 16): 4–5.

———. 1992b. "For David Kessler, a Year of Compromise: The FDA Chief Faces New Political Pressures in the Fight for Labeling Reform." *Adweek's Marketing Week* 33, no. 3 (January 20): 4–5.

Weaver, David R. 2000. "Leadership as a Political Process." *Michigan Academician* 32, no. 3 (July): 253–56.

Wechsler, Jill. 2001. "FDA: History of Leadership, Partnership, and Transformation." *Pharmaceutical Technology* 25, no. 7 (July): 14–16.

"What Is ACPM?" 2003. www.acpm.org (accessed January 2, 2003).

"What Is ASPH?" 2003. www.asph.org (accessed January 2, 2003).

Williams-Crowe, Sharon, and Terry V. Aultman. 1994. "State Health Agencies and the Legislative Policy Process." *Public Health Reports* 109, no. 3 (May–June): 361–67.

Wilson, Paula. 1997. "Rise and Fall of the Surgeon General: The Nation Wasn't Ready for Joycelyn Elders' Blunt Messages About Sexuality." *USA Today* (magazine) 125, no. 2624 (May): 58–59.

Wright, Kate, Louis Rowitz, Adelaide Merkle, Michael Reid, Gary Robinson, Bill Herzog, Diane Weber, Donna Carmichael, Tom Balderson, and Edward Baker. 2000. "Competency Development in Public Health Leadership." *American Journal of Public Health* 90, no. 8 (August): 1202–7.

Wright, Kathleen, Louis Rowitz, and Adelaide Merkle. 2001. "A Conceptual Model for Leadership Development." *Journal of Public Health Management Practice* 7, no. 4: 60–66.

3: The Politics of Public Health and Private Medicine

Barglow, Raymond. 2002. "Medicine at the Millennium: Still Caught Between Descartes and Spinoza." *Tikkun* 17, no. 2 (March): 28–32.

Beauchamp, Dan E. 1996. *Health Care Reform and the Battle for the Body Politic*. Philadelphia: Temple University Press.

Biggs, Hermann M. 1921. "The State Board of Health." *New York State Journal of Medicine* 21 (January): 7.

Brandt, Allan M. 1988. "AIDS in Historical Perspective: Four Lessons from the History of Sexually Transmitted Disease." *American Journal of Public Health* 78, no. 4: 367–71.

Brandt, Allan M., and Martha Gardner. 2000. "Antagonism and Accommodation: Interpreting the Relationship Between Public Health and Medicine in the United States During the 20th Century." *American Journal of Public Health* 90, no. 5 (May): 707–16.

Brieger, Gerth H. 1997. "Sanitary Reform in New York City: Stephen Smith and the Passage of the Metropolitan Health Bill." In *Sickness and Health in America: Readings in the History of Medicine and Public Health*, Revised, 3d ed., ed. Judith W. Leavitt and Ronald I. Numbers, 437–51. Madison: University of Wisconsin Press.

Brown, Richard E. 1979. *Rockefeller Medicine Men: Medicine and Capitalism in America*. Berkeley: University of California Press.

Burrow, James G. 1963. *AMA: The Voice of American Medicine*. Baltimore: Johns Hopkins University Press.

Callahan, Daniel. 1998. *False Hope: Why America's Quest for Perfect Health Is a Recipe for Failure*. New York: Simon & Schuster.

Cassil, Alwyn. 1998. "Politics, Patience, and Finally Medicare." *AHA News* 34, no. 4 (February 2): 7.

Centers for Disease Control and Prevention. 1997. "Smoking-Attributable Mortality and Years of Potential Life Lost—United States, 1984." *Morbidity and Mortality Weekly Reports* 46, no. 20: 444–52.

"Changes in the Public Health System." 1999. *Morbidity and Mortality Weekly Report* 48, no. 50 (December 24): 1141–42.

Condran, Gretchen A., Henry Williams, and Rose A. Cheney. 1997. "The Decline in Mortality in Philadelphia from 1870 to 1930: The Role of Municipal Services." In *Sickness and Health in America: Readings in the History of Medicine and Public Health*, Revised, 3d ed., ed. Judith W. Leavitt and Ronald I. Numbers, 452–66. Madison: University of Wisconsin Press.

Davis, Michael M. 1927. *Clinics, Hospitals, and Health Centers*. New York: Harper & Brothers.

Davis, Michael M. Jr., and Andrew R. Warner. 1918. *Dispensaries, Their Management, and Development*. New York: Macmillan Press.

Department of Health and Human Services. 1986. *Report of the Secretary's Task Force on Black and Minority Health*. Washington, DC: Government Printing Office.

Duffy, John. 1990. *The Sanitarians: A History of American Public Health*. Urbana: University of Illinois Press.

Egan, Mary C. 1994. "Public Health Nutrition: A Historical Perspective." *Journal of the American Dietetic Association* 94, no. 3 (March): 298–304.

Fee, Elizabeth, and Roy Acheson, eds. 1991. *A History of Education in Public Health: Health that Mocks the Doctors' Rule*. New York: Oxford University Press.

Fee, Elizabeth, and Theodore M. Brown. 2000. "The Past and the Future of Public Health Practice." *American Journal of Public Health* 90, no. 5 (May): 690–91.

———. 2002. "The Unfulfilled Promise of Public Health: Déjà Vu All over Again." *Health Affairs* 21, no. 6 (November–December): 32–43.

Fineberg, Harvey. 1990. "Distinctions Between Public Health and Medicine." www.sph.uth.tmc.edu/cbphp/phvsmed.htm.

Flexner, Abraham. 1910. *Medical Education in the United States and Canada: A Report to the Carnegie Foundation for the Advancement of Teaching*. New York: Carnegie Foundation.

Fox, Daniel M. 1975. "Social Policy and City Politics: Tuberculosis Reporting in New York City, 1889–1900." *Bulletin of History of Medicine* 49 no. 2 (summer): 169–75.

———. 1994. "The Public Health Service and the Nation's Health Care in the Post-World War II Era." *Public Health Reports* 109, no. 6 (November): 725–27.

Frieden, Thomas R., Barron H. Lerner, and Bret R. Rutherford. 2000. "Lessons from the 1800s: Tuberculosis Control in the New Millennium." *Lancet* 355, no. 9209 (March 25): 1088–92.

Garceau, Oliver. 1941. *The Political Life of the American Medical Association*. Cambridge: Harvard University Press.

Garrett, Laurie. 2000. *Betrayal of Trust: The Collapse of Global Public Health*. New York: Hyperion.

Gorin, Stephen H. 2001. "The Crisis of Public Health: Implications for Social Workers." *Health and Social Work* 26, no. 1 (February): 49.

Haller, John S. Jr. 1981. *American Medicine in Transition: 1840–1910*. Urbana: University of Illinois Press.

"History of CDC." 1996. *Morbidity and Mortality Weekly Report* 45, no. 25 (June 28): 526–30.

Houston, Thomas P. 1991. "The Roots of Public Health." *Journal of Family Practice* 32, no. 3 (March): 257–58.

Hunt, Edward L. 1921. "The Health Centers Bill of 1920." *New York State Journal of Medicine* 21, (January): 2.

Institute of Medicine. 1988. *The Future of Public Health*. Washington, DC: National Academy Press.

———. 1992. *Emerging Infections: Microbial Threats To Health in the United States*. Washington, DC: National Academy Press.

———. 2002a. *The Future of the Public is Health in the 21st Century*. Washington, DC: National Academy Press.

———. 2002b. *Who Will Keep the Public Healthy? Educating Public Health Professionals for the 21st Century*. Washington, DC: National Academy Press.

Kahn, Laura H. 2003. "A Prescription for Change: The Need for Qualified Physician Leadership in Public Health." *Health Affairs* 22, no. 4 (July–August): 241–48.

Kaptchuk, Ted J., and David M. Eisenberg. 2001. "Varieties of Healing: Medical Pluralism in the United States." *Annals of Internal Medicine* 135, no. 3 (August 7): 189–95.

Kelley, Stanley. 1956. *Professional Public Relations and Political Power*. Baltimore: Johns Hopkins University Press.

Lasker, Roe D. 1997. *Medicine and Public Health: The Power of Collaboration*. Chicago: Health Administration Press.

Link, Eugene P. 1992. *The Social Ideas of American Physicians (1776– 1976): Studies of the Humanitarian Tradition in Medicine*. London: Associated University Presses.

Lucaccini, Luigi F. 1996. "The Public Health Service on Angel Island." *Public Health Reports* 111, no. 1 (January–February): 92–94.

Lupton, Deborah. 1995. *The Imperative of Health: Public Health and the Regulated Body*. Thousand Oaks, CA: Sage Publications.

Malecki, Jean, and C.L. Brumback. 2003. "Need for Physicians Trained in Preventive Medicine and Public Health: Implications for a Bioterrorism Response." *Journal of Public Health Management and Practice* 9, no. 2 (March–April): 89–90.

Mann, Jonathan M. 1997. "Medicine, Public Health, Ethics, and Human Rights." *Hastings Center Report* 27, no. 3 (May–June): 6–14.

Markel, Howard. 1995. "A Gate To the City: The Baltimore Quarantine Station, 1918–1928." *Public Health Reports* 110, no. 2 (March–April): 18–19.

Marmor, Theodore. 1973. *The Politics of Medicare*. Chicago: Aldine Publishing.

McArthur, John H., and Francis D. Moore. 1997. "The Two Cultures and the Health

Care Revolution: Commerce and Professionalism in Medical Care." *Journal of American Medical Association* 277, no. 12 (March 26): 985–89.

McBeath, William H. 1991. "Health for All: A Public Health Vision." *American Journal of Public Health* 81, no. 12 (December): 1560–65.

Meckel, Richard. 1990. *Save the Babies: American Public Health Reform and the Prevention of Infant Mortality, 1850–1929.* Baltimore: Johns Hopkins University Press.

"Medicine, Public Health, and Environment: Panel Discussion." 1994. *Issues in Science and Technology* 11, no. 1 (fall): 68–74.

"Medicine/Public Health Initiative Aims at Collaboration for Health." 1995. *Nation's Health* 25, no. 10 (November): 3.

"Medicine, Public Health to Come Together for Groundbreaking National Congress in March." 1996. *Nation's Health* 26, no. 2 (February): 16.

Mermann, Alan C. 2001 *The Renaissance of American Medicine: A Century of New Learning and Caring.* New York: University Press of America.

Mullan, Fitzhugh. 1989. *Plagues and Politics: The Story of the United States Public Health Service.* New York: Basic Books.

"The Mutual Relations of the Medical Profession and the Public." 1996. *Journal of American Medical Association* 276, no. 12 (September 25): 1004.

Navarro, Vicente. 1994. "Future of Public Health in Health Care Reform." *American Journal of Public Health* 84, no. 5 (May): 729–30.

———. 2003. "Policy Without Politics: The Limits of Social Engineering." *American Journal of Public Health* 93, no. 1 (January): 64–67.

Peng, Rui-cong. 1999. "The Goals of Medicine and Public Health." In *The Goals of Medicine: The Forgotten Issue in Health Care Reform*, ed. Mark J. Hanson and Daniel Callahan, 174–80. Washington, DC: Georgetown University Press.

Phillips, Donald F. 2000. "Medicine-Public Health Collaboration Tested." *Journal of American Medical Association* 283, no. 4 (January 26): 465.

Pocket Guide To Cases of Medicine and Public Health Collaboration. 1998. New York: New York Academy of Medicine.

Poen, Monty M. 1979. *Harry S. Truman Versus the Medical Lobby.* Columbia, MO: University of Missouri Press.

Reiser, Stanley J. 1996. "Medicine and Public Health: Pursuing a Common Destiny." *Journal of American Medical Association* 276, no. 17 (November 6): 1429–30.

———. 1997. "Topics for Our Times: The Medicine/Public Health Initiative." *American Journal of Public Health* 87, no. 7 (July): 1098–99.

Ritchie, David, and Fred Israel. 1995. *Health and Medicine: Life in America 100 Years Ago.* New York: Chelsea House.

Romano, Michael. 2001. "Money and Politics." *Modern Healthcare* 31, no. 46 (November 12): 14.

Rosen, George. 1993. *A History of Public Health*, expanded edition. Baltimore: Johns Hopkins University Press.

Rosenberg, Charles E. 1967. The Practice of Medicine in New York a Century Ago." *Bulletin of the History of Medicine* 41, no. 3 (May–June): 223–52.

———. 1974. "Social Class and Medical Care in Nineteenth-Century America: The Rise and Fall of the Dispensary." *Journal of the History of Medicine and Allied Sciences* 29, no. 1 (January): 32–54.

Rosenberg, Charles, E., and Carroll Rosenberg. 1968. "Pietism and the Origins of the American Public Health Movement: A Note on John H. Griscom and Robert M. Hartley." *Journal of the History of Medicine* January: 16–35.

Shine, Kenneth I. 1998. "The Health Sciences, Health Services Research, and the Role of the Health Professions." *Health Services Research* 33, no. 3 (August): 439–45.

Sidel, Victor W. 1992. "Introduction." In *The Social Ideas of American Physicians (1776–1976): Studies of the Humanitarian Tradition in Medicine*, ed. Eugene P. London, 123–27. Associated University Presses.

Skidmore, Max. 1970. *Medicare and the American Rhetoric of Reconciliation*. University, AL: University of Alabama Press.

Smith, David R. 1994. "Porches, Politics, and Public Health." *American Journal of Public Health* 84, no. 5 (May): 725–26.

Starr, Paul. 1982. *The Social Transformation of American Medicine: The Rise of a Sovereign Profession and the Making of a Vast Industry*. New York: Basic Books.

Stevens, Rosemary. 1971. *American Medicine and the Public Interest*. New Haven, CT: Yale University Press.

Stokols, Daniel. 2000. "Social Ecology and Behavioral Medicine: Implications for Training, Practice, and Policy." *Behavioral Medicine* 26, no. 3 (fall): 129–39.

Terris, Milton. 1946. "Hermann Biggs' Contribution to the Modern Concept of the Health Center." *Bulletin of the History of Medicine* 20, (October): 387–412.

———. 1976. "Evolution of Public Health and Preventive Medicine in the United States." In *Academic Relationships and Teaching Resources*, ed. Duncan C. Clark, 1–10. Bethesda, MD: U.S. Government Printing Office.

Vaughan, Victor C. 1921. "Rural Health Centers as Aids to General Practitioners." *Journal of American Medical Association* 76, (April 9): 983–85.

Voelker, Rebecca. 1997. "Medicine and Public Health Join Forces." *Journal of American Medical Association* 273, no. 22 (May 28): 1579.

Weiss, Lawrence D. 1997. *Private Medicine and Public Health: Profit, Politics, and Prejudice in the American Health Care Enterprise*. Boulder, CO: Westview Press.

White, Kerr L. 1991. *Healing the Schism: Epidemiology, Medicine, and the Public Health*. New York: Springer-Verlag.

Wolinsky, Howard, and Tom Brune. 1994. *The Serpent on the Staff: The Unhealthy Politics of the American Medical Association*. New York: G.P. Putnam's Sons.

4: The Politics of Public Health and Law

Anders, Kelly. 1999. "The Brady Act and Its Aftermath." *LegisBriefs* 7, no. 6 (January).

Anderson, George M. 1995. "Gun Control: New Approaches." *America* 172, no. 8 (March 11): 26–29.

"APHA Promotes Public Health Legislation." 2001. *Nation's Health* 31, no. 7 (August): 2.

Ashe, Marice, David Jernigan, Randolph Kline, and Rhonda Galaz. 2003. "Land Use Planning and the Control of Alcohol, Tobacco, Firearms, and Fast Food Restaurants." *American Journal of Public Health* 93, no. 9 (September): 1404–8.

Auster, Bruce B. 1996. "A New Round For and Against Brady Bill." *U.S. News and World Report* (September 9).

Bai, Matt. 1999. "The Feds Fire a Round." *Newsweek* 134, no. 25 (December 20): 38–39.

Baker, Edward L., James S. Blumenstock, Jim Jensen, Ralph D. Morris, and Anthony D. Moulton. 2002. "Building the Legal Foundation for an Effective Public

Health System." *Journal of Law, Medicine, and Ethics* supplement 30, no. 3 (fall): 48–51.

Benjamin, Georges C. 2001. "Public Health Infrastructure: Creating a Solid Foundation." *Physician Executive* 27, no. 2 (March–April): 86–87.

Benjamin, Georges C., Wilfredo Lopez, and Angela Z. Monson. 2002. "Partners in Public Health Law: Elected Officials, Health Directors, and Attorneys." *Journal of Law, Medicine, and Ethics* supplement 30, no. 3 (fall): 17–21.

Bonnie, Richard. 2001. "Reforming United States Drug Control Policy: Three Suggestions." *Social Research* 68, no. 3 (fall): 863–65.

Bonta, Diana, Sandra Praeger, and Jan Schlichtmann. 2002. "New Perspectives on Litigation and the Public's Health." *Journal of Law, Medicine, and Ethics* supplement 30, no. 3 (fall): 33–40.

Brown, Peter H., and Daniel G. Abel. 2003. *Outgunned: Up Against the NRA.* New York: Free Press.

"California Cities, Counties File Gun Suits." 1999. *Nation's Health* 29, no. 6 (July): 11.

Campaign for Tobacco-Free Kids. 2004. *State Tobacco Settlement.* wwwtobaccofreekids.org/reports/settlements/.

Carney, Dan. 1997. "Brady Decision Reflects Efforts to Curb Congress' Authority." *Congressional Quarterly Weekly Report* 55, no. 26 (June 28): 1524–25.

Carter, Gregg L. 1997. *The Gun Control Movement.* New York: Twayne Publishers.

Carter, Sherry P., Stanley L. Carter, and Andrew L. Dannenberg. 2003. "Zoning Out Crime and Improving Community Health in Sarasota, Florida: Crime Prevention Through Environmental Design." *American Journal of Public Health* 93, no. 9 (September): 1442–45.

Centers for Disease Control and Prevention. 2003. "Cigarette Smoking-Attributable Morbidity—United States, 2000." *Morbidity and Mortality Weekly Report* 52, no. 35 (September): 842–44.

Clute, Kenneth F. 1973. "Law and Health: Some Current Challenges." In *Politics and Law in Health Care Policy*, ed. John B. McKinlay, 139–200. New York: Milbank Memorial Fund.

Cohen, Adam, and Julie Grace. 1998. "Guns in the Courtroom." *Time* 152, no. 1 (July 6): 53–54.

Colmers, John M., and Daniel M. Fox. 2003. "The Politics of Emergency Health Power and Isolation of Public Health." *American Journal of Public Health* 93, no. 3 (March): 397–99.

Cook, Philip J., and Jens Ludwig. 1997. *Guns in America: National Survey on Private Ownership and the Use of Firearms.* Washington, DC: U.S. Department of Justice, Office of Justice Programs, National Institute of Justice.

———. 2003. "The Effects of the Brady Act on Gun Violence." In *Guns, Crimes, and Punishment in America*, ed. Bernard E. Harcourt, 283–98. New York: New York University Press.

Corlin, Richard F. 2001. "The Secrets of Gun Violence in America: What We Don't Know Is Killing Us." *Vital Speeches of the Day* 67, no. 20 (August 1): 610–15.

Daynard, Richard A., and Mark Gottlieb. 2001. "Tobacco Class Actions Fire Up: Courts Are Certifying More Class Action Brought Against Tobacco Industry by Injured Consumers Seeking Damages or Help with Their Addiction and Other Parties Harmed by Cigarette Makers." *Trial* 37, no. 12 (November): 18–24.

"Death of the Tobacco Bill." 1998. Editorial. *New York Times*, June 18.

DeMarco, Vincent, and Glenn E. Schneider. 2000. "Elections and Public Health." *American Journal of Public Health* 90, no. 10 (October): 1513–14.

Department of Veterans Affairs. 2001. "America's Wars." www.va.gov/pressrel/amwars01.htm.

Diamond, Martin M. 1999. "It's Time to Treat Violence as a Public Health Issue." *AHA News* 35, no. 43 (November 1): 6.

Dinsmoor, Robert S. 1992. "Firearms: A Growing Threat to Public Health." *Priorities for Health* 4, no. 4 (fall): 33–35.

"Drug Reforms Sweeping States in Recent Years." 2003. *Nation's Health* 33, no. 9 (November): 11.

Durant, Thomas J. Jr. 1999. "Violence as a Public Health Problem." *Sociological Spectrum* 19, no. 3 (July–August): 267–80.

Erickson, Deborah L., Lawrence O. Gostin, Jerry Street, and Peter S. Mills. 2002. "The Power to Act: Two Model State Statutes." *Journal of Law, Medicine, and Ethics*, supplement 30, no. 3 (fall): 57–62.

Fielding, Jonathan E., James S. Marks, Bradford W. Myers, Patricia A. Nolan, Raymond D. Rawson, and Kathleen E. Toomey. 2002. "How Do We Translate Science into Public Health Policy and Law?" *Journal of Law, Medicine, and Ethics*, supplement 30, no. 3 (fall): 22–32.

Fleisher, Steven M. 1980. "The Law of Basic Public Health Activities: Police Power and Constitutional Limitations." In *Legal Aspects of Health Policy: Issues and Trends*, ed. Ruth Roemer and George McKray, 3–31. Westport, CT: Greenwood Press.

"For the First Time, a Majority in U.S. Favors Ban on Handguns." 1993. *Nation's Health* 23, no. 7 (August): 10.

Fox, Daniel M. 2001. "The Professions of Public Health." *American Journal of Public Health* 91, no. 9 (September): 1362–64.

Gardner, John. 1998. "Tobacco-Control Bill Stalls in Senate." *Modern Healthcare* 28, no. 23 (June 8): 11.

Gebbie, Kristine M. 2000. "State Public Health Laws: An Expression of Constituency Expectations." *Journal of Public Health Management Practice* 6, no. 2 (March): 46–54.

Gibeaut, John. 2000. "Gunning for Change." *ABA Journal* 86, no. 3 (March): 48–52.

Gostin, Lawrence O. 1986. "The Future of Public Health Law." *American Journal of Law and Medicine* 12, no. 3–4: 461–90.

———. 2000a. "Public Health Law in a New Century, Part II: Public Health Powers and Limits." *Journal of American Medical Association* 283, no. 22 (June 14): 2979–83.

———. 2000b. "Public Health Law in a New Century, Part I: Law as a Tool to Advance the Community's Health." *Journal of American Medical Association* 283, no. 21 (June 7): 2837–41.

———. 2000c. "Public Health Law in a New Century, Part III: Public Health Regulation: A Systemic Approach." *Journal of American Medical Association* 283, no. 23 (June 21): 3118–22.

———. 2000d. *Public Health Law: Power, Duty, Restraint.* Berkeley: University of California Press.

———. 2001. "Public Health Law Reform." *American Journal of Public Health* 91, no. 9 (September): 1365–68.

———. 2002. "Public Health Law: A Renaissance." *Journal of Law, Medicine, and Ethics* 30, no. 2 (summer): 136–40.

Gostin, Lawrence O., Allan M. Brandt, and Paul D. Cleary. 1991. "Tobacco Liability and Public Health Policy." *Journal of American Medical Association* 266, no. 22 (December 11): 3178–82.

Gostin, Lawrence O., James G. Hodge Jr., and Ronald O. Valdiserri. 2001. "Informational Privacy and the Public's Health." *American Journal of Public Health* 91, no. 9 (September): 1388–92.

Gostin, Lawrence O., and James G. Hodge Jr. 2002. *State Public Health Law— Assessment Report.* Washington, DC: Center for Law and the Public's Health, Georgetown University Law Center.

Gostin, Lawrence O., J.W. Sapsin, S.P. Teret, et al. 2002. "The Model State Emergency Health Powers Act: Planning for and Response To Bioterrorism and Naturally Occurring Infectious Diseases." *Journal of American Medical Association* 288, no. 5 (August): 622–28.

Gotsch, Karen E., Joseph L. Annest, James A. Mercy, and George W. Ryan. 2001. "Surveillance for Fatal and Nonfatal Firearm-Related Injuries: United States, 1993– 1998." *Morbidity and Mortality Weekly Report* 50, no. SS02 (April 13): 1–32.

"Government Figures Show Gun Crime Down, Brady Bill Successful." 2000. www.cnn.com/2000/ALLPOLITICS/stories/06/05/brady.guns/.

"Government v. Gun Makers." 1999. *Economist* 353, no. 8149 (December 11): 24.

Gray, James P. 2001. *Why Our Drug Laws Have Failed and What We Can Do About It.* Philadelphia: Temple University Press.

Gregoire, Christine O. 2002. "When Law Is Good Medicine." *Journal of Law, Medicine, and Ethics* supplement 30, no. 3 (fall): 41–44.

Guetzloe, Eleanor. 1999. "Violence in Children and Adolescents—A Threat to Public Health and Safety: A Paradigm of Prevention." *Preventing School Failure* 44, no. 1 (fall): 21–24.

"Gun Control Overview." 1999. *Congressional Digest* 78, no. 11 (November): 258–59, 288.

"The Gun Lawsuits." 1999. (Editorial) *Christian Science Monitor* 91, no. 46 (February 2): 10.

Gunderson, Linda. 1999. "The Financial Costs of Gun Violence." *Annals of Internal Medicine* 131, no. 6 (September 21): 483–84.

Heath, Iona. 2002. "Treating Violence as a Public Health Problem." *British Medical Journal* 325, no. 7367 (October 5): 726–27.

Heishman, Stephen J., Lynn T. Kozlowski, and Jack E. Henningfeld. 1997. "Nicotine Addiction: Implications for Public Health Policy." *Journal of Social Issues* 53, no. 1 (spring): 13–33.

Hobson, William. 1963. *World Health and History.* Baltimore: Williams and Wilkins.

Hodge, James G. Jr. 1997–1998. "The Role of New Federalism and Public Health Law." *Journal of Law and Health* 12, no. 2: 308–57.

Horton, Heather, Guthrie S. Birkhead, Christine Bump, Scott Burris, Kathy Cahill, Richard A. Goodman, Brian Kamoie, Paula Kocher, Zita Lazzarini, Karen McKie, Anthony D. Moulton, Montrece M. Ransom, Fredrick E. Shaw, Barbara Silverstein, and Jon S. Vernick. 2002. "The Dimensions of Public Health Law Research." *Journal of Law, Medicine, and Ethics,* supplement 30, no. 3 (fall): 197–201.

Horton, Richard. 2001. "Violence and Medicine: The Necessary Politics of Public Health." *Lancet* 358, no. 9292 (November 3): 1472.

Hyman, David A. 2000. "Medicine in the New Millennium: A Self-Help Guide for the Perplexed." *American Journal of Law and Medicine* 26, no. 2–3: 143–54.

"Injuries, Violence Pose Public Health Epidemic." 1999. *Nation's Health* 29, no. 2 (March): 5.

Institute of Medicine. 1985. *Injury in America: A Continuing Public Health Problem.* Washington, DC: National Academy Press.

Institute of Medicine. 1988. *The Future of Public Health.* Washington, DC: National Academy Press.

Institute of Medicine. 2002. *The Future of Public's Health in the 21st Century.* Washington, DC: National Academy Press.

Jacobs, James B., and Kimberly A. Potter. 1995. "Keeping Guns Out of the 'Wrong' Hands: The Brady Law and the Limits of Regulation." *Journal of Criminal Law and Criminology* 86, no. 1 (fall): 93–120.

Jacobson, Peter D., and Soheil Soliman. 2002. " Litigation as Public Health Policy: Theory or Reality?" *Journal of Law, Medicine, and Ethics* 30, no. 2 (summer): 224–40.

Jacobson, Peter D., and Kenneth E. Warner. 1999. "Litigation and Public Health Policy Making: The Case of Tobacco Control." *Journal of Health Politics, Policy, and Law* 24, no. 4 (August): 769–804.

Judis, John. 1989. "Nice Guys: An Officer and a Gentleman," *New Republic* 200, no. 19 (January 23): 19–22.

Kates, Don B., and Henry E. Schaffer. 1997. "Public Health Pot Shots." *Reason* 28, no. 11 (April): 24–29.

Kendall, Brent. 2003. "License to Kill." *Washington Monthly* 35, no. 1 (January–February): 11–14.

Kessler, David. 2002. *A Question of Intent: A Great American Battle with a Deadly Industry.* New York: Public Affairs Press.

Kim, Henny H., ed. 1999. *Guns and Violence: Current Controversies.* San Diego: Greenhaven Press.

Krisberg, Kim. 2003. "New Association Focuses on Field of Public Health Law." *Nation's Health* 33, no. 6 (August): 8.

LaFrance, Arthur B. 2000. "Tobacco Litigation: Smoke, Mirrors, and Public Policy." *American Journal of Law and Medicine* 26, no. 2–3: 187–203.

Late, Michele. 2003. "New Model Act Promises to Modernize Public Health Laws." *Nation's Health* 33, no. 3 (April): 6.

Lazzarini, Zita, and Deborah Elman. 2002. "Legal Options for Achieving Public Health Outcomes." *Journal of Public Health Management Practice* 8, no. 5 (September): 65–75.

"Legislation to Benefit Key Public Health Issues." 2001. *Nation's Health* 30, no. 11 (December): 1–2.

Levine, Art. 1999. "Taking Aim at the Weapon Makers." *U.S. News and World Report* 127, no. 22 (December 6): 84.

Levy, Barry S. 1999. "Twenty-First Century Challenges for Law and Public Health." *Indiana Law Review* 32, no. 3 (fall): 1149–60

London, William. 1995. "Will Legalizing Drugs Benefit Public Health? Yes." *Priorities for Health* 7, no. 2 (June): 24–27.

Ludwig, Jens, and Phillip J. Cook. 2000. "Homicide and Suicide Rates Associated with Implementation of the Brady Handgun Violence Prevention Act." *Journal of American Medical Association* 284, no. 5 (August 2): 585–91.

Maantay, Juliana. 2001. "Zoning, Equity, and Public Health." *American Journal of Public Health* 91, no. 7 (July): 1033–41.

McAfee, Robert E. 1996. "A Major Public Health Crisis." *Nieman Report* 50, no. 3 (fall): 13–14.

McCann, Michael W. 1994. *Rights at Work: Pay Equity Reform and the Politics of Legal Mobilization*. Chicago: University of Chicago Press.

McKinley, John, and Lisa Marceau. 2000. "U.S. Public Health and the 21st Century: Diabetes Mellitus." *Lancet* 356, no. 9231 (August 26): 757–61.

Moulton, Anthony D., Richard A. Goodman, Kathy Cahill, and Edward I. Baker Jr. 2002. "Public Health Legal Preparedness for the 21st Century." *Journal of Law, Medicine, and Ethics* 30, no. 2 (summer): 141–43.

Moulton, Anthony D., and Gene W. Matthews. 2001. "Strengthening the Legal Foundation for Public Health Practice: A Framework for Action." *American Journal of Public Health* 91, no. 9 (September): 1369.

Musto, David F. 1990. "The Problem of Drugs is Nothing New in America." *Human Rights: Journal of the Section of Individual Rights and Responsibilities* 17, no. 2 (summer): 1.

Nolan, J., ed. 1916. *City Planning*. New York: D. Appleton.

Northridge, Mary E., and Elliot Sclar. 2003. "A Joint Urban Planning and Public Health Framework: Contributions to Health Impact Assessment." *American Journal of Public Health* 93, no. 1 (January): 118–21.

Oaks, Laury. 2001. *Smoking and Pregnancy: The Politics of Fetal Protection*. New Brunswick, NJ: Rutgers University Press.

Parascandola, John. 1997. "The Surgeon General and Smoking." *Public Health Reports* 112, no. 5 (September–October): 440–42.

Parmet, W.E., and R.A. Daynard. 2000. "The New Public Health Litigation." *Annual Review of Public Health* 21, no. 1: 437–54.

Perdue, Wendy C., Lesley A. Stone, and Lawrence O. Gostin. 2003. "The Built Environment and Its Relationship to the Public Health: The Legal Framework." *American Journal of Public Health* 93, no. 9 (September): 1390–94.

Pertschuk, Michael. 1998. "Tobacco's Newest Leaf." *Nation* 266, no. 15 (April 27): 6.

Quindlen, Anna. 2003. "Tort Reform at Gunpoint." *Newsweek* 141, no. 18 (May 5): 72.

Richards, Edward P., and Katherine C. Rathbun. 2003. *Legislative Alternatives to the State Model Emergency Health Powers Act*. LSU Program in Law, Science, and Public Health White Paper #2 at LSU Law Center's Medical and Public Health Law Site. biotech.law.lsu.edu/blaw/bt/MSEHPA_review.htm.

"Rethinking America's War on Drugs." 2001. Editorial. *Lancet* 357, no. 9261 (March 31): 971.

"Saved by Smokers: The Tobacco Settlement." 2001. *Economist* (US). November 24.

Scheingold, Stuart A. 1974. *The Politics of Rights: Lawyers, Public Policy, and Political Change*. New Haven, CT: Yale University Press.

Sclar, Elliot, and Mary E. Northridge. 2001. "Property, Politics, and Public Health." *American Journal of Public Health* 91, no. 7 (July): 1013–15.

Scott, Mel. 1971. *American City Planning Since 1890*. Berkeley: University of California Press.

Scutchfield, Douglas F., and William C. Keck. 1997. *Principles of Public Health Practice*. Albany, NY: Delmar Publishers.

Serafini, Marilyn W. 2003. "States Wrestle with Quarantine Laws." *National Journal* 35, no. 20 (May 17): 1568–69.

Shepherd, Jonathan P. 2001. "Criminal Deterrence as a Public Health Strategy." *Lancet* 358, no. 9294 (November 17): 492–93.

Sidel, Victor W., and Robert C. Wesley Jr. 1995. "Violence as a Public Health Problem: Lessons for Action Against Violence by Health Care Professionals from the Work of the International Physicians Movement for the Prevention of Nuclear War." *Social Justice* 22, no. 4 (winter): 154–71.

State of the States: Drug Policy Reforms, 1996–2002. 2003. Washington, DC: Drug Free Alliance.

Stevens, Jane E. 1998. "Integrating the Public Health Perspective into Reporting on Violence." *Nieman Report* 52, no. 4 (winter): 38–40.

Stolberg, Sheryl G. 2004. "Senate Leaders Scuttle Gun Bill Over Changes." *New York Times*, March 3.

Sullum, Jacob. 1998a. "Smoking and the Tyranny of Public Health." *Consumers' Research Magazine* 81, no. 7 (July): 10–14.

———. 1998b. *For Your Own Good: The Anti-Smoking Crusade and the Tyranny of Public Health.* New York: Free Press.

Teret, Stephen P. 1986. "Public Health and Law: Litigating for Public's Health." *American Journal of Public Health* 75, no. 8 (August): 1027–29.

Teret, Stephen P. et al. 1998. "Support for New Policies to Regulate Firearms." *New England Journal of Medicine* 339, no. 813 (September 17): 814–15.

Trafford, Abigail. 1992. "Violence as a Public Health Crisis." *Public Welfare* 50, no. 4 (fall): 16–17.

Tumulty, Karen. 2003. "Why No One Shoots Straight on Guns." *Time* 161, no. 21 (May 26): 40.

Turner, Leigh. 1997. "Bioethics, Public Health, and Firearm-Related Violence: Missing Link Between Bioethics and Public Health." *Journal of Law, Medicine, and Ethics* 25, no. 1 (spring): 42–48.

U.S. Department of Health and Human Services. 1986. *Surgeon General's Workshop on Violence and Public Health Report.* Rockville, MD: Office of Maternal and Child Health. DHHP Publication No. HRS-D-MC-86–1.

———. 1988. *The Health Consequences of Smoking: Nicotine Addiction.* A Report of the Surgeon General. Washington, DC: U.S. Government Printing Office. DHHS Publication No. CDC 88–8406.

U.S. Department of Health, Education, and Welfare. 1979. *Healthy People: The Surgeon General's Report on Health Promotion and Disease Prevention 1979.* Washington, DC: U.S. Government Printing Office. DHEW Publication No. 79–55071.

U.S. Department of Treasury. 2000. *Commerce in Firearms in the United States.* Bureau of Alcohol, Tobacco and Firearms. www/atf/treas.gov.

Vernick, Jon S., and Julie S. Mair. 2002. "How the Law Affects Gun Policy in the United States: Law as Intervention or Obstacle to Prevention." *Journal of Law, Medicine and Ethics* 30, no. 4 (winter): 692–704.

Vernick, Jon S., and Stephen P. Teret. 1993. "Firearms and Health: The Right to Be Armed with Accurate Information About the Second Amendment." *American Journal of Public Health* 83, no.12 (December): 1773–77.

———. 2000. "A Public Health Approach to Regulating Firearms as Consumer Products." *University of Pennsylvania Law Review* 148, no. 4 (April): 1193–211.

Voelker, Rebecca. 1995. "Taking Aim at Handgun Violence." *Journal of American Medical Association* 273, no. 22 (June 14): 1739–40.

"Welcome to the Center for Law and the Public's Health." 2003. www.publichealthlaw.net/index.html.

White, Larry C. 1991. "Cigarettes on Trial: The Public Health Balancing Act." *Priorities for Health* 3, no. 4 (fall): 5–8.

Winett, Liana B. 1998. "Constructing Violence as a Public Health Problem." *Public Health Reports* 113, no. 6 (November): 498–503.

Wing, Kenneth R. 1999. *The Law and the Public's Health.* Chicago: Health Administration Press.

Wittman, Friedner D., and M. Hilton. 1987. "Uses of Planning and Zoning Ordinances to Regulate Alcohol Outlets in California Communities." In *Control Issues in Alcohol Abuse Prevention: Strategies for States and Communities*, ed. Harold D. Holder, 337–66. Greenwich, CT: JAI Press.

Young, John T., David Hemenway, Robert J. Blendon, and John M. Benson. 1996. "The Polls—Trends: Guns." *Public Opinion Quarterly* 60, no. 4 (winter): 634–49.

5: The Politics of Science and Public Health

Agency for Toxic Substances and Disease Registry. n.d. "A Primer on Health Risk Communication Principles and Practices." Washington, DC: U.S. Department of Health and Human Services.

Altman, Lawrence K. 2004. "Study Finds No Link Between Abortion and Breast Cancer." *New York Times*, March 26.

Anderson, Glen. 2000. "The Politics of Peanut Butter." *State Legislatures* 26, no. 6 (June). Online from infotrac.

Behn, Robert D., and James W. Vaupel. 1982. *Quick Analysis for Busy Decision Makers.* New York: Basic Books.

Bennett, James T., and Thomas J. DiLorenzo. 2000. *From Pathology to Politics: Public Health in America.* New Brunswick, NJ: Transaction Publishers.

Bero, Lisa A., Theresa Montini, Katherine Bryan-Jones, and Christina Mangurian. 2001. "Science in Regulatory Policy Making: Case Studies in the Development of Workplace Smoking Restrictions." *Tobacco Control* 10, no. 4 (December): 329–36.

Brigham and Women's Hospital. n.d. "Nurses' Health Study." www.channing.harvard.edu/nhs/.

British Broadcasting Company. n.d. "Medicine Through Time—Hippocrates." www.bbc.co.uk/education/medicine/nonint/prehist/dt/prdtbi2.shtml.

Broder, David S. 2002. "A Shot in the Dark: Swine Flu's Vaccine Lessons." *Washington Post*, May 27.

Burns, Scott. 1997. "The Invisibility of Public Health: Population-level Measures in a Politics of Market Individualism." *American Journal of Public Health* 87, no. 10 (October): 1607–10.

Centers for Disease Control and Prevention. n.d.a. "Background: The Virus' History and Distribution." www.cdc.gov/ncidod/dvbid/westnile/background.htm.

———. n.d.b. "Cholera." www.cdc.gov/ncidod/dbmd/diseaseinfo/cholera_g.htm#What%20is%20cholera.

———. 1999. "Ten Great Public Health Achievements in the 20th Century." *Morbidity and Mortality Weekly Report.* www.cdc.gov/od/oc/media/tengpha.htm.

Clymer, Adam. 2002. "U.S. Revises Sex Information, and a Fight Goes On." *New York Times*, December 27.

Collins, Chris, and Thomas J. Coates. 2000. "Science and Health Policy: Can They

Cohabit or Should They Divorce?" *American Journal of Public Health* 90, no. 9 (September): 1389–90.

Commission on Life Sciences. 1983. *Risk Assessment in the Federal Government*. Washington, DC: National Academy Press.

Davis, Devra. 2002. *When Smoke Ran Like Water: Tales of Environmental Deception and the Battle Against Pollution*. New York: Basic Books.

Department of Health and Human Services. 2000. *Health People 2010*, 2d ed. Washington, DC: U.S. Government Printing Office.

DES Cancer Network. n.d. "DES Frequently Asked Questions." Washington, DC: DES Cancer Network. www.descancer.org/des.html.

Easterbrook, Gregg. 1995. *A Moment on the Earth: The Coming Age of Environmental Optimism*. New York: Viking Press.

———. 1999. "America the O.K." *New Republic* 4381–4382 (January 4 and 11): 19–25.

———. 2003. "The Smart Way to be Scared." *The New York Times*, February 16.

Efron, Edith. 1984. *The Apocalyptics: Cancer and the Big Lie: How Environmental Politics Controls What We Know About Cancer*. New York: Simon & Schuster.

Environmental Protection Agency. 1987. *Unfinished Business: A Comparative Assessment of Environmental Problems*. Washington, DC: U.S. Environmental Protection Agency.

Faigman, David L. 1999. *Legal Alchemy: The Use and Misuse of Science in the Law*. New York: W.H. Freeman.

Fielding, Jonathan E. et al. 2002. "How Do We Translate Science into Public Health Policy and Law? *Journal of Law, Medicine, & Ethics* 30, no. 3 (fall): 22–32.

Fioina, Morris P., Samuel J. Abrams, and Jeremy C. Pope. 2004. *Culture War? The Myth of a Polarized America.* New York: Pearson Longman.

"Funding Can Taint Findings." 2003. (Editorial) *Los Angeles Times*, January 24.

Glantz, Stanton A., John Slade, Lisa A. Bero, Peter Hanauer, and Deborah E. Barnes. 1996. *The Cigarette Papers*. Berkeley: University of California Press.

Goldstein, Martin, and Inge F. Goldstein. 1978. *How We Know: An Exploration of the Scientific Process*. New York: Plenum Press.

Gordis, Enoch. 1997. "Alcohol Problems and Public Health Policy." *Journal of the American Medical Association* 278, no. 21 (December 3): 178–79.

Gostin, Lawrence O. 2000. *Public Health Law: Power, Duty, Restraint*. Berkeley, CA: University of California Press.

Gray, George M., and David P. Ropeik. 2002. "Dealing with the Dangers of Fear: The Role of Risk Communication." *Health Affairs* 21, no. 6 (November–December): 106–16.

Hacker, Sandra. 1998. "An Overview of the Known Health Effects of Smoking During Pregnancy." A presentation by Dr. Sandra Hacker (AMA federal vice president) for the AMA Smoking and Pregnancy Consensus Conference. June 17. www.domino.ama.au/AAAWEB/health.nsf.

Hall, E.J. 1998. "From Chimney Sweeps to Astronauts: Cancer Risks in the Work Place." *Health Physics* 75, no. 4 (October): 357–66.

Henderson, Donald A. 1997. "Edward Jenner's Vaccine." *Public Health Reports* 112, no. 2 (March–April): 116–21.

"HHS Urged to Use Science, Not Sectarian Beliefs, to Shape Policy." 2003. *U.S. Newswire*, February 20.

Hippocrates. "On Airs, Waters and Places," trans. by Francis Adams. Copyright statement: The Internet Classics Archive by Daniel C. Stevenson, Web Atomics. World Wide Web presentation is copyright © 1994–2000. http://classics.mit.edu/Hippocrates/airwatpl.mb.txt.

Hunter, Donald. 1969. *The Diseases of Occupation*. London: English Universities Press.

Hunter, James Davison. 1991. *Culture Wars: The Struggle to Define America*. New York: Basic Books.

Hurt, Richard D., and Channing R. Robertson. 1998. "Prying Open the Door to the Tobacco Industry's Secrets About Nicotine (Health Law and Ethics)." *Journal of the American Medical Association* 280, no. 13 (October 7): 1173.

Ibsen, Henrik. 1981. *Four Great Plays by Henrik Ibsen*, trans. R. Farquharson Sharp, with an introduction and a preface to each play by John Gassner. New York: Bantam Books.

Isaacs, Stephen, and Steven A. Schroeder. 2001. "Where the Public Good Prevailed." *American Prospect* 123, no. 10 (June 4): 26–30.

Kleiner, Kurt. 2000. "Tobacco Wars." *New Scientist* (March 4).

Kreinin, Tamara. 2002. "Abstinence-Only Program Risky Business." *Seattle Post-Intelligencer*, October 18.

Kuhn, Thomas S. 1970. *The Structure of Scientific Revolutions*, 2d ed. Chicago: University of Chicago Press.

Lindaman, Kara, and Donald P. Haider-Markel. 2002. "Issue Evolution, Political Parties and the Culture Wars." *Political Research Quarterly* 55, no. 1 (March): 91–109.

Lynn, Frances M. 1983. "The Interplay of Science and Values in Assessing Environmental Risks." PhD dissertation, University of North Carolina at Chapel Hill.

Maginnis, Robert L. 2000. "Injecting Drug Use: A 2000 Overview." Family Research Council. www.frc.org.

McKinlay, John, and Lisa Marceau. 2000. "U.S. Public Health and the 21st Century: Diabetes Mellitus." *Lancet* 356, no. 9231 (August 26). Infotrac.

McQueen, D.V. 2002. "The Evidence Debate: Evaluating Evidence for Public Health Interventions" (Editorial). *Journal of Epidemiology & Community Health* 56, no. 12 (February): 83–84.

Milloy, Steven J. 2001. *Junk Science Judo: Self-Defense Against Health Scares & Scams*. Washington, DC: Cato Institute.

Morrone, Michele, and Timothy W. Lohner. 2002. *Sound Science, Junk Policy: Environmental Health Science and the Decision-Making Process*. Westport, CT: Auburn House.

Mouw, Ted, and Michael E. Sobel. 2001. "Culture Wars and Opinion Polarization: The Case of Abortion(1)." *American Journal of Sociology* 106, no. 4 (January): 913–43.

Nathan, Richard P. 1983. *The Administrative Presidency*. New York: John Wiley & Sons.

National Heart, Lung, and Blood Institute. n.d. "Framingham Heart Study: 50 Years of Research Success." Washington, DC: National Heart, Lung, and Blood Institute. www.nhlbi.nih.gov/about/framingham.

"Needle-Exchange Programs Are Slowly Finding Greater Acceptance, Needle Prescriptions Are New Possibility." 2002. *AIDS Alert* 17, no. 6 (June): 69–73.

Noah, Timothy. 2004. "Information is Treason, Why Bush Is Worse Than Reagan." Salon.com (March 16).

Occupational Safety and Health Administration. 1980. "Identification, Classification, and Regulation of Potential Occupational Carcinogens." *Federal Register* 45 (January 22): 5002–296.

Office of Management and Budget. n.d. John D. Graham, administrator, OMB's Office of Information and Regulatory Affairs. www.whitehouse.gov/omb/inforeg/bio.html.

Ong, Elisa K., and Stanton A. Glantz. 2001. "Constructing 'Sound Science' and 'Good Epidemiology': Tobacco, Lawyers, and Public Relations Firms." *American Journal of Public Health* 91, no. 11 (November): 1749–57.

Pressman, Jeffrey, and Aaron Wildavsky. 1984. *Implementation*, 3d ed. Berkeley: University of California Press.

Rampton, Sheldon, and John Stauber. 2001. *Trust Us, We're Experts: How Industry Manipulates Science and Gambles with Your Future.* New York: Penguin Putnam.

Rennie, Drummond, Annettee Flanagan, and Richard M. Glass. 1991. "Conflicts of Interest in the Publication of Science." *Journal of the American Medical Association* 266, no. 2 (July 10): 266–67.

Report of the Advisory Committee to the Surgeon General. 1964. *Smoking and Health.* Washington, DC: U.S. Department of Health, Education and Welfare, Public Health Service.

Rourke, Francis E. 1976. *Bureaucracy, Politics and Public Policy.* Boston: Little Brown.

Rushefsky, Mark E. 1984. "The Misuse of Science in Governmental Decisionmaking." *Science, Technology, & Human Values* 9, no. 2 (summer): 47–59.

———. 1986. *Making Cancer Policy.* Albany: State University Press of New York.

———. "Elites and Public Policy." In *Politics and Policy: Theories and Evidence Environmental*, ed. James P. Lester, 261–86. Durham, NC: Duke University Press.

Rychetnik, L., M. Frommer, P. Hawe, and A. Shiell. 2002. "Criteria for Evaluating Evidence on Public Health Interventions." *Journal of Epidemiology & Community Health* 56, no. 12 (February): 119–127.

Samet, Jonathan M., and Thomas A. Burke. 2001. "Turning Science into Junk: The Tobacco Industry and Passive Smoking." *American Journal of Public Health* 91, no. 11 (November): 1742–44.

Schecter, Martin T. 2002. "Science, Ideology, and Needle Exchange Programs." *Annals of the American Academy of Political and Social Science* 582, no. 7 (July): 94–101.

Schierow, Linda-Jo. 1994. "Risk Analysis and Cost-Benefit Analysis of Environmental Regulations." Washington, DC: Congressional Research Service.

Schneider, Mary-Jane. 2000. *Introduction to Public Health.* Gaithersburg, MD: Aspen Publications.

Scott, Patrick. 1999. "Edward Jenner and the Discovery of Vaccination." Department of Rare Books and Special Collections, University of South Carolina. www.sc.edu/library/spcoll/nathist/jenner.html.

Shilts, Randy. 1987. *And the Band Played On: Politics, People and the AIDS Epidemic.* New York: St. Martin's Press.

Skrzycki, Cindy. 2003. "OMB Proposes Changes in Rulemaking." *Washington Post*, February 4.

Snow, John. 1856. *On the Mode of Communication of Cholera*, 2d ed. Delta Omega. www.deltaomega.org/snowfin.pdf.

Stone, Deborah. 2002. *Policy Paradox: The Art of Political Decision Making*, rev. ed. New York: W.W. Norton.

Sullum, Jacob. 1998. "Smoking and the Tyranny of Public Health." *Consumers' Research Magazine* 81, no. 7 (July). Infotrac.

Sunstein, Cass R. 2002. *Risk and Reason: Safety, Law and the Environment.* Cambridge: Cambridge University Press.
"Syringe Exchange Proves Effective." 2002. *Medical Letter on the CDC & FDA* (December 22). Infotrac.
Taubes, Gary. 1998. "The (Political) Science of Salt." *Science* 281, no. 5379 (August 14).
———. 2001a. "The Soft Science of Dietary Fat." *Science* 291, no. 5513 (March 30).
———. 2001b. "Rethinking the Paradigm Paradigm." *Technology Review* 104, no. 9 (November).
Teifer, Charles. 1994. *The Semi-Sovereign Presidency: The Bush Administration's Strategy for Governing Without Congress.* Boulder, CO: Westview Press.
Thompson, Frank J. 1981. *Health Policy and the Bureaucracy: Politics and Implementation.* Cambridge, MA: MIT Press.
Vig, Norman J., and Michael E. Kraft. 1997. "Environmental Policy from the 1970s to the 1990s: An Overview." In *Environmental Policy in the 1990s,* ed. Norman J. Vig and Michael E. Kraft, 1–30. Washington, DC: CQ Press.
Walsh, Kenneth T. 2001. "A Brand New Front in the Culture Wars." *U.S. News & World Report* 131, no. 3 (July 23): 22.
Weiss, Carol. 1972. *Evaluation Research.* Englewood Cliffs, NJ: Prentice-Hall.
Weiss, Rick. 2003. "New HHS Panel Makeup Draws Ire of Patient Advocates." *Washington Post,* January 5.
Wetzstein, Cheryl. 2002. "Groups Seek Abstinence-Only Curbs: Say Teen Programs Are 'Unproven.'" *Washington Times,* September 2.
Wildavsky, Aaron. 1979. *Speaking Truth to Power: The Art and Craft of Policy Analysis.* Boston: Little Brown.
Yach, Derek, and Stella Aguinaga Bialous. 2001. "Junking Science to Promote Tobacco." *American Journal of Public Health* 91, no. 11 (November): 1745–48.
Zitner, Aaron. 2002. "The Bush Team Is Going to Great Lengths to Vet Members of Scientific Panels: Credentials, Not Ideology, Should Be the Focus, Critics Say." *Los Angeles Times,* December 23.
———. 2003. "Health Research Being Politicized, Critics Charge." *Los Angeles Times,* February 23.

6: The Politics of Genetics and Public Health

American Association of Health Plans. 2002. "Genetic Nondiscrimination: Issue in Brief." Washington, DC: American Association of Health Plans-Health Insurance Association of America. www.aahp.org/PrintTemplate.cfm?Section= Genetics&template=/ContentManagement/ContentDisplay.cfm&ContentID=4102.
American Civil Liberties Union. 2000. "Workplace Rights; Genetic Discrimination." Washington, DC: American Civil Liberties Union. www.aclu.org/WorkplaceRights/ WorkplaceRights.cfm?ID=9075&c=180.
Austin, Melissa A., and Patricia A. Peyser. 2000. "The Multidisciplinary Nature of Public Health Genetics in Research and Education." In *Genetics and Public Health in the 21st Century: Using Genetic Information to Improve Health and Prevent Disease,* ed. Khoury, Burke, and Thomson, 83–100. New York: Oxford University Press.
Begley, Sharon. 2004. "Bill Seeking to Ban DNA Discrimination Isn't Really Necessary." *Wall Street Journal,* February 6.

Blamire, John. 2000. "Science at a Distance." Distance learning course at Brooklyn College. www.brooklyn.cuny.edu/bc/ahp/BioInfo/GP/Definition.html.

Botto, Lorenzo D., and Pierpaolo Mastroiacovo. 2000. "Surveillance for Birth Defects and Genetic Diseases." In *Genetics and Public Health in the 21st Century: Using Genetic Information to Improve Health and Prevent Disease*, ed. Khoury, Burke, and Thomson, 123–39. New York: Oxford University Press.

Centers for Disease Control. 1998. "Preventing Emerging Infectious Diseases: A Strategy for the 21st Century; Overview of the Updated CDC Plan." Washington, DC: Department of Health and Human Services. www.cdc.gov/mmwr/preview/mmwrhtml/00054779.htm.

———. 2002. "Protecting the Nation's Health in an Era of Globalization: CDC's Global Infectious Disease Strategy." Washington, DC: National Center for Infectious Diseases, Department of Health and Human Services.

Children's PKU Network. n.d. "What Is PKU?" www.pkunetwork.org/PKU.html.

Cooper, Mary H. 2001. "Human Genome Research." *Issues in Health Policy* Washington, DC: CQ Press: 175–93

Coughlin, Steven S., and Wylie Burke. 2000. "Public Health Assessment of Genetic Predisposition to Cancer." In *Genetics and Public Health in the 21st Century: Using Genetic Information to Improve Health and Prevent Disease*, ed. Khoury, Burke, and Thomson, 151–71. New York: Oxford University Press.

Council for Responsible Genetics. n.d. "Genetic Testing, Discrimination & Privacy." www.gene-watch.org/programs/privacy.html.

———. 2001. "Genetic Discrimination: A Position Paper." Cambridge, MA.

Dorman, Janice S., and Donald R. Mattison. 2000. "Epidemiology, Molecular Biology, and Public Health." In *Genetics and Public Health in the 21st Century: Using Genetic Information to Improve Health and Prevent Disease*, ed. Khoury, Burke, and Thomson, 103–21. New York: Oxford University Press.

Easton, David. 1953. *The Political System: An Inquiry into the State of Political Science*. New York: Alfred A. Knopf.

Farrell, Philip M. et al. 2000. "Newborn Screening for Cystic Fibrosis: A Paradigm for Public Health Genetics Policy Development," ed. Khoury, Burke, and Thomson, 45–59. New York: Oxford University Press.

Fink, Leslie, and Francis S. Collins. 2000. "The Human Genome Project: Evolving Status and Emerging Opportunities for Disease Prevention." In *Genetics and Public Health in the 21st Century: Using Genetic Information to Improve Health and Prevent Disease*, ed. Khoury, Burke, and Thomson, 45–59. New York: Oxford University Press.

Garrett, Laurie. 2000. *Betrayal of Trust: The Decline of Global Public Health*. New York: Hyperion.

"Gene Differences May Alter Susceptibility to Multiple Sclerosis." 2003. ScienceDaily.com (December 16). www.sciencedaily.com/releases/2003/12/031216075004.htm.

"Genetic Privacy and Nondiscrimination Act." 1995. Washington, DC: U. S. House of Representatives. HR 1690 IH, 104th Congress, 1st Session. thomas.loc.gov/cgi-bin/query/z?c104:H.R.2690.

"Genetics Privacy and Legislation." n.d. Washington, DC: Department of Energy, Human Genome Project Information. www.ornl.gov/sci/techresources/Human_Genome/elsi/legislat.shtml.

Goldberg, Carey. 2000. "Big Gap In Screening U.S. Infants for Hereditary Ills." *New York Times*, February 26.

Goldie, Sue J., and April R, Levin. 2001. "Genomics in Medicine and Public Health: Role of Cost-Effectiveness Analysis." *JAMA, the Journal of the American Medical Association* 286, no. 13 (October).

Gostin, Lawrence O. 2000. *Public Health Law: Power, Duty, Restraint*. Berkeley: University of California Press.

Hellman, Deborah. 2003. "What Makes Genetic Discrimination Exceptional." *American Journal of Law and Medicine* 29, no. 1: 77–116.

Herrnstein, Richard J., and Charles Murray. 1994. *The Bell Curve: Intelligence and Class Structure in American Life*. New York: Free Press.

Holahan, John, and Marie Wang. 2004. "Changes in Health Insurance Coverage During the Economic Downturn: 2000–2002. *Health Affairs* (January 28). Web exclusive content.healthaffairs.org/cgi/reprint/hlthaff.w4.31v1.pdf.

Institute of Medicine. 1988. *The Future of Public Health*. Washington, DC: National Academy Press.

———. 2003. *The Future of the Public's Health in the 21st Century*. Washington, DC: National Academy Press.

Ip, Gregg. 2004. "The Gap in Wages is Growing Again for U.S. Workers." *Wall Street Journal*, January 23.

Jencks, Christopher and Meredith Phillips, eds. 1998. *The Black-White Test Score Gap*. Washington, DC: Brookings Institution.

Khoury, Muin J. 1996. "From Genes to Public Health: The Applications of Genetic Technology in Disease Prevention." *American Journal of Public Health* 86, no. 12 (December): 1717–22.

Khoury, Muin J., Wylie Burke, and Elizabeth J. Thomson, eds. 2000a. *Genetics and Public Health in the 21st Century: Using Genetic Information to Improve Health and Prevent Disease*. New York: Oxford University Press.

———. 2000b. "Genetics and Public Health: A Framework for the Integration of Human Genetics into Public Health Practice." In *Genetics and Public Health in the 21st Century: Using Genetic Information to Improve Health and Prevent Disease*, ed. Khoury, Burke, and Thomson, 3–23. New York: Oxford University Press.

Khoury, Muin J., Linda L. McCabe, and Edward R.B. McCabe. 2003. "Population Screening in the Age of Genomic Medicine." *New England Journal of Medicine* 348, no. 1 (January 2): 50–58.

Krumm, Jennifer. 2002. "Why Congress Must Ban Genetic Testing in the Workplace." *Journal of Legal Medicine* 23, no. 4 (December).

Kuo, Deborah 2004. "Taiwan on High Alert Against Avian Flu." Taipei, Taiwan, Central News Agency (January 13). LexisNexis.

Lasswell, Harold. 1958. *Politics: Who Gets What, When, How*. Cleveland: World Publishing.

Lin-Fu, Jane S., and Michele Lloyd-Puryear. 2000. "Access to Genetic Services in the United States: A Challenge to Genetics in Public Health." In *Genetics and Public Health in the 21st Century: Using Genetic Information to Improve Health and Disease,* ed. Khoury, Burke, and Thomson, 273–89. New York: Oxford University Press.

McNicholl, Janet, Marie V. Downer, Michael Aidoo, Thomas Hodge, and Venkatachalam Udhayakumar. 2000. "Public Health Assessment of Genetic Susceptibility to Infectious Diseases: Malaria, Tuberculosis, and HIV." In *Genetics and Public Health in the 21st Century: Using Genetic Information to Improve Health and Prevent Disease*, ed. Khoury, Burke, and Thomson, 173–202. New York: Oxford University Press.

Mills, Robert J., and Shailesh Bhandari. 2003. "Health Insurance Coverage in the United States: 2002." Washington, DC: U.S. Department of Commerce, Census Bureau.

National Cancer Advisor Board. 2001. "Genetic Privacy, Discrimination and Medical Information." Washington, DC (December 3–5). www3.cancer.gov/legis/dec01/genetic.html.

National Conference of State Legislatures. 2003. "State Genetic Privacy Laws." Denver: National Conference of State Legislatures. www.ncsl.org/programs/health/genetics/prt.htm.

National Electronic Library for Health. n.d. "Antenatal and Newborn Screening Programme." United Kingdom, National Health Service. www.nelh.nhs.uk/screening/antenatal_pps/antenatal.html.

National Human Genome Research Institute. n.d. "Genomic Research." Washington, DC: U.S. Department of Health and Human Services. www.nhgri.nih.gov/About.

National Organization of Rare Disorders. 2002. "Issue Brief: Genetic Nondiscrimination in Health Insurance and Employment Act S. 318/H.R. 602. Danbury, CT: National Organization of Rare Disorders. www.rarediseases.org/nord/washington/washington/employmentact.

O'Leary, Leslie A., and Debra L. Collins. 2000. "Using the Internet to Disseminate Genetics Information for Public Health." In *Genetics and Public Health in the 21st Century: Using Genetic Information to Improve Health and Prevent Disease*, ed. Khoury, Burke, and Thomson, 603–15. New York: Oxford University Press.

Olney, Richard S. 2000. "Newborn Screening for Sickle Cell Disease: Public Health Impact and Evaluation." In *Genetics and Public Health in the 21st Century: Using Genetic Information to Improve Health and Prevent Disease,* ed. Khoury, Burke, and Thomson, 431–46. New York: Oxford University Press.

Omenn, Gilbert S. 2000. "Genetics and Public Health: Historical Perspectives and Current Challenges and Opportunities." In *Genetics and Public Health in the 21st Century: Using Genetic Information to Improve Health and Prevent Disease*, ed. Khoury, Burke, and Thomson, 25–44. New York: Oxford University Press.

Pass, Kenneth A. 2000. "Lessons Learned from Newborn Screening for Phenylketonuria." In *Genetics and Public Health in the 21st Century: Using Genetic Information to Improve Health and Prevent Disease,* ed. Khoury, Burke, and Thomson, 385–404. New York: Oxford University Press.

Patel, Kant, and Mark E. Rushefsky. 2002. *Health Care Policy in an Age of New Technologies.* Armonk, NY: M.E. Sharpe.

Petersen, Alan. 1998. "The New Genetics and the Politics of Public Health." *Critical Public Health* 8, no. 1: 59–71.

Petersen, Alan, and Robin Bunton. 2002. *The New Genetics and the Public's Health.* New York: Routledge.

Press, Nancy, and Ellen Wright Clayton. 2000. "Genetics and Public Health: Informed Consent Beyond the Clinical Encounter." In *Genetics and Public Health in the 21st Century: Using Genetic Information to Improve Health and Prevent Disease*, ed. Khoury, Burke, and Thomson, 505–26. New York: Oxford University Press.

"Public Health Genetics Crucial to Treatment, Expert Says." 2000. *TB & Outbreaks Week* (October 17). NewsRx.com.

Reagan, Michael D. 1999. *The Accidental System: Health Care Policy in America.* Boulder, CO: Westview Press.

"Remembering Tuskegee: Syphilis Study Still Provokes Disbelief, Sadness." 2003.

Morning Edition, National Public Radio (July 25). www.npr.org/programs/morn-ing/features/2002/jul/tuskegee/.

Reynolds, Ted. 2003. "Study Clarifies Risk of Breast, Ovarian Cancer Among Muta-tion Carriers." *Journal of the National Cancer Institute* 95 (December): 1816–18.

Rochefort, David A. 1998. "The Role of Anecdotes in Regulating Managed Care." *Health Affairs* 17, no. 6 (November–December): 142–49.

Roeber, Carter, Bryan O. Les, and John Massad. 2001. "Genetics Literacy Project; Literature and Materials Review: A Working Report." Takoma Park, MD: LTG Associates. http://genes-r-us.uthscsa.edu/LTGliterature.pdf.

Rossi, Peter H., Mark W. Lipsey, and Howard E. Freeman. 2004. *Evaluation: A Sys-tematic Approach.* Thousand Oaks, CA: Sage Publications.

"Roundtable: The Politics of Genetic Testing." 1996. *Issues in Science and Technol-ogy* 13, no. 7 (fall): 48–54.

Rushefsky, Mark E. 2002. *Public Policy in the United States: At the Dawn of the Twenty-First Century*, 3d ed. Armonk, NY: M.E. Sharpe.

Rushefsky, Mark E., and Kant Patel. 1998. *Politics, Power and Policy Making: The Case of Health Care Reform in the 1990s.* Armonk, NY: M.E. Sharpe.

Schneider, Mary-Jane. 2000. *Introduction to Public Health Genetics.* Gaithersburg, MD: Aspen Publishers.

Schulte, Paul A., and DeBord D. Gayle. 2000. "Public Health Assessment of Genetic Information in the Occupational Setting." In *Genetics and Public Health in the 21st Century: Using Genetic Information to Improve Health and Prevent Disease*, ed. Khoury, Burke, and Thomson, 203–19. New York: Oxford University Press.

"Senate Passes Genetic Discrimination Bill." 2003. *Science + Technology in Con-gress* (November). Washington, DC: American Association for the Advancement of Science.

Shin, Hyon B., and Rosalind Bruno. 2003. "Language Use and English-Speaking Ability: 2000." Washington, DC: U.S. Census Bureau, Department of Commerce (October).

Soucie, J. Michael, Frederick R. Rickles, and Bruce L. Evatt. 2000. "Surveillance for Hemophilia and Inherited Hematologic Disorders." In *Genetics and Public Health in the 21st Century: Using Genetic Information to Improve Health and Prevent Disease*, ed. Khoury, Burke, and Thomson, 141–50. New York: Oxford University Press.

Paul Starr. 1984. *The Social Transformation of American Medicine.* New York: Basic Books.

Stone, Deborah. 2002. *Policy Paradox: The Art of Political Decision Making.* New York: W.W. Norton.

Thernstrom, Abigail, and Stephen Thernstrom. 2003. *No Excuses: Closing the Racial Gap in Learning.* New York Simon & Schuster.

"UCLA Study Uses Genetic Profiling to Distinguish Different Types of Leprosy." 2003. *ScienceDaily* (September 15). www.sciencedaily.com/releases/2003/09/030915073021.htm.

U.S. Census Bureau. 2003. "Poverty: 2002 Highlights." Washington, DC: U.S. De-partment of Commerce. www.census.gov/hhes/poverty/poverty02/pov02hi.html.

Watkins, Hugh, and Kaprio Jaako. 2000. "Genetic Epidemiology: Science, Medicine and the Future." *British Medical Journal*, no. 7244 (May 6): 1257–59.

Watson, Michael S. 2000. "Medical and Public Health Strategies for Ensuring the Quality of Genetic Testing." In *Genetics and Public Health in the 21st Century:*

Using Genetic Information to Improve Health and Prevent Disease, ed. Khoury, Burke, and Thomson, 223–41. New York: Oxford University Press.

Wedeen, Richard P. 2000. "Consent in Epidemiology: Implications of History for Public Health." *Archives of Environmental Health* 55, no. 4 (July–August 2000): 231–39.

White House. 2000. "Executive Order to Prohibit Discrimination in Federal Employment Based on Genetic Information." Washington, DC: Office of the Press Secretary, the White House (February 8). www.opm.gov/pressrel/2000/genetic_eo.htm.

Wilfond, Benjamin S., and Elizabeth J. Thomson. 2000. "Models of Public Health Genetic Policy Development." In *Genetics and Public Health in the 21st Century: Using Genetic Information to Improve Health and Prevent Disease*, ed. Khoury, Burke, and Thomson, 61–81. New York: Oxford University Press.

Yen, Rhoda. 2003. "Tourette's Syndrome: A Case Example for Mandatory Genetic Regulation of Behavioral Disorders." *Law and Psychology Review* 27 (spring): 29–54.

7: The Politics of Environment and Public Health

American Council on Science and Health. 1999a. "Endocrine Disruptors: A Scientific Assessment." New York: American Council on Science and Health. ww.acsh.org/publications/booklets/enddis.pdf.

———. 1999b. *Environmental Tobacco Smoke: Health Risk or Hype?* New York: American Council on Science and Health.

Baillar, John C., III, and A. John Bailer. 2002. "The Science of Risk Assessment." In *Life Support: The Environment and Human Health*, ed. Michael McCally, 231–38. Cambridge, MA: MIT Press.

Balbus, John. 2002. "Water Quality and Water Resources." In *Life Support: The Environment and Human Health*, ed. Michael McCally, 39–63. Cambridge, MA: MIT Press.

Barrett, Katherine, and Carolyn Raffensperger. 1999. "Precautionary Science." In *Protecting Public Health & the Environment: Implementing the Precautionary Principle*, ed. Carolyn Raffensperger and Joel Tickner, 106–22. Washington, DC: Island Press.

Bayer, Ronald, and James Colgrove. 2002. "Science, Politics, and Ideology in the Campaign Against Environmental Tobacco Smoke." *American Journal of Public Health* 92, no. 6 (June): 949–54.

Bookchin, Murray. 1971. *Post-Scarcity Anarchism*. Berkeley, CA.: Ramparts Press.

Brockovich, Erin, and Edward L. Masry. 2003. "Beverly Hills Ignores Belmont's Toxic Lessons." *Los Angeles Times*, November 17.

Brown, Phil, Stephen Zavestoski, Brian Mayer, Sabrina McCormick, and Pamela S. Webster. 2002. "Policy Issues in Environmental Health Disputes." *Annals of the American Academy of Political and Social Science*, special issue (November 2002): 175–202.

California Environmental Protection Agency. n.d. www.calepa.ca.gov/.

Carson, Rachel. 1962. *Silent Spring*. Boston: Houghton Mifflin.

Caulfield, Henry P. 1989. "The Conservation and Environmental Movements: An Historical Analysis." In *Environmental Politics and Policy: Theories and Evidence*, ed. James P. Lester, 13–56. Durham, NC: Duke University Press.

Centers for Disease Control and Prevention. n.d. "CDC Lyme Disease Home Page." Washington, DC: Centers for Disease Control and Prevention, Division of Vector-Borne Infectious Diseases. www.cdc.gov/ncidod/dvbid/lyme/.

Children's Environmental Health Network. 1997. "Endocrine Disrupting Chemicals: Fact Sheet from a Congressional Briefing Conducted by the Children's Environmental Health Network." Washington, DC: Children's Environmental Health Network. www.cehn.org/cehn/CongBriefEndo.html.

Christiani, David C., and Mark A. Woodin. 2002. "Urban and Transboundary Air Pollution." In *Life Support: The Environment and Human Health*, ed. Michael McCally, 15–37. Cambridge, MA: MIT Press.

"Christie Whitman, Head of EPA, announced October 31 that the Bush Administration would retain the 10 parts per billion (ppb) standard for arsenic in drinking water that the Clinton Administration had set." 2001. *Public Works* 132, no. 13 (December): 8.

Clapp, Richard W. 2002a. "Cancer and the Environment." In *Life Support: The Environment and Human Health*, ed. Michael McCally, 201–9. Cambridge, MA: MIT Press.

———. 2002b. "Popular Epidemiology in Three Contaminated Communities." *Annals of the American Academy of Political and Social Science*, special issue (November): 35–46.

Clark, John. 1999. "The Politics of Social Ecology: Beyond the Limits of the City." *Democracy and Nature* 5, no. 3 (November): 523–60.

Clarkson, Frederick. 2003. "They Ban Textbooks, Don't They?" Salon.com (November 5).

Colborn, Theo, Dianne Dumanoski, and John Peterson Myers. 1997. *Our Stolen Future: Are We Threatening Our Fertility, Intelligence, and Survival? A Scientific Detective Story*. New York: Plume.

Commission on Life Sciences. 2000. *Hormonally Active Agents in the Environment*. Washington, DC: National Academy of Sciences. www.nap.edu/books/0309064198/html/.

Committee on Government Reform, Minority Staff. 2003. "Politics and Science in the Bush Administration." Washington, DC: U.S. House of Representatives. Staff report prepared for Rep. Henry A. Waxman (D-California). www.house.gov/reform/min/politicsandscience/pdfs/pdf_politics_and_science_rep.pdf.

Committee on Toxicology. 2001. *Arsenic in Drinking Water: 2001 Update*. Subcommittee to update the 1999 Arsenic in Drinking Water Report, Committee on Toxicology, Board on Environmental Studies and Toxicology, National Research Council. Washington, DC: National Academy Press.

Corn, David. 2003. *The Lies of George W. Bush: Mastering the Politics of Deception*. New York: Crown Publishers.

Cornwell, Ruppert. 2002. "Iraq, the Threat of War: Analysis: Saddam's Latest Move Is the Sign of an Adroit Tactician." *The (London) Independent*, September 17. Retrieved from Lexis-Nexis, June 6, 2003.

Cranor, Carl F. 1999. "Asymmetric Information, the Precautionary Principle, and Burdens of Proof." In *Protecting Public Health & the Environment: Implementing the Precautionary Principle*, ed. Carolyn Raffensperger and Joel Tickner, 74–99. Washington, DC: Island Press.

———. 1999b. Introduction. "To Foresee and Forestall." In *Protecting Public Health & the Environment: Implementing the Precautionary Principle*, ed. Carolyn Raffensperger and Joel Tickner, 1–11. Washington, DC: Island Press.

Davis, Debra. 2002. *When Smoke Ran Like Water: Tales of Environmental Deception and the Battle Against Pollution*. New York: Basic Books.

Davis, Debra Lee, and Pamela S. Webster. 2002. "The Social Context of Science:

Cancer and the Environment." *Annals of the American Academy of Political and Social Science*, special issue (November 2002): 13–34.

de Gruijl, Frank R., and Jan C. van der Leun. 2002. "Ozone Depletion and Ultraviolet Radiation." In *Life Support: The Environment and Human Health*, ed. Michael McCally, 136–45. Cambridge, MA: MIT Press.

Easterbrook. 1995. *A Moment on the Earth: The Coming Age of Environmental Optimism*. New York: Viking Press.

Easton, David. 1953. *The Political System: An Inquiry into the State of Political Science*. New York: Alfred A. Knopf.

Endocrine Disruptor Screening and Testing Advisory Committee. 1998. Final Report. Washington, DC: U.S. Environmental Protection Agency. www.epa.gov/oscpmont/oscpendo/history/finalrpt.htm.

Enstrom, James E., and Geoffrey C. Kabat. 2003. "Environmental Tobacco Smoke and Tobacco Mortality in a Prospective Study of Californians, 1968–98." *British Medical Journal* 326, no. 7398 (May 17): 1057–62.

Environmental Protection Agency. n.d.a. "Background on Endocrine Disruptors: EPA's Endocrine Disruptor Screening and Testing Advisory Committee (EDSTAC)." Washington, DC: U.S. Environmental Protection Agency. www.epa.gov/scipoly/oscpendo/history/edstac.htm.

———. n.d.b. "Endocrine Disruptor Screening Program Overview." Washington, DC: U.S. Environmental Protection Agency. www.epa.gov/oscpmont/oscpendo/overview.htm.

———. n.d.c. "Human Health Assessment." Washington, DC: U.S. Environmental Protection Agency. www.epa.gov/ebtpages/humahealthassessment.html.

———. 1997. *Climate Change and Public Health*. Washington, DC: U.S. Environmental Protection Agency.

———. 1999. "U.S. Emissions Inventory—1999." Washington, DC: U.S. Environmental Protection Agency. www.epa.gov/globalwarming/publications/emissions/us1999/index.html.

———. 2003a. "EPA Announces Next Step to Improve the New Source Program Review." Washington, DC: U.S. Environmental Protection Agency, August 27. www.epa.gov/newsroom/headline2_082703.htm.

———. 2003b. "Prevention of Significant Deterioration (PSD) and Non-Attainment New Source Review (NSR): Reconsideration." 40 CFR 51 and 52. www.epa.gov/nsr/recon_fr_10–30–03.pdf

"Environmentalists Claim Bush Administration Is Undermining the National Environmental Policy Act." 2002. *All Things Considered* (National Public Radio), October 14.

Fritschler, A. Lee. 1996. *Smoking and Politics: Policy Making and the Federal Bureaucracy*, 5th ed. Upper Saddle River, NJ: Prentice-Hall.

Frum, David. 2003. *The Right Man: The Surprising Presidency of George W. Bush*. New York: Random House.

Garg, Anjali, and Philip J. Landrigan. 2002. "Children's Environmental Health: New Gains in Science and Policy." *Annals of the American Academy of Political and Social Science*, special issue (November 2002): 135–44.

Garrett, Laurie. 2000. *Betrayal of Trust: The Collapse of Global Public Health*. New York: Hyperion.

Gibbs, Lois. 2002. "Citizen Activism for Environmental Health: The Growth of a Powerful Grassroots Health Movement." *Annals of the American Academy of Political and Social Science*, special issue (November 2002): 97–109.

Glantz, Stanton A., John Slade, Lisa A. Bero, Peter Hanauer, Deborah E. Barnes. 1996. *The Cigarette Papers.* Berkeley: University of California Press.

Green Party USA. n.d. "Platform of the Greens/Green Party USA." www.greenparty.org/Platform.html.

Haines, Andrew, Anthony J. McMichael, and Paul R. Epstein. 2002. "Global Climate Change and Health." In *Life Support: The Environment and Human Health*, ed. Michael McCally, 99–117. Cambridge, MA: MIT Press.

Hatch, Maureen, and Michael McCally. 2002. "Radiation and Health." In *Life Support: The Environment and Human Health*, ed. Michael McCally, 211–29. Cambridge, MA: MIT Press.

Hilts, Philip J. 2003. *Protecting America's Health: The FDA, Business, and One Hundred Years of Regulation.* New York: Alfred A. Knopf.

Hu, Howard. 2002. "Human Health and Heavy Metals Exposure." In *Life Support: The Environment and Human Health*, ed. Michael McCally, 65–81. Cambridge, MA: MIT Press.

Institute of Health. 2003. *Microbial Threats to Health: Emergence, Detection, Response.* Washington, DC: National Academy of Sciences Press (March). http://books.nap.edu/html/microbial_threats/reportbrief.pdf.

Institute of Medicine. 2003. *The Future of the Public's Health in the 21st Century.* Washington, DC: National Academy Press.

Intergovernmental Panel on Climate Change. 2001. *Climate Change 2001: The Scientific Basis.* World Meteorological Organization/United Nations Environmental Program. Cambridge: Cambridge University Press.

Jameton, Andrew, and Jessica Pierce. 2002. "Sustainable Health Care and Emerging Ethical Responsibilities." In *Life Support: The Environment and Human Health*, ed. Michael McCally, 285–96. Cambridge, MA: MIT Press.

Jehl, Douglas. 2001. "House Demanding Strict Guidelines on Arsenic Levels." *New York Times*, July 28.

Kamrin, Michael. 2003. "Environmental Chemicals in the Human Body: Are They a Risk to Human Health?" New York: American Council on Science and Health. www.acsh.org/publications/booklets/traces2003.pdf.

Khoury, Muin J., Wylie Burke, and Elizabeth J. Thomson, eds. 2000. *Genetics and Public Health in the 21st Century: Using Genetic Information to Improve Health and Prevent Disease.* New York: Oxford University Press.

Krimsky, Sheldon. 2000. *Hormonal Chaos: The Scientific and Social Origins of the Environmental Endocrine Hypothesis.* Baltimore: Johns Hopkins University Press.

Landrigan, Philip, and Angali Garg. 2002. "Vulnerable Populations." In *Life Support: The Environment and Human Health*, ed. Michael McCally, 257–71. Cambridge, MA: MIT Press.

Lee, Jennifer S. 2003. "The Warming Is Global, But the Legislating, in the U.S., Is All Local." *New York Times*, October 29.

Lee, Jennifer S., and Andrew C. Revkin. 2003. "Senate Defeats Climate Bill, But Proponents See Silver Lining." *New York Times*, October 31.

Lichter, S. Robert, and Stanley Rothman. 1999. *Environmental Cancer: A Political Disease?* New Haven, CT: Yale University Press.

Loh, Penn, and Jodi Sugerman-Brozan. 2002. "Environmental Justice Organizing for Environmental Health: Case Study of Asthma and Diesel Exhaust in Roxbury, Massachusetts." *Annals of the American Academy of Political and Social Science*, special issue (November 2002): 110–24.

Lomborg, Bjørn. 2001. *The Skeptical Environmentalist: Measuring the Real State of the World*. Cambridge: Cambridge University Press.

Longman, Phillip J. 2003. "The Health of Nations." *Washington Monthly* 35, no. 4 (April). washingtonmonthly.org.

Markowitz, Gerald, and David Rosner. 2002a. "Corporate Responsibility for Toxins." *Annals of the American Academy of Political and Social Science*, special issue (November 2002): 159–74.

———. 2002b. *Deceit and Denial: The Deadly Politics of Industrial Pollution*. Berkeley: University of California Press.

Massey, Rachel, and Frank Ackerman. 2003. "Costs of Preventable Childhood Illness: The Price We Pay for Pollution." Global Development and Environment Institute, Working Paper No. 03–09 (September). Tufts University. http://ase.tufts.edu/gdae.

McCain, John. 2003. "Fight Global Warming for $20 a Year." *Wall Street Journal*, October 30.

McCally, Michael, ed. 2002a. *Life Support: The Environment and Human Health*. Cambridge, MA: MIT Press.

———. 2002b. "Environment, Health, and Risk." In *Life Support: The Environment and Human Health*, ed. Michael McCally, 1–14. Cambridge, MA: MIT Press.

McGinnis, J. Michael, Pamela Williams-Russo, and James R. Knickman. 2002. "The Case for More Active Attention to Health Promotion." *Health Affairs* 21, no. 2 (March–April): 78–93.

Mestel, Rosie. 2003. "SARS May Be Just the Start." *Los Angeles Times*, May 3.

Missouri Department of Health and Senior Services. 2003. "Strategic Plan 2000–2005: 2003 Update. Jefferson City, MO: Missouri Department of Health and Senior Services. www.health.state.mo.us/StrategicPlanning/StratPlan03.html.

Montague, Peter. 1999. "Precautionary Action Not Taken: Corporate Structure and the Case Study of Tetraethryl Lead in the United States." In *Protecting Public Health & the Environment: Implementing the Precautionary Principle*, ed. Carolyn Raffensperger and Joel Tickner, 294–303. Washington, DC: Island Press.

Morello-Frosch, Rachel, Manuel Pastor Jr., and James Sadd. 2002. "Integrating Environmental Justice and the Precautionary Principle in Research and Policy Making: The Case of Ambient Air Toxics Exposures and Health Risks Among Schoolchildren in Los Angeles." *Annals of the American Academy of Political and Social Science*, special issue (November 2002): 47–68.

Morse, Stephen. 2003. "From Ducks to Pigs to Humans?" *Wall Street Journal*, April 23.

Nakamura, David, and Carol D. Leonning. 2004. "EPA Urged to Tighten Rules on Tap Water." *Washington Post*, March 18.

National Center for Environmental Health. n.d. "NCEH Factsheet: Childhood Lead Poisoning." Atlanta, GA: Department of Health and Human Services, Centers for Disease Control and Prevention. www.cdc.gov/nceh/lead/factsheets/childhoodlead.htm.

———. 2003. "Second National Health Report on Human Exposure to Environmental Chemicals." Atlanta, GA: Department of Health and Human Services, Centers for Disease Control and Prevention.

National Conference of State Legislatures. 2003. "Environmental Public Health Tracking: Connecting Health and the Environment." *Environmental Health Series* 7 (September).

National Security Council. 2002. "The National Security Strategy of the United States of America." Washington, DC: White House. www.whitehouse.gov/nsc/nss.html.

Office of Disease Prevention and Health Promotion. 2001. *Healthy People in Healthy*

Communities: A Community Guide Using Healthy People 2010. Washington, DC: Office of Public Health and Science, U.S. Department of Health and Human Services.

Ophuls, William. 1977. *Ecology and the Politics of Scarcity: Prologue to a Political Theory of the Steady State*. San Francisco: W.H. Freeman.

Paehlke, Robert C. 2000. "Environmental Values and Public Policy." In *Environmental Policy: New Directions for the Twenty-First Century*, ed. Norman J. Vig and Michael E. Kraft, 77–97. Washington, DC: CQ Press.

Patel, Kant, and Mark E. Rushefsky. 2002. *Health Care Politics in a Technological Age*. Armonk, NY: M.E. Sharpe.

Powers, Shawn. 2003. "Chemicals in Water Supplies Producing Feminizing Effects, Lower Sperm Quality." *World-Watch* 16, no. 6 (November–December): 11.

Rabe, Barry G. 2000. "Power to the States: The Promise and Pitfalls of Decentralization." In *Environmental Policy: New Directions for the Twenty-First Century*, ed. Norman J. Vig and Michael E. Kraft, 32–54. Washington, DC: CQ Press.

Raffensperger, Carolyn, and Joel Tickner, eds. 1999a. *Protecting Public Health & the Environment: Implementing the Precautionary Principle*. Washington, DC: Island Press.

———. 1999b. Introduction. "To Foresee and Forestall." In *Protecting Public Health & the Environment: Implementing the Precautionary Principle*, 1–11. Washington, DC: Island Press.

Rogan, Walter J., and N. Beth Ragan. 2003. "Evidence of Effects of Environmental Chemicals on the Endocrine System in Children." *Pediatrics* 112, no. 1 (July): 247–52.

Rosenbaum, Walter A. 1977. *The Politics of Environmental Concern*, 2d ed. New York: Praeger Publishers.

Rushefsky, Mark E. 1986. *Making Cancer Policy*. Albany: State University of New York Press.

———. Mark E. 2002. *Public Policy in the United States: At the Dawn of the Twenty-First Century*, 3rd ed. Armonk, NY: M.E. Sharpe.

Samuelson, Paul A. 1964. *Economics: An Introductory Analysis*, 6th ed. New York: McGraw-Hill.

San Francisco Government. n.d. "SF Precautionary Principle Ordinance." www.sfgov.org/sfenvironment/aboutus/policy/legislation/precaution_principle.htm.

Santillo, David, Paul Johnston, and Ruth Stringer. 1999. "The Precautionary Principle in Practice: A Mandate for Anticipatory Preventative Action." In *Protecting Public Health & the Environment: Implementing the Precautionary Principle*, 36–50. Washington, DC: Island Press.

Schettler, Ted, Katherine Barrett, and Carolyn Raffensperger. 2002. "The Precautionary Principle: A Guide for Protecting Public Health and the Environment." In *Life Support: The Environment and Human Health*, ed. Michael McCally, 239–56. Cambridge, MA: MIT Press.

Seely, Hart. 2003. "The Poetry of D.H. Rumsfeld: Recent Works by the Secretary of Defense." Slate.com (April 2). http://slate.msn.com/id/2081042/.

Seelye, Katharine Q. 2001. "Arsenic Standard for Water Is Too Lax, Study Concludes." *New York Times*, September 11.

Siebert, Horst. 1981. *Economics of the Environment*. Lexington, MA: D.C. Heath.

Solomon, Gina M., and Ted Schettler. 2002. "Environmental Endocrine Disruption." In *Life Support: The Environment and Human Health*, ed. Michael McCally, 148–62. Cambridge, MA: MIT Press.

Springfield/Greene County (MO) Health Department. n.d. "Air Quality." www.ci.springfield.mo.us/health/pages/airquality.html.

Srinivasan, Shoba, Liam R. O'Fallon, and Allen Dearry. 2003. "Healthy People: Initiating a Research Agenda on the Built Environment and Public Health." *American Journal of Public Health* 93, no. 9 (September): 1446–50.

State and Territorial Program Administrators and the Association of Local Air Pollution Control Officials. 2003a. "New EPA Air Rule Strikes a Blow to Environmental Protection, Say State/Local Air Quality Officials." Washington, DC: State and Territorial Program Administrators and the Association of Local Air Pollution Control Officials, August 27. www.4cleanair.org/RMRRFinalRule-PressRelease-August2003.pdf.

———. 2003b. "State/Local Air Officials Develop Regulator Alternatives for New Source Review to Better Air Quality and Public Health." Washington, DC: State and Territorial Program Administrators and the Association of Local Air Pollution Control Officials, October 16. www.4cleanair.org/NSRMenu-PressRelease-101603.pdf.

———. 2003c. "Summary of EPA's NSR Rule Revisions and Regulatory Alternatives Presented in STAPPA and ALAPCO's *New Source Review: A Menu of Options.*" Washington, DC: State and Territorial Program Administrators and the Association of Local Air Pollution Control Officials, October 16. www.4cleanair.org/NSRMenu-TableofOptions.pdf.

Steinpress, Martin G., and Anthony C. Ward. 2001. "The Scientific Process and Hollywood: The Case of Hexavalent Chromium." *Ground Water* 39, no. 3 (May): 321–22.

Thornton, Joe, Michael McCally, and Jeff Howard. 2002. "Body Burdens of Industrial Chemicals in the General Population." In *Life Support: The Environment and Human Health*, ed. Michael McCally, 163–200. Cambridge, MA: MIT Press.

Tibbetts, John. 2003. "Building Civic Health." *Environmental Health Perspectives* 111, no. 7 (June): A400–3.

Tickner, Joel A. 2002. "The Precautionary Principle and Public Health Trade-Offs: Case Study of West Nile Virus." *Annals of the American Academy of Political and Social Science*, special issue (November 2002): 69–79.

Umansky, Eric. 2003. "Erin Brockovich's Weird Science." *New Republic Online*, November 13.

Vaidya, Jayant Sharad. 2003. "Study Was Flawed From Outset." *British Medical Journal* 327, no. 7413 (August 30): 501.

Vig, Norman J., and Michael E. Kraft, eds. 2000. *Environmental Policy: New Directions for the Twenty-First Century.* Washington, DC: CQ Press.

Walters, Jerome Mark. 2003. *Six Modern Plagues and How We Are Causing Them.* Washington, DC: Island Press.

Warnock, John W. 2003. "Joel Kovel: Capitalism as the Enemy of Nature." *Canadian Dimension* 37, no. 4 (July–August): 34–37.

Whitaker, John C. 1976. *Striking a Balance: Environment and Natural Resources Policy in the Nixon-Ford Years.* Washington, DC: American Enterprise Institute.

WHO European Centre for Environment and Health. 1999. "Children's Health and the Environment." Rome, Italy: World Health Organization. www.who.dk/document/e66809.pdf.

8: The Politics of Bioterrorism and Public Health

Annas, George J. 2002. "Bioterrorism, Public Health, and Human Rights." *Health Affairs* 21, no. 6 (November–December): 94–97.

Barbaro, Michael. 2003. "The High Cost of Making an Anthrax Drug: Human Genome Sciences Needs Commitment from Government to Proceed With Treatment." *Washington Post*, December 8.

Barry, John, and Mark Hosenball. 2004. "What Went Wrong." *Newsweek* CXLIII, no. 6 (February 9): 24–31.

Bayer, Ronald, and James Colgrove. 2002. "Bioterrorism, Public Health, and the Law." *Health Affairs*, 21, no. 6 (November–December): 98–101.

Biological Terrorism Response Manual. n.d. "History of Bioterrorism: A Chronological History of Bioterrorism Throughout the Ages." www.bioterry.com/HistoryBioTerr.html.

"Bioterrorism: Safeguarding the Public's Health." 2001. *Lancet* 358, no. 9290 (October 20).

Branigin, William. 2004. "President Signs Legislation to Fight Bioterrorism." *Washington Post*, July 21.

Brownlee, Shannon. 2001. "Under Control: Why America Isn't Ready for Bioterrorism." *New Republic* (October 29): 22–25.

Carroll, Michael Christopher. 2004. *Lab 257: The Disturbing Story of the Government's Secret Plum Island Germ Laboratory*. New York: William Morrow.

Center for Law and the Public's Health. 2001. "The Model State Emergency Health Powers Act." Washington, DC: Georgetown University Law Center.

Center for Strategic and International Studies. 2001. "Dark Winter: Bioterrorism Exercise." Washington, DC: Center for Strategic and International Studies. www.csis.org/press/ma_2001_0723.htm.

Centers for Disease Control and Prevention. n.d. "Bioterrorism Agents/Diseases." Washington, DC: U.S. Department of Health and Human Services. www.bt.cdc.gov/agent/agentlist-category.asp#adef.

Central Intelligence Agency. n.d. "The War on Terrorism, Terrorism FAQs." Washington, DC: Central Intelligence Agency. www.cia.gov/terrorism/faqs.html.

Chandler, David, and India Landrigan. 2002. "Bioterrorism: A Journalist's Guide to Covering Bioterrorism." Washington, DC: Radio and Television News Directors Foundation.

Clancy, Tom. 1994. *Debt of Honor*. New York: G.P. Putnam's Sons.

———. 1996. *Executive Orders*. New York: G.P. Putnam's Sons.

Clarke, Richard A. 2004. *Against All Enemies: Inside America's War on Terror*. New York: Free Press.

Conrad, J. Lyle, and James L. Pearson. 2003. "Improving Epidemiology, Surveillance, and Laboratory Capabilities." In *Terrorism and Public Health: A Balanced Approach to Strengthening Systems and Protecting People*, ed. Barry S. Levy and Victor W. Sidel, 270–85. New York: Oxford University Press.

Crowley, Michael. 2004. "Playing Defense." *New Republic* 230, no. 4652 (March 15): 17–21.

Daalder, Ivo H., and James M. Lindsay. 2003. *American Unbound: The Bush Revolution in Foreign Policy*. Washington, DC: Brookings Institution Press.

Erickson, Jim. 2002. "Fort Collins Bioterror Lab Eyed." *Rocky Mountain News*, February 7.

Etzioni, Amitai. 2002. "Public Health Law: A Communitarian Perspective." *Health Affairs* 21, no. 6 (November–December): 102–4.

Federal Bureau of Investigation. 1996. "Terrorism in the United States 1996." Washington, DC: U.S. Department of Justice, Federal Bureau of Investigation, Counterterrorism Threat Assessment and Warning Unit, National Security Division.

Federation of American Scientists. n.d. "U.S. Intelligence and Security Agencies." www.fas.org/irp/official.html.

"Finish Project BioShield." 2004. *Washington Times*, February 10.

Food and Drug Administration. 2003. "Administrative Detention of Food for Human or Animal Consumption Under the Public Health Security and Bioterrorism Preparedness and Response Act of 2002." *Federal Register* 68, no. 90 (May 9): 25241–71. www.fda.gov/OHRMS/DOCKETS/98fr/03–11459.html.

Garrett, Laurie. 2000. *Betrayal of Trust: The Collapse of Global Public Health*. New York: Hyperion.

General Accounting Office. 2001. "Bioterrorism: Review of Public Health Preparedness Programs." Washington, DC: U.S. General Accounting Office (October 10).

———. 2004. "HHS Bioterrorism Preparedness Programs: States Reported Progress but Fell Short of Program Goals for 2002." Washington, DC: U.S. General Accounting Office (February 10).

Gerstenzang, James. 2002. "Bush Budget Plan." *Los Angeles Times*, February 6.

Gorman, Siobhan. 2004. "On Guard, But How Well?" *National Journal* 36, no. 10 (March 6): 696–703.

Gostin, Lawrence O. 2000. *Public Health Law: Power, Duty, Restraint*. Berkeley: University of California Press.

———. 2002. "Public Health Law in an Age of Terrorism: Rethinking Individual Rights and Common Goods." *Health Affairs* 21, no. 6 (November–December): 79–93.

Gottron, Frank. 2003. "Project BioShield." Washington, DC: Congressional Research Service (April 28).

Harris, Elisa D. 2004. "The Evil Twins of Research: Bioterror." *Los Angeles Times*, March 16.

Henderson, Donald A., Thomas V. Inglesby, and Tara O'Toole, eds. 2002. *Bioterrorism: Guidelines for Medical and Public Health Management*. Chicago: AMA Press.

Henderson, Donald A., et al. 2004a. "Anthrax as a Biological Weapon." In *Bioterrorism: Guidelines for Medical and Public Health Management*, ed. Donald A. Henderson, Thomas V. Inglesby, and Tara O'Toole, 63–97. Chicago: AMA Press.

———. 2004b. "Smallpox as a Biological Weapon." In *Bioterrorism: Guidelines for Medical and Public Health Management*, ed. Donald A. Henderson, Thomas V. Inglesby, and Tara O'Toole, 99–120. Chicago: AMA Press.

———. 2004c. "Plague as a Biological Weapon." In *Bioterrorism: Guidelines for Medical and Public Health Management*, ed. Donald A. Henderson, Thomas V. Inglesby, and Tara O'Toole, 121–40. Chicago: AMA Press.

Hoffman, Richard E., and Jane E. Norton. 2000. "Lessons Learned from a Full-Scale Bioterrorism Exercise." *Emerging Infectious Diseases* 6, no. 6 (November–December). www.cdc.gov/ncidod/eid/vol6no6/hoffman.htm.

Hulse, Carl. 2004. "Tests Indicate Poison in Senate Mail Room of Majority Leader." *New York Times*, February 3.

Institute of Medicine. 1988. *The Future of the Public's Health*. Washington, DC: National Academy Press.

———. 2003. *The Future of the Public's Health in the 21st Century*. Washington, DC: National Academy Press.

Keck, C. William, and Marguerite A. Erme. 2003. "Strengthening the Public Health System." In *Terrorism and Public Health: A Balanced Approach to Strengthening Systems and Protecting People*, ed. Barry S. Levy and Victor W. Sidel, 245–69. New York: Oxford University Press.

Kortepeter, Mark G., and Gerald W. Parker. 1999. "Potential Biological Weapons Threats" *Emerging Infectious Diseases* 5, no. 4 (July–August): 523–27.

Lane, J. Michael, and Joel Goldstein. 2003. "Evaluation of 21st-Century Risks of Smallpox Vaccination and Policy Options." *Annals of Internal Medicine* 138, no. 6 (March 18): 488–94.

Levy, Barry S., and Victor W. Sidel, eds. 2003a. *Terrorism and Public Health: A Balanced Approach to Strengthening Systems and Protecting People*. New York: Oxford University Press.

———. 2003b. "Challenges that Terrorism Poses to Public Health." In *Terrorism and Public Health: A Balanced Approach to Strengthening Systems and Protecting People*, ed. Barry S. Levy and Victor W. Sidel, 3–18. New York: Oxford University Press.

Margolskee, Dorothy. 2003. "Improving Vaccines, Antimicrobials, and Antitoxins Through Research." In *Terrorism and Public Health: A Balanced Approach to Strengthening Systems and Protecting People*, ed. Barry S. Levy and Victor W. Sidel, 286–304. New York: Oxford University Press.

McCarthy, Michael. 2001. "Attacks Heighten U.S. Concern About Threat of Bioterrorism." *Lancet* 358, no. 9287 (September 29): 1071.

Miller, Judith, Stephen Engelberg, and William Broad. 2001. *Germs: Biological Weapons and America's Secret War*. New York: Simon & Schuster.

National Public Radio. 2001. "History of Biological Warfare." www.npr.org/news/specials/response/anthrax,features/2001/oct/011018.bioterrorism.

National Vaccine Information Center. n.d. "What You Need to Know About the Proposed Model State Emergency Health Powers Act in Your State." Vienna, VA: National Vaccine Information Center. www.909shot.com/ActionAlerts/what_you_need_to_know.htm.

Nichols, Bill. 2004. "UN: Iraq Had No WMD After 1994." *USA Today*, March 2.

Patel, Kant, and Mark E. Rushefsky. 1999. *Health Care Politics and Policy in America*, 2d ed. Armonk, NY: M.E. Sharpe.

"Patent Protection Versus Public Health." 2001. *Lancet* 358, no. 9293 (November 11): 1563.

Patton, Zach. 2003. "Study Says Federal Bioterrorism Spending not Preparing States." GovExec.com. www.govexec.com/dailyfed/1203/121103cdpm2.htm.

Phillips, Kevin. 2004. *American Dynasty: Aristocracy, Fortune, and the Politics of Deceit in the House of Bush*. New York: Viking Press.

Preston, Richard. 1998. *The Cobra Event*. New York: Random House.

Propst, Rod. 2002. "New Terrorists? New Attack Means? Categorizing Terrorist Challenges for the Early 21st Century." *Journal of Homeland Security* (March). www.homelandsecurity.org/journal/articles/displayArticle.asp?article=48.

Public Health Security and Bioterrorism Preparedness Response Act of 2002. www.fda.gov/oc/bioterrorism/bioact.html.

Purdum, Todd. 2003. *A Time of Our Choosing: America's War in Iraq*. New York: Times Books.

Ripley, Amanda. 2004. "How We Got Homeland Security Wrong." *Time* (March 22). www.cnn.com/2004/ALLPOLITICS/03/22/homesec.tm/#.

Rubin, Irene S. 2000. *The Politics of Public Budgeting: Getting and Spending, Borrowing and Balancing*, 4th ed. New York: Chatham House.

Rushefsky, Mark E. 2002. *Public Policy in the United States: At the Dawn of the Twenty-First Century*, 3d ed. Armonk, NY: M.E. Sharpe.

Russell, Philip K. 1999. "Vaccines in Civilian Defense Against Bioterrorism." *Emerging Infectious Diseases* 5, no. 4 (July–August): 531–33.

Sidel, Victor W., and Barry S. Levy. 2003. "Biological Weapons." In *Terrorism and Public Health: A Balanced Approach to Strengthening Systems and Protecting People*, ed. Barry S. Levy and Victor W. Sidel, 175–98. New York: Oxford University Press.

Siegrest, David W. 1999. "The Threat of Biological Attack: Why Concern Now?" *Emerging Infectious Diseases* 5, no. 4 (July–August): 505–8.

Smith, Daniel, Marcus Corbin, and Christopher Hellman. 2001. "Reforging the Sword: Forces for a 21st Century Security Strategy." Washington, DC: Center for Defense Information. www.cdi.org/mrp/reforging-full.pdf.

Southwick, Ron. 2001. "U.S. Spending on Bioterrorism Studies and Computer Security Is Set to Soar." *Chronicles of Higher Education* 48, no. 14 (November 30).

Starr, Paul. 1982. *The Social Transformation of American Medicine*. New York: Basic Books.

Stern, Jessica. 1999. "The Prospect of Domestic Bioterrorism." *Emerging Infectious Diseases* 5, no. 4 (July–August): 517–22.

Stevenson, Richard W. 2004. "Iraq Illicit Arms Gone Before War." *New York Times*, January 24.

Trust for America's Health. 2003. *Ready or Not: Protecting the Public's Health in an Age of Bioterrorism*." Washington, DC: Trust for America's Health. http://healthyamericans.org/state/bioterror/Bioterror.pdf.

Tucker, Jonathan B. 1999. "Historical Trends Related to Bioterrorism: An Empirical Analysis." *Emerging Infectious Diseases* 5, no. 4 (July/August): 498–504.

———. 2001. *Scourge: The Once and Future Threat of Smallpox*. New York: Grove Press.

United States Commission on National Security in the 21st Century. 2001. *Road Map for National Security: Imperative for Change*. Washington, DC: United States Commission on National Security in the 21st Century. www.nssg.gov/PhaseIIIFR.pdf.

U.S. House Select Committee on Homeland Security. 2004. "America at Risk: Closing the Security Gap." Washington, DC: U.S. House of Representatives, Democratic Minority. www.house.gov/hsc/democrats/pdf/press/report/FULLREPORT.pdf.

Versel, Neil. 2001. "Thinking Ahead: Public Health Officials Plan Responses to Bioterrorism Threat." *Modern Physician* 5, no. 14 (November): 2–3.

Waecklerle, Joseph F. 2001. "A Review of Federal Bioterrorism Preparedness Programs from a Public Health Perspective." Testimony before the Subcommittee on Oversight and Investigations, Committee on Energy and Commerce, U.S. House of Representatives, 107th Congress, 1st Session (October 10).

White House. 2002. "National Security Strategy to Combat Weapons of Mass Destruction." Washington, DC: White House. December. www.whitehouse.gov/news/releases/2002/12/WMDStrategy.pdf.

Zoon, Kathryn C. 1999. "Vaccine, Pharmaceutical Products, and Bioterrorism: Challenges for the Food and Drug Administration." *Emerging Infectious Diseases* 5, no. 4 (July–August): 534–36.

9: Conclusion

Brown, Lawrence D. 1986. "Introduction to a Decade in Transition." *Journal of Health Politics, Policy and Law* 11, no. 4 (winter): 569–83.

"Costs of Complacency." 2004. *Governing* (February).

Institute of Medicine. 2003. *The Future of the Public's Health in the 21st Century.* Washington, DC: National Academy Press.

Garrett, Laurie. 2000. *Betrayal of Trust: The Collapse of Global Public Health.* New York: Hyperion.

Gostin, Lawrence O. 2000. *Public Health Law: Power, Duty, Restraint.* Berkeley: University of California Press.

———. 2002. "Public Health Law in an Age of Terrorism: Rethinking Individual Rights and Common Goods." *Health Affairs* 21, no. 6 (November–December): 79–93.

Patel, Kant, and Mark E. Rushefsky. 1999. *Health Care Politics and Policy in the United States*, 2d ed. Armonk, NY: M.E. Sharpe.

Schneider, Mary-Jane. 2000. *Introduction to Public Health Genetics.* Gaithersburg, MD: Aspen Publishers.

Index

About the Authors

Kant Patel is a professor of political science at Southwest Missouri State University in Springfield. He has published numerous articles and books in the area of health care politics and policies. His most recent book, *Health Care Policy in an Age of New Technologies*, was published in 2002. Other books include *Health Care Politics and Policy in America*, second edition (1999), and *Politics, Power, and Policy Making: The Case of Health Care Reform in the 1990s* (1998). All books are coauthored with Mark Rushefsky.

Mark E. Rushefsky is a professor of political science at Southwest Missouri State University in Springfield. He has published numerous articles and books in the areas of health care politics and policies, environmental policy, and public policy in general. Recent books are *Health Care Policy in an Age of New Technologies* (2002) and *Public Policy in the United States: At the Dawn of the Twenty-First Century*, third edition (2002). He has also published *Health Care Politics and Policy in America*, second edition (1999), and *Politics, Power, and Policy Making: The Case of Health Care Reform in the 1990s* (1998). Most books are coauthored with Kant Patel.